Adapting Infrastructure to Climate Change

T0330639

Many of the challenges that decision-makers grapple with in relation to climate change are governance related. Planning and decision-making is evolving in ambiguous institutional environments, in which many key issues remain unresolved, including relationships between different actors; funding arrangements; and the sources and procedures for vetting data. These issues are particularly acute at this juncture, as climate adaptation moves from broad planning processes to the management of infrastructure systems. Concrete decisions must be made.

Adapting Infrastructure to Climate Change draws on case studies of three coastal cities situated within very different governance regimes: neo-corporatist Rotterdam, neo-pluralist Boston, and semi-authoritarian Singapore. The book examines how infrastructure managers and other stakeholders grappling with complex and uncertain climate risks are likely to make project-level decisions in practice, and how more effective decision-making can be supported. The differences across governance regimes are currently unaccounted for in adaptation planning, but are crucial as best practices are devised. These lessons are also applicable to infrastructure planning and decision-making in other contexts.

This book will be of great interest to scholars of climate change and environmental policy and governance, particularly in the context of infrastructure management.

Todd Schenk is an Assistant Professor in the Urban Affairs and Planning Program of the School of Public and International Affairs at Virginia Tech, USA.

Routledge Advances in Climate Change Research

For a full list of titles in this series, please visit www.routledge.com

Adapting Infrastructure to Climate Change

Advancing Decision-Making Under Conditions of Uncertainty

Todd Schenk

First published 2018
by Routledge

2 Park Square, Milton Park, Abingdon, Oxfordshire OX14 4RN
52 Vanderbilt Avenue, New York, NY 10017

Routledge is an imprint of the Taylor & Francis Group, an informa business

First issued in paperback 2018

© 2018 Todd Schenk

The right of Todd Schenk to be identified as author of this work has been asserted by him in accordance with sections 77 and 78 of the Copyright, Designs and Patents Act 1988.

All rights reserved. No part of this book may be reprinted or reproduced or utilised in any form or by any electronic, mechanical, or other means, now known or hereafter invented, including photocopying and recording, or in any information storage or retrieval system, without permission in writing from the publishers.

Trademark notice: Product or corporate names may be trademarks or registered trademarks, and are used only for identification and explanation without intent to infringe.

British Library Cataloguing-in-Publication Data
A catalogue record for this book is available from the British Library

Library of Congress Cataloging-in-Publication Data
A catalog record for this book has been requested

ISBN: 978-1-138-19419-9 (hbk)
ISBN: 978-0-367-19297-6 (pbk)

Typeset in Goudy
by Apex CoVantage, LLC

Contents

Figures

Tables

Boxes

Preface

This book grew out of my dissertation research in pursuit of a PhD in Public Policy and Planning in the Department of Urban Studies and Planning (DUSP) at the Massachusetts Institute of Technology (MIT). I was extremely fortunate to have the opportunity to work with a fantastic group of people both at MIT and beyond, not least in each of the three cities this research was conducted in. I owe a debt of gratitude to many people for their support – intellectually, materially, emotionally and otherwise.

I would like to start by thanking Lawrence Susskind for his incredible mentorship. I would next like to acknowledge and honor JoAnn Carmin, who sadly passed away in 2014; her mentorship and guidance are sadly missed. I am also grateful to Richard de Neufville and Adil Najam for the guidance and feedback they provided throughout this project.

I wish to thank the wider communities in MIT/DUSP, the Program on Negotiation at Harvard Law School and the Consensus Building Institute for the rich intellectual environments, support and friendship they provided. While an incomplete list, I am particularly grateful to the following friends and colleagues: Eric Chu, Ellen Czaika, Josh Ellsworth, Victor Eskinazi, Mattijs van Maasakkers, Danya Rumore, Michal Russo, Kerry Spitzer and Leah Stokes. I also thank my 'new' colleagues in the School of Public and International Affairs at Virginia Tech for their support as I completed this manuscript.

I am extremely grateful to TNO and the Dutch Knowledge for Climate Programme for their generous support of the Harboring Uncertainty research project, the outcomes of which undergird this book. I would like to thank some people in particular at TNO for their assistance, support and intellectual partnership: Nienke Maas, Lori Tavasszy, Roel Massink, Ruben Vogel and Elja Huibregtse. Outside of TNO, I am very grateful to Hans Groeneveld at Rijkswaterstaat for his extensive and very generous assistance and insights.

I would not have been able to successfully conduct this research in Singapore without the very generous hosting and support of the Civil Service College. I am particularly grateful to Iva Aminuddin, Adeline Chin and the CAST team. I am also very grateful to Jeffrey Siow at the Ministry of Transport for his support and advice.

I am grateful to the Boston Society of Architects, and Gretchen Schneider in particular, for hosting the workshop and providing extensive support and advice. Boston Harbor Now (formerly The Boston Harbor Association), and Julie Wormser in particular, provided extensive support and advice as well. I am also grateful to Carl Spector with the City of Boston for his extensive assistance and advice.

Beyond those listed above, I would like to thank the more than 100 people who participated in this research across the three cities. I have not listed them by name to protect their anonymity, but am grateful for the time they gave and insights they shared.

I am grateful to Routledge-Earthscan for accepting this manuscript. I would like to thank Margaret Farrelly and Annabelle Harris in particular for their support and patience.

Last but certainly not least, I owe a debt of gratitude to my family. I would like to thank my parents and sisters for their nurturing support. I cannot express sufficient appreciation to my wife, Radka, and children, Honzik and Maire, for their patience, love and support during this long and not always easy journey through the PhD and subsequent preparation of this manuscript.

1 Introduction

Adapting infrastructure to climate change

The need for adaptation

It has been 25 years since the United Nations Framework Convention on Climate Change was negotiated in Rio, and by now the issue is on the radars of many government agencies and other stakeholders around the world. However, most of the attention has been paid to how we can reduce greenhouse gas emissions from industry, vehicles and other sources to avoid the consequences of climate change. Climate change mitigation remains critically important to our long-term well-being, particularly if we are to reduce the chances of catastrophic impacts, but by now most experts agree that we are 'locked in' to fairly substantial climatic changes, including increases in temperature and associated sea level rise and shifts in weather patterns (IPCC 2014).

These changes pose a range of significant threats to our built environments and infrastructure, as climate change strains the ability of planners and decision-makers to sustainably manage urban environments, including key infrastructure systems (de Sherbinin, Schiller and Pulsipher 2007; Dorfman et al. 2011; HM Government 2011; Rosenzweig et al. 2011). The threats will vary from place to place, but include sea level rise and associated coastal flooding and saltwater intrusion, more frequent and intense storms, prolonged periods of drought and associated water scarcity, heat waves, shifting ecosystem ranges and disease vectors, and biodiversity loss (IPCC 2014). The way we plan and implement our infrastructure systems will need to be revised in response; planners, decision-makers and other stakeholders will need to *adapt*.

Adaptation will surely involve technical solutions, but it is not a purely technological problem. It will require fundamental changes not only to how we design our infrastructure, but also to how we fund and manage it over time and think of the various infrastructures as interconnected systems of systems (Bollinger et al. 2014). Adapting infrastructure to climate change is a particularly *wicked* challenge (i.e., one that is difficult to definitively solve and involves a complex web of interdependencies) for a number of reasons (Levin, Cashore, Bernstein and Auld 2012; Rittel and Webber 1973). First of all, the complex and interconnected nature of most climate threats leaves responsibility unclear among agencies and levels of government (Moser and Ekstrom 2010). Furthermore, the nascence of climate adaptation, and the fact that it often requires cooperation across traditional institutional boundaries, make it characteristic of what Hajer (2003) calls "policy-making in the institutional void". That is, policymaking in unestablished or weakly established institutional environments.

While our understanding of the impacts of climate change is getting better, significant uncertainty persists and climatic conditions are irreconcilably dynamic and complex (IPCC 2014; Walker, Haasnoot and Kwakkel 2013). We have traditionally used historical data when setting design standards but may no longer be able to use the past as a reliable predictor of the future. This leads to the critical question of what information we should use. Answering this question is not so simple, with competing knowledge claims (van Buuren and Edelenbos 2004) and climate information usability gaps (Lemos, Kirchhoff and Ramprasad 2012). Real or perceived uncertainty in climate forecasts further clouds this question. We typically build our infrastructure with the expectation that it will remain operational for decades, and most infrastructure has traditionally been fairly static once built. However, it is decreasingly clear what the future will look like. It is often expensive to retrofit, and our funding and management models are not set up to support ongoing adaptation.

A further challenge is that infrastructure decisions are often made in highly constrained budgetary environments; resources are scarce, so the costs and benefits of making projects more robust must be considered. In general, there is often competition among different interests and priorities (Susskind 2010). Finally yet importantly, our governance systems are often slow to change, even when challenges like the threats posed by climate change are acknowledged. Planning, design and management occur in complex institutional environments with various hurdles and leverage points.

Adaptation in an institutional context

Efforts to understand and intervene in complex systems have often neglected the governance challenges involved (Bea, Mitroff, Farber, Foster and Roberts 2009). This book focuses on how to manage uncertainty and complexity in decision-making, considering the institutional dynamics. It explores the challenges associated with adapting infrastructure to climate change and makes a variety of suggestions, including around how we can:

- institutionalize better praxis of flexibility in infrastructure planning and decision-making;
- implement good process design to bring multiple stakeholders together for decision-making in complex and ambiguous institutional environments;
- use decision-support tools, including multiple scenarios, to enhance these processes and frame uncertainties; and
- use role-play simulation exercises for stakeholder engagement and action research around nascent issues like climate change.

It makes these recommendations while acknowledging and describing the implications of the wider governance regimes and institutional frameworks that decision-makers and other stakeholders find themselves in. Responding to the risks posed by climate change does not happen in a vacuum; existing institutional environments provide both opportunities and constraints.

Paradigmatic shifts notwithstanding, planning and policymaking generally follows entrenched patterns, with policy subsystems slow to take up new challenges and moving only incrementally when they do (Howlett and Ramesh 1998). Policy communities are often reticent to take on issues outside of the explicit domains of responsible agencies and interests of the other stakeholders. Well-entrenched institutional norms, or patterns, can make systemic changes, cooperation outside of established, discrete relationships, and flexibility over time difficult (Baumgartner and Jones 2009; Downs 1967; Perrow 1986; Powell and DiMaggio 1991; Pressman and Wildavsky 1984). Emerging issues, like the impacts of climate change, can strain existing arrangements. The 'streams and windows' model of policymaking suggests that the strain of new issues and actors pushing against the policy subsystem is the source of periodic paradigm shifts in a world of 'punctuated equilibrium' (Baumgartner and Jones 2009). The problem is that issues that involve significant complexity, persistent uncertainty and dynamic conditions, like climate change, may require more flexible and dynamic planning and policymaking that goes beyond punctuated equilibrium. This is a tall order, but one this book tackles as it considers how we can better institutionalize climate change adaptation into our planning and decision-making.

The uncertainty factor

Uncertainty may be a significant X factor in climate change adaptation. Systems are by nature dynamic and difficult to predict; no one knows what the future will bring. In response, infrastructure planning typically involves established models or forecasts of the future, enshrined standards and informal but institutionalized heuristics (Rahman, Walker and Marchau 2008). Air quality, economic growth, traffic demand and other models play prominent roles in planning and decision-making. The procedures and variables for constructing these models and procedures are often dictated in government law and policy, and they are reinforced in organizational and professional norms and via the allocation of organizational resources. Forecasts cannot divine what will actually happen, but they get it right often enough. As poignantly put by Box and Draper (1987), "all models are wrong, but some are useful". Despite their fallibilities, they facilitate 'satisficing' and thus the advancement of decision-making (Simon 1956).

An important question is whether the models and forecasts that inform our climate adaptation efforts really are sufficient, given the particularly dynamic and uncertain nature of climate change and deviation from past trends. That is, are they satisfactory both technically and politically for our decision-making? Climate change may involve a higher degree of uncertainty and thus necessitate new approaches (Birkmann et al. 2010; Bollinger et al. 2014; Eakin and Lemos 2010; Lemos et al. 2012). There are multiple possible emissions scenarios, based on different economic growth and technological change trajectories, and different global circulation models of how greenhouse gas concentrations will actually alter the climate (Sainz de Murieta, Galarraga and Markandya 2014). Climate models used to support decision-making at the local level involve substantial additional uncertainty, because downscaling from global models compounds the higher-level model uncertainties (Termeer et al. 2011). Furthermore, the uncertainties are not only climatological in nature; they also result from unpredictability around how socioeconomic and biophysical systems will respond to climate change (Biesbroek, Klostermann, Termeer and Kabat 2011; Moser and Ekstrom 2010).

Rahman et al. (2008) categorize the situation that infrastructure planners and decision-makers find themselves in vis-à-vis climate change as 'deep uncertainty'. Deep uncertainty is a condition in which

> analysts do not know, or the parties to a decision cannot agree on, (1) the appropriate conceptual models that describe the relationships among the key driving forces that will shape the long-term future, (2) the probability distributions used to represent uncertainty about key variables and parameters in the mathematical representations of these conceptual models, and/or (3) how to value the relative desirability of the various outcomes.
>
> (Rahman et al. 2008, 43)

Uncertainty is not one element of the decision-making process, but pervades the cascade of plans and decisions. Mearns (2010) uses the term 'meta-deep uncertainty' to describe the fact that there is not even agreement among decision-makers, climate scientists and other stakeholders around how important it is to decision-making that uncertainty in climate models be reduced, and that consensus on this matter may be impossible to achieve. She is skeptical of the focus on constructing ever more complex climate models, asserting that we need "a truly balanced research program that also [provides] sufficient funding for in-depth vulnerability assessments and investment in improving or expanding decision making protocols under deep uncertainty" (Mearns 2010, 84). That is, we need to figure out how to work with uncertainty rather than focusing solely on how to resolve it.

Climate adaptation planning

While significant work remains, there is a growing body of literature and practice around climate adaptation planning. It is slowly emerging as an acknowledged necessity and increasingly sophisticated area of activity for government agencies in numerous sectors and at all levels around the world. At the local level, many municipalities, including all three focused on in this book, have prepared either standalone or integrated climate change adaptation strategies and initiated various activities. Some planning efforts are cross-sectoral, while others are sector-specific. The Intergovernmental Panel on Climate Change (IPCC), which devoted significant attention to climate impacts and adaptation in its most recent (5th) Assessment Report, defines adaptation as "The process of adjustment to actual or expected climate and its effects. In human systems, adaptation seeks to moderate or avoid harm or exploit beneficial opportunities" (2014, 5). Whether proactive or reactive, adaptation is the suite of responses to a changing climate, from heightening and strengthening levees to keep the rising sea at bay to planting trees to counteract the urban heat island effect as temperatures rise.

Adaptation *planning* involves the integration of concern for and responses to climatic changes and potential future climate risks into our governance systems. It is the process through which public officials and other stakeholders better understand, prepare for and respond to the risks and uncertainty climate change poses (Adger et al. 2007; National Research Council 2010; Schipper and Burton 2009). The actions communities take today are important, because they will shape the nature and degree of risk they face in the future (IPCC 2014). While adaptation often involves non-governmental actors, and a parallel set of activities are taking off in the private sector, this book largely focuses on public-sector-centric adaptation planning. It is important to note, however, that the public-private divide is often blurred. In many countries, significant proportions of various infrastructure systems are privately owned and operated – including electricity, water and sanitation and even transportation– albeit with significant government oversight. Furthermore, civil society organizations often play significant roles in influencing government decisions, including those around infrastructure. Nonetheless, government agencies often have critical parts to play in advancing climate change adaptation, whether directly through their own policy and investment decisions or indirectly through their oversight.

It is important to note that risks, adaptive capacity and resilience – which is the capacity of a system to cope with events or changing conditions – are not equally distributed within or among communities (Berrang-Ford, Ford and Paterson 2011; IPCC 2014). Different groups face different types and levels of threat, and they have varying capacity to prepare and respond based on spatial, socioeconomic and other factors. Unfortunately, if not surprisingly, disparities in both risks and adaptive capacity often overlap with other disparities. It is important to keep this in mind as we consider the uneven costs and benefits of different adaptive responses.

It is also important to note that this book is not a comprehensive 'how to' on the mechanics of adaptation planning. It focuses on how adaptation can be better institutionalized into planning and decision-making. Fortunately, a wide variety of guidelines and resources has been developed by government agencies, non-governmental organizations, private consultancies and academics to inform adaptation planning efforts.[1] At the local level, networks of municipalities are playing very important roles as sources of information, coordination and support. ICLEI-Local Governments for Sustainability's Resilient Cities program provides resources and support internationally and organizes an Annual Global Forum. The C40 Cities Climate Leadership Group is a network of many of the world's largest cities that makes its various resource materials available to all. C40 also supports thematic subnetworks, like the Connecting Delta Cities network, which is based in Rotterdam. Cities selected to participate in the Rockefeller Foundation's 100 Resilient Cities network receive funding and guidance to hire a 'Chief Resilience Officer' to lead their efforts, extensive expertise from the public and private sectors as they develop a 'robust resilience strategy', and networking opportunities with other member cities around the world. Members are expected to apply the City Resilience Framework, which focuses on the following 12 'drivers', rooted in four 'essential dimensions' (Rockefeller Foundation 2016):

- Health & Well-Being

  - Meets Basic Needs
  - Supports Livelihoods & Employment
  - Ensures Public Health Services

- Economy & Society

  - Promotes Cohesive & Engaged Communities
  - Ensures Social Stability, Security & Justice
  - Fosters Economic Prosperity

- Leadership & Strategy

  - Promotes Leadership & Effective Management
  - Empowers a Broad Range of Stakeholders
  - Fosters Long-Term & Integrated Planning

- Infrastructure & Environment

  - Provides & Enhances Natural & Man-Made Assets
  - Ensures Continuity of Critical Services
  - Provides Reliable Communication & Mobility

Of course, climate change adaptation planning is only successful if it is implemented in practice and has tangible impacts on decisions made, including around our critical infrastructure systems. Unfortunately, the evidence suggests that adaptation planning efforts thus far have been largely aspirational, rather than advancing concrete measures, and reactive to stimuli, rather than proactive in light of emerging threats (Berrang-Ford et al. 2011; Bierbaum et al. 2014). A variety of barriers prevent more substantial action on climate change adaptation, including (Bierbaum et al. 2014; Friend et al. 2014; Funfgeld 2010; Lemos et al. 2012; Levin, Cashore, Bernstein and Auld 2012; Moser and Ekstrom 2010):

- Weak signaling of the threats and low levels of concern
- Policy and legal restrictions
- Competing interests and priorities
- Insufficient climate information at the local level
- Problems with the saliency, credibility and legitimacy of the information that is available
- Resource constraints, including limited funding and staff capacity
- Insufficient arenas for making adaptation decisions
- Ambiguous allocation of responsibility across agencies and levels of government
- Institutional stickiness that limits the responsiveness of governance systems
- Irrational discounting of the future

It is notable that many of these barriers are governance related. They are not scientific or technical challenges, but constraints related to the institutional environments within which planning and decision-making takes place. It is factors like the *institutional context, competing planning agendas* and lack of *leadership* that are the most substantial barriers to adaptation (Measham et al. 2011). This is not surprising, given how important institutional norms and procedures are to the ways in which new issues are integrated into our governance systems (Marshall 2013). Despite the strength of the international networks focused on adaptation, the institutionalization of urban climate governance is being driven primarily by endogenous factors; local efforts are engaged in 'urban entrepreneurship' based on their particular goals, resources, barriers and opportunities (Anguelovski and Carmin 2011). Climate change adaptation efforts must account for the behaviors of individuals, organizations and institutions (Berkhout, Hertin and Gann 2006). Underscoring a key theme of this book, they must take the governance processes and planning tools seriously, and not focus solely on technical matters (Birkmann et al. 2010). They must also recognize the interconnected nature of infrastructure systems and governance challenges associated with approaching adaptation comprehensively, particularly in fragmented planning and decision-making environments (Bollinger et al. 2014; Camacho 2009).

The Harboring Uncertainty research project

This book draws from a research project funded through the Dutch Knowledge for Climate program that engaged a wide range of stakeholders from both inside and outside government in three coastal cities: Singapore, Rotterdam and Boston. The questions it set out to answer were: As infrastructure managers and other stakeholders grapple with complex and uncertain risks, like those posed by climate change, how are they likely to make decisions in practice? How can we support more effective decision-making? The four hypotheses made were that:

1   *Process is important*, and facilitated multi-stakeholder deliberation can help groups to advance adaptation planning and decision-making to address wicked problems with institutional ambiguity, uncertainty and conflicting interests and perspectives.
2   The presentation of *multiple scenarios* (i.e., multiple distinct yet plausible futures) can help stakeholders to better understand uncertainty and subsequently make decisions despite its persistence.
3   We will see important *differences across governance regimes* that are shaping and constraining how climate change adaptation is or may be institutionalized.
4   *Role-play simulation (RPS) exercises* can facilitate powerful reflection by bringing stakeholders together collectively to wrestle with a simulated yet realistic challenge, raising their awareness of the issues and how they might be resolved.

As illustrated in Table 1.1, these hypotheses translated into a set of three independent variables: the wider governance regime, which varied across the three case cities; the process for convening and facilitating deliberation among stakeholders, which was modeled in the role-play simulation exercise and contrasted with participants' traditional models of decision-making; and multiple scenarios versus a single risk assessment forecast as alternative ways to frame uncertainty, which were reflected in the two versions of the exercise. The dependent variables examined were the decision-making processes and outcomes of the various groups that participated in the role-play simulation exercise, and complementary research interventions with participants and others.

Table 1.1 Harboring Uncertainty research design

Independent variable 1 – Governance regime					
Neo-corporatist *Rotterdam*		Semi-authoritarian *Singapore*		Neo-pluralist/neo-liberal *Boston*	
Independent variable 2 – Stakeholder engagement					
Multi-stakeholder deliberation		Multi-stakeholder deliberation		Multi-stakeholder deliberation	
Versus status quo		*Versus status quo*		*Versus status quo*	
Independent variable 3 – Tool for framing uncertainty					
Scenarios	Risk assessment	Scenarios	Risk assessment	Scenarios	Risk assessment
Dependent variables: Decision-making process and outcomes *(reflected both in the exercise and in the debriefings and follow-up interviews)*					

In addition to the four core hypotheses, various sub-hypotheses were proposed at the outset of this research enterprise. Concerning the importance of process, it was assumed that strong facilitation and negotiation skills and participants' individual personalities would influence the outcomes of the deliberations.

Concerning the value of multiple scenarios, the assertions made were that they would:

- draw greater attention to the decision-making process, potentially complicating it;
- make those more familiar with making probabilistic decisions, in particular trained engineers, uncomfortable as they are encouraged to shift away from a single design standard, and that they would respond by defaulting to a single scenario and disregarding the others;
- precipitate the favoring of flexible approaches as a response to the highlighted uncertainty;
- provide ammunition to parties, with each favoring the scenario that best serves their interests, facilitating more persistent disagreement;
- lead to different coalitions and alliances among the parties; and
- lead to new forms of discourse because they make uncertainty more explicit.

With regards to the different governance regimes, it was hypothesized that deliberations in Singapore and Rotterdam would be more consensus-seeking while in Boston they would be more conflictual; stakeholders in Singapore would be more deferential and respectful of hierarchy than those in the other two cities; stakeholders in Rotterdam would be more aware and concerned about future risks than those in Boston; and participants in Rotterdam would also be more proactive. Furthermore, it was anticipated that these traits would influence how they might tackle climate change.

In terms of the role-play simulation exercise, the hypotheses were that it would help participants to better appreciate the climate risks they face; increase their recognition of the uncertainties involved; increase their confidence that they can and will find ways to tackle the climate risks; and foster new appreciation for multifaceted nature of the risks and thus the need for the kind of multi-stakeholder deliberation that the exercise simulated.

At the heart of the project were workshops held throughout 2013 and 2014 that brought together groups in each city for half a day. Participants grappled with how they might make better infrastructure investment decisions in the face of a changing and uncertain climate, while acknowledging the variety of other factors constraining their decision-making. As discussed in greater detail in Chapter 6, a key feature of the workshops was a role-play simulation exercise (i.e., serious game) that placed participants in a hypothetical situation involving a transportation infrastructure decision that needs to be made, but that is complicated by emerging climate threats. Participants took on roles different from those they hold in the real world and were given a range of possible options for moving forward, an overview of their various interests and priorities vis-à-vis those options, and information that they might use to make their decisions. The exercise had them deliberate and seek consensus around what they should do. Half of the groups were given a version of the exercise that featured multiple scenarios, while the other half was given a risk assessment forecast with a single, probabilistic forecast of future conditions. As discussed in Chapter 7, comparing and contrasting these two versions provided insights into the advantages and disadvantages of introducing multiple scenarios (i.e., possible futures) into planning and decision-making processes.

As illustrated in Figure 1.1, the workshops were at the core of the project, but were not the sole source of information. Background research and interviews were conducted early in the process to ground the project and provide a baseline understanding of the climate risks, adaptation initiatives underway, and wider institutional environments and modes of decision-making. In addition to desk research, preliminary interviews were conducted with approximately 80 individuals across the three cities.

At the workshops, lessons were learned from pre- and post-exercise surveys, focus-group-style debrief conversations with groups after the exercise runs, and the exercise runs themselves, which were video recorded and coded for analysis. The debriefings provided opportunities for participants to reflect on what happened during the exercise runs, how similar or different the simulated experiences were to what they face in their real-world settings, and how the differences and similarities may inform real-world planning and decision-making. These were critical opportunities to 'ground truth' what happened in the exercise and discuss the situations, opportunities and barriers in each city. The debriefings were focus-group style and informal, loosely following a set of broad questions, like 'Was there a drive among the group to seek consensus, or to extend conflict? How realistic is this compared to your real world?' The debriefings were also video recorded, transcribed and coded for analysis.

The pre- and post-exercise surveys helped to discern if and how the exercise had an impact on participants' perceptions. Many of the questions asked in the pre-exercise survey were asked again post-exercise to identify the ways in which the workshop experience altered participants' responses. The pre-exercise survey also served to get a better sense of who the participants were, while the post-exercise survey directly asked them about the RPS exercise and workshop experience to get a sense of how similar (or different) it was to their real-world experiences, and validate it as a tool for learning and research.

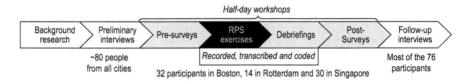

Figure 1.1 The Harboring Uncertainty research process
Used with permission of author

Finally, one-on-one semi-structured interviews were conducted with most of the 76 participants in the days following the workshops. These interviews, which typically lasted around an hour each, provided opportunities to better understand participants' perspectives and how they changed in light of this experience, delving deeper into the themes that emerged during the workshops. Participants' pre- and post-exercise surveys were not anonymous, so they could also be followed up on during the interviews. As with the preliminary interviews, these discussions were informal in nature and tailored to each interviewee's survey responses, previous comments and actions during the RPS exercise they participated in.

For later analysis, the preliminary and post-exercise interviews, RPS runs and debriefings were audio or video recorded. The recordings were transcribed and coded using standard qualitative research methods.[2] Statistical analysis was conducted on the pre- and post-exercise surveys. Participants identified themselves on both surveys, allowing for matched-pairs analysis. In particular, Wilcoxon signed-rank tests were run on various questions to test for statistical significance in shifts from pre- to post-exercise perspectives.

The exercise proved to be a rather novel and effective way to engage stakeholders and examine the nascent issue of climate change adaptation planning with them. Workshop participants came from a variety of agencies at all levels of government, including transportation, environment and urban planning authorities. For example, participants in Boston came from the city's transportation and planning departments, the state transportation and coastal zone management agencies, and the federal Department of Transportation. Some came from outside government, including from civil society and business organizations. All were recruited because they had relevance to the issue at hand – the impacts of climate change on infrastructure and how they might be addressed.

Introducing this book

This book is intended to help readers better understand possible pathways forward to enhance our climate adaptation planning and decision-making around infrastructure systems. As should be clear by now, the book is not technical in nature, but is rather about *improving governance*. It is hoped that this book can speak to wicked planning and policymaking challenges around climate change – and beyond – by contributing to our general understanding of how we can better account for complex risks characterized by uncertainty and dynamism in infrastructure planning and decision-making. It advances our understanding of how climate change adaptation may be integrated into infrastructure planning and decision-making, focusing on four themes in particular: (1) the importance of considering wider governance regimes when attempting to institutionalize adaptation; (2) the use of role-play simulation exercises for social learning and collaborative problem solving; (3) the use of multiple scenarios as a way to frame uncertainty; and (4) how we can advance more adaptive (i.e., flexible) *and* collaborative approaches to infrastructure planning, decision-making and management.

The rest of this book is divided into seven chapters, reflecting both the Harboring Uncertainty research process, and the themes identified above.

Chapter 2 compares and contrasts the three case cities – Singapore, Rotterdam and Boston – along various dimensions. It draws from both the RPS exercise run with participants and wider background research to examine how adaptation is evolving in these three cities. Particular attention is paid to how their respective governance regimes are shaping their activities. Issues explored include the relative levels of awareness, and degree and nature of action on climate adaptation; barriers to action; the nature of deliberations and the role played by stakeholder interests; the roles of governmental and non-governmental actors; how uncertainties are managed; and how priorities are established.

Chapters 3, 4 and 5 dive deeper into Rotterdam, Singapore and Boston respectively. Each of these case-based chapters starts with an overview of the Harboring Uncertainty project findings. This is followed by an introduction to each city's respective governance regime, discussing key characteristics and how they are (or might) influence the integration of climate resilience into infrastructure planning and decision-making. The next section in each introduces the climate-related threats that the city faces. Following that is a section that explores infrastructure planning and decision-making, particularly around transportation and coastal defense infrastructure. Interwoven throughout that section is information on the processes underway to address climate threats. The final section in each of these chapters draws synthesized conclusions on the state of affairs and how adaptation might evolve.

Chapter 6 explores the use of role-play simulation exercises for action research around emerging and complex threats like climate change. It introduces the use of RPSs – and serious games in general – and makes a case for their value, using data collected through the Harboring Uncertainty project. Project outcomes suggest that exercises can be valuable for increasing participants' recognition of climate risks, recognition of the presence and nature of uncertainties, confidence in their ability to adapt, understanding of the various interests and interdependencies present among different stakeholders, and appreciation for and understanding of good process in deliberative efforts.

Chapter 7 explores the use of multiple scenarios in project-level decision-making, based in large part on lessons learned through the RPS exercise run with Harboring Uncertainty participants. One version of the exercise – which was run with half of the groups across the three cities – contains multiple scenarios, and the other a single, probabilistic, risk assessment forecast. The findings suggest that scenario *planning* may very well be a valuable tool for groups grappling to make sense of uncertainties, particularly as part of higher-level strategic planning. Multiple scenarios can raise awareness of and bracket uncertainties and encourage the adoption of more flexible, adaptive decisions. However, officials are likely to confront significant challenges if they attempt to use scenarios to make project-level decisions. The need 'for a number' persists. For a number of reasons explored in this chapter, when it comes to infrastructure, agencies may inevitably need concrete forecasts that allow them to satisfice and make contingent decisions for now.

Chapter 8 responds to the calls for both flexibility and more effective processes in infrastructure management repeated throughout this book. Adaptive policy-making, collaborative adaptive management, anticipatory governance and other similar approaches to institutionalizing ongoing, iterative and responsive decision-making are explored. Tools for organizing more effective and efficient collaborative multi-stakeholder efforts, including the consensus building approach, are discussed. Joint fact finding is also introduced as a way to help groups devise shared information for decision-making.

Notes

1 An example of a resource produced by a government agency is the U.S. Environmental Protection Agency's *Being Prepared for Climate Change: A Workbook for Developing Risk-Based Adaptation Plans* (EPA 2014). Private consultancies are also contributing to the literature, including PricewaterhouseCoopers (2010) with their *Adapting to Climate Change in the Infrastructure Sectors* report. Non-governmental organizations play various prominent roles. The Georgetown Climate Center's Adaptation Clearinghouse is a major source of information, particularly for local and state officials in the United States.
2 The transcriptions were coded in a qualitative research program called TAMS Analyzer, using a code list that was initially developed based on the preliminary interviews but evolved throughout the project. Participants were also tagged based on their city, real-world position, role in the RPS exercise and version of the exercise they played. TAMS provides various tools for qualitative analysis. These tools were used to identify patterns and intensity, and extract quotations that illustrate key themes.

Works cited

Adger, W.N., S. Agrawala, M.M.Q. Mirza, C. Conde, K. O'Brien, J. Pulhin, R. Pulwarty, B. Smit and K. Takahashi (2007). Assessment of adaptation practices, options, constraints and capacity. Climate Change 2007: Impacts, Adaptation and Vulnerability. Contribution of Working Group II to the Fourth Assessment Report of the Intergovernmental Panel on Climate Change. M. L. Parry, O. F. Canziani, J. P. Palutikof, P. J. van der Linden and C. E. Hanson. Cambridge, UK, Cambridge University Press: 717–743.

Anguelovski, I. and J. Carmin (2011). Something borrowed, everything new: Innovation and institutionalization in urban climate governance. *Current Opinion in Environmental Sustainability*, 3: 1–7. doi:10.1016/j.cosust.2010.12.017

Baumgartner, F.R. and B.D. Jones (2009). *Agendas and Instability in American Politics*, Second Edition. Chicago, IL: University of Chicago Press.

Bea, R., I. Mitroff, D. Farber, H. Foster and K.H. Roberts (2009). A new approach to risk: The implications of E3. *Risk Management*, 11: 30–43. doi:10.1057/rm.2008.12

Berkhout, F., J. Hertin and D.M. Gann (2006). Learning to adapt: Organizational adaptation to climate change impacts. *Climatic Change*, 78: 135–156.

Berrang-Ford, L., J.D. Ford and J. Paterson (2011). Are we adapting to climate change? *Global Environmental Change*, 21: 25–33.

Bierbaum, R., A. Lee, J. Smith, M. Blair, L.M. Carter, F.S. Chapin, III, P. Fleming, S. Ruffo, S. McNeeley, M. Stults, L. Verduzco and E. Seyller (2014). Ch. 28: Adaptation. *Climate Change Impacts in the United States: The Third National Climate Assessment*. J.M. Melillo, T.C. Richmond and G.W. Yohe, Eds. U.S. Global Change Research Program. pp. 670–706. doi:10.7930/J07H1GGT

Biesbroek, R., J. Klostermann, C. Termeer and P. Kabat (2011). Barriers to climate change adaptation in the Netherlands. *Climate Law*, 2: 181–199.

Birkmann, J., M. Garschagen, F. Kraas and N. Quang (2010). Adaptive urban governance: New challenges for the second generation of urban adaptation strategies to climate change. *Sustainability Science*, 5: 185–206.

Bollinger, L.A., C.W.J. Bogmans, E.J.L. Chappin, G.P.J. Dijkema, J.N. Huibregtse, N. Maas, T. Schenk, M. Snelder, P. van Thienen, S. de Wit, B. Wols and L.A. Tavasszy (2014). Climate adaptation of interconnected infrastructures: A framework for supporting governance. *Regional Environmental Change*, 14: 919–931.

Box, G.E.P. and N.R. Draper (1987). *Empirical Model Building and Response Surfaces*. New York, NY: John Wiley & Sons.

Camacho, A.E. (2009). Adapting governance to climate change: Managing uncertainty through a learning infrastructure. *Emory Law Journal*, 59(1).

de Sherbinin, A., A. Schiller and A. Pulsipher (2007). The vulnerability of global cities to climate hazards. *Environment and Urbanization*, 19(1): 39–64.

Dorfman, M., M. Mehta, B. Chou, S. Fleischli and K.S. Rosselot (2011). *Thirsty for Answers: Preparing for the Water-Related Impacts of Climate Change in American Cities*. New York, NY: Natural Resources Defense Council.

Downs, A. (1967). *Inside Bureaucracy*. New York, NY: Little, Brown and Company.

Eakin, H. and M.C. Lemos (2010). Institutions and change: The challenge of building adaptive capacity in Latin America. *Global Environmental Change*, 20: 1–3.

EPA [United States Environmental Protection Agency] (2014). *Being Prepared for Climate Change: A Workbook for Developing Risk-Based Adaptation Plans*. Climate Ready Estuaries, EPA Office of Water.

Friend, R., J. Jarvie, S.O. Reed, R. Sutarto, P. Thinphanga and V.C. Toan (2014). Mainstreaming urban climate resilience into policy and planning; Reflections from Asia. *Urban Climate*, 7: 6–19.

Funfgeld, H. (2010). Institutional challenges to climate risk management in cities. *Current Opinion in Environmental Sustainability*, 2(3): 156–160.

Hajer, M. (2003). Policy without polity? Policy analysis and the institutional void. *Policy Sciences*, 36: 175–195.

HM Government (2011). *Climate Resilient Infrastructure: Preparing for a Changing Climate*. Presented to Parliament by the Secretary of State for Environment, Food and Rural Affairs by Command of Her Majesty. Norwich, UK: TSO (The Stationary Office).

Howlett, M. and M. Ramesh (1998). Policy subsystem configurations and policy change: Operationalizing the postpositivist analysis of the politics of the policy process. *Policy Studies Journal*, 26(3): 466–481.

IPCC (2014). Summary for policymakers. *Climate Change 2014: Impacts, Adaptation, and Vulnerability. Working Group II Contribution to the Fifth Assessment Report of the Intergovernmental Panel on Climate Change*. Field, C.B., V.R. Barros, D.J. Dokken, K.J. Mach, M.D. Mastrandrea, T.E. Bilir, M. Chatterjee, K.L. Ebi, Y.O. Estrada, R.C. Genova, B. Girma, E.S. Kissel, A.N. Levy, S. MacCracken, P.R. Mastrandrea, and L.L. White, Eds. Cambridge, UK and New York, NY: Cambridge University Press.

Lemos, M.C., C.J. Kirchhoff and V. Ramprasad (2012). Narrowing the climate information usability gap. *Nature Climate Change*, 2: 789–794.

Levin, K., B. Cashore, S. Bernstein and G. Auld (2012). Overcoming the tragedy of super wicked problems: Constraining our future selves to ameliorate global climate change. *Policy Sciences*, 45: 123–152.

Marshall, T. (2013). *Planning Major Infrastructure: A Critical Analysis*. Abingdon, UK: Routledge.

Mearns, L.O. (2010). The drama of uncertainty. *Climatic Change*, 100: 77–85.

Measham, T.G., B.L. Preston, T.F. Smith, C. Brooke, R. Gorddard, G. Withycombe and C. Morrison (2011). Adapting to climate change through local municipal planning: Barriers and challenges. *Mitigation and Adaptation Strategies for Global Change*, 16: 889–909.

Moser, S.C. and J.A. Ekstrom (2010). A framework to diagnose barriers to climate change adaptation. *PNAS*, 107(51): 22026–22031.

National Research Council [(U.S.) America's Climate Choices: Panel on Adapting to the Impacts of Climate Change] (2010). *Adapting to the impacts of climate change*. Washington, DC: National Academies Press.

Perrow, C. (1986). *Complex Organizations: A Critical Essay*. New York, NY: Random House.

Powell, W.W. and P. DiMaggio (1991). *The New Institutionalism in Organizational Analysis*. Chicago, IL: University of Chicago Press.

Pressman, J.L. and A.B. Wildavsky (1984). *Implementation: How Great Expectations in Washington Are Dashed in Oakland*. Berkeley, CA: University of California Press.

PricewaterhouseCoopers [LLP] (2010). *Adapting to Climate Change in the Infrastructure Sectors: Maintaining Robust and Resilient Infrastructure Systems in the Energy, Transport, Water and ICT Sectors*. A report for the Adapting to Climate Change Programme, UK Department for Environment, Food and Rural Affairs.

Rahman, S.A., W.E. Walker and V. Marchau (2008). *Coping With Uncertainties About Climate Change in Infrastructure Planning – An Adaptive Policymaking Approach*. Final Report. Rotterdam, NL: Ecorys Research and Consulting.

Rittel, H.W.J. and M.M. Webber (1973). Dilemmas in a General Theory of Planning. *Policy Sciences*, 4: 155–169.

Rockefeller Foundation (2016). *100 Resilient Cities*. www.100resilientcities.org

Rosenzweig, C., W.D. Solecki, R. Blake, M. Bowman, C. Faris, V. Gornitz, R. Horton, K. Jacob, A. Le Blanc, R. Leichenko, M. Linkin, D. Major, M. O'Grady, L. Patrick, E. Sussman, G. Yohe and R. Zimmerman (2011). Developing coastal adaptation to climate change in the New York City infrastructure-shed: Process, approach, tools, and strategies. *Climatic Change*, 106: 93–127.

Sainz de Murieta, E., I. Galarraga and A. Markandya (2014). An introduction to the economics of adaptation to climate change. *Routledge Handbook on Economics of Adaptation to Climate Change*. A. Markandya, I. Galarraga and E. Sainz de Murieta, Eds. London: Routledge.

Schipper, L. and I. Burton (2009). *The Earthscan Reader on Adaptation to Climate Change*. London, UK; Sterling, VA: Earthscan.

Simon, H.A. (1956). Rational choice and the structure of the environment. *Psychological Review*, 63(2): 129–138.

Susskind, L. (2010). Responding to the risks posed by climate change: Cities have no choice but to adapt. *The Town Planning Review*, 81(3): 217–235.

Termeer, C., A. Dewulf, H. van Rijswick, A. van Buuren, D. Huitema, S. Meijerink, T. Rayner and M. Wiering (2011). The regional governance of climate adaptation: A framework for developing legitimate, effective, and resilient governance arrangements. *Climate Law*, 2 159–179.

van Buuren, A. and J. Edelenbos (2004). Why is joint knowledge production such a problem? *Science and Public Policy*, 31(4): 289–299.

Walker, W.E., M. Haasnoot and J.H. Kwakkel (2013). Adapt or perish: A review of planning approaches for adaptation under deep uncertainty. *Sustainability*, 5: 955–979.

2 Learning across contrasting governance regimes

Contrasting governance regimes

Governance and policy regimes, including their institutional norms and standards and how they relate to infrastructure planning, are not universal (Marshall 2013). A variety of factors reflect and influence how and why they vary across space and time. This book focuses on Rotterdam in the Netherlands, Singapore and Boston in the United States, because they represent a good cross section of different governance regimes. Each city, and wider country, is archetypal of a different model: Decision-making in Rotterdam happens within a largely neo-corporatist paradigm; Boston within a neo-pluralist and neo-liberal paradigm; and Singapore within a top-down, semi-authoritarian paradigm. While not a comprehensive representation of all governance models, these cases reflect three distinct and important approaches to planning and decision-making.

The three succeeding chapters will discuss planning and policymaking vis-à-vis adaptation in each of these cities. This chapter compares and contrasts among them, with an eye towards what this says about tailoring adaptation planning to the governance context. It considers how their respective regimes may, comparatively speaking, influence their adaption decisions. Unique features of governance in each of the three case cities have implications on how the emerging issue of climate adaptation is being institutionalized. It is important to note, however, that there are also lessons to be learned from the similarities across the three case cities.

Neo-corporatist Rotterdam

The governance regime in Rotterdam is neo-corporatist in nature. This is clearest in economic policy and labor negotiations; employers, workers and the state formally negotiate as 'social partners' to reach sector and even economy-wide agreements on wages and other employment issues (Wiarda 1997). Rather than interacting in a predominantly adversarial fashion, the parties are expected to seek broad consensus. Scholars have variously emphasized and downplayed both the importance and collaborative nature of neo-corporatism, but generally agree that this model is significantly reflected in Dutch decision-making (Wiarda

1997; Woldendorp 2005). There is also debate around the degree to which neo-corporatism translates to policy spheres beyond economic policy, but evidence suggests that environmental issues can and do enter neo-corporatist agendas in countries with a strong tradition of following this model, including in the Netherlands (Glasbergen 2002; Jahn 1998; Schreuder 2001).

While the neo-corporatist model became popular throughout northwestern Europe after World War II, it may have deeper roots in the Netherlands in the form of the much older tradition of what the Dutch call 'poldering'. A polder is a low-lying piece of land, often reclaimed from the sea. The *polder model* of consensus seeking is rooted in the centuries-old practice of farmers and other landowners pooling their resources and reaching agreement on how they will maintain the dikes and manage the water within their shared polders. The model took on wider meaning in the 1980s to describe the practice of reaching broad consensus on economic and environmental policies in the neo-corporatist tradition (Schreuder 2001). In the course of the Harboring Uncertainty project, participants regularly described the 'polder mentality' as 'the way we do things'. There is also substantial academic literature suggesting that poldering is an important phenomenon in the setting of environmental policy (Glasbergen 2002; Schreuder 2001). It is notable, however, that some question the influence of the polder mentality in practice, noting that there is still substantial adversity (Woldendorp 2005). The transferability of the polder model to other countries has also been questioned (Schreuder 2001).

Neo-pluralist Boston

Decision-making in Boston can be considered neo-pluralist in nature. A range of interest groups continuously compete over the evolution of policies, ultimately shaping them in contention as much if not more than via consensus (Dahl 1962; Lindblom 1977). The prominent role that courts play in interpreting legislation and shaping how it is implemented in practice is evidence of this. While consensus may be reached in a neo-pluralist paradigm, many interactions are adversarial in nature. Parties compete for influence, with the outcome often requiring adjudication. Furthermore, the state is not a single actor, but a set of actors with varying interests across agencies, departments and levels of government, who are all seeking to influence decision-making. While early pluralist theory painted a rosier picture of balanced interests, Lindblom (1977), Domhoff (2010) and others have noted that certain groups can yield disproportionate influence in a world of vastly uneven power imbalances.

The governance regime in Boston may also be characterized as liberal or neo-liberal, as the state is a comparatively weaker actor in what is an overwhelmingly market-oriented economy that places high value on individual rights (Harvey 2007; Jahn 1998). The state plays a major role in the provision and management of infrastructure, but these activities are typically framed in the service of the private economy, and private companies under contract do much of the actual work. It is notable that the neo-liberal paradigm is dominant in most Western democracies – private management contracts have, for example, also become common in Dutch infrastructure provision. However, notably lower government expenditures on infrastructure and greater constraints on what the state can do – for example, in terms of public takings – suggest that the government is a relatively weaker actor in the United States. The laissez faire mentality and deference to individual liberty deeply entrenched in the underlying ethos are conducive to neo-liberalism.

Top-down Singapore

Singapore's decision-making environment is top-down and at least somewhat authoritarian in nature (Haley and Low 1998; Ortmann 2011; Rodan and Jayasuriya 2007). The city-state's highly professionalized civil service engages in extensive planning for all facets of the economy and society (Tan 2008). For example, over 80% of the population resides in government-built and -managed housing (Housing and Development Board 2016). The government plays a critical role in planning and service provision, but not to the exclusion of private enterprise; markets and central planning operate synergistically, facilitating an impressive run of economic growth and high social welfare (Huff 1995). The state also attempts to shape high-quality physical and sociocultural environments in what is in every way a highly constructed landscape (Henderson 2012).

The Singapore model is not, however, without its criticisms, including on human rights and democratic grounds. Singapore effectively operates as a single-party state with the government exerting its authority to maintain stability and advance what it sees as the interests of the nation (Henderson 2012; Ortmann 2011; Rodan and Jayasuriya 2007). Micro-management has historically led to significant prosperity and a high capacity to manage problems, but it has been criticized for its inflexibility. Critics contend that the focus on stability and planning at the expense of a more risk-taking entrepreneurial mentality could have negative economic consequences in an increasingly globalized world (Saywell 2002). In the political arena, there is concern that the traditionally meritocratic and highly capable civil service could, over time, devolve into an elite oligopoly that focuses on self-maintenance ahead of material performance (Tan 2008). As reflected in the chapter on Singapore, the state has opened windows for public participation, but very much on its own terms (Rodan and Jayasuriya 2007).

The way in which governance takes place is inevitably shaped by the wider structure of the government. The levels of government and mix of agencies involved in infrastructure planning vary across these three cities. In Boston, municipal, regional, state and national agencies all have roles. In contrast, Singapore is a city-state with only one layer of government. These differences are intertwined with their respective systems of governance. Fragmentation in Boston is both a result and product of its neo-pluralist nature. A more hierarchical model is possible in Singapore, in part, because there are not different levels of government to contend with each other.

Similarities among the three cities

Boston, Singapore and Rotterdam are archetypal of different governance regimes, but are also similar in important ways. All three are harbor cities with economically and culturally important infrastructure and built environments that are very vulnerable to climate change. A common threat is the impact of sea level rise (and storm surges) on low-lying lands reclaimed from the sea through fill and draining. While at different stages in the process, all three have climate adaptation efforts underway. They are part of many of the same global networks, including the Rockefeller Foundation's 100 Resilient Cities network and the C40 Cities Climate Leadership Group.

Comparing across the cases

There are lessons to be learned from comparing and contrasting across the three case cities. They approach planning and decision-making, including around infrastructure, in more or less unique ways. Some of the differences are understandable through the lenses of their respective governance models. Other differences and similarities may be attributable to their unique histories and institutional evolutions; sociocultural, economic and natural environments; and the dissemination of wider global norms and ideas. The similarities and differences shed light on how adaptation might be approached, hinting at what might be more universally valuable tactics, at least in a range of developed coastal cities, and which elements might require greater tailoring to context.

Key differences and similarities looking across the three cities are introduced in Table 2.1 and discussed further below. Comparisons are made in nine areas related to climate change, adaptation and the wider nature of decision-making in each place. As introduced in the first chapter, these findings are drawn from a variety of sources, including extensive desk research, interviews with key actors, a role-play simulation exercise run with key actors in each of the three cities, pre- and post-exercise surveys and post-exercise debriefings. These multiple sources of information provide a rich understanding of what is happening. As outlined in more detail in each of the case chapters, data collected via these various tools culminates in comprehensive pictures of how adaptation planning and decision-making is unfolding in each of the three cities and their wider countries, and how they might proceed in the future.

Lessons learned from the Harboring Uncertainty workshops

A role-play simulation exercise run with Harboring Uncertainty project participants was a primary source of information for this chapter and wider book. The exercise is discussed in greater detail in Chapter 6. Comparing and contrasting the processes followed and outcomes that the various groups participating in the exercise reached across the three cities provides insight into how their respective governance regimes might shape their approaches to adaptation planning and decision-making. Key outcomes for each group are summarized in Table 2.2 below,

Table 2.1 Cross-case comparison on adaptation and infrastructure planning

	Boston *Neo-pluralist/neo-liberal*	Singapore *Top-down/semi-authoritarian*	Rotterdam *Neo-corporatist*
Awareness of climate risks	Self-reported high degree of awareness; extensive documentation of risks	Self-reported low degree of awareness; little documented reporting of risks	Middling awareness reported; very high degree of documentation of risks
Nature of adaptation planning efforts	Many fragmented adaptation efforts, with relatively less coordination	Highly coordinated, hierarchically organized adaptation planning, but limited thus far	Multiple agencies and other actors engaged in sophisticated and well-coordinated efforts
Status of climate adaptation	Numerous assessments and guidance documents; little concrete investment in adaptation so far	Mostly evaluative so far, with some measures to enhance resilience	Strong, proactive adaptive measures on coastal risks; less, but increasing, for other infrastructure systems
Barriers to adaptation	Lack of resources; competing priorities; unclear/undefined responsibility	Lack of prioritization; (perceptions of) uncertainty around risks	Coastal defense network seen as the panacea; competing priorities
Role of interests	Adjudication and/or reconciliation of competing interests	Pursuit of 'national interests' and appeal to 'rationality'	Reconciliation of different interests ('poldering' tradition); appeals to notion of 'fairness'
Roles of state and nonstate actors	Non-governmental actors (both business and other advocacy groups) play key roles	Strong state role, with almost no involvement of non-governmental actors	Strong state role, with some non-governmental actors involved
Process of priority setting	Priorities and senior leadership can shift with administrations	Extremely stable, top-down management	Relatively stable priorities and management; division between 'political' and 'technical'
Nature of internal government deliberations	Different agencies can be at odds, requiring resolution of disputes; some policy entrepreneurship	Hierarchical governance, with internal debate at staff level but closed-door and not vertically	Opportunities for staff debate horizontally and vertically, within and across agencies
Response to uncertainties	Consult experts (current); flexibility and consult experts (preferred)	Flexibility, consult experts and robustness (current); flexibility (preferred)	Flexibility and consult experts (current); flexibility (preferred)

Table 2.2 Summary of outcomes for the 10 exercise groups across three cities

	Scenarios version	Risk assessment version
Rotterdam	Call for more research, but reflection that barriers were largely political. Information withheld by opinionated experts. Active chair	Leaning towards below-grade road. Impasse because full consensus rule invoked by chair. Strong expert opinions. Issue of 'fairness' around funding
Singapore	Improve existing road and freight rail service. Money for port transition to rail. Active environmental and port representatives, appealing to reason	Elevated road with pollution mitigation measures; alderwoman convinced on "merit of the arguments". 'Community consultation', but really just information provision. Active experts
	Improve existing road and freight. Further study of A and B as well. Fact-based process (vs. interests). Active chair, and prominent experts	Leaning towards phased approach based on improving existing road and expanding rail, but concerns around ability of rail to meet port's needs. Dominant chair controlled process, and wanted full agreement (i.e., unanimity)
Boston	Call for more research, with improved road and rail option popular. Financing emphasized. Introduction of other creative options, like alternative routes. Interests directly discussed; threat of lawsuit from environmentalist. Climate change ignored	Improve existing road with dedicated truck lanes, and passenger rail. If money found, broader rail investments – money not on table immediately. Strong port interests. Coalition building. Creativity
	Tentative agreement on improving road and freight, but call for more research. Possible additional road in future. Complaints of too much uncertainty, which the senior engineer emphasized. Actively considered scenarios, but assumed the 'wet and busy' scenario with sea level rise and high growth in decision-making. Creativity (e.g., moving port)	Improve existing road, and freight and passenger rail. Extra money from city, including for creative port compensation. Focus on competing interests, and threat of lawsuit from environmentalist (as in all Boston groups). Negotiation tactics, including port and city sidebar. Very skilled chair

with longer descriptions and further analysis provided within the respective case chapters (Chapters 3 through 5).

Some of the differences across exercise runs can be attributed to the particularities of each group and the individual actions of those involved, but interesting patterns emerge when the outcomes are compared across the 10 groups in three cities. These are summarized in Table 2.3. While the exercise runs invoked reflection among participants and were insightful, it is important to reiterate that they were not the only source of data for this research.

Table 2.3 Comparing and contrasting key features of exercise process and outcomes across the three cities

	Rotterdam	Singapore	Boston
Process	Little deference to hierarchy; experts opinionated and forthcoming with arguments Emphasis on information, but used to undergird interest-based arguments	Invocation of national priorities (economy in particular) as a reason to favor certain choices Appeal to 'rationality', and persuasion based on technical arguments	Explicit recognition of interests, and attention to them Clearest use of negotiation tactics Financing emphasized as a factor
Outcomes	No agreements reached. In one case, called for more information. The other reached an impasse while seeking full consensus	Emphasis on avoiding hardship to port, and creativity to do so Agreed upon community sacrifices for larger concerns, like wider economic growth	Chose options that are flexible and cost-effective today. Other options discounted because of strong stakeholder opposition (including fear of lawsuits)

Awareness of climate risks

Harboring Uncertainty participants were asked to self-report their level of awareness of 'climate change and the risks it may pose'. The average responses pre-exercise were 6 in Boston, 5 in Rotterdam, and 4.3 in Singapore on a 7-point Likert scale from 'not at all' at 1 to 'very' at 7. Comparatively speaking, these averages are not particularly significant absent any sort of common yardstick against which participants were asked to compare themselves. Nonetheless, they do concur with wider observations of the state of affairs in each city. More importantly, as discussed in Chapter 6, there was a statistically significant increase in the reported level of awareness from pre- to post-exercise. Unsurprisingly, the self-reported level of awareness was, on average, higher among those working directly on climate change and/or sustainability issues.

Compared with similar counterparts in the other two countries, self-reported awareness was highest in Boston across different groups of participants, including those coming from transportation agencies and engineering consulting firms. This suggests that information on the risks posed by climate change is permeating further throughout agencies, including to officials who would not typically think of their work as climate related. The expectation when the Harboring Uncertainty project was initiated was that the level of awareness would be highest in the Netherlands, given their long relationship with the sea and history of sophisticated water management. Flood control is highly institutionalized as a government priority. While still reporting relatively high levels of awareness of the risks climate change poses, some participants expressed concern that the excellent job done by flood control specialists has fostered complacency among other actors around the various other risks the country may face, and stifled discussion around whether continuing to reinforce hard coastal infrastructure is the best approach as conditions evolve. In contrast, there is widespread concern in Boston that far too little is being done to address the risks. The high level of self-reported awareness in Boston is not altogether surprising, given that numerous reports have been released by various agencies and other organizations detailing the risks climate change poses. In addition to attention within government, these assessments have received substantial press coverage. The feeling of vulnerability is increasingly widespread, with events like Hurricane Sandy in the New York City region serving as a wakeup call.

The level of attention being given to climate risks is relatively lower in Singapore, so it is not surprising that the self-reported level of awareness is as well. The government has relayed very little information on the country's climate vulnerabilities. The Resilience Working Group of the multi-agency National Climate Change Secretariat (NCCS) has conducted a vulnerability assessment but, according to interviewees, is reticent to release this information until they can also present solutions. As a result, not only the public but also government officials not involved in their agencies' climate change efforts are relatively unaware of the risks and potential adaptive responses.

Participants were also asked how significant of a factor they expect climate change to be in their organizations' planning and decision-making over the next 10 years. Here too, the average response was highest in Boston at 5.7 (pre-exercise on a 7-point Likert scale), compared to only 4.9 in Rotterdam and 4 in Singapore. Unsurprisingly, the responses were significantly higher among those already working on climate change issues. For example, a participant from the Massachusetts Department of Transportation in Boston who is managing one of their high-profile climate initiatives selected 7, while other employees from the same agency that answered this question ranked it 3 and 4. Similarly, a City of Boston participant involved in their climate initiatives responded with a 7, while others from the city (from various departments) answered 4 and 5. This suggests that there is still a gap in how deeply climate adaptation is integrated into agencies. This gap may be problematic insofar as climate adaptation becomes an important factor throughout all planning and decision-making.

Nature of adaptation planning efforts underway

Climate change adaptation planning efforts are underway in all three cities, but they vary in structure and character. This includes differences in which government agencies and/or other organizations are leading processes; the breadth of the different efforts in terms of how narrow or holistic of an approach they are taking; who is involved, including both the range of government and non-state actors, and the participation of technical versus lay stakeholders; and the degree to which, and how, different efforts are coordinated and interacting.

In Boston, there is a plethora of initiatives coming from various agencies at four different levels of government – municipal, regional, state and federal – and led by non-governmental organizations. At the municipal level, the Greenovate initiative is championing adaptation across city government. The city has released various reports, including its latest *Climate Ready Boston* report in 2016. A City-initiated Green Ribbon Commission draws membership from various key private and public organizations and municipal and state government in an effort to engender broad support and generate innovative ideas. As discussed in the next subsection, actual implementation of the various recommendations coming out of these planning processes varies.

One challenge is that the municipal landscape is fragmented in the metropolitan area, with over 100 different cities and towns, each with substantial autonomy on key issues like land-use planning. Some of these communities are working on climate adaptation, but most are not. The Metropolitan Area Planning Council (MAPC) attempts to play a coordinating role in the region, and maintains a Metro Boston Regional Climate Change Adaptation Strategy. According to many interviewees, a regional approach is needed and the MAPC could play a role, but unfortunately it lacks real authority. In the transportation domain, the Metropolitan Planning Organization (MPO), which is affiliated with the MAPC, has teeth insofar as any projects that receive federal funding must pass through its processes, but it is not yet accounting for climate change in its planning and project assessment.

Much of the infrastructure in the Boston area is managed by state agencies. Massachusetts passed the Global Warming Solutions Act in 2008, which, among other things, mandated the creation of an adaptation advisory committee. The committee's work culminated in the release of the Massachusetts Climate Change Adaptation Report in 2011. Since then, different agencies have taken various steps, as discussed in the next section of this chapter. Interagency adaptation planning is coordinated by the Executive Office of Energy and Environmental Affairs, which had a dedicated Policy Advisor for Climate Change Adaptation until the change of administrations in early 2015. Climate change adaptation does not appear to be a major priority for the current governor and his administration. Some agencies, including the Department of Transportation (MassDOT), have conducted vulnerability assessments (Bosma et al. 2015). This assessment is notable in that it originally focused on the vulnerability of the Central Artery tunnels in Boston but mushroomed into a partnership involving the cities of Boston and Cambridge, and is providing sophisticated information on the risks to the wider urban region and some potential adaptive responses. Many other agencies are now using the results of their inundation modeling, as it has implications on their own planning and decision-making.[1]

At the federal level in the United States, the previous (Obama) administration used its executive authority to take action. Various agencies have also taken steps to assess climate risks, develop responses, and share and support the implementation of best practices. The future of federal involvement is now uncertain, as the new (Trump) administration has downplayed the importance of climate change and vowed to significantly cut both regulations and agency budgets.

As discussed in more detail later in this chapter, non-governmental actors are playing key roles in adaptation planning in the Boston region. At the planning level, Boston Harbor Now (formerly The Boston Harbor Association) has been a key coordinator of climate assessments.[2] The Boston-based Barr Foundation has funded various efforts of both nonprofits and government agencies. Neighborhood organizations also support community-based adaptation.

In Singapore, climate change adaptation planning is coordinated through the National Climate Change Secretariat (NCCS), which is a multi-agency effort chaired by the deputy prime minister. The NCCS's work is conducted via a hierarchy of committees and subcommittees. The Resilience Working Group is responsible for adaptation planning and policymaking. It is comprised of senior representatives from the key agencies, including the Ministry of Environment and Water Resources, the Ministry of National Development, the Ministry of Finance and the Land Transport Authority. Below this are 'thematic clusters' focused on specific issues like 'infrastructure'. A representative from the Land Transport Authority chairs the infrastructure cluster. The absence of non-governmental actors on these committees is notable, yet unsurprising in government-dominated Singapore.

The NCCS released a National Climate Change Strategy in 2012 and is developing adaptation plans. Some agencies are starting to institutionalize adaptation into their processes. For example, the Building and Construction Authority established a Coastal and Project Management Department to address coastal protection and adaptation issues and is working on a Risk Map Study. The highly coordinated nature of governance in Singapore is a contributing factor to the organized way in which adaptation planning is occurring. The fact that there is only one level of government in the city-state also makes matters easier.

In Rotterdam, multiple agencies at different levels of government are engaged in climate adaptation planning. The Rotterdam Climate Initiative, which is a partnership between the municipal government, port, Deltalinqs (the port businesses' association), and DCMR (the regional environmental protection agency in the Rijnmond), has been planning for climate change since 2007. The Rotterdam Climate Proof program, which is the adaptation-focused component of the initiative, has established the goal of making the region 'climate proof' by 2025. Measures to achieve this goal are outlined in an ambitious climate change adaptation strategy. The city has a 'climate director' to coordinate its efforts, alongside dedicated staff in other organizations, including the port.

At the national level, there are various initiatives to enhance climate resilience. When it comes to coastal defense, the Dutch have been adapting to the climate since the 13th century, giving strong precedence to today's efforts. The Deltaplan, which was initiated in the 1930s but really accelerated after the disastrous floods of 1953, coordinated the construction of an extremely robust network of coastal defenses. A high-level Second Delta Commission was established in 2007, partly in recognition of the threats climate change might present to flood defense infrastructure. The Commission took an extremely long-range and holistic approach and recommended various investments and changes to spatial planning. The government is now implementing many of the recommendations and planning towards others. Rijkswaterstaat is the executive agency of the Ministry of Infrastructure and the Environment responsible for both the construction and management of water and transportation infrastructure at the national level. It is largely responsible for implementing the recommendations of the Delta Commission. From a planning perspective, its internal staff conduct vulnerability assessments and consider how climate risks can be integrated into decision-making. As in Boston, various climate adaptation planning processes are underway at the local/regional and national levels in the Netherlands, although with more coordination.

While attempts at better coordination are being made, adaptation planning efforts in the Boston region are fragmented across various agencies and other stakeholder groups, which is unsurprising in a neo-pluralist context. This fragmentation may contribute, however, to inefficient duplication of efforts, counteractive investments and narrow perspectives. On the other hand, the notion of and responsibility for adaptation is more widely disseminated. In contrast, adaptation planning in Singapore is highly coordinated and hierarchically organized, which may bring efficiencies, but leaves less room for innovation. Efforts in the Rotterdam region fall somewhere in between. Various efforts are underway by various agencies, but the level of coordination is higher than in Boston. Furthermore, climate risks are almost entirely framed as a flood defense issue in the Netherlands.

Status of climate adaptation in practice

Unfortunately, neither awareness nor planning necessarily translate into concrete action. Some action is taking place in all three cities, but it is relatively limited thus far, especially in Boston and Singapore. Rotterdam is further along in implementing concrete adaptive efforts.

In Boston, numerous assessments and guidance documents have been released, some with more formal directives and teeth than others have. For example, the Boston Planning & Development Agency (2015) requires that all large projects complete a Climate Change Preparedness and Resiliency Checklist, which includes questions like:

- What is the full expected life of the project?
- What is the full expected operational life of key building systems (e.g., heating, cooling, ventilation)?
- What time span of future climate conditions was considered?

Unfortunately, these standards are process rather than performance based. They are intended to draw attention to the risks but do not mandate any specific adaptive responses. In the absence of concrete adaptive requirements, some project proponents are diligent, while many are not. In terms of infrastructure, the Boston Water and Sewer Commission (BWSC) is furthest along in making concrete changes; the agency took future climate risks into account when developing their 25-year capital asset program. Investments and maintenance decisions are made with consideration of the risks. The Boston Transportation and Public Works Departments are starting to assess the risks climate change poses to their infrastructure, but have made few concrete changes thus far.

At the state level, various agencies, including the Office of Coastal Zone Management (CZM), have released guidance documents and provide technical and financial support through their initiatives, like the CZM office's StormSmart Coasts program. The CZM has also added future climate risks to the assessment processes it expects municipalities and private landowners to go through when conducting coastal and harbor planning. Unfortunately, similarly to the standards discussed above, these process requirements lack concrete performance standards. In the context of transportation infrastructure, there are examples of projects responding to climate risks, like the Morrissey Boulevard reconstruction in Boston, but these are rare instances thus far. In fact, Harboring Uncertainty interviewees reflected that some projects that may be acutely vulnerable have fallen short in adequately accounting for the risks. The Department of Conservation and Recreation, which is responsible for much of the coastal flood defense infrastructure, is starting to consider climate impacts as they assess and design projects. Unfortunately, according to interviewees, resource constraints and competing priorities severely limit how much is done in practice to advance adaptation.

At the federal level, agencies exert most of their influence via their grants programs, regulatory oversight and the provision of technical support. Regulations have been slow to change in response to changing climate risks. Some agencies that directly manage infrastructure – including the Army Corps of Engineers – are taking steps to consider future climate risks in their planning and design.

In Singapore, some concrete steps have been taken to integrate changing climate risks. The most prominent is an increase in the minimum elevation of newly reclaimed land from 1.25 meters above the highest recorded tide observed before 1991 to 2.25 meters. Some steps to enhance infrastructure for other reasons – including the ambitious efforts to achieve water independence by investing in water reclamation, desalinization, and aggressive capture and storage – may provide enhanced robustness as the climate changes. However, many agencies have made little or no progress on climate adaptation. On the transportation front, the Land Transport Agency (LTA) is at the table in the NCCS efforts, but this does not seem to be percolating into tangible decision-making yet, as evinced by the fact that the latest Master Plan, released in 2013, makes no mention of 'climate change', 'adaptation', 'flooding' or other climate keywords (LTA 2013). Three of four participants from the LTA engaged in this research concurred that it is not (yet) a high priority for the agency. "The problem is that climate change is too vague, and we operate at the specific level, so if the threat is so vague it is hard to translate into an operational plan that I can put on the ground", opined one of them, adding that they "need a very specific assessment to develop a plan; that is what is so tricky about climate change".

Rotterdam is the furthest along in taking concrete steps to advance climate adaptation. As discussed in the previous section, the national government is assessing when and how to shore up coastal defense infrastructure that is already designed to withstand 1-in-10,000-year storms. At the municipal level, there have been various projects, including the construction of a new multi-purpose parking garage close to the central train station that can serve as a water storage tank when needed; a new 'water square' that serves various recreational purposes when dry and stores rainwater when necessary, which was the product of an extensive participatory process with the surrounding community; and a 'paving out and plants in' campaign that is encouraging landowners to remove impermeable surfaces. Climate adaptation is not well integrated into land transportation infrastructure planning yet, although there have been some initial attempts. For example, 10-, 20- and 50-year water level projections were considered when designing an 'eco aqueduct' as part of the new A4 motorway extension currently under construction in the Rotterdam region.

Barriers to adaptation

While progress is being made, it is evident that significant work remains to integrate effective adaptation into planning and decision-making. Agencies and other stakeholders must find more effective ways to make sense of the risks and account for them. It is valuable to understand the obstacles to more effective adaptation. Looking across Boston, Rotterdam and Singapore, some barriers appear to be more universal in nature. Others are more unique, underscoring how intertwined they are with the respective governance norms and context-specific conditions.

Asked why climate change is not a higher priority, 'lack of resources' was the most popular choice among Harboring Uncertainty participants in Boston. During the exercise runs, the groups in Boston focused on funding more than did those in Singapore and Rotterdam, underscoring its importance as a factor in decision-making. Reflecting on the exercise experience, several participants identified chronic underfunding as a barrier to climate adaptation in infrastructure planning and decision-making. Projects are often already long overdue and underfunded, leaving little room for the consideration of other factors like future climate change. "A lot of bridge projects are accelerated almost to the case of being an emergency, so I don't know that [future climate vulnerability is] ever anybody's first question", said one participant.

Acute resource constraints exacerbate competition among priorities but are not the sole source of contention. As discussed further in the next section, the interests of the various stakeholder groups at the table came out most sharply among the Boston groups playing the RPS exercise. Participants felt compelled to reject certain route and design options based on likely community opposition, which they felt could have political implications or lead to long delays with legal challenges. While taking community interests and concerns seriously is very laudable, it can be a barrier to what might be wise but unpopular choices. Another significant barrier to climate adaptation in Boston is unclear and undefined responsibility in an environment with multiple initiatives but no clear coordination. "As far as regional planning is concerned, I think that's the biggest uncertainty because it's so difficult to come to consensus on what should happen on a larger basis. . . . I think we have a big problem with uncertainty insofar as planning is concerned", reflected a participant.

In contrast to Boston, the infrastructure systems in both Singapore and the Netherlands are robust and generally well funded. Both countries have put substantial resources into infrastructure systems when deemed a priority, namely the coastal flood defense network in the Netherlands and the 'four taps' strategy for water independence in Singapore.

The presence of 'competing priorities' was identified as an issue in Rotterdam as well. In contrast, in Singapore the emphasis is on shared 'national interests'. The primary barrier is subsequently that adapting to climate change has not yet been identified as a national priority. "I think a lot of agencies are having a wait-and-see attitude because . . . we will need a very strong mandate on 'Yes, let's do this, this is the broad, overarching strategy for Singapore', and then agencies, respective policies can come in", said a participant. She went on to note that "some agencies have started on their own, which is a good attempt, but . . . at the very top of this hierarchy, someone would probably have to decide 'this is the strategic direction we're going for Singapore' [and then] different plans, adaptation plans, mitigation plans [will] all have to fit into this broader strategy".

Participants in Singapore also reflected that the threats would have to be felt first. This stems, at least in part, from discomfort with the notion of persistent uncertainty. In Boston and Rotterdam, participants talked about uncertainty as a problem insofar as it challenges the assumption of static future conditions and has not yet been translated into usable design conditions. In Singapore, some participants still feel that the science itself is too uncertain to make decisions. In the words of a participant involved in the process, we are "still trying to better understand the impact of climate change on Singapore at this stage, so it is a bit premature to factor [into decision-making]". In an ostensibly rational, technocratic planning environment, parties want to feel like they are getting the necessary technical information to make the best possible decisions. Rather than embracing uncertainty, experts should be ready to 'speak with conviction' and 'justify why their models are sufficient', asserted a participant.

Given the adaptive measures already underway, Rotterdam would appear to have the fewest barriers. Nonetheless, in addition to competing priorities, one challenge is ensuring that all climate threats receive adequate attention. Planning mechanisms and resources have been trained on water management for decades, but climate adaptation will require action on other fronts as well, including in making transportation infrastructure more robust. Participants expressed some degree of concern that the robust coastal defense infrastructure has engendered a false sense of confidence that little else needs to be done to make systems climate ready.

The role of interests in planning and decision-making

The ways in which interests are understood and managed varies across the three cases, with the starkest difference being between Singapore and the other two countries. In Singapore, the emphasis is placed on shared 'national interests', whereas in the Netherlands and the United States there is wider acknowledgement of the various interests and priorities that different stakeholder groups hold, which often need to be reconciled or adjudicated. This is not to say that no attention is given to individual interests in Singapore, but rather that, relatively speaking, officials are focused on advancing what is perceived to be a set of shared national priorities. One example of this came by accident during a Harboring Uncertainty workshop; when reviewing the exercise instructions, two different participants independently asked what the 'national priorities' are, because they are not explicitly identified in the instructions. Discussing afterwards, some participants reflected that they were uncomfortable not knowing what the shared priorities were. In the absence of explicitly identified national priorities in the exercise, many participants assumed those that have dominated in Singapore, particularly economic growth. This is underscored by the fact that all four groups that played the exercise deferred to the port's interests one way or another. It could be interpreted from these outcomes that the port representatives were simply the most effective in fighting for their interests. However, the pattern of deliberations and reflections of the participants suggest that the situation was more one of parties coalescing around the importance of the economy and thus need to protect the port's viability.

In Singapore, the national priorities are well known, and planning and decision-making typically responds to them. Substantial resources have been invested, for example, in the state-of-the-art water system to secure freshwater independence. As discussed in the previous section, climate change is not yet deemed a national priority in Singapore. Participants' opinions on if and how climate change might become a greater priority varied. Some feel that it will inherently be reactive, although the work of the NCCS is laying the groundwork for it to emerge as a priority if and when deemed appropriate.

In contrast to Singapore, decision-making in Boston is characterized by the presence of various competing interests that need to be either reconciled or adjudicated. This came out very starkly in the exercise runs. The actors at the table representing specific constituencies or interest groups – i.e., the aldermen and -women speaking for a potentially impacted neighborhood, environmentalists and port representatives – were unabashed in explicitly stating their interests and fighting for them. While they did apply coalitional strategies in some cases, the notion of appealing to, or accepting, a wider or common cause did not emerge. In fact, the environmentalists in all four groups invoked the possibility of a lawsuit if their interests were ignored. Participants reflected afterwards that the threat of a lawsuit and community opposition were significant factors in shaping the perceived viability of different options and thus the ultimate outcomes. They also reflected that this is very realistic, as the courts have played prominent roles in many of the most important infrastructure projects in the region in recent decades. Furthermore, whether via legal avenues or other forms of pressure, the concerns of various interest groups regularly shape projects.

Stakeholders in the Boston context are forthright in expressing and pursuing their respective individual interests. It is important to note, however, that resolving tensions between competing interests and priorities does not always have to involve litigation or be adversarial; mechanisms are typically in place to consult different groups as projects are developed, although their efficacy is regularly questioned. The exercise conducted with participants modeled an alternative, deliberative approach in which parties seek mutually acceptable outcomes that address their various interests. Some participants reflected that they have participated in similar processes in practice, although it is not widespread as an approach. Those for whom it was a new experience reflected that they could see opportunities for similar processes in their work.

Competition among interests did not come out as sharply in Rotterdam as in Boston, but it still manifested. Exercise participants saw their task as reconciling these various interests, and looked for solutions that everyone could 'live with'. During the debriefings and follow-up interviews, they described the process of planning and decision-making, particularly around large projects, as one involving phases of parties lobbying for their interests, and attempts to 'balance' these interests and find mutually acceptable outcomes. "We try to build up a case; it will never be a perfect 100% win-win, but as much win as possible", said a participant from an important advocacy organization. The tradition of seeking consensus in the Netherlands is often referred to as the 'polder mentality'. Poldering does not inherently generate optimal outcomes; the 'wisdom of the crowd' is not always wise. Participants in Rotterdam were surprised when other interests overwhelmed climate adaptation goals in the exercise. The failure of both groups to reach agreement within the time allocated would seem to support another criticism often leveled at deliberative processes – that they can take more time.

The notion of 'fairness' also emerged as a factor in Rotterdam. Participants asserted that any outcome should be fair to all involved. Concern around the fair shouldering of responsibility was a significant complicating factor in one of the group's deliberations; the alderman was ready to commit the city to funding half of the cost of some extra remedial flood prevention measures, but only if the port would commit to funding the other half. This despite the fact that his instructions stated that he could fund all of it. To the participant, it was a matter of principle. The group failed to reach consensus within the time allotted anyway, but this issue was left unresolved with the port tasked with 'looking into' whether they could find funding. In contrast, groups in Singapore did what they could to accommodate the port, seeing its viability as a national priority. In Boston, the port representatives fought hard for their interests, and participants reflected that this is what they would expect, void of any sense of fairness.

In Singapore, climate adaptation will need to be integrated into the national priorities if it is to gain significant traction. Whether adversarial or collaborative, adaptation efforts in Boston and Rotterdam will need to explicitly account for different interests if they are to be successful. This is not necessarily an easy task, given that other interests are often well entrenched and impacts on them acutely felt, while long-term climate risks can seem more abstract and adaptation does not have the same type of constituency behind it.

Roles of state and nonstate actors in climate adaptation

Non-governmental actors are playing central roles in adaptation planning in the Boston region. Boston Harbor Now, which was formerly known as The Boston Harbor Association, has collaborated with the City, academics and other organizations to produce influential reports, organize events and generally raise the profile of climate risks and potential responses. Despite the fact that it is an advocacy organization, the group has significant credibility. The City of Boston has focused on integrating the institutional, business and nonprofit communities into its adaptation planning efforts, including via the Green Ribbon Commission. An interviewee actively involved in adaptation efforts in the city reflected that "in Boston, the business community and the institutional community are very involved in the climate change conversation, and we are very fortunate that that is the case", adding that "there are some deniers, there always are, but on the whole, we have an extremely supportive business community and benefit from that". Business organizations like A Better City (ABC) play prominent roles that go far beyond traditional lobbying. These groups leverage their resources, which can be scarce within government, and marshal support to advance research, planning, and decision-making. Private foundations like the Barr Foundation play important roles as sources of support in a resource-constrained environment. Barr has established climate change as a priority and funded various initiatives of both nonprofits and governmental agencies.

At the community level, organizations like Neighborhood of Affordable Housing (NOAH) in East Boston are also playing important roles. NOAH is partnering with academics to better understand the impacts climate change might have on this vulnerable community, and then directly engaging with residents to consider how they can adapt. While government officials are involved, the focus is on independent, community-based adaptation strategies. This is a markedly different approach from those in Singapore or Rotterdam, where government agencies are generally expected to plan and implement measures. Neighborhood-specific business and institutional organizations like the Medical, Academic and Scientific Organization (MASCO) in Boston's Longwood area are also playing coordinating roles between government agencies and their membership.

External consultants and contractors do much of the engineering, project assessment and construction in the Boston region. They are bounded by agency guidelines and their professional norms and standards, which will influence how adaptation is institutionalized into their work. Academics are also playing important roles vis-à-vis climate adaptation by, among other things, providing downscaled climate data.

In Singapore, planning and decision-making, including around climate adaptation, is almost exclusively the purview of government officials. Academics and other experts from both within and outside the country are consulted, but the various committees and working groups of the National Climate Change Secretariat involve only agency officials. This is characteristic of the governance paradigm in Singapore. The assumption is that interests-based participants would corrupt processes and make them too inefficient, while expert officials are able to rationally plan and make the decisions that best meet the aforementioned national priorities. Participants cited perceived unfairness in involving some actors and not others; capture by certain stakeholders, leading to biased outcomes; low capacity among civil society organizations; aversion to sharing information with external actors when it may be of national security or cause 'unnecessary fear'; inefficiencies, as different interests bloat proposals with their various issues; and time lost to deliberating as barriers or drawbacks to stakeholder engagement.

Ostensibly, 'grassroots' organizations in Singapore have traditionally focused on disseminating information and fostering cohesion, not coordinating interests-based opposition to government initiatives. It is, however, notable that the situation may be slowly changing. The strong network of formal and informal community groups that coalesced in opposition to the construction of a road through Bukit Brown, which is a historical cemetery that also serves as a nature area, is an example of citizens becoming increasingly vocal in demanding that government agencies consider their interests. Social media and changing societal expectations may necessitate more extensive stakeholder engagement in the future. Some of the workshop participants reflected that further engagement could be useful, particularly around issues like climate adaptation. "Increasingly, the problems that we face are getting a bit more complex and increasingly, at least in Singapore, there's a lot more demands for public engagement, so then decision-making has to evolve in a way such that we gather diverse views of the public, of the different stakeholders involved", reflected a participant.

In the Netherlands, the involvement of multiple stakeholders is a central component of the polder model. As noted previously, Deltalinqs (the port businesses' association) is a partner in the Rotterdam Climate Initiative. However, the involvement of non-governmental actors is not as extensive as in Boston. This is partly a matter of practicality – foundations and non-governmental organizations are filling important roles in the Boston region as facilitators, information providers and drivers of change. In contrast, government initiatives have taken the lead in filling these roles in the Netherlands. This may change as adaptation becomes a more prominent component of planning and decision-making and as various stakeholder groups expect a seat at the table. The neo-corporatist poldering tradition is well established in certain areas, like labor negotiations, but less so in other domains. Institutions for poldering would need to be created if actors are to effectively and efficiently come together around an issue, such as how to holistically integrate climate risks. The multi-stakeholder decision-making process around the Maasvlakte 2 expansion to the Port of Rotterdam is an example of how multi-stakeholder collaborative planning processes can be organized around complex projects with multiple dimensions. Representatives from nature protection, community, recreation, industry and other groups were brought together for a facilitated process that resulted in a package of design and other compensatory measures that everyone could accept.

Process of priority setting

Priorities often shift when administrations change in the United States, with some issues declining in importance or falling off the agenda and others emerging or increasing in importance. Sometimes a new administration actively rejects the priorities of the previous, and even works to reverse them. Issues like climate change that have not been deeply institutionalized into the norms and standards of decision-making are particularly vulnerable to the whims of changing administrations. One administration might prioritize climate issues, while the next disregards them and focuses on other things. Senior staff also typically change with administrations, often altering the focus and nature of efforts. "A lot of [what shapes the currency of issues] is varying shades of politics – whether it is the governor's priority, whether there are concerns with equity with each town or city or region getting their fair share", said an interviewee in Boston. This can contribute to instability, as the future viability of initiatives is in question with each election. 'Leadership' in the Boston context equates to bold political action to take a long-range perspective, despite the fact that electoral calculus might favor shorter-term thinking. Participants opined that this is unfortunately uncommon.

In contrast, the People's Action Party has governed in Singapore for more than 55 years. While criticized on democratic grounds, stability in government policy has allowed officials to make unpopular decisions that, they believe, will pay dividends in the longer term or for the greater good of society. The civil service and political class are generally integrated, with priorities permeating downwards in a hierarchical fashion – commands from above are to be followed, with relatively little room for discretion (Ho 2000). At the highest levels, the civil service and political elites intermingle. The civil service is generally perceived to be competent, blending elements of technocratic management and customer-centric and performance-oriented service delivery to provide high-quality governance across major swaths of the Singaporean economy and society. At least in theory, priorities are established and decisions made on rational grounds, based on dispassionate, sound analysis. In practice, both science and policy preferences have influence.

The ruling party or coalition has changed many times in the Netherlands, but there is typically substantial consistency from one administration to the next, both in terms of bureaucratic personnel and policies. This reflects broad consensus around major priorities, like the country's extensive flood control network. To this end, some functions of government are considered outside the realm of politics. For example, the Delta Commissioner – the czar overseeing the flood protection infrastructure – is seen to be outside, and in some ways above, the political fray. Similarly, the water boards responsible for polder management (i.e., regional water management and flood control) are independent institutions, with representation from various stakeholder groups, and are not beholden to other elected bodies. In other domains, Harboring Uncertainty participants reflected that both political and technical factors influence prioritization in planning and decision-making in the Netherlands.

Nature of internal government deliberations

Agencies both at the same and across different levels of government in the United States can find themselves at odds around proposed policies and projects. For example, environmental agencies at the state and federal levels might find themselves aligned, along with outside organizations, in demanding stricter regulations around resource extraction and pollution, while their counterpart resource management and economic development agencies are more aligned with the project proponents in industry. In some cases, disagreements can devolve into legal action. In addition to tension among agencies and across levels of government, agencies often have competing priorities, even internally. For example, while public transportation projects are often seen as net benefits environmentally, their progress can be complicated by, among other hurdles, Massachusetts Environmental Policy Act review.

Some Harboring Uncertainty interviewees in the United States spoke of how agencies or units can serve as intermediaries, and the importance of that role. An example of this is the GreenDOT team within the Massachusetts Department of Transportation. GreenDOT can act as a 'bridge' or 'convener' between colleagues within the DOT attempting to advance projects and external environmental regulators and other stakeholders. The team understands the objectives and constraints of all sides and can help them understand each other and find mutually acceptable solutions. An interviewee from the Massachusetts Office of Coastal Zone Management noted that they often find themselves playing the 'balancer' role, because they are able to use their position at the nexus of coastal development, environmental and other concerns to facilitate. This kind of bridging and convening is likely to be important as agencies grapple with how to adapt to climate change and confront the conflicting priorities of other agencies and external actors. During the Harboring Uncertainty exercise runs, some facilitators acted more neutrally than others did. Afterwards, participants reflected on the benefits of having a substantively neutral facilitator in practice.

Bridging and convening play important roles in facilitating the integration of climate adaptation into planning and decision-making, particularly in pluralistic governance environments. Another important element is effective policy entrepreneurship. Proponents of climate adaptation must be even savvier in environments with significant resource constraints and institutional barriers. On the one hand, many participants spoke of the need for leadership from the top. "There is that whole element – different priorities and not wanting to have to take on the burden of other people's priorities. So, it really needs to be a top down, at least [here in City Hall, with] people at the higher levels telling agencies [what they] are responsible for doing", said a participant in Boston. "People are going to move a lot quicker if they understand that the guy from the top is going to say do this, do this, and get it done", said another participant. On the other hand, participants noted the creative ways in which ostensibly less powerful policy champions can facilitate change. They noted the importance of 'strategic partnerships' and the ability to speak to people on their own terms. One participant said,

> You can't just be a tree hugger and [be effective], you have to be somebody who is able to say 'this is important' and be intelligent enough in a number of different realms . . . to speak to what other people are doing [to] what the status is in Boston in general, and be able to correlate that and lay it out in the simplest of terms to somebody like the mayor.

The personalities and skills of those involved can matter significantly. Various interviewees praised the now former chief of Environment, Energy and Open Space in Boston for his skills as a policy entrepreneur. They reflected that he and his team have been 'extraordinarily productive' in championing the climate issue, despite their small size and budget; they are able to 'articulately make the case' to other departments and external stakeholders. Partnerships with private foundations and nonprofits also raise their profile and provide necessary support.

While leadership and strong policy champions become important as issues increase in profile and require institutionalization to be implemented, participants also spoke of the important background work that can happen at the staff level in advance. Projects often gain traction because staff have built the necessary networks of support and proactively vetted options with their colleagues to ensure that they are palatable and will have buy-in.

> I think it's a good thing that there are these meeting of minds that happen independently from anything that is formal, because it's too early to know exactly the direction you want to go, so it's good to just trade information and not know how it's going to bear fruit necessarily,

said an in interviewee from the City of Boston, adding that "you are just letting people know things that you are interested in and vice versa, so when opportunities present themselves you know the right person to call". This background work often happens organically, and without official sanction. An interviewee referred to these efforts as 'stealth, independent organic initiatives' to build momentum that can translate into more formal programs when they reach key 'tipping points'.

As discussed earlier in this chapter, decision-making in Singapore is typically hierarchical in nature. Strong leadership manifests as the top-down definition of priorities. Hierarchy is important not only among staff, but also between organizations. For example, ministries would typically have more clout than would statutory authorities (i.e., implementing agencies). However, some interviewees noted that, similar to what was reported in Boston, informal deliberation among staff at similar levels across agencies is an important part of the planning process. Furthermore, the frequency and value of these informal interactions seem to be increasing over time with a new generation of civil servants that are more proactive in reaching out to their counterparts, rather than channeling everything vertically. As noted previously, these networks at the staff level can establish the groundwork for the institutionalization of new issues, like adaptation to climate change. Participants in Singapore reflected that strong hierarchy and the pursuit of technocratic optimization could come into conflict. On the one hand, civil servants pride themselves on being 'rational' people that are open to good arguments. On the other, participants acknowledged that there is generally little room to contradict once a directive has come from above, even if they might feel that it is not the best course of action.

In contrast to Singapore, decision-making in the Netherlands is relatively unconstrained by hierarchy and deference to authority. The way participants engaged in the Harboring Uncertainty exercise runs reflected this; they paid little or no attention to their stations vis-à-vis other participants. Those playing the roles of technical actors expressed their opinions strongly and directly, engaging in a much franker and open discussion than was done in either Singapore or Boston. As discussed earlier in this chapter, participants reflected that the 'poldering' mentality – which emphasizes open deliberation – is an important feature of decision-making in the Netherlands, both within government and among other stakeholders.

Response to uncertainties

Participants were asked about the nature of uncertainty as a challenge in planning and decision-making and how it should be addressed. There were relatively consistent findings across the three cities. Virtually all participants framed uncertainty as a governance challenge and not merely a technical issue. Uncertain institutional arrangements and lack of clarity around how climate risks should be incorporated into infrastructure planning and decision-making are confounding efforts to advance adaptation. As discussed in Chapter 7, participants were generally very positive about the use of multiple scenarios as a way to frame and explore uncertainties. However, the scenarios were largely ignored when it came time to make decisions, accentuating the challenges of moving beyond a single risk assessment in practice. Furthermore, the additional accentuation of uncertainties often complicated decision-making, making reaching consensus difficult.

When asked how uncertainty is currently managed, 'flexibility' and 'consult experts' were popular responses in all three cities. 'Flexibility' was also a favorite response to the question of how agencies *should* deal with uncertainties across all three cities. It was the overwhelming first choice in Singapore (56%) and Rotterdam (48%), and tied for most popular in Boston at 41%.

In Singapore, robustness (i.e., 'plan for the worst-case scenario') was also a relatively popular choice when participants were asked how uncertainty is managed – 24% of participants selected it, compared to only 7% in the Netherlands and 9% in Boston. It was also the second most popular choice in Singapore when participants were asked how uncertainty *should* be managed. As discussed previously,

Singaporean infrastructure can be typified as robust in areas that the government deems to be priorities. The 'four taps' program for securing water independence via major investments in desalinization, water reclamation and rainwater harvesting and storage is an example of this. Participants reflected that they see flexibility and robustness as complementary responses. They asserted that it is best to be pragmatic in designing to the worst-case scenario within reason, and then maintaining flexibility to allow for changes or unforeseen circumstances. An example provided was that they are elevating the entrances to new Mass Rapid Transit (MRT) stations to reduce flooding risks, but some flexibility in the design will allow for further protective measures if necessary in the future. While not explicitly linked to climate change, this represents an adaptive response to inland flooding risks that seem to be increasing over time.

In Boston, 'consult experts' tied with 'flexibility', with 41% support each, as the most frequent response to how uncertainty should be managed. Some participants expressed concern that flexibility can result in a 'wait-and-see' approach that leaves the region underprepared and is difficult to institutionalize. Instead, they expressed a preference for expert guidance that planners, decision-makers and other actors can act upon. Participants asserted that the data does not have to be perfect, but that they prefer the political and legal cover of having officially sanctioned and unambiguous models that they can plan towards. They acknowledged that there is a certain 'fear of admitting uncertainty' and discomfort in working flexibly, although it may be inevitable. Flexibility may become a necessity, but planners and engineers would still like to have someone else take responsibility for telling them what standards to design to. This is particularly true when much of the planning and engineering is done on contract by external consultants. They want to make sure that their contracting agencies set clear requirements that they can comply with and have little incentive to take risks and deviate from those standards, even when uncertainty and systemic complexity suggests that the standards are providing a poor representation of the future.

Conclusion

This chapter has compared and contrasted the situations across three case cities – Rotterdam, Boston and Singapore – chosen based on their distinct and archetypal governance regimes. While there are similarities across these three cities, there are also important differences, which are shaping their unique approaches to climate change adaptation.

Although there is a high degree of awareness of the threats climate change may pose in Boston, very little concrete action has been taken so far. Governance is fragmented in nature, with responsibilities divided across multiple governmental and non-governmental agencies and other actors. Non-governmental actors play a particularly notable role in leading and supporting efforts. The multiple adaptation planning efforts underway reflect the fragmentation. When prioritized and coordinated, multiple complementary efforts can effectively advance adaptation. Unfortunately, resource constraints are a significant barrier to advancing climate adaptation in practice. Competing priorities and lack of (or changes in) political will can also be very problematic, particularly in an environment in which there is often significant interests-based contestation around what should be done. Parties use the courts, the political arena and so on to pursue their interests. Civil servants and project consultants are subsequently reticent to take risks, favoring cover from leadership and/or expert guidance before they make a move.

The level of awareness of climate risks is lower in Singapore, in part because agencies engaged in examining them are guarded in sharing their findings. This reflects an ethos of highly coordinated and hierarchically organized governance in which the government applies technical rigor to dispassionately and ostensibly neutrally understand the issues and devise responses. Some actions have taken place, but relatively little has been done to advance climate adaptation so far. Non-governmental actors are virtually absent from planning and decision-making. Government is highly resourced and faces relatively little opposition, so the most significant barrier to integrating adaptation is the fact that it is not yet seen to be a priority. Should it become one, officials are confident that they will be able to respond. The preference is to take a more flexible approach so as to remain responsive to new information and changing conditions.

The risks posed by climate change are well documented in the Rotterdam region, with multiple agencies and other actors engaged in sophisticated and well-coordinated efforts. Rotterdam is the furthest along in taking concrete measures, in large part because it is a continuation of their centuries-long work to tame the sea and manage flooding. The Dutch see their expertise as an asset, and they are attempting to sell it around the world. There is some concern that the extremely high level of protection afforded by the country's flood defense network may be breeding complacency among other agencies and levels of government, including transportation infrastructure managers. However, nascent climate adaptation efforts are underway throughout those units. The state plays a strong role in managing infrastructure, in accordance with widely supported goals, but it engages other stakeholders in the 'poldering' tradition. Balancing interests and pursuing 'fair' outcomes is deemed important. Flexibility is seen as an effective way to manage uncertainty here, too; while Dutch infrastructure has traditionally been very fixed and inflexible, some of the latest projects emphasize ongoing, dynamic management.

The succeeding three chapters dig much deeper into each city, examining their particular styles and features of governance; their respective approaches to infrastructure planning, decision-making and management; how climate change is being integrated; and how the exercise and other elements of the Harboring Uncertainty project unfolded with the various groups in each place. The findings collected through this examination inform the remainder of this book, which focuses on the use of multiple scenarios for framing uncertainties, the use of role-play simulation exercises for engagement and learning, and how we can institutionalize more flexible and adaptive approaches to adaptation planning.

Notes

1 There is no material reason why MassDOT led such an assessment process with wider implications, but they received a grant from the U.S. Federal Highway Administration and so found themselves in that position.
2 The Boston Harbor Association merged with the Boston Harbor Island Alliance in 2016 to become Boston Harbor Now. The new organization identifies 'climate change preparedness' as one of its key activities under the banner of 'harbor policy'.

Works cited

Bosma, K., E. Douglas, P. Kirshen, K. McArthur, S. Miller and C. Watson (2015). *MassDOT-FHWA Pilot Project Report: Climate Change and Extreme Weather Vulnerability Assessments and Adaptation Options for the Central Artery*.

Boston Planning & Development Agency (2015). *Climate Change Preparedness and Resiliency Checklist – Performance Criteria*. Boston. www.bostonplans.org/planning/planning-initiatives/article-37-green-building-guidelines

Dahl, R.A. (1962). *Who Governs? Democracy and Power in an American City*. New Haven, CT: Yale University Press.

Domhoff, W. (2010). *Who Rules America? Challenges to Corporate and Class Dominance*. New York, NY: McGraw-Hill.

Glasbergen, P. (2002). The Green Polder Model: Institutionalizing multi-stakeholder processes in strategic environmental decision-making. *European Environment*, 12: 303–315.

Haley, U.C.V. and L. Low (1998). Crafted culture: Governmental sculpting of modern Singapore and effects on business environments. *Journal of Organizational Change Management*, 11(6): 530–553.

Harvey, D. (2007). *A Brief History of Neoliberalism*. Oxford, UK: Oxford University Press.

Henderson, J.C. (2012). Planning for success: Singapore, the model city-state? *Journal of International Affairs*, 65(2): 69–XIII.

Ho, K.L. (2000). *The Politics of Policy-Making in Singapore*. Oxford, UK: Oxford Press.

Housing and Development Board (2016). *Public Housing: A Singapore Icon*. www.hdb.gov.sg/cs/infoweb/about-us/our-role/public-housing–a-singapore-icon

Huff, W.G. (1995). What is the Singapore model of economic development? *Cambridge Journal of Economics*, 19(6): 735–759.

Jahn, D. (1998). Environmental performance and policy regimes: Explaining variations in 18 OECD-countries. *Policy Sciences*, 31: 107–131.

Lindblom, C.E. (1977). *Politics and Markets: The World's Political Economic Systems*. New York, NY: Basic Books.

LTA [Land Transport Authority] (2013). *Land Transport Master Plan 2013*. Singapore: Land Transport Authority.

Marshall, T. (2013). *Planning Major Infrastructure: A Critical Analysis*. Abingdon, UK: Routledge.

Ortmann, S. (2011). Singapore: Authoritarian but newly competitive. *Journal of Democracy*, 22(4): 153–164.

Rodan, G. and K. Jayasuriya (2007). The technocratic politics of administrative participation: Case studies of Singapore and Vietnam. *Democratization*, 14(5): 795–815.

Saywell, T. (2002). Re-imagining Singapore. *Far Eastern Economic Review*, 165(27): 44–48.

Schreuder, Y. (2001). The Polder Model in Dutch economic and environmental planning. *Bulletin of Science Technology & Society*, 21(4): 237–245.

Tan, K.P. (2008). Meritocracy and elitism in a global city: Ideological shifts in Singapore. *International Political Science Review*, 29(1): 7–27.

Wiarda, H.J. (1997). *Corporatism and Comparative Politics: The Other Great "Ism"*. Armonk, NY: M.E. Sharpe.

Woldendorp, J. (2005). *The Polder Model: From Disease to Miracle? Dutch Neo-Corporatism 1965–2000*. Alblasserdam, Netherlands: HAVEKA bv | De Grafische Partner.

3 Rotterdam

A neo-corporatist approach to adaptation

God created the earth, but the Dutch created the Netherlands.
— Dutch saying

Water naar zee dragen [Carrying water to the sea]
— Dutch expression for a futile activity

Introduction

Few places in the world have as intimate of a relationship with water as does Rotterdam and the surrounding province of South Holland. Ongoing dike building and maintenance, pumping and other infrastructure investments are essential to the viability of this prosperous and dynamic region of almost four million people at or below sea level. The costs are substantial, yet water is also integral to the region's success. Rotterdam's port is one of the largest in the world, thanks in large part to its location in the Rhine–Meuse–Scheldt river delta on the North Sea.

Climate change may exacerbate the threats the Rotterdam region faces, particularly from both coastal and inland flooding. Various agencies at all levels of government are considering these threats and how infrastructure may be adapted. Rotterdam, and the Netherlands in general, are at the forefront of climate adaptation planning. In fact, as is discussed later in this chapter, the Dutch are now looking to capitalize on their expertise by exporting their technologies and knowledge around the world. Yet, significant work remains in integrating climate adaptation into planning and decision-making, especially at the project level. This chapter considers how adaptation planning is evolving in Rotterdam – and the wider region and country – and may continue to evolve into the future.

The first section outlines the Rotterdam-specific findings of the Harboring Uncertainty project introduced in the first chapter of this book. The outcomes of the 'A New Connection in Westerberg' exercise run with participants and their reflections on the experience are briefly introduced and discussed. Many of the participants' experiences and reflections resonate with the management of infrastructure in the Netherlands, and are informative as decision-makers and other stakeholders continue their adaptation work. On that note, the second section introduces the distinctly Dutch 'polder model', and provides examples of how it manifests in practice. Governance arrangements in the Netherlands are situated within this broader neo-corporatist framework.

The next section introduces the various climate-related threats that Rotterdam and its broader region face. While significant, they are relatively well understood. The fourth section discusses how adaptation is evolving in Rotterdam, and the wider country, while concurrently introducing how infrastructure planning and decision-making is approached. Particular attention is paid to the evolving adaptive measures and institutional arrangements and processes followed in the contexts of flood protection and road transportation infrastructure. Both the status quo and some more novel approaches being taken with particular projects are introduced. The Dutch are at the forefront globally, and thus lessons can be learned from their evolving but already relatively well-developed methods for integrating climate risks into planning and decision-making.

The fifth section considers uncertainty as an important factor in climate adaptation planning. An interesting finding is that a myriad of uncertainties not directly related to climate change – like who might make certain decisions and when – are as substantial as the climatological uncertainties. That is, the governance challenges associated with advancing climate adaptation are as significant as the technical challenges, with new institutional arrangements necessary. Collaborative models of decision-making can help to advance adaptation efforts, and there is good precedent for their success in the Netherlands, but attention must be paid to process design. Participants broadly support more flexible and adaptive approaches as a way to proceed despite uncertainties, but they do not always integrate easily with established modes of making decisions and managing infrastructure over the long term. Participants also liked the notion of using multiple scenarios, but their experiences suggest that it is challenging in practice, with most reverting to single scenarios to frame their arguments rather than embracing and planning against the range of possible futures.

Research design and process in Rotterdam

The research undergirding the findings in this chapter closely followed the design and methods employed in the other two cities, as outlined in the first chapter of this book. As discussed in greater detail in Chapter 6, the Harboring Uncertainty project used a role-play simulation exercise to engage actual transportation infrastructure-related stakeholders from various agencies and other organizations. In Rotterdam, this included officials from both the 'wet' and 'dry' sides of Rijkswaterstaat (the implementing agency of the Ministry of Infrastructure and the Environment), the Port of Rotterdam, the port business association and top infrastructure consultancies. Fourteen participants in total participated in the two half-day workshops. In addition to the exercise, which was recorded and transcribed for coding and analysis, workshop participants filled out pre-exercise surveys; participated in exercise debriefs in which they reflected on what they learned and how it might inform their real-world planning and decision-making;

and were interviewed one-on-one in the days that followed. Other key stakeholders were also interviewed before or after the workshop.

The exercise – called A New Connection in Westerberg – puts participants into a fictitious yet realistic situation in which a group of key stakeholders has been assembled to consider if and how to incorporate climate risks into project-level planning around a proposed piece of transportation infrastructure. Participants fill roles other than those they hold in the real world. The case bears many similarities to the expansion of the A15 motorway through the Port of Rotterdam. There are two versions of the RPS – one asks participants to use four plausible qualitative scenarios of the future, and the other contains a single risk assessment forecast of future climate conditions. Playing these two different versions with similarly constituted groups provided insights into the efficacy of scenarios versus risk assessments. The deliberations that unfolded and outcomes reached by each group across the three cities are summarized in Table 2.2 in Chapter 2. Brief vignettes for the two groups in Rotterdam are also provided below. The findings in this chapter – and throughout the rest of this book – draw from these workshops, including the exercise runs and complementary research tools, and wider background research on infrastructure planning and decision-making in the Netherlands.

Risk assessment RPS group

The risk assessment group did not reach agreement. The majority of participants were willing to accept a proposal to build the road below grade, but with extra drainage pipes and a commitment from the city, and potentially port, to spend up to $500 million on additional pumping infrastructure in the future, should it become necessary due to climate change. The group did not reach agreement largely because the flood protection specialist was unwilling to acquiesce due to concerns about vulnerability. An option that involved shoring up and increasing the capacity of the existing road was also on the table, but opposed by some because it may not be a sufficient expansion and would not build in redundancy. The group came close to an agreement, but was unable to reach consensus. The chair invoked a unanimous consent decision rule, and the flood protection specialist blocked agreement. Had near-unanimity been accepted, the group would have reached agreement, underscoring how much process matters.

This was also the only group of the 10 across all three cities that leaned towards or chose the below-grade option (A in the exercise). One explanation for this is the inordinate amount of attention given to it; approximately 23 minutes during the first round of discussion, compared to only 11, 10 and 13 minutes respectively for the other three. It became the de facto default option, with participants acquiescing to its acceptability early on. This is further evidence of how process may influence the outcomes. Another, perhaps complementary, explanation in the Dutch context is that managing water in below-grade environments is a regular part of infrastructure management, and thus not deemed particularly risky.

The senior engineer was opinionated, guiding the group towards certain options and away from others, which also had implications. His perspective on what is *valuable* certainly ran counter to that of the port and could be considered opinion rather than technical fact. Other experts also brought in technical information when it was convenient for them, rather than as neutral resource people. For example, the municipal Transportation Department project manager, a character who was generally not particularly concerned about climate change, used the risk of increasingly strong winds as an argument against the alternative elevated route through a coastal wetland, which she did not favor for other reasons. In the exercise debrief, she acknowledged that it was a strategic move rather than a substantive concern, saying: "Yeah, for me it was very convenient . . . I just invented it, because I read about the impacts and I thought 'well wind'".

Key interest and value-based arguments emerged throughout the exercise, as did the notion of fairness. While his confidential instructions said that the municipality could allocate up to $1 billion towards the project if it would lead to a better outcome vis-à-vis the city's interests, the alderman was reticent to unilaterally guarantee up to $500 million in support for future flood mitigation. "We are willing to guarantee [a] budget for measures that might be needed over time, and I presume the port will do this too?" asked the city official. The port representative balked, stating that it is the government's responsibility, with the port doing its part by paying taxes and creating jobs. This almost led to an impasse, as both the alderman and other participants clearly felt this was an unreasonable response on the part of the port.

Uncertainty was a factor. At one point, it appeared that they were going to conclude by asking for more research, and the participants generated a list of topics: traffic robustness, climate effects and the relative benefits of different options. However, the senior engineer responded: "Well, my team did everything we could, so I don't expect that there will be any more new information . . . there are just too many uncertainties." This refocused the conversation. Participants defaulted to their initial preferences, albeit often using arguments that might resonate with others.

There is not one answer to the question of why the group failed to reach agreement, or to why they were gravitating towards the below-grade option. However, thorough analysis of the exercise 'play-by-play', debrief discussion, and follow-up interview transcripts indicate that procedural factors were at least as important as the technical. The inordinate attention given to option A, the flood protection specialist's unwillingness to accept it, and the chair's requirement of unanimity helped shape the outcome. The bias of the senior engineer, and the alderman's insistence on 'fairness', also appear to have been factors.

Scenarios RPS group

The group that played the *scenarios* version of the A New Connection in Westerberg RPS also failed to reach agreement, concluding with a call for more research. The below-grade option was still on the table, with questions around whether flooding could be remediated. The key question with the elevated route was whether measures could be taken to make it acceptable to the community. The open question around simply rebuilding the existing route was whether it would meet the long-term traffic capacity needs.

Some of the information on the risks associated with each option, and how they may be ameliorated, was provided in the confidential instructions of different players, but not shared. The Transportation Agency senior engineer is intended to serve primarily as a technical resource person for the group, and he introduced himself as such. However, shortly thereafter – and even before others had expressed their interests and preferences – he declared: "It seems clear to me that we are going for either A or B." He was vociferously against the rail and alternative route options. Asked immediately following the exercise by another participant why he shared cost information on the rail options so late in the game, he responded: "I [would] have given the information if people would ask for it; [the alderman] was the only one that actually asked." Others did not consider that additional information might be available, believing that it would naturally be put on the table, rather than that someone might be holding it back strategically. "I'm not an experienced negotiator, so this game makes me aware . . . I see it costs $2.5 billion, so I say 'OK that's 2.5 billion' and I don't think about what are the possibilities underneath that", said a participant with a more technical orientation in the real world. "We should have asked more questions to come to a better decision", said another participant. Another reflected that this dynamic is realistic, stating: "I also experienced this as a real-life experience, because that's the way we do discussions – everyone starts talking, giving up solutions" rather than seeking more information.

The chair (i.e., regional deputy director) played a dominant role in the process, intervening 67 times. In comparison, the second most active participant (the environmentalist) made 38 interventions. The chair attempted to run a considered and balanced process, but potentially discounted thorough consideration of the rail option, which was not in the general instructions but rather in the confidential instructions of a couple of players. He appeared somewhat frustrated when the environmentalist insisted that the rail option be considered, because it disrupted his clear sense of what was on the table and needed to be resolved.

While ostensibly it was information gaps that prevented the group from making a definitive decision, participants acknowledged that the uncertainties might have been an excuse when the choices were, in fact, political rather than technical. There are "two political pathways – livability and sustainability as a stake, [and the] short-term economic growth [of the] port as a stake", said the environmentalist, adding, "in the end it really is a political choice". This theme was dominant in the debrief conversation. Participants emphasized the tradeoffs that had to be made between different values, like climate risks, mobility, environmental protection and quality of life. "It was for some people too attractive to say 'let's do more research' instead of making a decision right now", said a participant. A participant actively involved in policymaking reflected that the exercise mirrored the real world in some important ways.

Some participants, including the chair, approached the negotiation as if it were a technical exercise. In the end, the group failed to choose among the options because information was withheld, biases precluded adequate consideration of what could have been a viable option, and the group, rightly or wrongly, concluded that more research would lead to an optimal outcome, despite the fact that they did not get all the information they had on the table. The group did not feel empowered *politically* to make a decision, and thus punted it when they could not reach consensus based on a nonexistent shared technical understanding. Even the deputy director, who had proposed gathering additional research, acknowledged that this is ultimately a decision around interests rather than facts. He concluded by saying: "I don't think it will be easy to find consensus, and in the end, it is a political decision and it is money that counts."

The polder model: the wider neo-corporatist framework for decision-making

Governance arrangements for climate adaptation are still emerging, but it seems likely that the ways in which infrastructure is managed, and by whom, will be bounded and shaped by wider norms of governance. Rotterdam is a particularly interesting case because it is archetypal of the neo-corporatist approach to decision-making (Slomp 2011). Traditionally, neo-corporatist institutions have focused on labor and the management of the economy; employers, workers and the state formally negotiate as 'social partners' to reach sector- and even economy-wide agreements (Slomp 2011; Wiarda 1997). Rather than interacting in an exclusively adversarial fashion, they come together and seek consensus. There is debate around the degree to which this model translates into other policy spheres, particularly given the relative absence of formal institutional arrangements, such as the Social and Economic Council, once you move beyond labor and economic issues. However, the evidence suggests that environmental issues can and do enter neo-corporatist agendas in countries with a strong tradition of following this model, including the Netherlands (Glasbergen 2002; Jahn 1998; Schreuder 2001).

The Dutch may have a particularly strong predilection towards and distinctive style of neo-corporatism, including in the area of environmental management, rooted in the long tradition of *poldering* or the *polder model*. A polder is a low-lying, flood-prone area that is kept dry by dikes, pumps and other infrastructure. That kind of water management is not feasible at the individual level, so starting in the Middle Ages, before the advent of professional bureaucracies, farmers and other residents would share collective responsibility. Poldering was the traditional manner in which they would seek consensus on how to manage their polders, precipitating "the thousand-year-old tradition of meeting and consulting" (Prak and van Zanden 2013). While much of the actual work is now conducted by experts, multi-stakeholder water boards persist to this day to make decisions. A key feature of the Dutch model vis-à-vis other neo-corporatist states may be the relative openness to debate and weak degree of deference to authority found in decision-making. Farmers, engineers and other stakeholders sit side-by-side in water board meetings.

In the 1980s, the polder model emerged as a descriptor for the well-entrenched practice of reaching broad consensus on economic, environmental and other policies far beyond water management (Schreuder 2001). The assertion is that there is a "distinctively Dutch style of policy making in the social and economic sphere [that is] consultation-intensive and consensus-seeking" (De Vries 2014, 100). Dutch officials and other stakeholders interviewed for this research regularly cited the tradition of poldering as 'the way we do things'. A government official involved in policy development and implementation reflected that:

> In general, in Holland . . . stakeholders are involved, that's part of our culture, what they call the 'polder mentality' . . . We have to think about the interests of others, it is important. And so, when you involve stakeholders, it helps to get a solution that is acceptable so there will be less opposition during the process, which makes the process easier. [Furthermore], involving stakeholders can maybe lead to different insights that can lead to a better solution – one that you maybe wouldn't think of when you do it on your own. . . . It would be easier to not have to take into account what all the other people want, but it's absolutely necessary.

The polder mentality has certainly gone through phases of prominence and popularity, but after a period of decline it seems to now be resurgent (Economist 2012). A planner from Rijkswaterstaat said,

> What I see over the past 15 years is that it goes up and down – in the 90s, it was very usual to work with participation, [and then] after that we went the other way, [with decision-makers] saying we know what the solution is and poldering is bad, [and] now we are going back . . . and a lot of projects are using participation again.

Eight Harboring Uncertainty participants (57%), including all of the participants with policy positions and from non-governmental stakeholder groups, reported that they had participated in 'facilitated multi-stakeholder decision-making processes' in the past. The frequency of their interactions with other stakeholders varies widely, however, largely depending on position; senior policy-oriented actors reported interacting with others multiple times per day.

Participants were generally bullish on the importance of poldering. The average response when asked 'how important is it that you engage with other decision-makers and stakeholders as you plan and make decisions' was 5.4 pre-exercise and 6.4 post-exercise, on a Likert scale from 1 to 7. It is notable that this is a statistically significant increase, suggesting that the simulated multi-stakeholder experience with the A New Connection in Westerberg exercise increased their already strong opinions on the importance of multi-stakeholder deliberation.[1] Participants also rated their previous experiences in multi-stakeholder deliberations relatively highly – the average rating was 4.6 on a 7-point Likert scale. It is notable, however, that interviewees largely framed poldering in utilitarian terms. That is, as something that needs to be done to move projects forward and generate the best outcomes, rather than in ethical or moral terms. "It is necessary, especially in a country like the Netherlands in which we use the word 'polder' also as a verb, which means you have to get together, otherwise it will not work", said a participant from Rijkswaterstaat, adding that "especially in the work we do, if somebody wants to block the process, they always can".

Poldering, however, can come at a cost. It takes time to seek consensus and processes can fall short, occasionally actually increasing rather than decreasing antagonism. "Sometimes it's quicker to skip all of this poldering and just make your legislation, and if the subject is not so [controversial] then it's probably easier just to go ahead", opined an interviewee. Furthermore, it is not clear that there is always adequate consultation across agencies and with external stakeholders in practice. An interviewee lamented the lack of greater communication between agencies, citing the lack of direct interaction between the Meteorological Institute and Rijkswaterstaat, even though they are both under the Ministry of Infrastructure and the Environment. Even within the same organization, there is not always sufficient dialogue. This is particularly true between more technical and policy-oriented actors. Harboring Uncertainty survey responses suggest that it is much less common for technical experts to be directly involved in multi-stakeholder decision-making. When asked whether they should be, participants universally reflected that there are benefits, including greater appreciation of the needs of decision-makers and vice versa, but that ultimate decision-making should be the purview of elected officials. One interviewee said,

> Decisions should be taken by those who are representing all people; you can't leave that to technicians. . . . Yes, it is good to involve [technical experts], but it requires something of them as well – it requires that they speak a language which is understandable for politicians, and not only understandable, but it has to be useful to them.

Reflecting on a conference he organized that involved both policy and technical actors, another participant reflected that both sides saw benefit in meeting, because "it's the whole chain of decision-making and interaction, and it works differently if the chain is connected . . . part of being very successful is that you have a good chain from the policy" through to project implementation.

Participants noted that the approach to poldering has not remained static over time or across sectors. While some participatory processes appear to be more professionalized, this is certainly not always the case. An interviewee involved in the Maasvlakte 2 Port of Rotterdam expansion process – which is discussed in the text box below – asserted that consultation around infrastructure projects has traditionally been very ad hoc in nature, but that their process followed a more structured approach; one that was relatively new in the Dutch context. This reflects a dichotomy between the more traditional, formalized neo-corporatist institutions that exist around particular labor and social welfare issues, and the informal and heterogeneous consultations that have often occurred around projects to discuss environmental and other issues outside the framework of those institutions. It is not clear that consultation is always done well in the Netherlands or that it inherently involves all stakeholders. In fact, the varied history of stakeholder engagement around the Maasvlakte 2 project suggests that, despite the underlying current of the 'polder mentality', relatively stable institutional arrangements have not yet emerged around how stakeholders should convene on issues like reconciling environmental and economic goals when considering infrastructure projects.

There were differences in opinion among Harboring Uncertainty participants around how formal or informal decision-making is, but in general, they described interwoven formal and informal interactions throughout the process. A technical expert said that he normally provides information via more formal memos and brief reports that his boss subsequently refers to in both formal and informal meetings with other actors, both within and outside the agency. A non-governmental actor described his participation in meetings every two months with counterparts in government to talk about issues, including how they can work together, their shared goals, the obstacles they face and who else they need to engage with. These more formal gatherings are interspersed with regular informal interactions. A more technically oriented participant lamented that project-level decision-making can be too informal at times, saying that decision-makers "try to sit around the table and discuss the pluses and minuses of each proposal and come to some agreement. There is some connection to the [established] criteria, but it's not very concrete . . . It's too flexible at this point actually". In contrast, a senior expert that regularly participates in decision-making processes complained that processes could be too rigid: "I would hesitate to say that most of the work is done informally. Certainly, we will call each other now and then, but the processes are very well delineated and known, and they are very regular – so we are an overplanned, overregulated country!" The interplay between the formal and the informal suggests coalitional negotiation dynamics at work as coalitions are formed and expanded around policy options, and then those coalitions achieve success by formalizing the consensus they reach. A participant from an important lobbying group described these dynamics:

> At first you always have the phase of let's say planning and trying to convince others of the need. With the example of the new tunnel, until two years ago there was nothing official. Still, we . . . were already for let's say five years urging for a new tunnel. We had some arguments, we had some facts and figures, and we were supported by some other organizations. But it was not official. And it became official when the planning of the national government took this new tunnel into their program. And then it starts. But during that first phase of let's say not official planning, but lobbying you saw that also the environmental pressure groups were saying "no, we don't need that", so that was a sort of national debate, informal debate, and it became formal when the national government [began] doing something.

A senior government official presented a similar picture, highlighting the fact that this kind of interests-based negotiation and coalition building is not simply the purview of external stakeholders. He stated that the issues "are going to manifest in the newspapers or whatever, and that's the phase when, in my experience in the Dutch setting, it's still possible to have a good conversation", adding that

> even though you have very different positions, you can still put everyone around the table and try to exchange them, both in the informal and more formal, depending on what you need in your decision-making. Usually there is an informal round, then more formal for the decision-making. [It's] really about trying to organize and balance your powers.

Local politicians also put pressure on agencies and national government officials to influence transportation infrastructure planning and decision-making. "[Local officials] are lobbying the parliament, the politicians, but also the directors; [my boss] is in all kinds of conversations with the municipality of Rotterdam, the region around the Hague, the Province of South Holland, [as] they are trying to put in their ideas", said an interviewee.

As discussed in greater detail in Chapter 8, more collaborative, multi-stakeholder approaches to decision-making will likely become all the more necessary as climate change threatens our infrastructure systems. It is not clear that the governance arrangements in place around much of the world are fully up to the challenge. A great deal can be learned from the Dutch tradition of poldering. On the other hand, the Dutch model will undoubtedly need to adapt and evolve to meet this challenge.

Box 3.1 Maasvlakte 2: negotiating an ambitious expansion to the port of Rotterdam

Lessons can be learned from how other complex environmental, land-use and infrastructure disputes have been managed and applied in the context of adaptation. One such case is the recent expansion to the Port of Rotterdam.

Anticipating growing demand and faced with limited options for expansion, the Rotterdam Mainport Development Project was initiated in the 1990s, bringing together representatives from relevant national, regional and local government agencies, and nine non-governmental stakeholder groups, including environmental and labor organizations (Kelly 2005). The objectives were to consider how the port's viability could be maintained and the quality of life in the region enhanced, all under very tight space constraints in this very densely populated region. The option favored by the Port Authority from the beginning was to expand further into the North Sea on new fill.

The process faced various hurdles, including a change in national government mid-stream and tensions among ministries that, while ostensibly on the 'same team' had different interests. This tension is informative, given that agencies may need to coordinate much more extensively as they grapple with emerging threats like climate change that do not fall neatly into a single area of responsibility. Even in the Netherlands, various arms of government can be more aligned with external stakeholder groups in their respective areas of responsibility – agriculture, the environment, the economy and so on – than they are with their peer agencies (Sabatier and Jenkins-Smith 1993).

Disillusioned with the process and seeing a window of opportunity, a group of environmental NGOs initiated a sidebar process with the Port Authority and Municipality of Rotterdam that ultimately led to 'what if' conversations around what the environmentalists would want should an expansion go ahead, rather than continuing to focus on why it should not proceed (Kelly 2005). They ultimately reached tentative agreement on a set of parameters for the project that involved altering the design of the expansion and implementing a set of compensatory measures. However, they still required buy-in from others, including the wider environmental community, other stakeholder groups, and, not least, the relevant national government ministries.

Others were unhappy with the substance of the agreement and that they were left out of the conversations, and the prospects of a consensus agreement waned. A professional neutral was subsequently brought in in 2005 to reorganize and reinvigorate the multi-stakeholder process (WesselinkVanZijst 2015). The new process focused on rebuilding relationships and helping parties to engage one another to better understand their respective points of view, map issues, engage in joint fact-finding and seek out packages that all could live with (Vellinga 2007). It is noteworthy that they hewed closely to the 'mutual gains' approach developed largely in the United States (Susskind and Field 1996). That reflects the particular approach of the firm hired, but is interesting in the context of a society that points towards its long tradition of poldering.

The process ultimately yielded an agreement that all stakeholders were prepared to buy into. The comprehensive and creative package was designed to address the multiple interests. Features include (Vellinga 2007): agreement that the two thousand hectare Maasvlakte 2 expansion would go ahead; the creation of a 25,000-hectare marine protected area; a 35-hectare dune restoration project elsewhere along the coast; measures to make the new facility more sustainable, including a commitment to a landside modal split favoring rail and inland water over road and the clustering of facilities to encourage lifecycle integration; measures to maintain acceptable air quality, including restrictions on trucking fleets; and the construction of a 'multifunctional seawall' that would provide adequate coastal defense while featuring distinct zones for recreation nature protection and wind turbines for energy production. The Dutch Parliament approved the project in 2006 and Rotterdam's municipal council in 2007. Construction began in 2008 and officially concluded in 2013. The first ships arrived in 2014, and the construction of quayside infrastructure is ongoing. Key stakeholders from a dozen different constituencies continue to meet intermittently to assess progress towards the commitments made in the initial agreement and discuss any new issues as they emerge and require attention.

This extensive multi-stakeholder process illustrates the consensus-seeking mentality in Dutch decision-making. The Port of Rotterdam and government agencies were willing to genuinely engage in extensive deliberations with other stakeholders out of a belief that this could generate stable and wise outcomes. However, the various hurdles encountered along the way and the time it took to reach agreement suggest that these processes do not always go smoothly. Furthermore, the techniques ultimately employed drew from global best practices at least as much as from specific cultural traditions of poldering.

For more information, see www.maasvlakte2.com/en. Kelly (2005) provides an excellent analysis of the initial stakeholder engagement around this case. Information on the later stakeholder engagement process came from interviews, Vellinga (2007) and Vellinga and de Jong (2012).

Climate vulnerabilities in the Rotterdam region

Large swaths of the extremely densely populated province of South Holland are built on land reclaimed from the North Sea and former coastal wetlands. Approximately 90% of Rotterdam is below sea level, some by as much as six meters (ICLEI 2014). This makes the city vulnerable to sea level rise (SLR) and storm surge, both of which are expected to increase as a result of climate change (City of Rotterdam 2013). The city is also sensitive to more extreme precipitation patterns.

Scenarios from the Royal Netherlands Meteorological Institute (KNMI) project SLR by 2050 ranging from a minimum of 15 cm with a low global mean temperature increase (1 degree Celsius) and little change in global air circulation up to a maximum of 40 cm with a model based on a higher global temperature increase (2 degrees) and a larger change in air circulation (KNMI 2014). By around 2085, the range is 25 cm to 80 cm. Mean annual precipitation is projected to increase or decrease under different models, but not significantly. However, it is expected to become much more seasonally concentrated, with as much as a 30% increase in mean winter and a 23% decrease in mean summer precipitation by around 2085 (KNMI 2014). Winter storms could also become more frequent; the number of winter days with more than 10 mm of precipitation is projected to increase by 9.5–35% in the 2050 range, and 14–60% in the 2085 window (KNMI 2014). While overall drier, the intensity of summer storms could increase, with extreme rain showers and more severe hail and thunderstorms.

Existing dikes and other flood protection infrastructure becomes less robust as sea levels rise and storms become more intense, making what was traditionally an extremely rare flood event increasingly likely over time. Likewise, areas outside the dike network become increasingly vulnerable as tides become higher and storms stronger (City of Rotterdam 2013).

While SLR and coastal storm surge may be the most obvious climate-related threats facing the Rotterdam region, they are not the only ones. More frequent and intense storms and concentrated seasonal precipitation not only threaten coastal defenses, but also increase the risks of inland flooding from swelling rivers and canals and higher groundwater levels, which can overwhelm pumping and drainage capacity (City of Rotterdam 2013; Delta Programme 2013). Conversely, prolonged droughts can lead to lower inland water levels, which can threaten freshwater supplies by facilitating saltwater intrusion, especially when coupled with SLR (Rotterdam Climate Initiative 2009). Lower water levels in rivers and canals can also inhibit inland shipping, which is an important part of Rotterdam's economy (City of Rotterdam 2013). While Rotterdam's northern European climate has traditionally been quite moderate, the average number of summer days per year over 25 degrees Celsius is projected to increase from 21 at present to approximately 36 by around 2050, and 48 by 2085 under a high temperature and air circulation change model (KNMI 2014). Heat waves decrease comfort and increase mortality, threaten flora and fauna, and damage infrastructure (City of Rotterdam 2013). On the upside, warmer winters can lead to reduced mortality and decrease the frequency and intensity of challenges to mobility from ice and snow (KNMI 2014).

Harboring Uncertainty project participants reported that they expect climate change to be a fairly significant factor in their organizations' planning and decision-making over the next 10 years, with an average ranking of 4.9 (pre-exercise) on a 7-point Likert scale from 'not at all' at 1 to 'very' at 7. In comparison, the averages in Singapore and Boston were 4 and 5.7 respectively.

Infrastructure planning, decision-making, and adaptation to climate change

While the risks are significant, arguably no other city or country has done as much to address the climate-related threats they face. A variety of initiatives associated with different levels and branches of government and external private and quasi-governmental firms are trained on addressing the risks. The Dutch have emerged as world leaders in evaluating and preparing for climate change. It is beyond the scope of this chapter to exhaustively detail all of them, but this section gives a snapshot of the state of adaptation planning in Rotterdam, and the Netherlands in general, and how it fits within planning and decision-making. It also shares insights from how Harboring Uncertainty participants see climate adaptation and its place in their infrastructure planning and decision-making.

Participants reported that they are quite aware of 'climate change and the risks it may pose', with an average response (pre-exercise) of 5 on a 7-point Likert scale. The average response was only slightly lower (4.6) when participants were asked to rank the degree to which climate change is already on their organizations' radars. There was variability in responses to both questions. Those in research and higher-level policy positions self-reported as more aware than did those in technical positions. Those working in land transportation units, especially those working in the field rather than in research, generally gave lower responses than those working around the port or on water issues. However, a representative of port users (i.e., businesses) ranked current engagement around the issue at only two, reflecting that his members are not willing to engage in conversations around adapting to climate change, and some even question why he is investing time in this: "They say 'it is so far away, it's not my interest at the moment', [but] when it is problematized, for example if a flood occurs, they will probably say 'well, not anymore!'"

In terms of how *confident* participants are that they and other stakeholders will be able to manage the risks and uncertainties climate change poses, participants entered the workshop somewhat skeptical, with an average ranking of only 3.7 on a 7-point Likert scale. Skepticism was common across participants coming from different organizations and from both technical and policy positions. While still low (4.1), it is noteworthy that there was a statistically significant increase in participants' confidence from pre- to post-exercise.[2] This increase would suggest that the exercise experience enhanced participants' confidence that climate-related threats can be successfully addressed.

Adaptation to climate change necessarily takes place within the wider context of policymaking and public administration. Adaptation is implemented when it is institutionalized into ongoing systems of planning, decision-making, and building and managing infrastructure. This book focuses primarily on transportation infrastructure, but given the key interrelationship with water management in the Dutch context, this section starts with an examination of planning and decision-making around flood protection, including climate adaptation activities. Examining flood protection also offers important insights into the Dutch approach to infrastructure planning and decision-making writ large, as this is the sector in which governance innovations have often first emerged.

Flood protection

The Dutch have always lived with the water and have been actively managing it since at least the 13th century (Jonkman 2009). It was the advent of the aforementioned polders that allowed the country to urbanize and emerge as a powerful state with cities and agricultural lands largely immune to regular flooding (Hooimeijer 2007). Rotterdam only exists as the city it is today because an extensive network of dikes and other flood protection measures keep the sea at bay. As mandated in the Deltaplan, most of the South Holland region sits behind an impressive coastal flood defense system that is designed to handle 1-in-10,000-year flood events (Ministerie van Verkeer en Waterstaat 2007). The high level of protection is deemed necessary because failure would be catastrophic; hundreds if not thousands of lives would likely be lost and an important economic hub for all of Europe crippled, should the defenses fail.

The Deltaplan was initiated in the 1930s, but picked up considerable momentum after the catastrophic floods of 1953. The subsequent Delta Law, which was passed in 1959, established a technical and economic framework for making what are supposed to be objective 'risk-based flood protection' decisions on what infrastructure investments will be made and where, all coordinated by a standalone Delta Commission (Deltacommissie 2008; Jonkman 2009). Delta management is supposed to operate above the fray of politics, with decisions rooted in ongoing modeling and robust cost-benefit analysis. Expert engineers and bureaucrats have subsequently reshaped the Dutch coast even further than it was already, constructing one of the most complex and expansive public infrastructure networks ever – the Delta Works. The network of dikes, storm surge barriers, locks, sluices, and various other infrastructure cost over $7 billion and took over 40 years to complete (Krystek 2011).

The Delta Works are very characteristic of the 'manipulative' phase of flood management that they fell squarely within (Hooimeijer 2007). The Delta Commission tasked planners and engineers with making the country safe, which meant putting water in its place and keeping it there. It was a project full of scientific hubris and grand government planning; protecting the country from the possibility of future disasters by building the largest, strongest infrastructure system possible and further realigning the flow of water throughout the low-lying country was deemed a national priority and funded accordingly.

Box 3.2   Watershed event: the 1953 floods

While their aggressive approach to coastal adaptation may be rooted in the Netherlands' long-standing, intimate relationship with water, the catastrophic floods of 1953 are regularly evoked as the event that drove home the importance of strong water management and coastal defense.

Communities are typically reactive when it comes to addressing climatic risks; concrete adaptive measures are often precipitated by extreme events rather than by ongoing change or forecasted but unexperienced threats (Amundsen, Berglund and Wetskog 2010; Berrang-Ford, Ford and Paterson 2011). While the Dutch are often evoked to counter this claim – given their proactive approach to climate adaptation – a longer and wider view of history might suggest that their efforts are, at least in part, reactive.

Those interviewed for this project regularly cited the 1953 floods, which claimed more than 1,800 lives, displaced 70,000 people and destroyed a significant proportion of the nation's farmland, as *the* watershed event that precipitated major investments in flood prevention and ongoing vigilance to this day (Floodsite 2008). While likely unrelated to climate *change*, the event was a wakeup call that still resonates. The Delta Commission was created 20 days after the catastrophic event, and the country quickly went to work building the most extensive flood protection system in the world (Deltawerken 2004). The Dutch government has invested billions of euros over the decades, and most of the region is now behind dikes and other barriers designed to withstand 1-in-10,000-year flood and storm surge levels (Jonkman 2009). What is interesting is that the vigilance persists 60 years later. The massive Maeslantkering storm surge barrier on the Meuse River in Rotterdam, which was completed in 1997 at a cost of approximately 450 million euros, is a more recent example of how the Dutch have continued to take flood protection very seriously (Deltawerken 2004). Furthermore, as the works originally envisioned were nearing completion, planners and decision-makers acknowledged that the task of keeping floods at bay will never be complete – climate change, subsidence, development and other forces of change will continuously alter the conditions, necessitating ongoing, adaptive management (Delta Programme 2013).

Events beyond the Netherlands similar to the 1953 floods have served to reinforce the Dutch predilection to invest in strong coastal defense. In particular, interviewees cited Hurricane Katrina as a seminal event that raised the profile of climate risks. In many ways, New Orleans and Rotterdam are similar; they are both delta cities largely below sea level, and thus at the mercy of their dike networks to hold back the sea. However, the levels of protection are vastly different. An incomplete network of levees poorly protected New Orleans before Katrina. Post-Katrina, $14.5 billion has been spent on a new flood protection and pumping network, but it is still only designed to withstand 1-in-100-year storms, which some feel is woefully inadequate, especially in light of climate change (Schwartz 2012). This is a stark contrast to the comprehensive Dutch network designed to withstand 1-in-10,000-year events. Nonetheless, Katrina vividly reminded decision-makers and other stakeholders of the risks and was a key impetus behind the creation of the Second Delta Committee in 2007.

Recognizing that coastal defense remains a work in progress, a high-profile second Delta Committee was appointed by the Dutch cabinet in 2007 with the explicit mandate of considering the management of water 100 or even 200 years into the future. While deeming flood risks 'critically important' and increasingly so over time, the group did not find that they are 'acute' given the strength of the Delta Works. The Committee concluded that sea level rise of 0.65 to 1.3 meters by 2100 and 2 to 4 meters by 2200 should be taken into account, and subsequently made 12 recommendations that, if implemented, are projected to cost 100 to 300 million euros per year (Deltacommissie 2008). The recommendations are much more holistic than are those of the first Commission, taking the long-term sustainability of the region and various interests and sectors, including transportation, into account. They include increasing the flood protection levels in areas behind dikes by a factor of 10 in the medium term, with further strengthening likely necessary later; securing land to allow higher flow rates in the Muse and Rhine Rivers; avoiding externalizing the costs of vulnerable developments; and creating a well-funded and politically independent organization to support ongoing delta works.

The Delta Committee's report was generally well received, with some criticism leveled for using SLR projections significantly higher than those of the Royal Netherlands Meteorological Institute (Jonkman 2009). Nonetheless, the government and other stakeholders have largely accepted the premise that sea levels are rising and that this will eventually render the existing flood protection infrastructure insufficient. The government implemented many of the recommendations, or is currently doing so, including by adopting a new Delta Act in 2012. The act established a Delta Programme for ongoing infrastructure development and management; a Delta Fund to finance the works; and a new high-level 'Delta Commissioner' position to coordinate and oversee the efforts (Delta Programme Commissioner 2014). According to interviewees, the Delta Commissioner is highly regarded and seen as a voice for logical delta management that is relatively immune to the whims of politicians. The Programme involves relevant actors from the central, regional and local governments, the water boards and other non-governmental actors, including representatives of the business community.

While the Delta Programme (2013) provides a high-level process for establishing the overall direction of Dutch water management and coordinating activities, it has a limited staff of its own. On the ground, Rijkswaterstaat – which is the executive (i.e., implementing) agency of the Ministry of Infrastructure and the Environment – is typically responsible for larger-scale infrastructure design, construction, management and maintenance. Regional water boards are responsible for most water management at the local level. While typically much larger today due to consolidation, these boards are direct descendants of those established in the 13th century to manage each polder. They are still independent institutions with members both directly elected by residents and appointed by stakeholder groups like farmers and private industry. They maintain the right to levy taxes to fund their operations.

Confronted with the ongoing need to actively manage water, the Dutch continue to invest heavily in research in this area, including through world-renowned institutes like Deltares, which has the motto of "enabling delta life". As discussed later in this chapter, these organizations are capitalizing on Dutch expertise by selling their consulting and engineering services around the world.

The Delta Programme, and contemporary flood management practices in the Netherlands in general, have become somewhat less exclusively technocentric over time. Technicians and decision-makers no longer have complete faith that they can engineer the entire system to meet established goals, especially as a complex web of other issues, like environmental protection, gain prominence. Experts and decision-makers are also increasingly aware that they do not have all of the answers, and that they must accept persistent uncertainty and dynamic conditions, particularly with climate change (Delta Programme 2013). The nascent 'adaptive manipulation' management paradigm puts greater emphasis on living and working with water and integrating multiple planning processes, including spatial planning (Hooimeijer 2007). The Room for the River Programme (2014), which is advancing more natural approaches to inland flood control, is an example of this new approach. Nonetheless, while these ambitious initiatives underscore a serious commitment to more flexible and holistic approaches to water management, this paradigm has not yet been fully embraced throughout all organizations. Participants noted that progress is slow. One factor is the professional norms and training of the engineers who are actually designing and implementing projects. "We have to reeducate our engineers, because [they] are educated in a linear world – it's true or not true . . . so they learned to discuss risks, but they didn't learn to discuss [or manage] uncertainty", said a participant.

The management and adaptation of the road network

Different levels of government are responsible for different parts of the Dutch road network. The Ministry of Infrastructure and the Environment is responsible for overall policy and planning, and is guided by the Traffic and Transport Planning Act. As with water infrastructure, the design, construction, management and maintenance of national and regional arterial highways is handled by implementing agency Rijkswaterstaat. The agency is responsible for over 3,000 kilometers of motorways and major highways (Rijkswaterstaat 2017).

Strategic planning involves actors from various agencies and organizations and external stakeholders. At the highest level, the national cabinet provides long-term guidance, including via the National Traffic and Transport Plan. The current plan establishes mobility, safety and quality of life as the triumvirate core aims for the transportation system and, among other things, recommends a greater market orientation (i.e., 'putting a price on mobility'). Others respond to these plans, often in an effort to shape implementation. For example, the Social and Economic Council – which is a typical neo-corporatist entity with representation from employers and employees – released a report expressing support but raising some concerns (Sociaal-Economische Raad 2001).

Longer-term strategic planning translates into medium-term priority setting by the Ministry and Rijkswaterstaat, in consultation with other stakeholders. The Multiannual Infrastructure and Transport Program provides a framework for moving from overarching priorities to specific goals, project selection, design and implementation for transportation and water management infrastructure at the national level. Key projects like the widening of the A15 motorway into the Port of Rotterdam are framed at this stage, including their financials and timelines. Priority projects are put into the Multi-Year Investment Program for government funding and other resources. Throughout this process, technical assessment plays a role, but so do political and other considerations. The minister and cabinet ultimately make decisions on which major projects to fund, typically after consultation with relevant local politicians and other stakeholders and a review of technical analysis provided by Rijkswaterstaat and Ministry staff. That analysis involves assessment against various quantitative and qualitative criteria, including RAMSHE (reliability, availability, maintainability, safety, health and economics) variables.

Project implementation is largely carried out through Rijkswaterstaat's seven regional offices. Rotterdam falls within the Western Netherlands South region, which is coterminous with the province of South Holland. Regional staff play front-line roles in network development, management and operations. Private engineering and construction firms and outside research organizations also play various roles in the road transportation system. Technical consultants are involved in infrastructure analysis and research around the world, but what is unique in the Dutch context is that much of this work is done by quasi-public and nonprofit organizations such as TNO and Deltares. As elsewhere in the world, most of the actual construction of new road infrastructure is contracted to private firms. They typically work with Rijkswaterstaat throughout the project design and construction phases. While late to adopt compared to some other countries, liberalization is putting a greater proportion of road network design, construction and management into the hands of private firms. Rijkswaterstaat has largely shifted from a 'design-bid-build' model of project implementation to a 'design-build' model over the past decade, under which a single contractor is responsible for the entire design and construction process, with the expectation that they will deliver infrastructure that meets a range of pre-established standards (Altamirano 2010). In some cases, the government is employing an even more market-oriented 'design-build-finance-operate/maintain' approach, under which private operators are responsible for financing, constructing and maintaining the infrastructure under long-term lease agreements. This is the case with the A15 expansion project discussed below.

As discussed previously, Rijkswaterstaat is responsible for the construction and maintenance of much of the country's water management infrastructure, and thus climate change is very much on their radar. However, according to interviewees, climate change is much less of an issue on the 'dry' side of the organization (i.e., among those responsible for land transportation infrastructure). However, it may be increasing in prominence. According to an agency expert that advises on environmental issues and regulatory compliance:

> I think it is going to be a very important issue, but at this moment it isn't . . . Because we are in the birth of climate change, and like with noise pollution, for example, at the beginning it's about searching for what are we going to do? How are we going to do it? That then settles, we get used to it, and it becomes business as usual. And climate change is . . . a new thing, it's not business as usual. I think, I hope, in three to five years [it will be] just a part of every project . . . I think people are not [yet] aware enough [of] what the impact is.

However, the same expert noted that it is starting to emerge at the project level, citing the 'eco aqueduct' being constructed as part of a new highway extension as an example. "One of the issues was how we are going to keep the water in the aqueduct after 10, 20, 50 years because the water is rising and the land is sinking – that was one of the first times I heard something about climate change", said the expert.

There is a small group within Rijkswaterstaat's Center for Transport and Navigation dedicated to investigating the potential impacts of climate change on road infrastructure, and how they may be addressed in planning and decision-making. This group is working to integrate climate change into various guidelines, including the 'Werkwijzer Aanleg', which a participant described as the "bible for building and maintaining things in Rijkswaterstaat", and the environmental impact assessment guidelines, which are the set of factors like air pollution and noise that projects must take into account and are assessed against. Participants characterized this integration as a somewhat organic process of making the case to a variety of different stakeholders throughout the organization and then making it easy for them to adopt. This group commissioned an extensive 'Investigation of the Blue Spots in the Netherlands National Highway Network', which provides very specific quantitative risk assessments on the various parts of the Dutch road network (Bles et al. 2012; Pereboom, van Muiswinkel and Bles 2014). According to an interviewee directly involved, this data is now being used to identify and address particularly vulnerable 'blue spots' in the road network, including in and around the Port of Rotterdam. It is also starting to translate into regular decision-making practices, even if the result is not always to take the most robust path. Citing a situation in which their analysis concluded that the extra costs required to make a tunnel completely flood proof were not worth it, given the relatively minor risks, a participant reflected that "we don't say you have to make everything climate proof, just [that you] have to think about it".

In addition to considering the climate impacts on transportation infrastructure, experts from the 'dry' side of Rijkswaterstaat are increasingly at the table for conversations around holistic flood risk management and spatial planning with their 'wet' (i.e., water management) colleagues. The organization has been reorganizing in recent years to, among other things, break down the divide and better integrate employees. The goal is to facilitate greater collaboration and knowledge sharing, particularly as the lines of responsibility are blurred; flood protection specialists are increasingly forced to consider other infrastructure networks and the built environment, while transportation infrastructure planners consider how they might plan in a wetter environment.

In the Dutch system, the provinces are responsible for the bulk of the highway network that is not managed by Rijkswaterstaat. The Province of South Holland manages 550 kilometers of roadway, with a transportation budget of 370 million euros for 2015 (Provincie Zuid Holland 2015). The province follows a somewhat similar process to Rijkswaterstaat; it elaborates its own Multiannual Infrastructure and Transport Program to establish priorities, and carries out both capital projects and maintenance via various forms of public-private partnerships. It is not clear that climate risks have yet emerged on the agenda of transportation network managers at the provincial level.

The Gemeente (City of) Rotterdam's Planning Department (Stadsontwikkeling) contains a unit responsible for the tertiary transportation network in the municipality. According to an interviewee, the city's focus in recent years has been on redesigning roads to increase pedestrian and cyclist safety and improve overall streetscape and quality of life. Traffic flow and safety remain core priorities, but issues like noise are also being addressed via improvements like the increasing use of quiet asphalt. According to interviewees, environmental concerns are regularly factored into the unit's decision-making. However, the risks associated with climate change are not yet on their radar. This is curious in a city that, as discussed elsewhere in this chapter, is both very vulnerable to climate change and at the forefront of adaptation in other areas. It suggests that, while receiving significant attention at the broader planning level, adaptation is not fully integrated throughout departmental planning and decision-making. Furthermore, as noted earlier, adaptation in Rotterdam, and the Netherlands more widely, focuses largely on flood protection as a discrete management challenge, rather than on its integration into the management of various infrastructures.

The Metropolitan Region Rotterdam Hague (Metropoolregio Rotterdam Den Haag 2015) does not directly manage road infrastructure, but plays a key coordinating role among municipalities, the province and other actors in this highly integrated region. While transportation planning is a key component of the partnership, it is not clear that coordinated adaptation to climate change is yet on their radar. Other forums for collaboration have also emerged in the region, including for project-specific challenges like the Traffic Management Company that formed to manage mobility during the A15 highway expansion project.

Box 3.3   Coordinated infrastructure management: the Traffic Management Company

The adaptation of infrastructure will invariably require strong partnerships among various stakeholders from both within and outside government. Fortunately, we can learn from other innovative examples of actors collaborating to tackle shared challenges, like the Traffic Management Company.

The efficient and unencumbered movement of goods and people into and out of the Port of Rotterdam is imperative to its operations. Furthermore, approximately 90,000 people work in the port, commuting in and out daily. The A15 motorway is a key artery for the port and wider city. It was already experiencing congestion, and demand is expected to increase significantly with the major Maasvlakte 2 port expansion. Plans to widen the highway were welcome, but introduced a challenge: how to minimize disruptions and maintain acceptable levels of mobility during this major infrastructure project, which ran from 2011 to 2015.

The City, Regional Authority, Port Authority and Ministry of Infrastructure and the Environment responded with an innovative partnership called De Verkeersonderneming (2014), the Traffic Management Company, to devise and coordinate solutions to help manage this challenge. A further advisory board includes representatives from the business community, port workers and other municipalities in the region. Rather than each party assuming that the problem is someone else's, they took collective responsibility for identifying and implementing creative ways to minimize disruption, including coordination and the staggering of shift changes among different firms; new integrated shuttle bus services; smartphone apps; recreational sports activities during peak travel times to stagger commutes; and e-bike leasing. Many solutions emerged through a 'Marketplace for Mobility' program that was designed to help private firms launch ultimately self-sustaining mobility services; port users and employees benefit from these services directly, while overall peak demand is reduced.

The company was very successful in achieving its mission. "[It] is the complete example of [cooperative] behavior, were all the [branches of government] put in their money and their people, and not officially but unofficially their responsibilities . . . It's the most state of the art there is in terms of working together and daring to let go", said an interviewee. Some port users and other levels of government did initially suggest that it was the central government's project and thus their responsibility to deal with the problem, but the Ministry refuted this argument by providing data to suggest that the bulk of the traffic on the A15, particularly at peak times, is local. Furthermore, it is the users and local authorities that would bear much of the consequences if significant congestion manifests. This interdependence was motivating.

An indicator of success is that rather than being dissolved when the A15 reconstruction drew to a close, as was the original plan, the company has been given an extension and new mandate to implement the Beter Benutten ('Optimizing Use') program. This collaborative effort between the national and regional governments, which has a joint investment of 600 million euros, is working to reduce congestion and shorten journey times by addressing key bottlenecks around the country (Platform Beter Benutten 2017). As with the A15 project, strong emphasis is placed on collaborating with the private sector. The cornerstone is 'smart deals' arrangements with businesses, including tax measures, flexible work programs, e-bike campaigns and other instruments.

The Traffic Management Company is an example of a problem-oriented, multi-stakeholder organization setup to address a challenge that is best handled collaboratively rather than by a single agency or other actor. It is innovative and uncommon, but also not wholly unique. In fact, it is somewhat similar to the multi-stakeholder forum that emerged around the Central Artery (i.e., 'big dig') project in Boston in the late 1990s, which is discussed in Chapter 5.

Asked why the partnership works, an interviewee directly involved noted the common objective and feeling among the parties that something needed to be done, but realization that responsibility was unclear. The interviewee also stressed the importance of groundwork laid via ongoing, informal cooperation among agency staff. Another factor is the importance of each actor continuing to feel a sense of ownership. "[This type of cooperation is] only possible if the organizations keep on recognizing that it's [their initiative]", said an interviewee. The neo-corporatist Dutch model may make this easier, as employer and employee organizations are well established, familiar with playing roles in planning and policymaking efforts, and recognized by government agencies.

The company provides a venue for groups of stakeholders facing significant shared challenges in an uncertain institutional environment to collaboratively devise approaches that maximize the individual and collective benefits while minimizing the costs. Similar arrangements may be appropriate when tackling wicked challenges, like adapting infrastructure to climate change. New forums may, in fact, already be emerging around climate adaptation, although it is unclear that they are adopting best practices from these other, similar initiatives.

Adaptation planning at the local level: city of Rotterdam

The Rotterdam Climate Initiative – which was initiated as a partnership between the municipal government, the Port of Rotterdam, Deltalinqs (the port businesses' association), and DCMR (the environmental protection agency for the Rijnmond region) – has been working to both reduce emissions and assess and prepare for the risks posed by climate change since 2007. The initiative has established ambitious emissions mitigation and climate change adaptation goals aimed at making Rotterdam a leading center for climate change knowledge and action. The City of Rotterdam was the first in the Netherlands to appoint a 'climate director' to coordinate its efforts. The Rotterdam Climate Proof program, which is the adaptation-focused component of the initiative, was established to ensure that "Rotterdam will be climate proof by 2025", while maintaining an accessible port, enhancing quality of life and placing the city at the forefront of innovative "water knowledge cities and an inspiring example for other delta cities" (Rotterdam Climate Initiative 2009). Rotterdam's most recent Resilience Strategy (2016) echoes these same themes while suggesting tighter integration with the Rockefeller Foundation–led 100 Resilient Cities initiative, including with the appointment of a 'chief resilience officer'. The vision for Rotterdam espoused is a city where (Rotterdam Climate Initiative 2016, 6):

- strong citizens respect each other and are continuously developing themselves;
- the energy infrastructure provides for an efficient and sustainable energy supply in port and city;

- climate adaptation has penetrated into the mainstream of city operations and water has added value for the city and our water management system is cyber proof;
- the underground is being used in such a way that it supports the growth and development of the city;
- we have embraced digitization without making us dependent, and we have ensured a best practice level of cyber security;
- self-organization in the city gets enough room and a flexible local government supports if really needed; and
- resilience is part of our daily thinking and acting.

One key difference in the pivot to 'resilience' is that the latest document is much more holistic in nature, encompassing social, economic, physical and resource issues. For example, it includes goals around equipping young people with '21st century skills', improving public health and defending infrastructure against cyber-attacks. The strategy also aims to integrate these various goals, creating, among other things "climate proof plus cyber proof critical infrastructure".

From a climate change perspective, Rotterdam's strategy is built around the robust infrastructural foundation that already protects and serves the city well, and it is expected to do so reasonably into the future. However, recognizing that this foundation may not be sufficient, the strategy promotes "the large-scale application of small-scale" adaptation measures to increase flexibility (Rotterdam Climate Initiative 2013). The strategy emphasizes that stakeholders from both the private and public sectors need to work together to advance adaptation, given the shared responsibilities. It also calls for linking adaptation into other projects and programs, including transportation infrastructure management, to ensure that objectives are met efficiently and effectively.

Information provision is emphasized, with the assumption that stakeholders are not aware of the risks and adaptive measures they can take, and that shared responsibility requires shared understanding. The initiative has employed various high- and low-tech tools to disseminate information and engage stakeholders at all levels. These range from a serious game called *Rotterdam Climate Game Feijenoord* that focuses on climate proof spatial development to a *climate adaptation barometer* that outlines the phases of the adaptation process, and assesses ongoing progress towards established goals (Rotterdam Climate Initiative 2013).

An explicit goal of Rotterdam's adaptation strategy is to create substantial corollary benefits from adaptation measures, rather than seeing them as costs. This is driven home in the Resilience Strategy, which presents a bright 2030 'Rotterdam of tomorrow' that capitalizes on the 'opportunities' adaptation provides (Rotterdam Climate Initiative 2016, 30):

The irony is that the climate crises actually turned out to be tremendous opportunities for Rotterdam. Precisely because they posed a really fundamental challenge to our city. Rotterdam's centuries old capacity for reflection and knowledge about living in a river delta was a vital survival tool during the period when the sea level began to rise steadily, rain and river flow patterns became more extreme, and the ground began to sink ever deeper. Rotterdam's climate adaptation strategy proved to be a unique tool that has grown into a fully-fledged and robust sector of the city's economy in recent decades. Whereas Rotterdam once flourished as a centre for offshore activities, it is now the epicentre of the 'watershore' sector. We can take pride in a rich ecosystem of companies, institutions, events, infrastructure, maker spaces, institutions and public resilience programmes, and the city's resourcefulness and integrated approach mean that the city stands out from the rest. Rotterdam receives consultancy projects from cities and countries around the world who need support with the introduction of customized local and regional watershoring and water adaptation programmes. And all because we have developed and applied so many new techniques and methods successfully ourselves, in order to ensure that our own city continues to thrive.

Rotterdam is very outward looking with its adaptation initiatives. The publication in English of most of its strategies and reports is evidence of this, as is the hosting of major events, like the Deltas in Times of Climate Change conferences. Rotterdam is a leading partner in various initiatives, including 100 Resilient Cities and the C40 Cities (2017) Climate Leadership Group, with which it created the C40 Connecting Delta Cities Network. The strategy also suggests that added value can be provided for the *environment* by, among other things, enhancing parklands along waterways; the *ecology* by adopting technologies that keep more water in the city and create natural habitats for flora and fauna; the *community* by encouraging trends like urban gardening that provide health, recreational and social benefits; and the *economy* by protecting assets and keeping the port and other economic engines safe and viable, and by developing world-class expertise that can consult elsewhere around the world (Rotterdam Climate Initiative 2013).

While many have failed to move from planning and aspiration to concrete practice, Rotterdam's strategy has facilitated some degree of success in advancing concrete adaption measures. Examples include the construction of a new multi-purpose parking garage/water storage tank close to the central train station; a new 'water square' that serves various recreational purposes when dry and stores rain-water when necessary, which was the product of an extensive participatory process with the surrounding community; and a 'paving out and plants in' campaign encouraging landowners to remove impermeable surfaces (Molenaar, Aerts, Dircke and Ikert 2013).

Adaptation planning: the Port of Rotterdam

The Port of Rotterdam is the major economic engine of the Rotterdam region. It is the largest port in Europe, and one of the largest in the world. Beyond shipping, it is home to numerous oil and chemical refineries and other processing industries. The Port Authority is an independently managed corporation jointly owned by the City of Rotterdam and the national government. The Port is acutely aware of the dynamic environment it operates in, and uses sophisticated long-range planning techniques to evaluate and prepare for risks like climate change. It employs a subject matter expert on climate change and mobility and has devoted resources to evaluating vulnerabilities and potential adaptation strategies.

The Port has identified challenges associated with both climate change and certain potential adaptive measures, including that access could be restricted under some scenarios, especially if the storm surge barrier is closed more frequently; freshwater supplies critical to some industries could be disrupted by saltwater intrusion; flooding risks are not substantial on elevated quays and in other areas now, but could be in the future; and inland shipping could be adversely impacted by lower water levels (van der Meer 2010). Interestingly, interviewees associated with the Port downplayed the potential risks associated with climate change, at least in the short and medium term. If anything, many of them were more concerned about conveying confidence that they are on top of this, and that some evaluations may be too precautionary in nature, as adaptive measures can come at substantial cost. One interviewee gave the example of closing and reinforcing the Maeslantkering storm surge barrier and forcing ships to travel through locks. "The biggest risk is that you do certain things that are not good, or take the wrong decisions in which you can't see the consequences", said the interviewee. While the Port's adaptation work may be motivated by the desire to stay ahead of the curve and proactively shape both users' perspectives and government regulations, it is engaging in some concrete adaptive measures. For example, there are higher elevation requirements in the new Maasvlakte 2 area of the port to reduce the chances of chemical industries being flooded. Furthermore, the Port Authority is experimenting with alternative approaches to planning that are adaptive in the face of significant uncertainties, rather than static based on fixed assumptions (Taneja, Walker, Ligteringen, Van Schuylenburg and Van Der Plas 2010).

Uncertainty: challenges and solutions in Rotterdam

As discussed throughout this book, uncertainty is a pervasive factor in planning and decision-making. When asked 'how significant of a problem is uncertainty (not just from climate change) to you as you plan and make decisions (1 being not at all and 7 being very)?' the average response of participants in Rotterdam was 5. In the words of one participant,

> [there] are so many things, like how much is the population going to grow, how much is car use going to develop, what is the economic development going to be – there are so many interests that you have to deal with . . . so this climate change is just one aspect of a very, very wide range of aspects that you have to value, that you have to judge as a politician.

In other words, uncertainty is an inescapable factor for planners and decision-makers as they grapple with how to make wise infrastructure decisions not only for the present but also for the future.

Climate change exacerbates the degree and nature of uncertainty, while adaptation planning is confounded by persistent uncertainties. Participants were also asked more specifically about the degree to which 'uncertainty is a factor in climate change adaptation'. The average response was surprisingly slightly lower than that for uncertainty in general in the pre-exercise survey (4.6). However, there was a statistically significant increase to 5.9 post-exercise.[3] This would suggest that the exercise enhanced participants' perceptions of how much of a factor uncertainty may be as they start to tackle adaptation challenges.

A clear lesson from the workshops is that climate uncertainties cannot be separated from other factors and treated as purely scientific or technical issues. Participants struggled most when they discussed climate-related uncertainty without acknowledging the interplay with interest-based factors, like who will benefit from and who will pay for any deviations from the status quo. Uncertainty can quickly become a proxy for parties to argue their respective cases. In the exercise runs, those who would lose from adaption proposals on the table used uncertainty as an argument to wait and see, while others used the potential risks as an argument for their respective preferred options.

Managing uncertainty: flexibility in infrastructure systems

Asked how they typically deal with uncertainties, participants responded as follows:[4]

- three participants 'follow official policies or guidelines';
- five 'consult experts for their best projections';
- two 'plan for worst-case scenario'; and
- five 'maintain flexibility'.

Three participants said they take 'other' approaches, but the written-in responses of two may be interpreted as flexibility: "Adaptive monitoring of situation" and "monitor and adapt – roadmapping". The third said they "perform risk analysis".

Post-exercise, participants were asked to rank how they think uncertainty *should* be dealt with. As illustrated in Figure 3.1, 'maintain flexibility' was the most popular option – it was the first choice of six of participants, and the second of a further six of fourteen. This positive sentiment was echoed throughout the exercise debriefs and follow-up interviews. "[We need to] learn to live with uncertainties, and think adaptively", said one participant, adding that we need to "think in scenarios and make the solution that can be no-regrets, that can be adapted for each scenario". Another participant argued that we should go beyond scenarios to truly embrace uncertainty, and consider how we can be "completely agile or adaptive".

Taking *flexible* or *adaptive* approaches entails making decisions today based on the best information available, while explicitly leaving room for modifications and additions in the future as conditions change. As an approach to engineering, there are examples of flexible design in practice as a response to potential climate change. For example, the Botlek Tunnel in Rotterdam is being reconstructed with

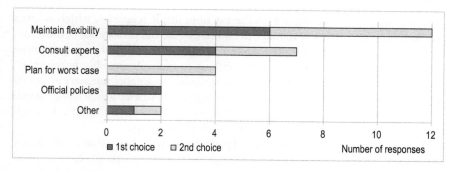

Figure 3.1 Preference ranking of how agencies should deal with uncertainties
First and second choices of respondents

extra cellar capacity so that larger pumps can be installed in the future, should more intense precipitation events become increasingly common, as projected. Rather than oversizing the pumping capacity today, this approach allows for the easy accommodation of additional infrastructure in the future. While a wise design philosophy, this research suggests that there are some significant *governance* challenges preventing widespread implementation of flexibility in practice. These challenges may be surmountable, but must be recognized and attended to if decision-makers are to make progress.

One challenge is that different departments – and sometimes completely different agencies or private firms – are typically responsible for different phases, and in particular for the construction versus the management of infrastructure. Those concerned with initial design and construction are responsible for delivering pieces of infrastructure that meet the defined specs on time and within budget. Those responsible for maintenance then monitor the state of the infrastructure over time and make repairs and adjustments as needed. As discussed in more detail in Chapter 8, these parties must work together much more directly in an adaptive paradigm so that designers understand the technical capacities, operating procedures and options generally open to those who maintain, and those charged with maintenance explicitly understand the opportunities for flexibility that have been built in. This requires enhanced interactions and mechanisms for information sharing and the right incentives. The more novel forms of 'design-build-finance-operate/maintain' privatization that the Netherlands is experimenting with may help to align incentives and foster more lifecycle-oriented approaches, but only if properly designed and implemented. Ambiguity around responsibility across infrastructure systems may make this extremely difficult, as firms may find it more cost-effective to argue for limited liability than to proactively consider factors that are ostensibly peripheral to their core activities. Even if the alignment is there, adaptive management requires clear monitoring processes and mechanisms for iterative decision-making, like the use of decision (or 'scenario') trees with multiple pathways.

Decision support: multiple scenarios

This research explicitly focused on the use of multiple scenarios, which is often invoked as an effective way to make decisions despite the persistence of unresolvable uncertainties. Rather than comparing options to a single forecast of future conditions, decision-makers compare options to multiple possible futures (i.e., scenarios). Scenario planning is being employed to support adaptation efforts around the world. The Rotterdam Climate Change Adaptation Strategy developed four qualitative 'Delta Scenarios' that are very similar to those in the exercise run with Harboring Uncertainty research participants.

Because the RPS exercise introduced participants to either scenarios or unitary risk assessment forecasts as a way to manage uncertainty, participants were asked in advance whether they use either one in their own planning and decision-making. All of the participants in the scenarios version reported prior experience with considering multiple futures when framing uncertainty. When asked how useful it is to consider multiple scenarios, they were very positive, with an average response of 6 on a 7-point Likert scale. All but one of the participants in the risk assessment group stated that they had prior experience with 'risk assessments or reports'. In contrast to the positive responses regarding the use of scenarios, when asked 'how useful those single risk assessments are', the average response was not particularly high pre-exercise at 4.5 on the same 7-point Likert scale. However, there was a statistically significant increase in the average to 6 post-exercise, suggesting that the experience increased participants' opinions on the value of this kind of probabilistic risk assessment forecast.[5]

During the discussions, participants consistently reflected that they like the idea of scenarios, as they provide a way to think about uncertainty. Nonetheless, as discussed in much greater detail in Chapter 7, their value in practice when it came to the simulated project-level decision-making in the exercise was questionable. The scenarios were often disregarded or downplayed. Despite the explicit encouragement and guidelines in the instructions, participants largely reverted to the single scenario that best matched their respective estimations of what the future will look like to justify their positions. Those most concerned about climate change suggested that the option chosen should be able to handle the worst-case scenario, as that is the one they see as most likely. Those who wish to maintain the status quo used the scenarios to emphasize the uncertainty and thus promote a 'wait-and-see' approach. Scenario planning may be very useful when developing high-level strategies, but the value of the resulting scenarios when making subsequent project-level decisions is questionable.

Learning from the exercise

The benefits and challenges of running role-play simulation exercises with stakeholders to learn with them and help them think about how they might better integrate climate adaptation into their planning and decision-making is addressed thoroughly in Chapter 6. This section briefly summarizes the lessons learned in

Rotterdam, which largely reflect the general findings. Participants engaged in the exercise to gain exposure to some of the core topics – like the use of scenarios – in a sandbox-like experimental environment. This allowed for rapid, inexpensive and vivid exposure to a set of concepts that they subsequently reflected on during both the group debrief and individual follow-up interviews.

Participants were asked a series of questions post-exercise to gather feedback on how much the exercise mirrored their realities and whether it was valuable as a learning tool. In terms of how similar the 'situation or problem presented' is to their own worlds, the average ranking was 5.2 on a 7-point Likert scale from 'very different' (1) to 'very similar' (7). The 'characters' involved were also similar (average of 5). The 'interaction between the characters' in the RPS was also seen as relatively similar (average of 4.8). One factor that was poorly represented in the game is the interpersonal history among the actors. "In the real world, sometimes it's more politics – give some, get some – I think that's the difference", said a participant, adding that "people in the real world have a history together, so you know 'last time he did this, so I am going to do this', and most people [in our group] were new faces to me".

Participants in the risk assessment and scenarios groups reported that these respective 'tools introduced' were somewhat but not very realistic, with an average rating of 4 for the former and 4.3 for the latter. The most common comment here was that they were very simple. "[The scenarios] are rather abstract now – it's more traffic and more weather influence, you have to be very visionary to see what the pressures will be", reflected a participant. The 'options or solutions' presented in the game were realistic to participants (average of 5.1). The multi-stakeholder, collaborative 'method of decision-making' used in the exercise was also regarded as somewhat similar to participants' real-world situations (average 4.8). Interestingly, some of the more technically oriented participants were surprised by how 'political' the discussion was, while more policy-oriented participants had the opposite opinion. "In the final phase, it gets much more political – it isn't so much about all the technical elements, they aren't so relevant any more – it's more about positions; who wants what and why", said a senior participant from the Ministry. He added that the exercise more closely resembled the early phases in a project, when "the discussion is still about technical issues and so on, and later it gets much more political". Participants in the risk assessment group reflected that it was unrealistic for a technical expert to block the entire process, as was the case with their simulated deliberation.

As examined in more detail in Chapter 6, participants unanimously reported that they learned from the exercise experience. What they learned varied, but their takeaways were largely related to process and negotiation. Common answers included: what *uncertainty* means, how it might complicate decision-making, and what might be done about it; the gap between how engineers and other technical experts view this challenge and how those on the more political and policy side view it; and the need to also account for the various stakeholders' interests when devising responses to climate change, rather than seeing the task as one of purely optimizing to climate models. Participants felt that the exercises provided a great way to initiate and frame their conversations with participants from other agencies with whom they had not previously talked about climate change. Some participants noted that they were surprised how much impact the uncertainty factor had on the process and outcome. One cited it as the primary reason why the risk assessment group did not reach agreement. Differences in opinion around what the future will look like allowed different opinions around what should be done to persist.

Conclusion

The broad picture that emerges when examining climate adaptation in Rotterdam and the wider region and country is of actors grappling with how to effectively integrate emerging threats, characterized by uncertainty and dynamism into ongoing decision-making, and the process-related obstacles they face. The fact that neither role-play group in Rotterdam was able to reach agreement on how to proceed underscores the difficulties. The challenges stakeholders face in *institutionalizing* the management of new threats like climate change into planning and decision-making are significant.

Institutionalizing climate change adaptation into planning and decision-making in a tangible way is difficult, in part, because stakeholders find themselves in an *institutional void* (Hajer 2003). As discussed further in Chapter 8, greater collaboration among stakeholders may be fundamentally necessary, yet there are significant barriers. In the Dutch context, this is most apparent in the divided responsibilities for 'wet' and 'dry' infrastructure. Transportation infrastructure owners have traditionally paid little attention to the resilience of their infrastructure to flooding because their counterparts responsible for flood control and drainage have done a stellar job of keeping water at bay. As noted earlier in this chapter, that dynamic might have to change as the Dutch learn to 'live with water'.

The challenges associated with institutionalizing climate adaptation into planning and decision-making are compounded by persistent uncertainty and the dynamic nature of the changing climate. This research suggests that uncertainty is a substantial factor in adaptation planning and decision-making, particularly when it involves making concrete, project-level decisions. While fostering new institutional arrangements to address emerging issues may always be difficult work, it seems particularly challenging when many of the threats are not yet acutely felt and no one is certain when, or even if, they will be. However, as discussed previously, explicitly climate-related factors are not the only, or even the most critical, sources of uncertainty in adaptation planning. Uncertainties around policy and political choices – like who should act, when actions will be taken and what resources will be available – are also significant factors.

The exercise outcomes and associated debriefs, interviews and follow-up research conducted under the Harboring Uncertainty project suggest that multi-stakeholder forums for decision-making can serve as effective avenues for addressing wicked challenges like adapting to climate change. The well-entrenched neo-corporatist tradition in the Netherlands and associated 'polder mentality' may make this kind of collaborative boundary work easier to implement – the notion of working with other stakeholders to tackle problems and make public policy and planning decisions is not foreign. However, the neo-corporatist model is well institutionalized in certain arenas, like labor negotiations, and less so in others. Processes like that around the Maasvlakte 2 expansion to the Port of Rotterdam suggest that multi-stakeholder collaborative planning can work in other domains, but they also accentuate the importance of good process design, rather than assuming that it will happen naturally.

In the Netherlands – as elsewhere – tools like scenario planning are being proposed, and even implemented on a limited basis. These process innovations and decision-support tools may add significant value. However, their experimental use here would suggest that they must be contextualized within the governance regimes that they will operate. The interplay of substantive and interest-based factors as participants strived to make decisions underscores the notion that adapting to climate is not an optimization problem that can be managed exclusively via the deployment of more sophisticated decision-support methods. Rather, processes need to account for ongoing learning and changing conditions, *and* the various interests, priorities and perspectives of the different stakeholders. Potentially viable decision-support tools, like scenario planning, have been identified and are being experimented with, but work remains in devising the best approaches for their integration.

Notes

1 Hypothesis: Exercise participation increases respondents' opinions on the importance of engagement. Question asked: 'How important is it that you engage with other decision-makers and stakeholders as you plan and make decisions?' The results were significant at the $p = 0.01$ level, using a Wilcoxon matched pairs signed ranks ($N = 13$, $T = 12$; one-tailed hypothesis). Therefore, the null hypothesis can be rejected.
2 Hypothesis: Exercise participation increases respondents' confidence in the ability of their organizations and other stakeholders to adapt to climate change. Question asked: 'How confident are you that your organization and other stakeholders will be able to manage the risks and uncertainties climate change poses?' The results were significant at the $p = 0.05$ level, using a Wilcoxon matched pairs signed ranks test ($N = 7$, $T = 3.5$; one-tailed hypothesis). Therefore, the null hypothesis can be rejected.
3 Hypothesis: Exercise participation will shift respondents' opinions on how much of a factor uncertainty is in climate change adaptation. Question asked: 'To what degree is uncertainty a factor in climate change adaptation?' The results were significant at the $p = 0.05$ level, using a Wilcoxon matched pairs signed ranks test ($N = 13$, $T = 16$; two-tailed hypothesis). Therefore, the null hypothesis can be rejected.
4 Note that the number of responses is greater than the number of participants because some chose more than one option, although asked to 'choose only the most common or important'.

5 Hypothesis: Exercise participation will shift respondents' opinions on the value of risk assessment forecasts. Question asked: 'How well do these forecasts prepare you and other stakeholders for making decisions in the face of uncertainty?' The results were significant at the $p = 0.10$ level, using a Wilcoxon matched pairs signed ranks test ($N = 5$, $T = 0$; two-tailed hypothesis). Therefore, the null hypothesis can be rejected.

Works cited

Altamirano, M.A. (2010). *Innovative Contracting Practices in the Road Sector: Cross-National Lessons in Dealing With Opportunistic Behavior*. Delft, NL: Next Generation Infrastructures Foundation.

Amundsen, H., F. Berglund and H. Wetskog (2010). Overcoming barriers to climate change: Adaptation a question of multilevel governance? *Environment and Planning C: Government and Policy*, 28(2): 276–289.

Berrang-Ford, L., J.D. Ford and J. Paterson (2011). Are we adapting to climate change? *Global Environmental Change*, 21: 25–33.

Bles, T.J., M.R. van der Doef, R. van Buren, J.T. Buma, R.J. Brolsma, A.A.M. Venmans, J.J. van Meerten (2012). *Investigation of the Blue Spots in the Netherlands National Highway Network*. Delft, NL: Deltares.

C40 Cities (2017). www.c40.org

City of Rotterdam (2013). *Rotterdam Climate Proof: Adaptation Programme*. Rotterdam, NL: Rotterdam Climate Initiative.

Deltacommissie (2008). *Working Together With Water*. Findings of the Deltacommissie, 2008.

Delta Programme (2013). *Delta Programme 2014. Working on the Delta: Promising Solutions for Tasking and Ambitions*. The Hague, NL: The Ministry of Infrastructure and the Environment; The Ministry of Economic Affairs.

Delta Programme Commissioner (2014). www.deltacommissaris.nl/english

Deltawerken (2004). *The Delta Works*. www.deltawerken.com/23

De Verkeersonderneming (2014). www.verkeersonderneming.nl/english/

De Vries, J. (2014). The Netherlands and the Polder Model: Questioning the Polder Model concept. *BMGN – Low Countries Historical Review*, 129(1): 99–111.

Economist (2012, November 3). Dutch politics. Same old Dutch: Is the polder model back? *The Economist*.

Floodsite (2008). *The Disaster of the 1953 Flood*. www.floodsite.net/juniorfloodsite/html/en/student/thingstoknow/hydrology/1953flood.html

Glasbergen, P. (2002). The Green Polder Model: Institutionalizing multi-stakeholder processes in strategic environmental decision-making. *European Environment*, 12: 303–315.

Hajer, M. (2003). Policy without polity? Policy analysis and the institutional void. *Policy Sciences*, 36: 175–195.

Hooimeijer, F.L. (2007). The relation between design and technology of polder cities. *Urbanism Laboratory for Cities and Regions: Progress of Research Issues in Urbanism 2007*. F.D. van der Hoeven and H.J. Rosemann, Eds. Amsterdam, NL: IOS Press.

ICLEI-Local Governments for Sustainability (2014). *Member in the Spotlight: Rotterdam, the Netherlands*. www.iclei-europe.org/members/member-in-the-spotlight/archive/rotterdam

Jahn, D. (1998). Environmental performance and policy regimes: Explaining variations in 18 OECD-countries. *Policy Sciences*, 31: 107–131.

Jonkman, S.N. (2009). Flood risks and climate change. *BOSS Magazine*, 35: 16–21.

Kelly, S.D. (2005). *Toward a More Deliberative Port Planning: The 'Vision and Daring' of Environmental NGOs in Negotiations on the Second Maasvlakte, Port of Rotterdam, the Netherlands*. Master in City Planning Thesis. Cambridge, MA: Massachusetts Institute of Technology.

KNMI [Royal Netherlands Meteorological Institute] (2014). *KNMI '14 Climate Scenarios for the Netherlands*. De Bilt, NL: KNMI, Ministry of Infrastructure and the Environment.

Krystek, L. (2011). *The Zuiderzee and Delta Works of the Netherlands*. www.unmuseum. org/7wonders/zunderzee.htm

Metropoolregio Rotterdam Den Haag (2015). http://mrdh.nl

Ministerie van Verkeer en Waterstaat (2007). *Water veiligheid, Begrippen begrijpen*. Den Haag, NL: Ministerie van Verkeer en Waterstaat, Directoraat-Generaal Water.

Molenaar, A., J. Aerts, P. Dircke and M. Ikert (2013). *Connecting Delta Cities: Resilient Cities and Climate Adaptation Strategies*. Rotterdam, NL: City of Rotterdam.

Pereboom, D., K. van Muiswinkel, T. Bles (2014). *Risk Assessment of Flooding of Highways in the Netherlands*. Transport Research Arena 2014, Paris.

Platform Beter Benutten (2017). www.beterbenutten.nl/english

Prak, M. and J.L. van Zanden (2013). *Nederland en het poldermodel: De economische en sociale geschiedenis van Nederland, 1000–2000*. Amsterdam: Prometheus.

Provincie Zuid Holland (2015). *Verkeer en Vervoer*. www.zuid-holland.nl/onderwerpen/ verkeer-vervoer

Rijkswaterstaat (2017). *Highways*. www.rijkswaterstaat.nl/english/highways

Room for the River Programme (2014). www.ruimtevoorderivier.nl/english/ room-for-the-river-programme

Rotterdam Climate Initiative (2009). *Rotterdam Climate Proof*. www.rotterdamclimateini-tiative.nl/documents/2015-en-ouder/RCP/English/RCP_adaptatie_eng.pdf

Rotterdam Climate Initiative (2013). *Rotterdam Climate Change Adaptation Strategy*. www. rotterdamclimateinitiative.nl/documents/Documenten/20121210_RAS_EN_lr_ versie_4.pdf

Rotterdam Climate Initiative (2016). *Rotterdam Resilience Strategy: Ready for the 21st Century*. Rotterdam: City of Rotterdam.

Sabatier, P.A. and H.C. Jenkins-Smith, Eds. (1993). *Policy Change and Learning: An Advocacy Coalition Approach*. Boulder, CO: Westview.

Schreuder, Y. (2001). The Polder Model in Dutch economic and environmental planning. *Bulletin of Science Technology & Society*, 21(4): 237–245.

Schwartz, J. (2012, June 14). Vast defenses now shielding New Orleans. *New York Times*. www.nytimes.com/2012/06/15/us/vast-defenses-now-shielding-new-orleans.html

Slomp, H. (2011). *Europe, A Political Profile: An American Companion to European Politics*. Santa Barbara, CA: ABC-CLIO, LLC.

Sociaal-Economische Raad (2001). *National Traffic and Transport Plan 2001–2020*. Abstract 01/03E. The Hague, NL: Social and Economic Council.

Susskind, L. and P. Field (1996). *Dealing With an Angry Public: The Mutual Gains Approach to Resolving Disputes*. New York, NY: The Free Press.

Taneja, P., W.E. Walker, H. Ligteringen, M. Van Schuylenburg and R. Van Der Plas (2010). Implications of an uncertain future for port planning. *Maritime Policy & Management*, 37(3): 221–245.

van der Meer, R. (2010). *Port Development and Climate Change Adaptation*. Presented at the International Conference Deltas in Times of Climate Change, 29th of September to 1st of October, 2010. Rotterdam, NL: The Port of Rotterdam.

Vellinga, T. (2007). *Mutual Gains Stakeholder Management for Rotterdam Port Expansion Maasvlakte 2*. Presentation for CEDA Dredging Days 2007. Rotterdam, NL: Port of Rotterdam.

Vellinga, T. and M. de Jong (2012). Approach to climate change adaptation in the port of Rotterdam. *Maritime Transport and the Climate Change Challenge*. R. Asariotis and H. Benamara, Eds. New York: Routledge.

WesselinkVanZijst (2015). *Maasvlakte 2*. www.wesselinkvanzijst.nl/cases/maasvlakte-2

Wiarda, H.J. (1997). *Corporatism and Comparative Politics: The Other Great "Ism"*. Armonk, NY: M.E. Sharpe.

4 Singapore
Adapting a strong city-state

Introduction

Like Rotterdam, Singapore has an intimate relationship with the sea, which has brought great success yet also creates vulnerabilities. The city-state is highly engineered; approximately 20% of the land is fill claimed from the sea (Koh 2005). Economic success and a vibrant multicultural society are products of its strategic location on important shipping routes, and the port remains one of the largest in the world. Because of its unique geography, Singapore has not historically faced significant coastal flooding, although some predict that this might change with the climate. The city has experienced significant inland flooding from intense rain showers during monsoon seasons, and the frequency and intensity of these events seem to be increasing. Awareness of the threats and uncertainties associated with a changing climate is increasing and the government is devoting resources to understanding and adapting to them. Nonetheless, climate change is not yet as prominent of an issue for planners and decision-makers as it is in Rotterdam or Boston.

From a governance perspective, Singapore is quite different from Rotterdam and Boston. Singapore is a city-state with only one level of government, which obviates the issues of coordination and negotiation among levels of government found in most other countries. Coordination between agencies is, however, still a factor. While democratic and increasingly open, the state plays a dominant role in planning and decision-making in Singapore, and is rarely challenged. This chapter considers how adaptation planning is evolving and may continue to evolve into the future in this small island city-state.

The first section discusses the research process conducted via the Harboring Uncertainty project, which undergirds the findings presented throughout this chapter. The second introduces various characteristics of Singapore's distinct approach to governance, and how they are (or might in the future) shape the city-state's response to climate change. The particular characteristics explored include the dominant and semi-authoritarian role of the state, the importance placed on shared 'national priorities', the strong belief in rational and objective decision-making, the nature of cross-agency coordination and the emerging place of civil society. It is clear that the social contract between society and the state is evolving in Singapore. However, norms of deference to hierarchies and state control remain entrenched and are likely to shape how climate adaptation evolves for the foreseen future.

The third section briefly introduces the climate threats Singapore faces. The next discusses how the adaptation of infrastructure in response to those threats is evolving, in terms of both planning and infrastructure management. Interwoven is an overview of how infrastructure planning and decision-making happen in Singapore writ large, including who the major players are and which pieces of the puzzle they work on.

Uncertainty is a persistent factor in any planning and decision-making, but may be particularly pronounced when the climate change X factor is introduced. The fifth section discusses how actors in Singapore currently manage uncertainty and believe it is best managed moving forward. The use of multiple scenarios as a way of framing uncertainty is also considered. The final section discusses what people learned from participating in the role-play simulation exercise that was a key component of the Harboring Uncertainty project.

Research design and process in Singapore

This chapter draws its findings from the Harboring Uncertainty project. Success hinged on engaging actual infrastructure-related stakeholders, which required strong local project partners. In this case, that was the Singapore Civil Service College. The college supported this work by hosting the two workshops in 2013 and soliciting participants under the auspices of a training "workshop exploring the management of risks and uncertainty in infrastructure-related planning and decision-making". Approximately 35 individuals participated in the workshops and/or in interviews. As in both Rotterdam and Boston, participants were solicited based on their real-world relationships to the decision-making simulated in the exercise. They came from various branches of government: The Land Transport Authority (LTA), the Centre for Public Project Management, the Housing and Development Board, the Public Service Division of the Prime Minister's Office (which does strategic planning), the Urban Redevelopment Authority, the Ministry of the Environment and Water Resources, the Ministry of Defense, the Ministry of National Development and the Civil Service College. All participants but one – a university faculty member – came from inside government. While the absence of other non-governmental actors may appear unfortunate, this reflects decision-making in Singapore; private firms may be at the table when directly relevant (e.g., in the case of public-private partnerships), but civil society groups are largely absent.

The half-day workshops followed the same routine as in Rotterdam and Boston; the process is introduced in greater detail in the first chapter. The A New Connection in Westerberg exercise placed participants in a fictitious yet realistic situation in which a group of stakeholders has been brought together as a special working group to consider if and how to reconcile some recently identified and still uncertain climate risks with plans to construct a new road, which may be vulnerable if certain design options are chosen. While the case presented in the role-play simulation exercise is highly simplified and clearly not Singapore, elements bear some similarities to challenges Singapore faces. For example, the trade-offs between constructing roads below grade versus elevating them are actively discussed in Singapore; most of the 12-km Kallang-Paya Lebar Expressway, which opened in 2008, is underground, and the LTA is considering building a much more extensive underground road network (Tan 2013a). Underground roads mitigate visual, noise and air pollution and leave more land for development, but may also be more vulnerable to flooding. As evinced by the Bukit Brown case discussed later in this chapter, there has also been tension in Singapore in recent years around putting roads through ecologically sensitive areas, which is another dimension in the RPS. The two versions of the exercise – one with multiple scenarios and the other with a single risk assessment forecast – provided an opportunity to explore how different tools for framing uncertainty have implications as stakeholders consider the adaptation challenge.

The higher number of participants, compared to Rotterdam, meant that there were four exercise groups in Singapore – two for each of the versions. This allowed for greater comparison. The nature of the deliberations that unfolded and outcomes reached by each group across the three cities are summarized and compared in Table 2.2 in Chapter 2. Brief vignettes for the four groups in Singapore are provided below.

Scenarios group #1

One of the two groups that played the *scenarios* version of the exercise reached agreement on an option that involved enhancing the capacity of the existing road, climate proofing the infrastructure and enhancing freight rail service. They also recommended that passenger rail service be kept open as an option for the future. This package left $250 million of the $2.5 billion project budget unallocated, so they made the novel recommendation that these remaining funds be used to assist port users with the transition to rail. This was a response to the port representative's insistence that they not suffer negative economic consequences from the decisions made and the rest of the group's acquiescence.

In contrast to both cases in Rotterdam and the second scenario group in Singapore, the deputy director (i.e., meeting chair) was not particularly active, allowing participants to interact directly with little facilitation. In fact, the process was more or less hijacked by the environmentalist. The environmentalist made influential statements on both the climate risks and uncertainty around demand needs with emerging technologies like autonomous vehicles. In general, the environmental NGO and port representatives dominated the discussion. Quantitatively, they spoke most frequently, with 71 and 70 interventions respectively. By comparison, the other participants made 20–24 interventions each. Qualitatively, the environmentalist was particularly forceful and persuasive in her arguments for the option the group ultimately chose, making forceful arguments such as

> [We] all know what happens when you build a road, you get more vehicles –
> it's only a temporary fix to the congestion problem . . . 20 years down the
> line, if you haven't expanded the railway infrastructure, you are just going to
> be back to getting more demand for more roads, and you are going to be back
> to spending billions more.

The environmentalist was also quick to challenge the competing arguments of others.

When asked why they listened to the environmentalist in the post-exercise debriefing, particularly given that she was the only non-governmental actor at the table, participants emphasized that they wanted to make 'data-driven decisions'. They said that they assessed her arguments and that she made a convincing case. In other words, she succeeded based on the perceived merit of her arguments. However, participants acknowledged in retrospect that her arguments were clearly rooted in her interests. Furthermore, they stated that it is not very realistic for a 'greenie' to have an equal seat at the table in the real world, even if it might add value. In practice, "the process of engagement is actually very, very downstream, so by the time people are brought into the discussion it's really for info and for reference, rather than for [their] inputs", reflected a participant. While they saw advantages to engagement, many were also concerned about potential disadvantages, including wasting time and the misuse of sensitive information. Many expressed faith in the government as the most capable of making 'rational' choices, even if the exercise reflected the importance of different interests.

While the environmentalist was the dominant force, the port representative did continue to express great concern with the option chosen, arguing that it would not satisfy his clients' needs and preferences for road over rail. In particular, he made persuasive arguments that the pricing models of rail over road were unfair. Realizing that there was still funding on the table and that he was not going to succeed in blocking the rail-dependent option, toward the end of the negotiation he creatively pitched that the remaining $250 million be used for subsidizing the transition for operators from road to rail. The environmentalist was the first to agree, placating the port was a priority for others, and a 'win-win' compromise had been found. It was clearly not the port's first choice, but it was an option he could live with.

Information was shared relatively freely. The senior engineer disclosed the rail option, including costing details, very early, and without being asked by anyone else. In most other instances, it was the environmentalist that proposed the rail idea and the engineer provided data on it more or less freely when asked. The port was unhappy with this proposal, but the others accepted it as a viable option, and it was on the table from an early stage. Similarly, the flood protection specialist noted early on that dikes on which part of the existing road is built would need to be strengthened in the near future, and freely volunteered that his agency has funds available to support this work, which could be complementary to the renovation. The availability of this extra money made the renovation option look all the more attractive.

Scenarios group #2

The other scenarios group also concluded with a recommendation that involved renovating the existing road and enhancing the freight rail, but not passenger service, in the near future. The group agreed that they would leave the option open to build a new road (above or below ground level) and suggested further feasibility studies of each. This last, creative, component was added to ameliorate the concerns of the port representative who felt that not building the road would come at too great an opportunity cost.

The interactions were relatively balanced among the various actors in this group, with the exception that, in stark contrast to the first group, the environmentalist was the least active. The project manager from the municipal Department of Traffic and the senior engineer from the National Transport Agency played outsized roles, insofar as they emerged as sources of information that others saw as objective and trustworthy. It is notable that they approached this task differently. The municipal project manager tackled the interests and concerns of others head-on, framing his recommendations accordingly. He attempted to reconcile the various concerns of the different stakeholders, playing the role of what might be called an 'objective and rational consensus builder'. In contrast, the senior expert disregarded the interests of the different stakeholders, going so far as to make comments such as: "I would like to just put some facts and figures on the table; for us, from the engineering point of view, we don't really consider all your [political] considerations – it's a design matter". Both experts attempted to act objectively, but what they saw as an objective approach differed – to the project manager, it was considering the various concerns and attempting to reconcile them in a balanced way, given the information at hand. To the senior expert, it was disregarding the interests and focusing on 'the facts'.

The option chosen was not strongly advocated for by anyone initially, but gained traction based on its perceived merits as the participants methodically considered the options. The municipal traffic project manager came to champion it, which is notable because the confidential instructions for that role are actually negative on this option. Despite this, the participant filling this role examined the facts on the table and concluded that

> from a purely numbers point of view it seems to fit, because currently our shortfall is 15%, so purely by upgrading the rail network you are already covering the shortfall. And then the future growth is about 15%, which, by [renovating the existing road] you are able to cover, to plan for future growth, and at the same time you are fixing the dike, reduce the environmental impact, we don't affect Bloomland, and we do it at a lower cost than [other] options.

It may be said that the group had a *facts-based*, rather than *interests-based*, deliberation. However, the port still played an important, interests-driven role, as evinced by the fact that the final agreement called for further research on the need for a new road.

While largely facts-based, process still mattered. In fact, the process followed was a substantial reason why the deliberations were more facts-based. The deputy director (i.e., chair) played a key role in focusing the group on technical questions, and gave the technical participants more legitimacy by explicitly and repeatedly calling on them for input. As in the first group, technical information was disclosed relatively freely. On the other hand, the senior engineer was somewhat less forthright than her counterpart was in the other scenarios group, responding to others when asked but putting less out proactively. In fact, the rail option emerged relatively late in the deliberation because the environmentalist, who was supposed to be the champion of this option, remained quiet and the engineer did not share her information on it. When asked why not, she replied, "People didn't ask!" She saw herself as a technical expert that was very happy to share information, but was at arm's length and reticent to get involved with the interests-based preferences of others.

It is notable that – as in Rotterdam and Boston – the scenarios had little influence on the proceedings. In the first group, the chair introduced the 'assessment of robustness' as a goal for the meeting upfront, but the scenarios were not used or referred to at all thereafter. Many participants implicitly defaulted to the 'wet and busy' scenario. In the second scenarios group, the flood protection specialist did invoke the scenarios in explaining his preferences, saying that choosing the alternative route for the new road "does well against most of the scenarios we developed – the dry and quiet, wet and busy, etcetera", but went on to argue for this option largely vis-à-vis the worst-case scenario. Otherwise, the scenarios were not mentioned.

Risk assessment group #1

The first risk assessment group settled on the elevated road option, with additional investments in noise, air and visual pollution mitigation. The downside of this option is the negative impacts on the residential neighborhood of Bloomland, so the group also agreed to fund community outreach. However, it is important to note that this outreach was framed as more educational than truly consultative in nature. "[We] can support you to do a public consultation, an exhibition to educate the members of the community of Bloomland . . . we actually have traffic data and noise data and pollution data that we are able to share [to show] it's actually not really a big issue", said the Municipal Traffic Department project manager. Parties saw the task as one of explaining decisions made based on objective criteria, rather than truly listening and responding to community concerns. In fact, whether and how to consult citizens became an important, recurring theme. It was proposed at one point that the elevated and below-grade road options simply be put to residents for their consideration, but many parties were hesitant.

> The residents are also very short term in their thinking; they will, of course, say that they want [the road] to go underground because it effects the property price and rental in the next three years, but for us as government officers we need to think of the long term, so we must be very careful when we go and consult,

said the senior engineer. Again, even proponents of engagement framed it more as a process of education; "there may be good points we can sell", said the port representative. The debate around if and how to engage citizens and other stakeholders is real in Singapore today.

The mitigative measures the group agreed upon – including sound walls and state-of-the-art pavement – were intended to allay the concerns of the alderwoman that constituents would be highly impacted by an elevated road through their community and subsequently punish her in the next election. The challenge was financing; simply constructing the elevated road was projected to consume the entire \$2.5 billion project budget, and these extra measures were estimated to cost an additional \$750 million. The alderwoman had up to \$1 billion in additional funding noted in her confidential instructions, which she could reveal and commit to using at her discretion. However, it is surprising that she agreed to this road option in the first place, and even more surprising that she agreed to fund these extra measures. In fact, her instructions suggested that this is her least favorite option, and that she would certainly not want to fund it. While she expressed concerns with the elevated road, the alderwoman ultimately acquiesced. During the debrief, she said that she was convinced based on the 'merit of the arguments', stating that she

> did start to buy it, because I do have to look the greater welfare and not just the air quality or the noise . . . if you look at the jobs that will be created if there is a good network, and good accessibility to different parts of the city, I thought this could actually be good.

In other words, she was convinced that other goals – like enhanced mobility and the jobs it would supposedly bring – were more important than minimizing the impacts on the residents of the neighborhood that the elevated road would pass through. This reflects her perceived prioritization of issues and commitment to rational decision-making, even at the expense of her constituents' immediate interests.

While ostensibly technical experts, and seen as credible because of this, the senior engineer from the National Transportation Agency and the project manager from the Municipal Traffic Department were very influential actors in this group. They provided extensive advice to the group, but it was arguably colored by their preferences. This was particularly evident in the case of the project manager, who even made up information to advance his case, saying things like

> The traffic department has received many, many complaints from residents in Bloomland because of congestion, because they need to make a big detour . . . and it can become a political [issue] for the alderman . . . if the residents' request for traffic help is not handled well; that is why, from our perspective [a new road is] still worth considering, although you might have to deal with residents' complaints of noise and so on.

The traffic complaints cited were not in his confidential instructions, but rather made up to advance his case. The technical experts had an outsized influence because of the legitimacy their expertise bestowed and because, like the environmentalist in the first scenarios group, they used ostensibly fact-based arguments to advance positions that others might accept as 'rational'.

The chair played an important, but not dominant role, allowing the group to proceed without her intervention for periods of time, but when she saw them going down what she felt was an unproductive path, she would step in. She attempted to make sure that parties were able to get their concerns and information on the table, carefully tracking on flipchart paper and shepherding the process along. She also employed active listening techniques, saying things like "I understand your point; what you are saying is you don't think option D is viable, even if we approve [the rail], correct?" Her style largely reflected what might be considered best practice in facilitation techniques.

Risk assessment group #2

The other risk assessment group reached only a tentative agreement. Most participants had come to support an option based on a phased approach, reconstructing the existing road and enhancing freight rail as soon as possible, and then passenger rail if and when necessary and financially feasible in the future. However, the port representative remained unsupportive of this option and the regional deputy director (i.e., chair) was seeking unanimous agreement. They subsequently concluded that they should conduct further research on why port users prefer road to rail and if their capacity needs can be met by improving the existing road and rail, and then convene again to review this information before finalizing their recommendation. It is notable that the unanimity decision rule invoked by the chair played a substantial role here, as was the case with the risk assessment group in Rotterdam.

While the additional research they called for may have provided value to the group, this conclusion appeared to be the product of persistent protests on the part of the port representative that his interests were not being met, rather than of genuine knowledge gaps. He was concerned that the opportunity costs associated with not building a new road would be too high, based on the information he had that his users prefer road to rail. The group had the capacity data on hand confirming that they could meet current and projected future demands, but the representative was successful in arguing that it may not be sufficient. One factor was the deputy director's attentiveness to the port representative's concerns; she attempted to reconcile his opposition by concluding that they should do more research. Even this outcome left the port representative unhappy; one of his final comments as they wrapped up was, "The recommendation we made is bad for business [and] bad for the economy; what we need is something that is quick, and that can solve the problem at the moment". However, a delay to gather more information was a good way to prevent the group from making a decision that he did not like.

Another barrier that may have prevented the group from reaching an agreement was that relatively less information was put on the table. For example, neither the alderman nor the flood protection specialist disclosed that extra funding might be available from their respective organizations. A key factor behind why more information was not disclosed appeared to be the deputy director's hold on the process. She attempted to tightly manage the deliberations, focusing participants on what was known and discouraging creativity and the sharing of information that did not immediately help the group move along. In general, she played an extremely dominant role in the deliberations, intervening 100 times, which is more than twice as many as the second most active (the port representative). She attempted to train participants' attention on the A39 and avoid other issues and possibilities, particularly at the early stages of the meeting. When the environmentalist initially brought up rail as a potential new option, she responded that their focus is on reducing congestion problems on the *road*. The rail option was almost left off the table, but the senior expert stepped up and supported it, saying, "There is actually an additional option, which connects very closely to what [the environmentalist] has been bringing up". The chair interjected again, noting that they have a limited budget and need to be realistic, but allowed the senior expert to proceed.

The deputy director was seeking consensus, but was particularly attentive to the port representative. She regularly checked in to see if and how his concerns might be met and made supportive comments. In contrast, when the environmentalist stated strong opposition to the alternative route through the wetland, the Port's preference, the chair said, "It is a green land – what does it do, besides provide habitat? Does it really create any value?" This reflected her prioritization of the economy, and thus the port, over other issues. Later in the deliberations, she acknowledged this directly, stating: "let's talk about how we can quickly meet [the capacity] need, because we cannot have the economy impacted; [let's] see how we can do a phased approach that would meet [port users'] needs as quickly as possible".

While particularly acute in the case of the second risk assessment group, the concerns of the Port Authority seemed to be taken more seriously in Singapore in general than in Rotterdam or Boston. During the debriefs, participants spoke of the 'national interest' (i.e., priorities), with economic growth as being high among them. A participant reflected,

> I think the option we ended up with in both [scenarios] groups is actually one of the worst options ever . . . because it is not economically

forward-looking . . . [Had] I known the national interest or the government interest, I would have pushed for this a little bit more, and there would have been a bit more tension, because if I know that economic growth . . . is the national interest, the other agencies will know that, and everyone will have that in their head.

Participants expressed discomfort with not knowing what the 'national interest' was in the exercise, as it would have guided their decision-making. Two different participants approached me one-on-one before the RPS runs to ask what the national priorities are in the exercise, because they were not explicitly identified. Similar concerns did not emerge in either Rotterdam or Boston.

Singapore's semi-authoritarian model

The ways in which infrastructure is managed and by whom – including how policies are crafted and implemented – are bounded and shaped by the wider norms of governance in the country. In contrast to neo-corporatist Rotterdam and neo-pluralist Boston, the overarching approach to governance in Singapore may be characterized as *semi-authoritarian, top-down,* and *pragmatic* (Haley and Low 1998; Ortmann 2011; Rodan and Jayasuriya 2007; Tan 2012). While a democracy, the People's Action Party (PAP) has governed since independence in 1959 and used various measures to limit viable opposition (Chee 2011; Economist 2011; Singh 2007). Founding Prime Minister Lee Kuan Yew spoke openly about the risks of democracy and importance of a strong state, and argued that economic development must precede democracy: "[Democracy's] exuberance leads to undisciplined and disorderly conditions which are inimical to development . . . The ultimate test of the value of a political system is whether it helps . . . improve the standard of living for the majority of its people" (in Abdoolcarim and Chowdhury 2015). The state presents the semi-authoritarian nature of their governance regime as the most effective and rational way to proceed with public administration (Tan 2012).

The Singapore model is not without its critics, which have concerns on human rights and democratic grounds (Henderson 2012; Ortmann 2011; Rodan and Jayasuriya 2007). Furthermore, micro-management has historically led to prosperity and a high capacity to manage problems, but has been criticized for its inflexibility; critics contend that the focus on stability and planning at the expense of a more risk-taking entrepreneurial mentality could have negative economic consequences in an increasingly globalized world (Haley and Low 1998; Saywell 2002). In the political arena, there is concern that the traditionally meritocratic civil service could devolve into an elite oligopoly that focuses on self-maintenance ahead of material performance (Tan 2008).

It is notable that the authoritarian nature of Singaporean planning and decision-making may be softening over time. The Economist Intelligence Unit's Democracy Index 2014 (2015) moved Singapore up a category from its previous ranking from 'hybrid regime' to 'flawed democracy', in part due to increasing tolerance of protests. Government agencies are increasingly making their planning and decision-making public and are including consultative elements, as discussed further later in this section. The first Concept Plan in 1971 was not made public, while today's Concept and Master Planning processes include explicit public participation components (Barter 2008; URA 2016c). In the arena of electoral democracy, the opposition parties received 40% of the votes in the 2011 elections, which was the highest proportion in decades and some believe a sign that Singaporeans are willing to consider alternatives to the PAP (Economist 2011).[1]

An important question is how climate change adaptation planning is evolving, given Singapore's governance model. Will the propensity to master plan, risk adversity and capable civil service lead to proactive and appropriate adaptation measures? Conversely, will the absence of public dialogue and broad stakeholder engagement leave actors blind to the risks of climate change or lead to maladaptive measures? How will this model manage uncertainty? This section explains the semi-authoritarian and pragmatic Singapore model and what it looks like in practice.

National cohesion and shared priorities

One reason why the semi-authoritarian features of Singapore, including central planning and limited direct public engagement, are accepted is the invocation of a set of overarching shared values and importance placed on national harmony. These are key components of the *social contract* between the government and the citizenry (Tan 2010). Singapore is a very young country that has faced significant hurdles, including hostilities with its neighbors, a dearth of resources, and internal racial and political tensions. The leadership strategically pursues the construction and maintenance of a national identity, with a shared vision and shared values, as a means to overcome these challenges and maintain stability (Chong 2010; Singh 2007). The education system reinforces these values by promoting ethnic harmony, stressing academic performance in areas like mathematics, and emphasizing skills that will contribute to economic growth (Singh 2007). Compulsory military service for all male citizens exists not only for defense purposes, but also to foster national harmony and interracial cohesion (Singh 2007).

Intertwined with these shared values is the prescription of shared national interests and priorities. These are the substantive matters that the government deems most important, and thus that are prioritized in planning and decision-making. Water has been identified as a national priority from the early days, because it is seen as an issue of national security and survival (Ong 2010). In response, significant resources have been put into enhancing Singapore's water independence, even when ongoing reliance on water sales from Malaysia may have been more cost effective. Economic growth is also a long-standing national priority; the government played a significant role in nurturing and supporting the emergence of the dynamic and high-performing economy that took Singapore from 'the third world to the first' in less than 30 years. The government focused on developing human resources and infrastructure for economic development, and nurtured the economy with a web of state-controlled enterprises and strategic partnerships to attract international investment (Choy 2010; Tan 2010; Tan 2012; Trocki 2006; Worthington 2003). These shared priorities can obfuscate interests-based deliberation, as parties ostensibly know which issues have priority vis-à-vis others. The *rational*, and thus naturally appropriate, option is the one that best addresses the national interests.

As noted previously, Harboring Uncertainty project participants were unsettled by the lack of clear national priorities in the RPS instructions. Some found it disconcerting that no priorities were established, and asked for further guidance. Others just assumed and applied Singapore's own national priorities. In particular, economic growth was given preeminent consideration; two groups made concessions for the port, and the alderwoman in a third group acquiesced to an elevated road option, despite the fact that this was explicitly against the interests of her constituents because it would ultimately be in the 'national interest' by supporting job growth and greater mobility. The fourth group concluded with a call for more research (i.e., no agreement) in large part because the port representative was unwilling to acquiesce to an outcome involving no new road, and the chair was deferential to his concerns.

It is clear that climate change is not yet deemed a national priority in Singapore.

> I think an area of concern would be that, at this particular point of time, the government as a whole, Singapore as a whole, has quite a lot issues on their radar – for example, the immigration issue, the transport issue, and stuff like that – so I can imagine people then would have less capacity to think about this climate change issue,

said an interviewee. Participants' opinions on if and how climate change might become a greater priority varied. Many feel that it will inherently be reactive, and they see recent flooding and the air quality issues associated with major forest fires in Indonesia as potential windows of opportunity to raise its profile. Interviewees emphasized that the government is investing resources in understanding the problem so that it can aggressively respond as conditions change.

Strong hierarchies, deference to authority

Singapore's national values and shared priorities involve adherence to and respect for hierarchies (Tan 2010). *Consensus* often involves deference to the most senior figure or institution, making it quite different from both the Dutch poldering tradition and modern deliberative consensus-building techniques. Several interviewees noted the importance of hierarchy in decision-making. One ascribed it, at least in part, to the legacy of Lee Kuan Yew, and reflected that "there is a certain hierarchy in Singapore; this goes straight into the internal workings of government". Another interviewee described how this plays out internally in government, with deference to certain ministries and officials over others. Another noted that

> in a sense, we do give a certain amount of respect – it's there in the Asian culture system, or society – so we do give certain respect to people who hold a higher position because, inherently you'll think that the guy actually has a bigger picture, he oversees a bigger project.

This deference to authority is important both within government and vis-à-vis the citizenry and media (Ho 2000). It is noteworthy that this hierarchical arrangement is generally one of cohesion, rather than might.

As discussed in greater detail later in this chapter, one element of the exercise Harboring Uncertainty participants found unrealistic was the lack of deference. They noted that in the real world the alderman would probably be the highest ranking, as an elected official, and thus "whatever they say, we will probably take heed, and some people will be a bit more wary". A policy maker put it this way:

> Although we try to listen to staff feedback a little bit more, very often it's top-down, so I think there is a little bit less teamwork, in terms of conversations around the table; we are trying to do more going around the table, but there is not so much of it right now. . . . Maybe it's the culture, maybe staff are not so open to it.

Participants were quick to note that these strong hierarchies do not preclude debates; they just tend to happen behind closed doors and among staff at similar levels, both within and across agencies. Interviewees involved in policymaking explained that proposals are typically more or less agreed upon before they are brought to higher-level meetings, but that they are the products of iterative processes of, often informal, discussion among staff before they get to that point. Nonetheless, the hierarchical nature of decision-making can have important implications when it comes to raising the profile of nascent issues like climate change. Issues may be given less attention if they are coming from weaker organizations. A participant noted that this is the advantage of the way the National Climate Change Secretariat (NCCS) is structured, with key ministers from across government, and their lieutenants, chairing various committees, rather than operating as a standalone effort of the Ministry of Environment and Water Resources. This does leave the initiative dependent on abilities and willingness of these key actors from various ministries and agencies to advance the climate resilience agenda. "The strength of the people controlling this platform is very important", reflected the participant, adding that "it's not just about capability, but even the right knowledge, skillsets to push it, to know how to manage and push a process to send policies along, and even, in a sense, to manage their bosses, to garner buy-in among their bosses". When asked how an important issue like climate change can be disseminated across a powerful organization like the Land Transport Authority, a policy maker responded that "the bosses will have to tell [each organization] how to prioritize the resources", as it is the allocation of resources that signals prioritization.

Participants emphasized that strong leadership is particularly important in this hierarchical environment.

> Given the nature of bureaucracy, I think the impetus must come from . . . senior leaders in the government, where they are enlightened enough to think "okay, actually we have this problem 10 years down the road and not five years down the road, but we have to start doing it",

said an interviewee. To the degree that they take place, meetings like that modeled in the RPS exercise would typically involve strong chairs shepherding the process. Strong leadership is seen as an ability to take in the concerns of different stakeholders, devise an appropriate plan and build cohesion around it. Considering what is needed to advance climate change, a participant reflected that

> You need people who have the kind of singular talent to really set a direction . . . When you have an overload of information, basically, you need somebody to say "look everybody, make a decision" and move from there; it's the inability to make a decision which already is a stumbling block.

Strong civil service

The city-state's civil service is extensively engaged in all facets of the economy and society (Tan 2008; Worthington 2003). For example, over 80% of the population resides in government-developed and -managed housing (Housing and Development Board 2016). The services provided are generally of good quality, particularly when contrasted with the substandard state of infrastructure and services only 50 years ago (Quah 2010; Singh 2007). The civil service is largely subservient to the political class, but there is emphasis placed on professionalism and elements of negotiated 'collaborative partnership' between the political and bureaucratic elites (Worthington 2003). The government does not operate to the exclusion of private enterprise; neo-liberal economic policy with its emphasis on global economic competitiveness and central planning operate in synergistic ways, which has facilitated impressive economic growth and social welfare, while maintaining the hegemony of the state (Huff 1995; Tan 2012).

Significant emphasis is placed on maintaining a high-quality civil service; the government aims to recruit the 'best and the brightest', they are paid comparatively well, and it is seen as a prestigious career (Quah 2010; Singh 2007). There are also significant opportunities for career development and ongoing education. Singapore's civil service blends elements of scientific management and customer-centric and performance-oriented service delivery, as is clear from the dual objectives of the PS21 'change movement' of the Public Service Division (2015): high-quality, responsive and courteous service to citizens and the application of state-of-the-art management tools and techniques to constantly increase the efficiency and effectiveness of service delivery. Quah (2010) characterizes the main features of public administration in Singapore as

> Macho-meritocracy; competing with the private sector for the best talent; low level of corruption; reliance on institutional and attitudinal administrative reforms; reliance on statutory boards for implementing socio-economic development programs; effective policy implementation; improving service to the public; and using policy diffusion to solve problems.

Rational model

The government takes a very rationalist approach to setting goals and fine-tuning delivery. Tools like scenario planning and mechanisms for cross-agency collaboration are used to enhance government performance, while the introduction of potentially conflicting interests is shunned because they might corrupt the process (Singh 2007). Formal policy evaluation and program appraisal methods are widely employed to promote efficient and effective service delivery, but they come with risks, including tunnel vision and unresponsiveness to public concerns (Ho 2000). The power put in the hands of the bureaucracy represents trust put in experts to get things done. This may be easier for relatively uncontroversial and straightforward challenges, but not for messier problems that inherently create winners and losers, or that do not have obvious answers.

This positivist paradigm is reflected in how the government and civil service are viewed, and how they view themselves. They claim to be following a "non-ideological, pragmatic approach" in tackling challenges (Mutalib 2010). Civil servants subsequently tend to be technocrats with backgrounds in law, engineering, science and business management, with "a sort of 'non-ideological' or positivist commitment to 'universal' standards of rationality and professionalism" (Trocki 2006: 130). Interestingly, interviewees in this research noted that *rationality* can even trump *hierarchy* in the Singaporean civil service. Said one,

> We are all rational people – if something is put on the table that we all feel is serious, valuable, we will not throw it away, even if it is from the most junior person. [I am] proud to say that in the Singaporean civil service we are very rational, and very practical at the same time,

In the context of climate change and the lower clout of climate agencies, another reflected that

> a lot of times people describe the Singapore civil service, as technocrats; we are fairly driven by the hard sciences, the hard numbers . . . [So] if an agency who is doing some of these projections and modeling doesn't have the legitimacy or is very new, I think if they have the science behind it to back it up, and the numbers to back it up, I think people will still look to them.

In the RPS exercise runs, there were various examples of participants taking stances based not on their interests, as described in their role-specific confidential instructions, but rather because they were convinced that it was the *rational* choice. The best example of this is the alderwoman who went against her constituents' interests because she was convinced that the elevated road option would be better for the common good for the wider city. In general, participants reflected that their decision-making was 'rational'. One participant reflected after the exercise that "once the numbers and the considerations were written on the flipchart, it pretty much was a one-sided contest; the poor port guys were like, 'okay, you win' once they saw the facts". He was surprised that other groups did not naturally reach the same conclusion.

The identification of universally rational positions and policies may be particularly challenging in ambiguous situations with high degrees of uncertainty and dynamic conditions, like adapting to climate change. While it is not yet clear how Singaporean decision-makers might adapt their sense of the rational to incorporate the risks associated with climate change, it appears that it will involve an ambitious research agenda. The government is investing resources and nurturing partnerships with academic institutions both domestically and internationally, with the aim of developing a fuller understanding of the risks and possible responses. The emphasis is on enhancing knowledge and technical capacity.

Cross-agency coordination and collaboration

It is noteworthy that strong hierarchies and a positivist bent do not preclude coordination. As in Rotterdam and Boston, Harboring Uncertainty participants generally feel that engagement with other stakeholders is an important element in public sector decision-making. When asked 'how important it is that they engage with other decision-makers and stakeholders as they plan and make decisions', the average response was 5.7 pre-exercise and 6 post-exercise, on a Likert scale from 1 to 7. However, participants' reflections suggest that they feel differently than do their counterparts in Boston and Rotterdam on the question of *who* should be engaged. Participants in Singapore universally emphasized the importance of cross-agency coordination, particularly around nascent issues that are not well institutionalized yet, like adapting to climate change. Said one participant,

> "It is human nature that . . . our focus can be limited . . . for example, if I'm working [on] transport, every single thing I see will be related to transport, the things I do, but then there might be other dimensions that I've not looked at, so that's why [it is important that you engage with] people from the other areas.

While cross-agency coordination may be common, structured forms of multi-stakeholder decision-making are less so in Singapore than in Rotterdam or Boston. Only 12 of 29 participants (41%) stated that they had prior experience in 'facilitated multi-stakeholder decision-making processes', compared to 57% of participants in Rotterdam and 79% in Boston. Those with prior experience rated them relatively highly (4.7 on a 7-point Likert scale). On the other hand, the frequency of interaction with stakeholders outside participants' respective departments were comparable to those in Rotterdam and Boston. Some noted that the nature of these interactions is becoming less formal over time as a new generation of civil servants foster informal networks to get things done.

> Traditionally, our approach was to go straight to the permanent secretaries, do a song and dance for them, and expect that they would pass directives down; more recently, because it's a small service everyone knows everyone, it's very common for us to reach out to others and say that we have this project, ask them for recommendations, meet them in workshops . . . and [these networks] help, because let's say you are starting this climate change work, you can tap into [them].

Hierarchies are important, but more-informal interactions among staff at different levels and stages in processes are key to the development of policies and plans. Nonetheless, interactions across layers are much more formal; lower-level technical experts, mid-level policy makers and political decision-makers rarely find themselves at the same table, and when they do, their interactions are highly constrained.

Citizen engagement

Despite the primacy given to national priorities and ostensibly uncorrupted rationality, it is clear that differences in opinion and conflicting interests exist in Singapore. While universally praising interagency coordination, participants were much more conflicted on the importance of engaging external stakeholders. The exercise introduced the notion of directly engaging external stakeholders in policy and planning deliberations, which was foreign to many participants and not well received by all. Some expressed support for public engagement and see it expanding over time. "We haven't done really grounded stakeholder engagement, but from the exercise I thought it's really important to engage people right at the beginning", reflected a participant, adding that "it [struck me] even stronger after the exercise that yeah, it could be potentially more effective and efficient to engage stakeholders at an earlier time as compared to after we have made our decision and telling them 'Okay, this is what we want to do'". Others were more guarded, citing various barriers and drawbacks to stakeholder engagement, including perceived unfairness in involving some actors and not others; capture by certain stakeholders, leading to biased outcomes; low capacity among civil society organizations; aversion to sharing information with external actors when it may be of national security or cause 'unnecessary fear'; inefficiencies, as different interests bloat proposals with their own issues; and time lost to deliberating.

A participant from the LTA stated that they try to inform residents what is going on and engage them, but that there must be limits because

> a lot of people just want to get their ideas through, and then they will just keep carrying on, writing in, until you give way to them, [but in Singapore], because as a small country, if we want to survive, we really have to get things moving fast . . . we cannot just let the public stop us from moving forward.

Another opined that in Singapore, "efficiency is one of the things that we are very, very proud of, [but] the more you have [engagement], the slower you become, [and] then, our advantage is lost". Concern was also expressed that other actors do not have the capacity to engage. "In Singapore, the expertise is disproportionately within government, resources are within government; we don't even have that strong of industry lobby groups . . . and the nonprofit sector, frankly, is not that strong", said an interviewee. To some, engaging external stakeholders can corrupt the pursuit of the common good and add unnecessary inefficiencies.

Interviewees did note that the civil service is rapidly learning how to engage the public, and that enhanced participation seems increasingly inevitable, given social media, public expectations and the general trajectory of society. However, existing outlets for citizen engagement are typically on the government's terms (Rodan and Jayasuriya 2007). The government provides avenues for citizen engagement at different levels and stages in planning and decision-making processes. For example, the *reaching everyone for active citizenry @ home* (REACH) agency was established by the government in 2006 to "Gather and Gauge Ground Sentiments; Reach Out and Engage Citizens; and Promote Active Citizenry through Citizen Participation and Involvement" (REACH 2014a). REACH works with ministries and agencies throughout government to facilitate consultation on a wide variety of issues, including a *Public Consultation on Climate Change and Singapore* (NCCS 2015). A *Citizen Engagement Handbook* uses cartoons and accessible language to make the case and set the terms for public participation (REACH 2014b). Singapore's long-term planning processes also provide avenues for citizen engagement; the latest round of review for the Concept Plan involved a lifestyle survey, focus group discussions and an online survey. The URA (2016c) affirms that "Public consultation is an important component of the Concept Plan process. Through engaging our stakeholders and the public at large, we can better understand our people's concerns and aspirations as we plan for the future."

While clearly more open than in the past, these efforts are still bounded. They are framed as tools for optimizing policy design and implementation; the heavy use of focus groups and surveys makes these efforts more akin to business market research than to truly collaborative processes. Citizens are asked for their opinions and recommendations, and the government incorporates or disregards as it wishes, leading to potentially wiser, more informed decisions, but not necessarily to policies with greater support or that are the products of multi-stakeholder deliberations.

Access to information is a cornerstone of citizen engagement. In Singapore, the government tightly controls what it releases; this, in part, reflects the sentiment widely held in government that they should have answers to problems before acknowledging them openly. It is also a product of regulations limiting access to information, rather than mandating it. The preponderance of information that is released by government agencies appears to be designed to promote their work to engender public support. The publications made readily available – including most of those cited throughout this chapter – are more promotional in nature than deep policy documents that are nuanced and acknowledge tradeoffs and heretofore unaddressed challenges.

While there is a close relationship between elected officials and the civil service, members of parliament can hold the government accountable and advocate on behalf of their constituents. In the context of the flash flooding discussed later in this chapter, for example, MPs called agency officials to the mat to demand action and inquire into what could be done. However, they were also defensive of the civil service, at least publicly, in noting the extraordinary nature of the events and outlining the solutions already being implemented (see PAP 2013).

Civil society organizations and emerging opposition

Civil society organizations can play key roles in organizing and representing the interests of stakeholder groups. Singapore has a strong network of 'grassroots organizations' that implement government policies; collect feedback and inform government of citizens' sentiments; organize activities and awareness campaigns; and coordinate citizens in times of crisis (Singh 2007). They are organized at both the neighborhood level and around specific issues, like women's welfare, youth support and the particular issues of ethnic minorities. However, these organizations have traditionally been more complementary to the objectives of the government, rather than oppositional; they are parapolitical in nature (Ho 2010; Mutalib 2010; Singh 2007). Most were created by the state to promote racial harmony, sponsor government programs and advance nation building, not as truly grassroots organizations that sprouted from citizens' dissatisfactions.

There are, however, signs that true dissent is becoming more accepted. Civil society organizations are increasingly willing and able to organize and speak out against the government on issues. Protests are only permitted in one park, Speakers' Corner, but the number and size of these demonstrations has been growing – from 85 in 2011 to 98 in 2012, then 169 in 2013 (Harjani 2014). Furthermore, both individually and in groups, citizens are increasingly willing and able to develop comprehensive critiques of government proposals. Strong opposition to the development of transportation infrastructure and housing in the Bukit Brown area, which is discussed in box 4.1 below, is an example of civil society cautiously organizing to challenge government proposals, conducting research to support their arguments, promoting their causes in the public sphere, and engaging with government agencies to resolutely make their case. The delay of work on a new transit station because of vociferous opposition from residents of the Maplewoods condominium complex is another example; while the LTA ultimately proceeded with few amendments, citizens were able to force various public meetings and delay the project by months (Chan 2011). According to an interviewee from the LTA that thought the process could have been handled much better, the government lost almost a year on the project, and learned that they need to do better and more targeted stakeholder engagement in the future.

There are various reasons why civil society may be becoming more independent and able and willing to challenge the government. First of all, the traditionally important national priorities like economic growth and national security may be diminishing in their centrality as the problems they address become less acute; Singapore is wealthy and its neighborhood more stable, so other issues are becoming increasingly important to citizens. Second, the population is increasingly educated and confident, and thus expects greater access to information and decision-making (Harjani 2014; Ho 2010). Social media also plays a role, insofar as it allows uncensored information to travel more freely, and facilitates truly grassroots organizing. The government is also playing a role by allowing, and even facilitating, greater civil society engagement in decision-making. In the words of an interviewee from inside government:

> The climate now is that the government wants to come across as doing more – more engagement, more open to hearing different views, making sure that there are sufficient channels for feedback and comments. So, I think it has become a little bit more overt [that] yes, we need to consciously think about if we should engage more than before . . . [the last election] catalyzed the need for broad new policies . . . And I think underlying all that is that the citizens really wanted to be heard a lot more . . . politically, the climate has shifted that way, partly because of the reaction from the ground, [but also because] some of the more senior leaders have stepped down [and] there are new ministers pushing for doing things a little bit differently.

Box 4.1 Bukit Brown: civil society in Singapore

Singapore is extremely densely populated with few areas in which nature is largely left alone. Most of the green spaces in this 'garden city' are artificially constructed and highly managed (Tan, Wang and Sia 2013). Rapid development over the past 50 years has also displaced many historical landmarks and cultural places, including former cemeteries (Tan 2013b). Bukit Brown is thus a rarity – an abandoned cemetery almost one square kilometer in size with 80,000 to 100,000 graves that has become a sanctuary for wildlife, as well as for those looking for peace, nature and cultural heritage (*Economist* 2012). One can find rare birds and statues honoring the deceased, making the area an important space for an eclectic mix of environmental and cultural heritage activists, recreational users and decedents of those buried there.

It is against this backdrop that the government has faced opposition to a planned eight-lane road through Bukit Brown, dissecting it and portending the development of a Housing and Development Board (HDB) housing estate in the future (Lamb 2013; URA 2014). Only 4,000 graves will need to be exhumed to make way for the highway, but opponents charge that it will fundamentally change its character. For a country in which challenges to the state are rare and typically muted, the activism to protect Bukit Brown is an interesting phenomenon. While still very civil, various opponents have employed a range of tactics to mobilize and bring pressure to bear.

The Nature Society (2011, 2012) released a position paper that catalogues the species of flora and fauna and makes various recommendations, including that the area become a heritage park and government address traffic challenges in other ways. Notably, the paper makes proactive suggestions that respond to the government's priority of traffic congestion and attempts to present this as an opportunity to 'showcase' the country's talent and set a 'benchmark' in sustainable development. The Singapore Heritage Society also released a position paper, which is critical of the government's decision to build the road, stating that it is "deeply disappointed with the plans". The paper details the historical significance of the cemetery; calls for alternatives to the new road; suggests that a proper cost-benefit analysis and an environmental impact assessment should be transparently done; calls for 'genuine' consultation, criticizing the shortcomings of the process conducted; and suggests that Bukit Brown be listed as a heritage site (Singapore Heritage Society 2012). The criticism of the government's decision-making process and frank calls for 'genuine consultation' are particularly surprising, especially from an established civil society organization. However, the Society is careful to compliment the prime minister on his call for 'inclusive dialogue'.

All Things Bukit Brown is a truly grassroots initiative, with the motto *Heritage. Habitat. History.* The group has become extremely active and well organized, with a range of ongoing activities, including guided walks, exhibitions to raise awareness, academic publications, widespread media coverage and a partnership with the World Monuments Fund. The group was awarded in the inaugural Singapore Advocacy Awards (2014). SOS Bukit Brown (2014) is another grassroots group. Their primary effort was collecting signatures for a petition urging the government to reconsider the project.

The role of Facebook and other social media in the emergence and success of these grassroots groups is notable. They were able to materialize outside the formal channels and restrictions placed on traditional civil society groups (Kai, Pang and Chan 2013). Social media allows for the rapid exchange and sharing of unfiltered information and facilitates coordination among likeminded but previously disconnected activists. Interviewees in this research concurred on the importance of social media and its ability to help more-informal networks emerge and thrive outside the traditional channels. In the words of one, reflecting on Bukit Brown: "I think what's happening now is just that their voices are getting louder because of social media, [it] actually amplifies the voice of these minority groups."

Ultimately, the activists' efforts did not sway the government to cancel the project. Construction is underway and the latest plans reaffirm that much of the cemetery should eventually be removed for housing. Nonetheless, the activism around Bukit Brown may be a harbinger of increasing willingness and capacity to organize and speak up. Among other factors, citizens, both individually and in networks, are increasingly vocal and expect a genuine hearing of their concerns. The aforementioned Singapore Advocacy Awards are evidence that activists are becoming organized and are increasingly tolerated. Interviewees reflected that this kind of public pushback over a proposed infrastructure project is traditionally uncharacteristic of Singapore, but increasingly common. An interviewee reflected that the government:

> needs to understand other actors and what they want, and then we can work around their 'pressure points' – It's not a question of who you want to engage, but how. Sometimes we come across as dogmatic, but [we increasingly] appreciate that we can't go into a meeting and say "we know that this is what is best for you, and this is the way we will do it". That is the way it used to be done, but it wasn't working anymore. Now it's more 'co-solutioning'.

While they did not alter their plans, the government did respond, including with a Bukit Brown Cemetery Documentation Project that is cataloging the graves being exhumed and the wider sociocultural history in the area. The government ultimately coopted some of the civil society concerns and advocates, including by involving them in the documentation project, as they moved ahead with the project but attempted to ameliorate the fallout.

For more information on the Bukit Brown case, see All Things Bukit Brown's active website (www.bukitbrown.com). The government-sponsored Bukit Brown Cemetery Documentation Project may be found at www.bukitbrown.info.

Climate vulnerabilities in Singapore

Singapore is a densely populated city-state close to the equator in Southeast Asia. It faces a variety of climate-related challenges, including (NCCS 2012, 2016a):

- coastal flooding from rising sea levels;
- water supply threatened by more frequent and severe droughts;

- infrastructure hit with more frequent and intense rainfall, sea level rise, stronger winds and temperature changes;
- shifting wind patterns decreasing air quality (e.g., more haze);
- impacts to biodiversity and greenery, including trees from wind damage and species from shifts in temperature and rainfall;
- brush fires due to temperature increases and droughts;
- impacts of higher temperatures on human health;
- shifting disease vectors and pest populations resulting from changing weather patterns;
- disrupted food supplies and price spikes from impacts on agriculture elsewhere; and
- slope instability due to rainfall.

Much of Singapore's territory is close to sea level. A substantial proportion of the country's low-lying areas are built on reclaimed land, and Singapore plans to add additional land and grow by another ~14% over the next 50 years (Koh 2005). This geography makes Singapore vulnerable to sea level rise (SLR). Mean SLR in the Straits of Singapore has averaged approximately 3 mm per year recently, and the rate could increase dramatically as the earth warms and rainfall increases (NCCS 2012). Projections of global mean sea level rise by the end of the century range from 26 cm to almost a meter (IPCC 2013). Average increases of millimeters per year may sound minor, but they add up when many critical assets – including the airport, marine ports, business district and critical freshwater storage reservoirs – are less than two meters above sea level (Arnold 2007). A thorough inundation analysis concluded that between 4 km^2 and 17 km^2 of Singapore's territory could be completely lost by 2100 if protection measures are not taken; the value of this land is estimated to be between 3.7 and 16.2 billion USD (Ng and Mendelsohn 2005).

Furthermore, sea level rise exacerbates the risks posed by storm surges, because it reduces the protective height that seawalls, barrages and other coastal defenses provide. Because of its location so close to the equator and in straits between Malaysia and Indonesia, Singapore has not historically faced major tropical cyclones. However, Typhoon Vamei, which was the first recorded cyclone near the equator, passed just north of Singapore in 2001, causing significant flooding and damage in the region; some forecast that climate change might make this type of event more common and/or intense (Chua 2013; NCCS 2012).[2] Because Singapore's coastal defenses were not constructed to withstand major tropical storms, the country would be extremely vulnerable should they increase in frequency or intensity.

Singapore may be unaccustomed to tropical cyclones, but it is very familiar with extreme precipitation, especially during monsoon seasons. Unfortunately, climate change may be increasing the frequency and intensity of heavy rain events. There were, on average, only five days a year in which rainfall exceeded 70 mm in an hour around 1980, while by 2012 the average was ten (PUB [Public Utilities Board] 2014a; Zengkun 2013). There has also been a statistically significant upwards trend in the 'annual maximum hourly' rainfall total from 80 mm in 1980 to 110 mm in 2010 (PUB 2014b). Recent years have seen a spate of severe flash floods, damaging property, disrupting activity and even causing death. Infrastructure systems, including key arterial roads, are disrupted when flood control infrastructure is overwhelmed (Yahoo Newsroom 2013).

While more intense rain events may be increasingly common under climate change, the country could also face periods of prolonged drought. In fact, February 2014 was Singapore's driest month since 1869, necessitating water conservation measures (BBC News 2014). Singapore historically relied on Malaysia for freshwater, but it has invested heavily in recent years in various technologies – including water retention, water recycling and desalinization – to advance water independence and thus security (PUB 2016b). Singapore's ability to achieve its ambitious goals around water self-sufficiency may be challenged as precipitation patterns change, while water scarcity elsewhere in the world increases concerns around the long-term stability of imports not only of water, but also of food supplies because of their vulnerability to drought conditions.

Singapore is an equatorial country familiar with very high temperatures and humidity and is largely adapted to its tropical environment; climate-controlled buildings are the norm, tree canopies are maintained to provide shade, and infrastructure is built to handle high temperatures. Nonetheless, even higher temperatures could strain the country's capacity to manage. The annual mean surface temperature rose from 26.8°C in 1948 to 27.6°C in 2011, and even conservative estimates suggest that Southeast Asia is likely to face an increase in mean temperatures of 1.7°C this century, which is higher than the projected mean global increase of 1.1°C (NCCS 2012). Much higher increases are possible, which could precipitate upticks in heat-related mortality and infrastructure failures. For example, electricity grids can collapse when energy demand for cooling is excessive and transmission lines are stressed by high temperatures. Temperature increases, and more extreme and intense heat events, may also threaten Singapore's biodiversity and food supplies from both domestic and imported sources, as species are no longer able to cope (NCCS 2012). Changing coastal environments may also impact biodiversity, particularly in coastal mangroves and coral reefs. From a public health perspective, temperature and other climatic changes may shift disease vectors with public health consequences.

Finally, climate change may involve shifting wind patterns, which could increase the frequency and intensity of days with poor air quality due to forest fires in neighboring Indonesia (NCCS 2012). Both 2013 and 2014 saw periods of particularly intense fire-related smog, with severe implications for public health and quality of life (Watts 2014).

Infrastructure planning, decision-making, and adaptation to climate change

While not as extensive as those in and around Rotterdam and Boston, various initiatives are underway in Singapore to tackle climate change. These efforts feature cross-agency collaboration and expert consultation, but with very little engagement of external stakeholders. The government sees enhancing resilience as primarily an internal responsibility and is acting accordingly. Efforts are also largely technical in nature, looking for engineering solutions to enhance climate resilience. This section introduces both how infrastructure planning and decision-making is organized in Singapore, and how climate adaptation is being integrated. It also shares insights from the Harboring Uncertainty project.

Project participants reported middling awareness of 'climate change and the risks it may pose', with an average response pre-exercise of 4.3 on a 7-point Likert scale from 'not at all' at 1 to 'very' at 7. In comparison, the average was 5 in Rotterdam and 6 in Boston. The level of awareness varied across participants. Not surprisingly, the two participants from the Ministry of the Environment and Water Resources self-reported that they are quite aware (6 and 7). The Land Transport Authority participants self-reported slightly lower awareness (two 5s and a 3). It is notable that there was a statistically significant increase in self-reported level of awareness from pre- to post-exercise.[3] This change would suggest that the exercise experience enhanced participants' awareness.

In general, participants expect climate change to be a somewhat significant factor in their organizations' planning and decision-making over the next 10 years, with an average ranking of 4 (pre-exercise) on a 7-point Likert scale. In comparison, the averages in Rotterdam and Boston were 4.9 and 5.7 respectively. However, the average response increases to 4.9 if participants from the Civil Service College are excluded. That organization is much less likely to play a direct role in tackling climate change. The average response was similar – 3.9 overall and 4.9 with Civil Service College participants excluded – when participants were asked to rank the degree to which climate change is already on their organizations' radars. There was variability in responses to both questions across organizations. In addition to the college, lower responses came from participants from the Prime Minister's Office (i.e., in strategic planning) and the highest came from those working directly on environmental issues.

In terms of how *confident* participants are that they and other stakeholders will be able to manage the risks and uncertainties climate change poses, participants entered the workshop somewhat skeptical, with an average ranking of only 3.8 on a 7-point Likert scale. Skepticism was common across participants coming from different organizations, although it is notable that those directly involved in climate adaptation and/or infrastructure planning and decision-making were more confident on average. One reason for skepticism is widespread belief that adaptive measures will only be implemented in response to climate-related events. Seven different participants speculated in the follow-up interviews that climate adaptation would be reactive, stating things like "I hate to say this, but something must happen close to us and real – it has to show that there is a clear and imminent danger". The good news is that most participants believe the government can react decisively if and when it becomes necessary. "In situations like SARS, [the government can] jump into action very quickly; even the slightest hint of this kind of epidemic, we go all out to protect the country", said a participant. On the other hand, climate change could emerge rather quickly, making a wait-and-see approach inappropriate. "The real issue is that we don't really exactly know how much things will change, whether or not Singapore will be drowned . . . climate could change faster than we think", opined a participant.

As discussed earlier in this chapter, concerted action in Singapore typically takes place once an issue has been deemed a national priority. Participants largely do not see climate change as a priority thus far. In the words of one,

> I think a lot of agencies are having a wait-and-see attitude because . . . we will need a very strong mandate on "yes, let's do this, this is the broad, over-arching strategy for Singapore", and then agencies, respective policies can come in . . . I think, at some level, at the very top of this hierarchy, someone would probably have to decide that this is the strategic direction we're going for Singapore so different plans, adaptation plans, mitigation plans all have to fit in and draft into this broader strategy.

Should climate change adaptation increase in prioritization, it will involve the establishment of standards and greater coordination.

It is important to note that, while still low (4.1), there was a statistically significant increase in participants' confidence from pre- to post-exercise.[4] This increase would suggest that the exercise experience enhanced participants' confidence that climate-related threats can be successfully addressed. Participants were also asked to self-report on whether the exercise changed their level of confidence. Eleven of 28 reported no change, four reported feeling less confident, and the remaining 13 reported increased confidence. Interestingly, there is no discernable pattern in which participants reported feeling more or less confident.

Coordinated adaptation planning

The National Climate Change Secretariat (NCCS), which is based in the Prime Minister's Office, is the primary coordinating body on climate change adaptation and mitigation efforts. The NCCS was established in 2010 to "develop and implement Singapore's domestic and international policies and strategies to tackle climate change", with responsibility to "facilitate efforts to mitigate carbon emissions in all sectors; help Singapore adapt to the effects of climate change; harness economic and green growth opportunities arising from climate change; and encourage public awareness and action on climate change" (NCCS 2016). At the highest level in the NCCS is the Inter-Ministerial Committee on Climate Change, which is led by the deputy prime minister. Thematic working groups – International Negotiations, Long Term Emissions and Mitigation, and Resilience – bring together senior staff from each of the relevant ministries and statutory boards (NCCS 2016).[5] The Resilience Working Group, which is responsible for adaptation planning and policy, brings together representatives from the 16 different ministries and agencies with responsibility over areas in which climate impacts are foreseen, and thus adaptive actions are being considered. This includes the Housing Development Board, the National Environment

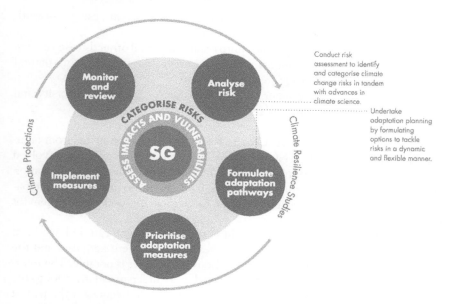

SINGAPORE'S RESILIENCE FRAMEWORK

Figure 4.1 Singapore's resilience-based approach to adaptation

Source: Ministry of the Environment and Water Resources, and Ministry of National Development (2016). Singapore's Climate Action Plan: A Climate-Resilient Singapore, For a Sustainable Future. p. 9. Used with permission.

Agency and the Land Transport Authority. There are issue-specific sub-groups like 'coastal defense' and 'infrastructure'.

Recognizing the high degree of uncertainty and evolving understanding of the risks climate change poses and thus the need to take a flexible approach, the NCCS applies a *resilience framework* to its adaptation planning (see Figure 4.1). This framework suggests that the government is taking an iterative approach – understanding the changing climate and its impacts, devising and assessing adaption options, implementing chosen options, monitoring and evaluating their efficacy, and revising strategies in an ongoing cycle over time.

The NCCS Secretariat has released publications on the potential impacts of climate change, what the government is doing and may do in the future, and how citizens can do their part. These include a National Climate Change Strategy, which was released in 2012, and *Singapore's Climate Action Plan: A Climate-Resilient Singapore, For a Sustainable Future* in 2016. The strategy introduces measures that have been taken or are planned with climate change in mind, including (NCCS 2012):

- an increase in the minimum elevation of newly reclaimed land from 1.25 meters above the highest recorded tide observed before 1991 to 2.25 meters;

- the creation of a Coastal and Project Management Department devoted to coastal protection and adaptation issues within the Building and Construction Authority;
- a revamping of the drainage and flood management systems, using a forward-looking risk management-based approach;
- suppressing and monitoring mosquito populations and other disease vectors;
- constructing buildings, infrastructure and urban spaces to promote natural cooling and reduce energy consumption; and
- enhancing tree management and maintenance to protect biodiversity and counteract the urban heat island effect.

A *Public Consultation on Climate Change and Singapore* was conducted from January through March of 2015 (NCCS 2015). The consultation primarily involved online e-polls (i.e., questionnaires) in five 'areas of action', and the focus was on climate mitigation rather than adaptation. The questionnaires were accompanied by brief background documents to inform participants and prepare them for participation.

While some information and guidelines on what citizens can do have been disseminated, the NCCS is primarily focused on government activities and the absence of external stakeholders in the various committees is notable. The information made public has also been very general in nature, particularly prior to the more recent (2016) Climate Action Plan. This reflects reticence on the part of the government to 'raise alarm bells' until plans are developed. Officials interviewed before the action plan was released admitted that they had more detailed analysis internally, but did not want to share it with citizens until they fleshed out the solutions. When asked about their reticence to share information, one interviewee put it this way:

> We don't want to get people [worked up], saying "Okay, your area is flood-prone, so in the long run . . . maybe you have to sell your house, the property price will drop", for instance. [So, we give a lot of] consideration before releasing certain information to minimize the potential, the situation whereby people would start to get afraid. I guess the other reason is because when we want to do something, and climate change is happening slowly, it's moving very slowly, so I guess for us we want to do, or to have some concrete plans before releasing it to the public. For instance, we have actually done quite a number of things . . . we have come up with risk assessment and adaptation plans . . . but we haven't released to the public because . . . when you tell them about the risk, the idea is to also tell them what is the solution . . . so they wanted something that is more complete before going to the public. Which might not be the same for other countries because they may [say] "okay, this is the risk, we are looking at the adaptation plans", but I think in Singapore that is not the approach . . . people generally want to have solutions before releasing to the public.

There is little place for stakeholders outside government, beyond local and domestic experts brought in to provide technical knowledge. In contrast to the Netherlands and United States, the norm in Singapore is that government generally knows best and is expected to plan and make 'rational' policy decisions that advance the common good for the long term.

An important question then is whether the NCCS is successfully promoting the issue internally with other agencies. One participant was positive about other agencies using their work, stating that

> I can tell you that, before new projects are coming up, we have agencies coming up to us to ask us for our opinion. . . . And the reason why they want us or they are engaging us at early stages is because they want to minimize potential destructions that could result due to climate change.

Another interviewee was more guarded, stating that information shared with agency representatives "does not permeate through their ranks, or across the organization as we would like it to" for many reasons, including prioritization and organizational hierarchies. It is notable that the level or engagement may be changing quickly; these interviews were conducted in 2013, long before the release of the latest action plan (2016).

While the NCCS is the coordinating body, adaptive measures, whether explicitly linked to climate change or not, typically must be implemented by various relevant statutory boards (i.e., agencies) and ministries. In most cases, these activities must be integrated into their ongoing infrastructure management tasks. In Singapore, agencies engaged in coastal and inland flood defense, and land transportation infrastructure, which is the focus of this book, are certainly relevant. The challenge is to find ways to institutionalize adaptation. An important first step is understanding how decision-making takes place. The following subsections introduce the institutional arrangements in place to facilitate infrastructure planning and decision-making in Singapore and how climate change is being integrated. One key feature of governance in Singapore is that, as a city-state, there is only one level of government. This naturally eliminates the challenges associated with coordinating across different levels of government with overlapping and interconnected authorities, and both conflicting and complementary interests. However, coordination across different ministries and agencies within the Singaporean government is still important. Central planning is a key feature of the state.

Land transportation planning

Singapore's transportation infrastructure is extensive and growing rapidly. The rail network increased from 138 km to 178 km and two new expressways were opened between 2008 and 2013 alone (LTA 2013). There are plans to add dozens of new trains and buses in the coming years and to increase the rail network to around 360 km by 2030. Construction is beginning on a major new 'North-South integrated transport corridor' and an extensive underground road system is being considered for the city center. The government has also established cycling policies and plans to add infrastructure there too (LTA 2013).

The Ministry of Transport sets overarching transportation policies, which are largely implemented by its statutory boards. In the context of roads and rail, including public transport, the Land Transport Authority plays a particularly important role, with responsibility for "planning, operating, and maintaining Singapore's land transport infrastructure and systems" (LTA 2017a). The Ministry devises higher-level transportation strategies and drafts relevant policies and legislation in response to government priorities, but delegates a substantial proportion of the responsibility for planning and decision-making to the LTA (May 2004). Other agencies – including the Public Transport Council, the Traffic Police and the Ministry of the Environment – play smaller roles around the development and management of the system. For example, the Ministry of the Environment deals with noise and air quality issues; the LTA is tasked with taking remedial action when the Ministry finds that ambient standards are being breached (May 2004).

A feature of governance in Singapore is strong central planning and coordination. The Ministry of Transport and its affiliated statutory boards coordinate closely with the Ministry of National Development and Urban Redevelopment Authority as they devise their plans and make investments. Transportation infrastructure is both a central theme of the Concept Plan and a critical component of meeting various other planning goals, including livability and sustainability ambitions. The Master Plan dictates where and how growth should be directed, and transportation infrastructure investments are coordinated to complement. There is a long-standing and deeply entrenched commitment to dense, transit-oriented development; a good public transportation system; and discouraging car ownership (Barter 2008; May 2004). While not without its shortcomings, Singapore's transportation planning addresses social, economic and environmental sustainability objectives rather than focusing exclusively on the traditional pillars of mobility and safety (Barter 2008; May 2004; Sharp 2005). This comprehensive approach reflects Singapore's broader characteristics of strong state involvement and a commitment to professional management, modernization and the pursuit of 'excellence' (Barter 2008). This approach requires a long-term perspective on transportation planning, rather than focusing on particular problems and how they may be addressed in the short term.

The LTA is somewhat unique in that it is responsible for virtually all ground transportation, giving it a wider perspective and ability to make decisions across transportation infrastructure systems (May 2004). In other cities and regions, public transportation systems are managed separately from roads, and road management is often fragmented across levels of government, increasing the likelihood of competition for resources rather than coordination towards shared ends. The LTA is also structured internally such that some of the key groups – including Policy & Planning, Engineering, and Corporate Planning & Research – focus on all aspects of the system (LTA 2017b). The LTA releases updated Land Transport Master Plans (LTMP) every five years to guide their work. Given the goals and priorities, it is not surprising that the current LTMP takes a commuter-centric perspective and emphasizes increasing connectivity, enhancing service levels, and promoting livability and inclusivity (LTA 2013). The plan reinforces the goals established in the Ministry of National Development's Concept Plan, including the target of 75% of trips by public transit during peak hours.

Overall strategic planning and project-level appraisal are conducted using various model-based systems, which predict variables like projected car ownership, commuting patterns and expected responses to different interventions. A nested set of models are used, with an overall 'policy model' informing a 'strategic model', which in turn informs 'local models' that consider particular interventions (May 2004). These are constructed using modeling techniques based on household surveys, trends analysis and other data sources. Accurate forecasting is made much easier by the multiple command and control levers the LTA has to directly influence patterns over time to bend reality to the predictions (May 2004). For example, the number of cars is more or less controlled through the Vehicle Quota System and associated auctions for Certificates of Entitlement, and peak demand loads can be at least somewhat managed through dynamic road pricing (LTA 2012).

Environmental monitoring is integrated, with reducing noise pollution highlighted as a goal (LTA 2013). The LTMP emphasizes environmental sustainability, including around nature protection, although the Bukit Brown case suggests that stakeholders do not always view these efforts as sufficient or feel adequately consulted. Financially, projects are assessed using cost-benefit analysis that considers travel time, operating costs and the safety implications for the various stakeholders. However, there is clearly a political element. Furthermore, financing is typically less of a constraint than other factors, making the economic evaluation of projects a less rigorous component of infrastructure planning and decision-making (May 2004). This is a stark contrast to infrastructure systems in other cities, including Boston, that are constantly underfunded, and thus in which financing is one of the prime drivers of infrastructure planning and decision-making. While strongly regulated by the government and centrally planned, elements of the system – including the operations and maintenance of the public transportation system – are tendered to private contractors.

The LTA is an important player in the climate change arena, although concrete action thus far has largely been on the mitigation side. Singapore's strict controls on private automobile use and emphasis on public transportation, while not driven primarily by climate concerns, complement greenhouse gas emissions reduction efforts (NCCS 2012). On the adaptation side, the LTA has started taking steps to protect assets and maintain service levels to the degree possible during major weather events; these include enhancing road drainage systems, in concert with the Public Utilities Board (PUB), and installing flood barriers at 19 of the most vulnerable mass rapid transit stations (Sim 2013a, 2013b). However, despite these initial efforts, it is notable that climate change does not appear to be a high priority for the agency. The fact that the latest Master Plan, released in 2013, makes no mention of 'climate change', 'adaptation', 'flooding' or other climate keywords is evidence of this (LTA 2013). Small steps are being made and LTA representatives are engaged in the NCCS process, but it is not (yet) high on their agenda.

While keen to emphasize that climate change is emerging as an issue, the majority of participants from the LTA engaged through this research concurred that it is not yet an organizational priority. One downplayed the importance of climate change, stating that

> there is a team that looked at climate change but they said that right now the risk is low, so for now, because there are other things that are a little bit more important . . . I think climate change may be taking a little more of a backseat.

Another framed it as other agencies' responsibility, stating that the "LTA is quite concerned about it, but it's not within our control". In particular, he identified it as a PUB concern, because it affects their 'key performance indicators'. Yet another LTA participant reflected that the 'vagueness' associated with climate change is a barrier to integration into the organization's planning and decision-making, stating that "it is hard to translate into an operational plan that I can put on the ground; [we] need a very specific assessment to develop a plan". On the other hand, LTA representatives that have been more involved in the NCCS and other climate efforts were more upbeat.

> Definitely before they build something, they already consider climate and the changes across the years, so our structures, even underground structures, are built . . . with considerations of these flooding issues, the flood levels . . . looking to the future, we also look at the risk,

said one. He added that

> the new climate change report has come out and the different agencies will have to evaluate our own structures, whether they are resilient enough or not, [and] in terms of risk management . . . climate change is something that . . . we are looking at and we will have to work with other agencies like the National Environment Agency, PUB, to ensure that we are prepared.

Coastal and inland flood defense

The Ministry of Environment and Water Resources (2017) has overarching responsibility for water management, including drainage and flood protection. It establishes overarching policies on water management, including flood protection, to ensure that government legislation is enacted (Ong 2010). The Public Utilities Board is the statutory board under the Ministry with comprehensive responsibility for the collection, production, distribution and reclamation of water in Singapore (PUB 2016a). Among the infrastructure they manage is 8,000 km of drains, canals and rivers (PUB 2014a). Water collection, management and supply tasks are consolidated under the PUB because they are explicitly understood and managed within a closed 'water loop'. As outlined in the 'Four National Taps' box (4.2) below, collecting and storing virtually every drop of water that falls on the island is a key component of the country's water security strategy. The challenge is that Singapore receives substantial rainfall on an annual basis, but it is largely concentrated in the monsoon seasons, resulting in contrasting periods of disruptive flooding and low supply (Ong 2010). The PUB must thus contend not only with securing and storing water for use, but also with providing adequate drainage to handle flash flood events.

Flash floods seem to be increasingly frequent and intense in Singapore in recent years as a result of both climate change and urbanization (PUB 2014b; Yahoo Newsroom 2013). While not historically unprecedented, these events suggest a reversal from the trend of declining flood risks over the past 45 years. In response, the PUB developed a *flood resilience plan*, which makes recommendations around how the system can be improved in three areas: *Source solutions* involve controlling water where it falls, and include hard infrastructure like on-site detention basins and softer solutions like rain gardens; *pathway solutions* enhance conveyance by upgrading canals and constructing centralized detention tanks; and *receptor solutions* involve protecting flood-prone infrastructure, including elevating roads and the platform levels of developments and safeguarding underground infrastructure (PUB 2014a). As is the case with transportation infrastructure, Singapore's water planning is tightly integrated with its overall land-use planning; canals and other water-related infrastructure are designed in concert with other elements of the built environment (Ong 2010).

Singapore's flood risks have traditionally been inland from extreme precipitation events. However, as noted in the 'climate vulnerabilities' section above, the island may be increasingly vulnerable to coastal flooding as sea levels rise and tropical storm patterns change (NCCS 2012; Ng and Mendelsohn 2005). This is a component of water management that the PUB does not manage. The Building and Construction Authority (BCA) is the statutory board of the Ministry of National Development responsible for the built environment, including coastal defenses. The BCA created a Coastal and Project Management Department in 2008 to examine coastal protection and adaptation issues, and it is working with other agencies and external experts to map risks and devise a *Coastal Adaptation Strategy*. Little information on the BCA's research and future plans has been made public thus far, but they have already implemented some measures, including stipulating that any new land reclamation projects are elevated an additional meter above the previous standard, to 2.25 meters above the highest recorded tide (NCCS 2012). The BCA is also managing 14.6 km of coastal defense infrastructure and experimenting with different approaches, like 'geobag seawalls' and Dutch-style flood barriers (Arnold 2007; BCA 2013). Like the PUB, the BCA is engaging technical experts and studying various approaches from around the world as it develops its understanding and capacity (BCA 2013).

Box 4.2   Four National Taps: Singapore's water security

> *I never believed [water security] would be impossible forever. I thought, some-time, some place, technology will be found that would make it nearly possible.*
> – Prime Minister Lee Kuan Yew (in PUB 2015)

Maintaining a stable supply of freshwater has long been a priority for Singapore. From the early days, founding Prime Minster Lee Kuan Yew was very uneasy about the city-state's reliance on Malaysia – from which it had separated and had a tense relationship – for almost all of its freshwater supply. This is unsurprising, given that Malaysia used the threat of cutting off the supply as leverage in their negotiations (Lee 2013). The fact that a major drought overlapped with Singapore's independence in 1963 only exacerbated concerns. In response, water sustainability was deemed a matter of national security. Various efforts have been made over the decades to increase Singapore's water self-sufficiency. This is an extremely challenging task on a densely populated island; Singapore sees substantial rainfall on an annual basis (2,400 mm on average), but it is largely concentrated within two monsoon seasons (Ong 2010).

Singapore's ambitious freshwater program, which is managed by the Public Utilities Board, is illustrative of what can happen when the government rallies around a complex environmental management challenge. The Four National Taps program is focused on developing and maintaining a sustainable supply from four sources (PUB 2016b):

- *Local catchment water* – An elaborate network of 17 reservoirs are fed by drains and canals, allowing for the capture and storage of rainfall on more than half of the land area. There are ambitious plans to increase this to 90% of the land surface by 2060. This is one of the most extensive rainwater harvesting systems in the world, and it depends on large-scale infrastructure, including barrages that enclose all of the major estuaries and extensive monitoring to maintain high water quality.
- *NEWater reclamation* – A state-of-the-art water recycling system uses membrane and ultra-violet disinfection technologies to turn wastewater into 'new' water that exceeds normal drinking water standards. The current NEWater plants can meet up to 30% of Singapore's water needs, but there are plans to increase capacity to supply up to 55% of the country's forecasted water demands in 2060.
- *Desalinated water* – Two desalinization plants are capable of meeting up to 25% of today's water demand. Both were constructed and are operated as public-private partnerships. There are plans to increase desalinization production capacity so that it can continue to supply approximately 25% of water as demand increases.
- *Imported water* – Despite major investments, Singapore continues to purchase approximately 40% of its water from neighboring Malaysia.

However, one agreement expired in 2011 and the remaining will expire 2061. Efforts to enhance self-sufficiency made renewing the first agreement unnecessary, and the goal is to have the capacity to be completely self-sufficient by 2060, should renegotiating the second agreement prove impossible or unattractive.

The system is understood as a closed *water loop*. While supply-focused technical solutions are most prominent, the water management strategy also promotes water conservation on the demand side, using regulations, pricing strategies and education initiatives to encourage private and commercial users to reduce consumption (Ong 2010).

While not originally climate related, Singapore's investments in long-term water security should enhance climate preparedness (NCCS 2012). The country's approach to water security may also be indicative of its wider approach to enhancing resilience and managing emerging threats. It suggests an emphasis on long-term security and independence, adopting solutions that are technical in nature and highly orchestrated within strong government institutions. Singapore's water strategy involves citizens, especially through conservation measures, but is largely government-driven, with little consultation and stakeholder engagement.

Master planning

A certain level of integrated long-range planning is practiced in all three cities examined through the Harboring Uncertainty project. In Boston, the Metropolitan Planning Organization (MPO) is one arena in which proposed transportation infrastructure projects are considered against long-range land-use plans and other projections of and aspirations for the future. However, the MPO is a relatively weak actor and, while it factors spatial planning into transportation infrastructure planning, these processes are not truly integrated. In Rotterdam, initiatives like the Delta Programme (2013) are influential, well-funded, and touch upon multiple infrastructure systems and land-use planning. The Dutch government also prepares an integrated National Policy Strategy for Infrastructure and Spatial Planning (Ministry of Infrastructure and the Environment 2011). Still, transportation infrastructure planning is largely siloed.

In Singapore, the Ministry of National Development (MND) is a very powerful arm of government, with a variety of responsibilities both directly and through its various statutory boards, including land-use planning, urban redevelopment, public housing, and parks and open spaces (MND 2016). The MND and the Urban Redevelopment Authority (URA) – which is one of the Ministry's statutory boards – engage in extensive strategic planning. The relatively top-down nature of governance in Singapore gives the plans much greater teeth compared to the more aspirational plans developed elsewhere in the world.

The planning and development process is comprised of three nested phases (URA 2016a): The overarching *Concept Plan* sets the overall vision for land-use and transportation planning over the next 40–50 years, and is reviewed on a decadal basis. The *Master Plan* translates the broad vision into detailed implementation plans, guiding both public and private investment decisions. *Implementation* involves shepherding both public and private actors towards the goals established in the Master Plan. The URA works with other branches of government to coordinate targeted infrastructure investments. The last review of the Concept Plan resulted in the publication of *A High Quality Living Environment for all Singaporeans: Land Use Plan to Support Singapore's Future Population* in 2013. The plan uses 2030 as the planning horizon, although elements look further into the future. The current Master Plan, which was released in 2014, is comprised of a map providing parcel-level detail on what land uses are permitted where and what complementary infrastructure exists or is planned, and a 'Written Statement' that describes how the plan should be interpreted (URA 2016b). The MND and URA coordinate with other ministries and statutory boards around the provision of infrastructure services to ensure that their development plans are complementary.

It is notable that planning happens within the various ministries and statutory boards as well. One vehicle for this is the *Strategic Futures* offices, which exist within many agencies. According to an interviewee directly involved in one of these offices:

> We try to anticipate the trends that would shape the operating environment for Singapore and then contextualize it to [our statutory board]. Obviously, climate change is affecting the wider operating environment . . . So, [it] is one of the driving forces that we have identified and we are trying to assess the impact and we find that it's not quite easy because, I think, internationally the experts are still trying to better understand the impact. And you might understand the global impact or the macro impact, but you need to scale it down to Singapore and this is where NCCS is trying to come in. . . . So, this is just one trend, . . . we're also doing things like demographic changes, social changes, economic changes, and political changes.

The Strategic Policy Office in the Prime Minister's Office supports long-range planning, including 'strategic foresight' work, and conducts strategic planning at the whole of government level. A key component of the Office is the *Centre for Strategic Futures*, which is an internal think tank with a mission to help the government understand future trends and manage risks accordingly (Centre for Strategic Futures 2015). The Centre employs various tools, including what they call 'scenario planning plus', which mixes scenario planning with other tools to facilitate thinking on 'black swans and wild cards'. The Risk Assessment and Horizon Scanning Programme (2015) is yet another arm of government focused on helping policy makers examine and prepare for uncertain futures, employing scenario planning and other tools, including a proprietary software tool. It is clear that centralized comprehensive planning – including both physical master planning and more strategic long-range scenario planning – is highly institution-alized in Singapore.

According to an interviewee, the Urban Redevelopment Authority, which is the agency responsible for planning, has a small group assessing how they might respond to a changing climate. They are considering factors like the urban heat island effect and how it might be mitigated through changes to their planning guidelines. The interviewee also noted that the climate adaptation portfolio recently shifted from the Strategic Research to the Planning Policies Department. This signifies a shift from climate adaptation being framed as a research concern for long-range consideration to it being a more immediate issue that warrants attention in terms of policy development. Still, planning agencies are taking a cautious approach. "I think we definitely recognize climate change as a potentially major threat, because we're an island state, but at the same time, we're also taking time to really understand the science behind it, understand the projections [and then] try to downscale it to what it means for Singapore", opined an interviewee, adding that in her opinion that is the right approach because they are "not jumping too quickly into making solutions now, when there are still a lot of these studies ongoing".

While climate change adaption is framed largely as a government responsibility, there is an emphasis on engaging experts from academia and research institutes both within Singapore and abroad. The NUSDeltares 'knowledge alliance', which is a partnership between the National University of Singapore and Dutch research institute Deltares, is an example of this. The alliance is focused on finding 'meaningful solutions' to 'essential societal challenges', including climate change, high-density living and urban water management. It's portfolio of projects thus far focus largely on implementing more sophisticated monitoring regimes to enhance understanding of dynamic and potentially vulnerable systems over time (NUS-Deltares 2016). These partnerships only underscore that climate adaptation in Singapore is an expert-driven affair.

Uncertainty: challenges and solutions in Singapore

The first chapter in this book discusses the pervasive nature of uncertainty in planning and decision-making. When participants in Singapore were asked 'how significant of a problem is uncertainty (not just from climate change) to you as you plan and make decisions (1 being not at all and 7 being very)?' the average response was 5.1 pre-exercise, which is the same as the average response in Rotterdam.[6] As in Rotterdam and Boston, participants see uncertainties resulting from numerous sources. "I think it's what we are all grappling with, you know, a lot of uncertainty. [The] environment [is] volatile, uncertain, complex . . . The main sources are social demographic changes, and [cultural changes]. I think things are changing more rapidly with technology and all that", said a participant, adding that "there are many driving forces that cause this change and uncertainty".

Participants do not see uncertainty in the context of climate adaptation as any more significant of a factor than uncertainty is in general in decision-making.

When asked 'to what degree is uncertainty a factor in climate change adaptation?' the average response was, in fact, lower than that for uncertainty in general in the pre-exercise survey at 4.1. There was, however, a statistically significant increase in the average ranking of how much of a factor uncertainty is in climate adaptation from pre- to post-exercise (5.1).[7] This would suggest that the exercise enhanced participants' perceptions of how much of a factor uncertainty may be as they start to tackle adaptation challenges.

Insofar as interviewees reflected that uncertainty *is* an important factor in climate change adaptation, their comments largely related more to governance challenges and the interpretation of models than to physical uncertainty. Issues like the establishment of common standards and challenges associated with raising the profile of a nascent issue are key here, according to interviewees. "It does seem fair to say that people are not aligned on this issue", said one.

> Before the game, I didn't think [uncertainty] was really that much of a problem because it was coming from my own point of view, and after the game, after interacting with the different people who have different agendas, different priorities, I realized how, when those come together, the uncertainty can increase,

said another, reflecting on the experience. To some, it is a matter of paralysis because of perceived uncertainties – "It's not like a known unknown, but people seem to keep complicating the issue", said an interviewee. She went on to note that the continuous interrogation and revision of climate models erodes trust and makes policymaking difficult, and asserted that the proponents of these climate models must be ready to speak with conviction, justify why their models are sufficient, and stand prepared to accept the consequences when they are far off. Otherwise, potential users of this information remain confused and unconfident in their applicability and accuracy.

It is notable, however, that other interviewees did reflect that the climate science is still too uncertain. In the words of one:

> We don't pass over the climate change indicators to the different departments or groups [in our organization] for consideration . . . because there is a lot of uncertainty with those forecasts, there's still a lot of uncertainties. . . . [The] NCCS is still trying to better understand the impact of climate change on Singapore at this stage, so it is a bit premature to factor in.

Managing uncertainty in Singapore

Asked how they typically deal with uncertainties in practice, participants responded as follows:[8]

- two participants 'follow official policies or guidelines';
- ten 'consult experts for their best projections';

- ten 'plan for worst-case scenario'; and
- twelve 'maintain flexibility'.

The ratio of responses here is similar to that in Rotterdam, with the exception that more respondents said 'plan for worst-case scenario'.[9] This is curious, given that Rotterdam's infrastructure planning is, at least from a climate risks perspective, arguably guided more by worst-case estimates of the future, such as the 10,000-year storm threshold used for the dike system protecting most of Holland. However, outside the climate issue, Singapore is perhaps just as cautious in their planning and decision-making, as evinced by the significant investments put into water security.

Post-exercise, participants were asked to rank how they think uncertainty *should* be dealt with. As illustrated in Figure 4.2, 'maintain flexibility' was the most popular option – it was the first choice of 15 of participants, and the second of a further 9. This positive sentiment was echoed throughout the exercise debriefs and follow-up interviews. Participants see value in flexibility in both policymaking and physical design and engineering. "The form of flexibility I like is having a plan B – what if A fails, then we can go to plan B", said an interviewee, adding that on the design side flexibility involves "the scalability of the solution, meaning, for example, now we can put up a [flood protection] barrier to 1.5 m, but what if tomorrow I want it to 5 m? Can it be done easily?" Another equated flexibility with being 'nimble' and "revising policies and adapting to the situation as it changes". He noted that most policies in Singapore have sunset clauses so that they are revisited at defined intervals.

Many participants explicitly talked about the interrelationship between maintaining flexibility and robustness (i.e., planning for the worst-case scenario). "I think what people normally do is think of the worst-case scenario and try to be a bit more flexible, in a sense, having additional resources and the space to react", said one. In a similar vein, others talked about building robust infrastructure while being flexible to different alternatives at the policy level, suggesting that the best

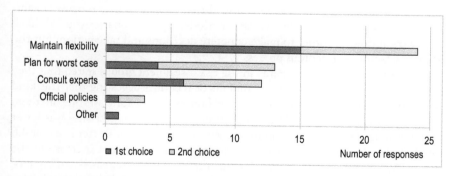

Figure 4.2 Preference ranking of how agencies should deal with uncertainties
First and second choices of respondents
Used with permission of author

approach is to "plan according to what was forecast . . . and then continuously evaluate". A participant opined that

> in terms of how [we] actually deal with uncertainty is really putting enough cushioning into our system; [in terms of flexibility], there are a lot of policies that we make, and sometimes it goes down to how we implement certain things, so policies cannot be too rigid. . . . So, flexibility on the top is important.

Participants also discussed the need to maintain efficiency by planning for the worst case and creating opportunities for adaptation as conditions change, but while concurrently looking for efficiencies and opportunities to optimize.

Decision support: multiple scenarios

Because the RPS exercise introduced participants to either scenarios or single risk assessment forecasts as a way to manage uncertainty, participants were asked in advance if they use either in their own planning and decision-making. All but two of the scenarios group participants stated that they have previously used multiple scenarios. As was the case in Rotterdam, this suggests widespread use of this decision-support tool in planning. Participants were also asked how useful the consideration of multiple scenarios is; they were very positive, with an average response of 5.6 pre-exercise and 5.5 post on a 7-point Likert scale. When asked why they are useful, participants reflected that it is really the scenario planning *process* rather than outcomes that they find valuable. This would explain why the scenarios – which were presented more as objects – were not really considered during the RPS runs. "I find [scenario planning] valuable as a process, [but] I wouldn't use it as a prescriptive kind of thing. . . . I would question the value of these scenarios, but I would say that the process is definitely very much valuable", reflected a participant with extensive experience using them, adding that "you wouldn't put so much stock into trying to predict certain things but the attempt to understand where you are, how you got there and what you're most likely to, where you might be heading – that process is valuable". She went on to explain that after considering the scenarios you still have to narrow it down in order to make concrete decisions and take action, but the scenarios facilitate a rigorous process.

All but three of the participants in the risk assessment groups stated that they had prior experience with 'risk assessments or reports', suggesting that this kind of report is widespread as well. When asked how well these forecasts prepare them for making decisions in the face of uncertainty, the average response was lower than for multiple scenarios – and in line with the average for Rotterdam – at 4.6 on the same 7-point scale. There was a statistically significant increase in the average to 5.4 post-exercise, suggesting that the experience increased participants' opinions on the value of this kind of probabilistic risk assessment forecast.[10] This increase brought risk assessments to the same level of support as the already high opinions participants had, on average, of considering multiple scenarios.

Learning from the exercise

As discussed in greater detail in Chapter 6, participants were asked a series of questions to gather feedback on how much the RPS mirrored their realities and was valuable in their opinion as a learning tool. Their responses shed light on the usefulness of this approach to action research and stakeholder engagement. Interestingly, RPS exercises are already being used in Singapore to help decision-makers gain exposure to issues and experiment with new tools and approaches. In particular, the Civil Service College has an Applied Simulation Training (CAST) team that is developing exercises for use in their various training programs. The support they have from the highest levels of the civil service underscores the value RPSs and other serious games can provide in helping civil servants and other stakeholders to grapple with 'wicked problems' like adapting to climate change.

In terms of how similar the 'situation or problem presented' is to their own worlds, the average ranking was only 4.4 on a 7-point Likert scale from 'very different' (1) to 'very similar' (7); this is lower than the averages in Rotterdam and Boston. One key difference is that there is only one level of government in Singapore, while the exercise features separate local and national levels. The 'characters' involved were also comparatively less similar, with an average of 4.6. As noted previously, non-governmental actors would not typically be involved in this kind of process in Singapore. "We don't involve the greenies as much", reflected a participant, adding that officials "usually come to some consensus first and then they go on to the private people".

The average for 'interaction between the characters' was also low at 4.3. According to interviewees, this kind of multi-agency meeting happens regularly in Singapore, but the outcomes are typically more predetermined. Some participants found the experience "overly democratic". Meeting chairs typically play central roles in this respect, which was the case with some RPS groups but not others. "Typically, in our setting the chair does have a lot more say, and people will give more respect", said a participant. On the other hand, many did not find the 'collaborative method of decision-making' completely foreign, noting that they do "find ways to negotiate" at the staff level. In fact, a couple of participants reflected that there might be *more* tension in a similar real-world situation, depending on who is at the table and the stage in the process.

> I guess culturally in Singapore there is a lot more respect for hierarchy – so what you will see at the table is that they may not show their points so much, but [in the background], outside the scope of when the bigger bosses come together, I think it happens like that at the lower level, but when it goes up you don't see this as much,

said a participant. "I think, in our culture, what you would typically see is that when someone wants to raise a particular point, they do it in a more discreet manner", said another. Debate occurs informally, off the record at the staff level, to forge broadly supported agreements before more senior officials meet.

Participants in the risk assessment and scenarios groups reported that these respective 'tools introduced' were somewhat similar to those they employ in the real world, with an average of 4.6; this is roughly comparable to the averages in Rotterdam (4.2) and Boston (4.4). As noted previously, scenarios are widely used in Singapore. The 'options or solutions' presented in the game were also somewhat realistic to participants, with an average of 4.6. As discussed earlier in this chapter, the Singaporean government is starting to consider options like floodwalls and question the robustness of buried roads with changing climate conditions.

While clearly not fully reflective of their realities, the accuracy of the RPS exercise is not necessarily a direct measure of its value. In fact, participants noted that, in some cases, they learned from what was different. Exercises can provide safe spaces for experimentation that may not be possible in the real world. "I guess that's also the beauty of having a simulation exercise whereby people can actually use the safe environment to kind of test some of the ideas and actions", reflected a participant. The lack of clear hierarchy and open debate between technical experts and more political and policy-related actors that occurred in the RPS runs was not realistic to participants, but nonetheless interesting and potentially informative. "We have been discussing and it is of interest in Singapore what is the relationship between the political office holder and the public servant", noted one interviewee, adding that they are grappling with questions like what neutrality means and what they should do when they disagree with politicians and senior bureaucrats. The exercise and surrounding workshop provided an opportunity to explore these important issues.

Process matters and interpersonal communications

Literally all of the participants stated that they 'learned something from the exercise that they might be able to apply in their own planning and decision making'. When asked *what*, most identified negotiation and interpersonal skills, and process considerations. For many, the fact that the process matters so much was an important lesson in its own right. In the words of one astute participant that is regularly involved in this kind of multi-stakeholder deliberation:

> My main takeaway was around how do you put in a process that [allows for] everyone's opinions [to be] heard, and I think that can be quite difficult. If you are not sensitive to the process, you can inadvertently lead to a lot of cognitive bias, and whoever shouts loudest wins, which is not conducive to this kind of multi-stakeholder engagement. [Groupthink is] a challenge in all governments, because to get that high in the first place you need to conform to a certain behavior. . . . But there are techniques you can use, [including] systematically bringing in an outsider. There are ways of doing this, and for civil servants, of being sensitive to that – the order, where you put people and so on. There are a lot of benefits, and improvements to the quality of the discussion you can have just by thinking through those issues more strategically.

On a similar note, many realized that there are many pathways and potential outcomes in a process like this, depending on the procedure followed, personalities involved and other factors that are not directly substantive. "It is quite interesting to . . . see how there are more ways than one that the decision could be altered, or affected, or influenced in one way or another", reflected a participant. The personalities of individual participants is a critical confounding factor in attempting to generalize and learn from what happens in RPS exercises, but must be recognized nonetheless − it mirrors the messy reality around how individual personalities shape real-world deliberative processes. The process was not one of simply optimizing plans based on objective evaluation of the risks and opportunities; despite the emphasis participants placed on 'rational' and 'objective' decision-making, values and interests had influence. Procedural factors − like what and when information was shared and who dominated discussions − also had significant implications. There is value in objectively evaluating the strength and weakness of different options and the veracity of different information, including around climate change, but it is impossible, and arguably undesirable, to remove the intertwined interests, values and perspectives of the different actors involved. This appears to be true even when the actors are coming together from within government, let alone from external interest groups.

On a related note, another common theme among participants' reflections on what they learned was the value of perspective taking and the benefits that this kind of RPS can provide by placing them in role of a different stakeholder.

> One thing I find very useful about this gaming exercise is that you force participants to put on different hats, and so they put themselves in the shoes of that role, and that helps to get them out of their own comfort zone, the role that they are playing in office,

reflected a participant with a policy background, adding that

> They are [subsequently] able to see the other side of the argument, the other argument, the counter-arguments, and that . . . sensitizes them to certain issues. And when they return to their portfolio, they are better able to formulate plans or strategies for that particular issue. So, it broadens their perspective.

In a similar vein, another participant argued that perspective taking encourages parties to get information on the table:

> I think, a lot of people tend to consider their own position too much, and sometimes it impedes certain decisions or stalls certain ideas, so, if someone is forced to speak a different language altogether, that's [how] more of the truth gets to come out, and they . . . may be more willing to consider other options.

The perspectives of actors outside government are rarely directly heard in this kind of deliberative process in Singapore. To some participants, the exercise suggested that there might be value in bringing non-governmental actors to the table. In the words of one participant,

> One key thing is that the government doesn't have all the answers to any solutions the country probably is facing. . . . So that was something interesting which I learned, because in our particular group, actually the NGO gave the most interesting perspective . . . and that never occurred to me and that's really sometimes very true to agencies that we are working in. Sometimes we don't realize a different perspective would actually really help.

The importance of, and a chance to hone, negotiation skills was the most commonly cited thing that participants took away from the RPS runs. "To me, the emphasis of the workshop was how do we become stronger negotiators, because that's not something we are typically good at in the Singaporean civil service", said one participant, adding, "failing in negotiations at the government level, there's a hell of a lot at stake!" Another participant with extensive experience in infrastructure project management situated negotiation dynamics in contrast to the traditionally prioritized elements of scientific management, saying:

> The exercise was definitely useful for training in negotiation skills, which is really needed. Negotiation is an art. Value engineering is easy because you have a target in mind, but with value management you want to set goals and each stakeholder has a different thing in mind. The question is how can we get everyone to move forward with a driving mission, and reach a simple outcome in which everyone is to get something. There are techniques you need to know, best approaches, like understanding others. Negotiation is part of what we do every day. The dynamics of groups is also a factor; the chairman calls the shots, so how they approach matters, including the degree of dissent that they tolerate, versus being more hierarchical. For example, if they look at seniority around the room it may not be the best in policymaking if the climate change rep is a junior and the chairman is from trade, we know how it is going to turn out before it starts. The same is true at the political level, between ministers.

Substantively, the exercise exposed participants to certain climate risks and to methods and approaches for managing them. A participant involved in pedagogy from the Civil Service College reflected that "just telling people that climate change is important, they might not be convinced, but when they do a simulation, being in the role, actually, [helps] them to appreciate the fact that climate change is [an] important considering factor". A participant that is actively involved in Singapore's climate adaptation work increased his evaluation of how much of a factor climate change will be in Singapore in the future from before to after the exercise, and reflected during the interview: "I guess why it changed would be that I saw the people there, it was unexpected to me, but they seemed a bit more interested and aware of the subject than I expected."

Conclusion

Various insights may be gleaned from the exercise proceedings and outcomes, interviews, pre- and post-exercise surveys and background research on infrastructure planning and decision-making in Singapore. These findings suggest how the adaptation of infrastructure systems both is emerging and may continue to evolve.

Issues deemed to be 'national priorities' receive extraordinary attention in planning and decision-making in Singapore, guiding the allocation of resources. Current priorities, and in particular economic growth, may influence how adaptation planning evolves. Climate resilience is not yet a national priority, but could emerge as one as risks become more acute. The strong civil service is generally deferential to hierarchies at both organizational and interpersonal levels. Strong leadership willing and able to champion climate resilience is thus critical if climate adaptation is to grow in prominence as an issue. That being said, the civil service and political elite pride themselves on being rational and 'data-driven'. Ideas are, at least ostensibly, vetted on their merits. Climate adaptation, therefore, may simply grow in importance as the data becomes clearer and more widely understood. However, wicked problems like adapting to climate change can threaten the rational paradigm, given the ambiguity around what is the most appropriate response in uncertain situations; how the state will respond remains to be seen, but early indications suggest that agencies are holding information on uncertain risks close to the vest, at least until they feel confident in their response plans. The wider governance regime significantly influences how planning and decision-making take place in Singapore and thus must be considered as adaptation evolves.

Uncertainty is a significant factor in governance, including around climate change. Scenario planning is widely employed in Singapore as a way to explore uncertainties and is generally viewed positively. However, important nuance emerged around when and how scenario planning adds value. Participants that played the scenarios version of the RPS reflected that they were not really used in the exercise because they needed to base their decision-making on something concrete, and they implicitly settled on the worst-case scenario because it was not particularly controversial or unbelievable, and it would encourage them to be robust. However, these same participants noted that they have found scenario planning extremely valuable in other situations because the *process* encourages stakeholders to methodically consider current and potential future conditions and how they can best be accounted for. Scenario planning can add value, but more as a tool to foster broader thinking in decision-making processes than for the scenarios that result. Participants in this research also reflected that flexibility and robustness might be complementary responses to uncertainty. Many participants expressed support for approaches to infrastructure planning that emphasize the worst-case scenario, but leave options open.

Civil society has typically played a relatively minor role in Singaporean governance, with tight controls and limited opportunities to engage directly with decision-makers in any sort of genuine deliberation. Structured and facilitated multi-stakeholder forums for decision-making are subsequently uncommon. Recent events suggest that this could change, with implications for who is involved in planning and the degree of influence 'outside' actors have. The increasing involvement of non-governmental actors and the complex and wicked nature of climate adaptation – including institutional ambiguity within government – may necessitate greater attention to process design. A key takeaway is the importance of good deliberative processes and the impact that negotiation skills can have on the government's ability to pursue its most important objectives. While they may learn from the collaborative approaches employed elsewhere in the world – including in Rotterdam and Boston – new modes of deliberation in Singapore will need to account for the unique characteristics of their governance regime and institutional arrangements.

Finally yet importantly, RPS exercises can help stakeholders grapple with how to manage wicked problems, like adapting to climate change. They can introduce participants to certain risks and provide safe, low-cost spaces for experimentation and public learning. Serious games are already being used in Singapore to train civil servants. Participants reflected that they drew both procedural and substantive lessons. There were statistically significant increases from pre- to post-exercise in various areas, including participants' self-reported awareness of the risks posed by climate change, confidence in the ability of themselves and their colleagues to address these risks, and impressions of how much of a factor uncertainty is in adaptation planning.

Notes

1 It is noteworthy that the PAP's take of the popular vote returned to 70% in the 2015 general elections, underscoring that their hold on power is still quite strong.

2 Tropical cyclones (including hurricanes and typhoons) are extremely rare close to the equator because of the Coriolis force (Irion 2003). From a meteorological perspective, Vamei was an almost improbable event.

3 Hypothesis: Exercise participation increases respondents' awareness of climate change and the risks it may pose. Question asked: 'How aware would you say you are of climate and the risks it may pose?' The results were significant at the $p = 0.025$ level, using a Wilcoxon matched pairs signed ranks test ($N = 12$, $T = 12$; one-tailed hypothesis). Therefore, the null hypothesis can be rejected.

4 Hypothesis: Exercise participation increases respondents' confidence in the ability of their organizations and other stakeholders to adapt to climate change. Question asked: 'How confident are you that your organization and other stakeholders will be able to manage the risks and uncertainties climate change poses?' The results were significant at the $p = 0.01$ level, using a Wilcoxon matched pairs signed ranks test ($N = 16$, $T = 22$; one-tailed hypothesis). Therefore, the null hypothesis can be rejected.

5 Statutory Boards are the implementing agencies of government with legally mandated authority in their respective domains. For example, the Housing and Development Board (HDB) is responsible for public housing and the Land Transport Authority (LTA) is responsible for land-based private and public transportation, including the public transit system, roads and vehicle registration and regulation. Statutory Boards typically report to a single ministry (Transport for the LTA and National Development for the HDB), which are responsible for broader policymaking.

6 There was a slight increase to 5.5 post-exercise, but this is not a statistically significant shift (Wilcoxon test; $p = 0.01$; $N = 18$; $T = 52.5$; two-tailed hypothesis).

7 Hypothesis: Exercise participation will shift respondents' opinions on how much of a factor uncertainty is in climate change adaptation. Question asked: 'To what degree

is uncertainty a factor in climate change adaptation?' The results were significant at the $p = 0.01$ level, using a Wilcoxon matched pairs signed ranks test ($N = 12$, $T = 6$; two-tailed hypothesis). Therefore, the null hypothesis can be rejected.

8 Note that the number of responses (34) is greater than the total number of respondents ($N = 29$) because some chose more than one option, although asked to 'choose only the most common or important'.

9 Only two of 18 responses in Rotterdam were 'plan for worst-case scenario'.

10 Hypothesis: Exercise participation will shift respondents' opinions on the value of risk assessment forecasts. Question asked: 'How well do these forecasts prepare you and other stakeholders for making decisions in the face of uncertainty?' The results were significant at the $p = 0.10$ level, using a Wilcoxon matched pairs signed ranks test ($N = 7$, $T = 2.5$; two-tailed hypothesis). Therefore, the null hypothesis can be rejected.

Works cited

Abdoolcarim, Z. and N. Chowdhury (2015, March 22). 'Father of Singapore' Lee Kuan Yew dies at 91. *Time*. http://time.com/3748684/lee-kuan-yew-obituary/.

All Things Bukit Brown (2015). *Bukit Brown: Heritage, Habitat, History*. http://bukitbrown. com

Arnold, W. (2007, August 29). Vulnerable to rising seas, Singapore envisions a giant seawall. *New York Times*. www.nytimes.com/2007/08/29/world/asia/29iht-Dikes.2.7301576. html?_r=0

Barter, P.A. (2008). Singapore's urban transport: Sustainability by design or necessity? *Spatial Planning for a Sustainable Singapore*. Wong, T.-C., B. Yuen and C. Goldblum, Eds. Netherlands: Springer. pp. 95–112.

BBC News (2014, March 5). February was Singapore's driest month since 1869. www.bbc. com/news/business-26445373.

BCA [Building and Construction Authority] (2013). *Inspiring Change for a Better Tomorrow: BCA Annual Report 2012/2013*.

Centre for Strategic Futures (2015). www.csf.gov.sg

Chan, R. (2011). Condo's MRT woes at stalemate. *AsiaOne*. www.asiaone.com/News/ AsiaOne%2BNews/Singapore/Story/A1Story20110630-286699.html

Chee, S.J. (2011, May 10). Singapore is taking the first steps to true democracy. *The Guardian*. www.theguardian.com/commentisfree/2011/may/10/singapore-election-democracy-new-media.

Chong, T. (2010). Introduction: The role of success in Singapore's national identity. *Management of Success: Singapore Revisited*. T. Chong, Ed. Singapore: Institute of Southeast Asian Studies. pp. 1–20.

Choy, K.M. (2010). Singapore's changing economic model. *Management of Success: Singapore Revisited*. T. Chong, Ed. Singapore: Institute of Southeast Asian Studies. pp. 123–138.

Chua, G. (2013, October 22). Cyclone unlikely to hit Singapore, experts say. *The Straits Times*. www.straitstimes.com/the-big-story/extreme-weather-asia/story/cyclone-unlikely-hit-singapore-experts-say-20131022.

Delta Programme (2013). *Delta Programme 2014. Working on the Delta: Promising Solutions for Tasking and Ambitions*. The Hague, NL: The Ministry of Infrastructure and the Environment; The Ministry of Economic Affairs.

Economist (2011, May 12). Banyan: Low expectations. *The Economist*. www.economist. com/node/18681827.

Economist (2012, March 17). A Singapore cemetery: Brown study. *The Economist*. www. economist.com.ezp-prod1.hul.harvard.edu/node/21550321.

Economist Intelligence Unit (2015). *Democracy Index 2014: Democracy and Its Discontents*. www.eiu.com/democracy2014

Haley, U.C.V. and L. Low (1998). Crafted culture: Governmental sculpting of modern Singapore and effects on business environments. *Journal of Organizational Change Management*, 11(6): 530–553.

Harjani, A. (2014). Balmy Singapore contends with rising protests. *CNBC*. www.cnbc.com/id/101918954

Henderson, J.C. (2012). Planning for success: Singapore, the model city-state? *Journal of International Affairs*, 65(2): 69–XIII.

Ho, K.L. (2000). *The Politics of Policy-Making in Singapore*. Oxford, UK: Oxford Press.

Ho, K.L. (2010). Political consolidation in Singapore: Connecting the party, the government and the expanding state. *Management of Success: Singapore Revisited*. T. Chong, Ed. Singapore: Institute of Southeast Asian Studies. pp. 67–79.

Housing and Development Board (2016). *Public Housing: A Singapore Icon*. www.hdb.gov.sg/cs/infoweb/about-us/our-role/public-housing–a-singapore-icon

Huff, W.G. (1995). What is the Singapore model of economic development? *Cambridge Journal of Economics*, 19(6): 735–759.

IPCC (2013). Summary for policymakers. *Climate Change 2013: The Physical Science Basis. Contribution of Working Group I to the Fifth Assessment Report of the Intergovernmental Panel on Climate Change*. Stocker, T.F., D. Qin, G.-K. Plattner, M. Tignor, S.K. Allen, J. Boschung, A. Nauels, Y. Xia, V. Bex and P.M. Midgley, Eds. Cambridge, UK and New York, NY: Cambridge University Press.

Irion, R. (2003, April 8). The Rarest Typhoon. *Science*. http://news.sciencemag.org/2003/04/rarest-typhoon

Kai, K.L., N. Pang and B. Chan (2013). New media and new politics with old cemeteries and disused railways: Advocacy goes digital in Singapore. *Asian Journal of Communication*, 23(6): 605–619.

Koh, G.Q. (2005, April 12). Singapore finds it hard to expand without sand. *Planet Ark*. www.planetark.com/dailynewsstory.cfm?newsid=30328

Lamb, K. (2013, January 25). Singapore cemetery demolition angers residents. *Voice of America*. www.voanews.com/content/singapore-cemetery-demolition-sparks-debate/1590643.html.

Lee, K.Y. (2013). *One Man's View of the World*. Singapore: Straits Times Press.

LTA [Land Transport Authority] (2012). *Managing Traffic & Congestion*. www.lta.gov.sg/content/ltaweb/en/roads-and-motoring/managing-traffic-and-congestion.html

LTA (2013). *Land Transport Master Plan 2013*. Singapore: Land Transport Authority.

LTA (2017a). *About LTA*. www.lta.gov.sg/content/ltaweb/en/about-lta.html

LTA (2017b). *What We Do*. www.lta.gov.sg/content/ltaweb/en/about-lta/what-we-do.html

May, A.D. (2004). Singapore: The development of a world class transport system. *Transport Reviews: A Transnational Transdisciplinary Journal*, 24(1): 79–101.

Ministry of the Environment and Water Resources, & Ministry of National Development (2016). *Singapore's Climate Action Plan: A Climate-Resilient Singapore, For a Sustainable Future*. Singapore. https://www.nccs.gov.sg/sites/nccs/files/NCCS_Adaptation_FA_webview%20 27-06-16.pdf

Ministry of Environment and Water Resources (2017). *Managing Our Water: Flash Floods*. www.mewr.gov.sg/topic/flash-floods

Ministry of Infrastructure and the Environment (2011). *Summary National Policy Strategy for Infrastructure and Spatial Planning: Making the Netherlands Competitive, Accessible, Liveable and Safe*. The Hague: Ministry of Infrastructure and the Environment.

MND [Ministry of National Development] (2013). *A High Quality Living Environment for all Singaporeans: Land Use Plan to Support Singapore's Future Population*. Singapore: Ministry of National Development.

MND (2016). *About Us*. http://app.mnd.gov.sg/About-Us/Introduction

Mutalib, H. (2010). PM Lee Hsien Loong and the "third generation" leadership: Managing key nation-building challenges. *Management of Success: Singapore Revisited*. T. Chong, Ed. Singapore: Institute of Southeast Asian Studies. pp. 51–66.

Nature Society (Singapore) (2011). *Nature Society (Singapore)'s Position on Bukit Brown*. www.nss.org.sg/documents/Nature%20Society's%20Position%20on%20Bukit%20Brown.pdf

Nature Society (Singapore) (2012). *Nature Society (Singapore)'s Response to the Bukit Brown Expressway Plan*. www.nss.org.sg/documents/BB_Response_HHC_AS_CL_v3-9.260312.pdf

NCCS [National Climate Change Secretariat] (2012). *Climate Change & Singapore: Challenges. Opportunities. Partnerships*. Singapore: NCCS.

NCCS (2015). *Public Consultation on Climate Change and Singapore*. www.nccs.gov.sg/consultation2015

NCCS (2016). *About NCCS*. www.nccs.gov.sg/about-nccs

Ng, W.-S. and R. Mendelsohn (2005). The impact of sea level rise on Singapore. *Environment and Development Economics*, 10: 201–215.

NUSDeltares (2016). www.nusdeltares.org.

Ong, B.L.I. (2010). Singapore water management policies and practices. *International Journal of Water Resources Development*, 26(1): 65–80.

Ortmann, S. (2011). Singapore: Authoritarian but newly competitive. *Journal of Democracy*, 22(4): 153–164.

PAP [People's Action Party] (2013, November 1). *Alleviating the Floods*. www.pap.org.sg/news-and-commentaries/news-reports/alleviating-floods

Public Service Division (2015). *PS21*. www.psd.gov.sg/about-us/ps21

PUB [Public Utilities Board] (2014a). *Managing Stormwater for Our Future*. www.pub.gov.sg/managingflashfloods/Documents/ManagingStormwater.pdf

PUB (2014b). *Flood Resilience Plan Needs to Evolve With New Challenges*. www.pub.gov.sg/managingflashfloods/floodresilienceplan/Pages/floodplan.aspx

PUB (2015). *In Memory of Mr. Lee Kuan Yew*. www.pub.gov.sg/water/memory_LKY/Pages/default.aspx

PUB (2016a). *About Us*. www.pub.gov.sg/about

PUB (2016b). *Our Water, Our Future*. PUB Report. www.pub.gov.sg/Documents/PUBOurWaterOurFuture.pdf

Quah, J.S.T. (2010). *Public Administration Singapore-Style*. Research in Public Policy Analysis and Management, vol. 19. Bingley, UK: Emerald.

REACH [reaching everyone for active citizenry@ home] (2014a). *Overview*. www.reach.gov.sg/AboutREACH/Overview.aspx

REACH (2014b). *Citizen Engagement Handbook*. www.reach.gov.sg/NewsPublication/Publications/CitizenEngagementHandbook.aspx.

Risk Assessment and Horizon Scanning Programme (2015). www.rahs.gov.sg

Rodan, G. and K. Jayasuriya (2007). The technocratic politics of administrative participation: Case studies of Singapore and Vietnam. *Democratization*, 14(5): 795–815.

Saywell, T. (2002). Re-imagining Singapore. *Far Eastern Economic Review*, 165(27): 44–48.

Sharp, I. (2005). *The Journey: Singapore's Land Transport Story*. Singapore: SNP Editions.

Sim, R. (2013a, December 3). LTA calls tender to flood-proof 19 MRT stations. *The Straits Times*. http://transport.asiaone.com/news/general/story/lta-calls-tender-flood-proof-19-mrt-stations?page=0%2C0.

Sim, R. (2013b, October 7). First MRT stations equipped with flood barriers. *The Straits Times*. www.nccs.gov.sg/news/straits-times-first-mrt-stations-equipped-flood-barriers.

Singapore Advocacy Awards (2014). *All Things Bukit Brown*. http://singaporeadvocacyawards. org/saa2014/honourees/all-things-bukit-brown

Singapore Heritage Society (2012). *Position Paper on Bukit Brown*. www.singaporeheritage. org/wp-content/uploads/2011/11/SHS_BB_Position_Paper.pdf

Singh, B. (2007). *Politics and Governance in Singapore*. Singapore: McGraw-Hill.

SOS Bukit Brown (2014). https://sosbukitbrown.wordpress.com

Tan, C. (2013a, October 16). More roads to be built underground; LTA studying plan to build subterranean roads. *The Straits Times*. www.straitstimes.com/the-big-story/marina-coastal-expressway/story/more-roads-be-built-underground-lta-studying-plan-buil.

Tan, D.W. (2013b, April 14). UNESCO bid: How about Tiong Bahru, Bukit Brown? *The Sunday Times*. www.bukitbrown.org/2013/04/unesco-bid-how-about-tiong-bahru-bukit. html.

Tan, E.K.B. (2010). The evolving social compact and the transformation of Singapore: Going beyond *Quid Pro Quo* in governance. *Management of Success: Singapore Revisited*. T. Chong, Ed. Singapore: Institute of Southeast Asian Studies. pp. 80–99.

Tan, K.P. (2008). Meritocracy and elitism in a global city: Ideological shifts in Singapore. *International Political Science Review*, 29(1): 7–27.

Tan, K.P. (2012). The ideology of pragmatism: Neo-liberal globalisation and political authoritarianism in Singapore. *Journal of Contemporary Asia*, 42(1): 67–92.

Tan, P.Y., J. Wang and A. Sia (2013). Perspectives on five decades of the urban greening of Singapore. *Cities*, 32: 24–32.

Trocki, C.A. (2006). *Singapore: Wealth, Power and the Culture of Control*. London, UK: Routledge.

URA [Urban Redevelopment Authority] (2014). *Tender to Construct New Road Across Bukit Brown Awarded*. www.ura.gov.sg/uol/media-room/news/2013/aug/pr13-48.aspx

URA (2016a). *Our Planning Process*. www.ura.gov.sg/uol/master-plan/vision-and-principles/Our-Planning-Process.aspx

URA (2016b). *Master Plan 2014*. www.ura.gov.sg/uol/master-plan.aspx?p1=View-Master-Plan&p2=master-plan-2014

URA (2016c). *Concept Plan – Public Consultation*. www.ura.gov.sg/uol/concept-plan. aspx?p1=Participate

Watts, J.M. (2014, October 7). Singapore grapples with 'unhealthy' haze from Indonesia. *The Wall Street Journal*. www.wsj.com/articles/singapore-grapples-with-unhealthy-haze-from-indonesia-1412661625.

Worthington, R. (2003). *Governance in Singapore*. London: RoutledgeCurzon.

Yahoo Newsroom (2013, September 5). AYE flooding: Tidal gate to be built at expressway-adjacent canal. https://sg.news.yahoo.com/-not-acceptable – for-major-expressway-to-close-due-to-flooding – minister-balakrishnan-151937577.html

Zengkun, Feng (2013, October 1). S'pore could see hotter, wetter days next century. *The Straits Times*. www.asianewsnet.net/Spore-could-see-hotter-wetter-days-next-century-52283.html

5 Boston

Many hands on deck in the neo-pluralist U.S.

Introduction

Boston's history is intertwined with the sea. At 400 years, Boston Harbor is the oldest continuously active port in the Western Hemisphere (Massport 2015a). The city emerged around the harbor as the preeminent port in New England during the colonial era and remained a major shipping center post-independence, landing cargo and immigrants from around the world and hosting a large naval presence. Commercially and militarily, the Boston Harbor is not as important as it once was, but nonetheless remains a hub on the East Coast; as of 2013, it was the 35th largest port in the United States by cargo volume (AAPA 2013).

Boston was literally built around or – more accurately in many cases – in the harbor. A large proportion of the city of Boston as it exists today was built on reclaimed land, including much of the downtown. Land reclamation allowed the city to grow while maintaining its proximity to the sea. Unfortunately, builders over the centuries only filled as much as they had to, given the water levels and storm patterns they were familiar with, and thus significant portions of the city are less than twelve feet above mean sea level. Given historical tides and the protective buffer the harbor islands provide from storms, this elevation has largely proven sufficient. Boston has experienced minor flooding, but nothing catastrophic. That may, however, be changing. Sea levels are rising and tropical storms seem to be tracking further north, potentially threatening the city. Hurricane Sandy was a wakeup call; had it hit Boston a few hours earlier or later (i.e., at high tide), the region could have experienced the kind of damage and disruption that ravaged New York and New Jersey, with up to 6% of the city flooded (Douglas, Kirshen, Li, Watson and Wormser 2013). Add an additional 2.5 feet of sea level rise, and over 30% of the city would be flooded under a similar event.

Awareness of the threats climate change poses to Boston is high among relevant stakeholders. Various governmental and non-governmental actors are involved in studying the threats and devising responses. Yet, concrete action has been slow to take hold. This may be, in part, a consequence of the governance regime within which Boston operates. The pluralistic nature of decision-making is characterized by fragmentation in decision-making; different agencies, levels of government and neighboring jurisdictions are responsible for various tasks and do not always coordinate well. Furthermore, the laissez faire paradigm, predilection towards individual rights and widespread suspicion of government leave many decisions in private hands and government agencies with relatively fewer resources for infrastructure and other projects. Civil society organizations play outsized roles in shaping and advocating for policies. This chapter considers how adaptation planning is evolving in Boston and may continue to evolve into the future.

The first section discusses the Harboring Uncertainty research interventions carried out with infrastructure stakeholders in Boston, including summaries of the processes and outcomes of the four groups that participated in the A New Connection in Westerberg exercise. The data drawn from these exercise runs – along with the complementary surveys, debriefing and interviews – informs the rest of this chapter. The second section characterizes the nature of the neo-pluralist and neo-liberal paradigm that Boston operates within, including the fragmented nature of decision-making, lack of investment and strong roles civil society organizations play. The next section briefly introduces the climate-related threats that the city and wider region face. Following that is a section that explores infrastructure planning and decision-making in the Boston region – particularly for transportation and coastal defense infrastructure – interweaving how these processes are responding to climate-related threats.

The final section of the chapter draws a synthesized set of conclusions from this research and provides a background examination of planning and decision-making in Boston. The key conclusions emphasized in this section are:

- Governance in the Boston region is typified by fragmentation across multiple different agencies at four different levels of government. There is coordination among agencies, but it is often weak, particularly at the regional level.
- Nonprofit organizations, including environmental advocacy organizations and business groups, play key roles in planning and decision-making, especially around emerging issues like climate change. Many of these organizations are highly regarded and integrated into governance systems.
- The disparate interests of different stakeholder groups strongly influence the development and vetting of policies and plans. Stakeholders use lawsuits and other mechanisms to influence processes, setting boundaries around what is possible.
- Infrastructure systems are often subpar because of underinvestment. Resource scarcity is a key factor in how infrastructure is constructed and managed. Lack of trust in government, and thus unwillingness to fund it, may be a factor behind underinvestment.
- Political leadership is often important to the emergence of issues like climate change adaptation on policy agendas, leaving initiatives open to cancellation or significant revision when administrations change.
- Uncertainty is a pervasive factor in decision-making, although certainly not only – or even primarily – because of climate change. Uncertainties result from changing political conditions and agency preferences, and various other factors. Participants see 'flexibility' as a good way to proceed despite

uncertainty, while recognizing that there are substantial barriers, including the linear nature of decision-making, and professional norms and standards.

- Considering multiple scenarios can add value in planning and decision-making but is difficult in practice, especially at the project level. Their real value is in making the nature of uncertainties explicit.
- Role-play simulation exercises can help participants to take perspective and experiment with others, providing valuable process lessons.

Research design and process in Boston

The research process followed in Boston was essentially the same as that employed in Rotterdam and Singapore. As outlined more extensively in the first chapter, the primary means of engaging project participants was via a half-day workshop that featured two different versions of the A New Connection in Westerberg role-play simulation exercise – one version with multiple scenarios and the other with a single risk assessment forecast. Half of the 32 participants played each version, allowing for two groups of each.[1] Pre- and post-exercise surveys, debriefing conversations and one-on-one follow-up interviews with many participants in the days that followed facilitated reflection and learning.

The success of this project was contingent on directly engaging actual infrastructure-related stakeholders. Strong local partners – the Boston Harbor Association (TBHA),[2] the Boston Society of Architects (BSA) and the City of Boston – were integral to recruitment. Participants were solicited based on their real-world relationships to the decision-making simulated in the exercise. They came from various agencies, including The U.S. Department of Transportation (USDOT); the Massachusetts Department of Transportation (MassDOT); the Boston Transportation Department; the City of Boston's Office of Environment, Energy and Open Space; the Massachusetts Office of Coastal Zone Management; Massport; and the Boston Redevelopment Authority. There were also participants from various consultancies and nonprofit organizations, including two local community groups.

While the case presented in the RPS is highly simplified and clearly not Boston, it does bear some similarities. In particular, the road project is loosely comparable to the Central Artery. While climate risks were not considered during design and construction, MassDOT is now evaluating its vulnerabilities and considering how it might be adapted retroactively (Bosma et al. 2015). The exercise challenges participants to consider what they might do differently if dynamic and uncertain climate risks are explicitly on their radars.

The process and outcomes reached by the four groups in Boston – and groups in Rotterdam and Singapore – are briefly summarized and compared in Table 2.2 in Chapter 2. Brief vignettes for the groups in Boston are provided below. Each of these summaries discusses the nature and substance of key interventions; the style of the deliberations that unfolded; which players were more or less active; and some preliminary themes that may be drawn, which recur throughout this chapter.

Scenarios group #1

The first group that played the *scenarios* version of the exercise came close to reaching agreement but was unable to within the time allowed. An option that involved enhancing the capacity of the existing road and enhancing freight rail service was popular, but vociferously opposed by the Port Authority representative, because of his constituents' preference for road over rail and unhappiness that a new road would not be built. In response, the group was considering if, how and when they might use extra funding to build a new road, in addition to the option on the table. This creative new option would follow an alternative route between the neighborhood of Bloomland and the wetland, avoiding the flooding risks associated with putting the road below grade, the neighborhood opposition associated with putting it through Bloomland, and the environmental impacts associated with going through the wetland. The group was debating whether this could be financed and on what timeline when the session concluded.

The deputy director (i.e., meeting chair) was very active, largely controlling the group's progression and speaking most frequently. Many of her interventions were procedural, but did significantly influence the proceedings. For example, she frequently answered questions raised, even when others might have had more, or different, information. She also had participants raise their hands and wait for her acknowledgement before they could speak, which limited dialogue between participants. She colored the consideration of the options based on her preferences; very little attention was given to the wetland option after she concluded her introduction of it by saying that it would cost "1.5 times the budget my agency is looking at, so it really makes this option prohibitive from our stand point, and this option does not address the urban congestion directly". The port representative still attempted to make a case for it, but clearly already saw that it was unlikely to pass.

After the deputy director, the most active participants were the port representative, alderwoman and environmentalist. This reflects deference to the concerns of their respective constituencies and recognition that this deliberation was in large part about addressing stakeholder interests. The chair, and others, repeatedly asked or deferred to these interest group representatives on whether an option was something 'their constituents could live with'. For example, when the port representative tried to revive the wetland route option, he asked the environmentalist, "If, by some miracle, [it] worked out, would you guys be open to replicating wetlands equal to the impacted area [elsewhere]?" Compared to Singapore, where the participants framed the process as one of achieving a shared national goal, even if they were de facto making arguments based on their respective interests, the interest group representatives were unabashed in declaring their interests and how they should be met. For example, the port representative stated, "I don't care about the future; I have the problem now!"

The interest group representatives were also unabashed in presenting their alternatives to a negotiated agreement and using them as threats. When discussing the wetland option, the environmentalist declared, "I simply cannot let this [route] happen; this resource cannot be disturbed, and I will take any organization to court that wants this road". Similarly, the port representative made dire predictions if he did not get his way in securing a new road, repeatedly making statements like "if you guys can live with the layoffs [that will result from no new road], that's great". These ultimatums did not offend or turn others off; to the contrary, they attempted to allay their concerns. This was clearly a strategy that participants felt appropriate and wise strategically. At one point, the environmentalist stepped out of role and quipped, "I am the [Conservation Law Foundation] in this exercise", referring to an important organization based in Boston that has used the courts to successfully advance an environmental agenda.

Hardball ultimatums did not preclude interest group representatives from employing skills of coalition building. For example, the port representative attempted to ally himself with the alderwoman, after deducing that they had some of the same interests and that meeting her concerns would be key to seeing any project move forward quickly. To this end, he voted against the elevated road option in a straw poll mid-way through, despite the fact that it was, on paper, satisfactory to him. "I like [the below-grade option], because the neighborhood likes it, and it gets me a road quicker", said the rep, adding that "if the neighborhood is happy, I'm happy".

While they spoke infrequently and had less influence in the deliberations, the technical stakeholders did have some impact. The senior engineer from the Transportation Agency was able to share costing and capacity information on the rail option when the environmental representative raised it as an option. The flood protection specialist was relatively muted in raising the profile of the flood risks, but did introduce the possibility of combining dike work with rebuilding the existing roadway, and the possible extra funding this might attract from his agency. This caught the attention of participants; the ability to access extra money both from them and from the City, after the alderwoman reported that they might be able to find an additional $1 billion if the project will benefit the city, was very attractive to participants.

In general, financing was a central issue, coming up multiple times. In her opening statement, the deputy director said that "the one thing I have to let everyone know is that there is a strict [budget]; the agency itself only has $2.5 billion for the project, so any additional cost, such as if option C is chosen, would have to come from other sources". The senior engineer was reticent to share his preferences early in the deliberations, but did emphasize cost and, in general, applied a fiscal lens to his analysis. During the debrief, the first thing the participant that played the deputy director noted was how money made a difference in which option was chosen, reflecting that when the alderwoman said

> that she could throw in an additional $1 billion if we avoided going through their neighborhood, [that] really enticed a lot of us . . . [and then] the flood protection specialist said they had some extra money that could go in from federal funds, so, financially, it was the [option] that was in some ways most beneficial, because funds were coming from other sources . . . from our standpoint that was the best.

The group was very creative in coming up with alternative options, including a hybrid option that involved building sections of the new highway above and below grade, and the alternative route noted above. The regional deputy director from the National Transportation Agency also proposed an option that involved opening a second port further inland along the river so that it would be closer to the key motorways on the other side of the city. These creative options opened up a range of viable possibilities, but ultimately complicated matters, preventing the group from reaching agreement before the deliberations ended. They also added uncertainties that participants did not know how to deal with, because they did not have the information in their instructions.

It is notable that climate change was not prominent in the deliberations, and explicit questions of uncertainty even less so. The group did not refer to the scenarios at all and discussed the flood risks only once. Other issues, like the pressing capacity needs of the port, the environmental impacts of putting the highway through a wetland and the community impacts of putting it through a neighborhood far eclipsed any climate concerns in the deliberations. Some assumed that flooding risks are significant, and subsequently supported options that would enhance resilience. In contrast, others thought it was less of an issue relative to their other concerns.

Scenarios group #2

The second scenarios group also came close, but had difficulty finalizing an agreement within the time allocated. They concluded with general agreement that they would expand the existing route and add freight rail to start, and were deliberating on a proposal to build a new (below-grade) road as well. The port and municipal traffic department representatives were particularly adamant in getting an alternative route for network robustness and convenience in crossing the river. The group also concluded that they would want to do more research before making a decision – they felt that they did not know enough about the flooding projections; the cost estimates for different options; how much funding might be secured from both the Flood Protection Agency and the City for a more elaborate project; the construction timelines for the different options; and if and how the port users might be convinced to shift to rail. The environmental representative also noted that the port itself might be very vulnerable to climate change, given its coastal location, and insisted that a vulnerability assessment should be done on it as well before they invest all this money to build a road that may lead to a flooded area.

The discussion in this group was much more balanced among the participants. Substantively, everyone contributed to the discussion. The deputy director played a more facilitative role than did the chair of the first scenarios group, largely resisting shaping the outcome but employing effective facilitative techniques like active listening, asking questions like "When you say the transportation needs of the project . . . are you looking at the general overall traffic patterns, or simply the port?" and "It sounds like what I am hearing is that we like option D, with some initial improvements, and probably looking for some additional money?"

This was the *only* scenarios group across the three cities that paid significant attention to the multiple scenarios in their deliberations. The chair put them front and center – they systematically went through and identified which option(s) would be best in each case. This accentuated the uncertainties and instigated some discussion on robustness, but participants ultimately coalesced around assuming the worst-case scenario after the chair concluded the scenario review exercise by stating that "now is when we craft a recommendation . . . We talked about a lot of things, but if we had to come up with a recommendation, what do you think it should be? . . . [and] what type of scenario are we planning for?" The environmentalist and alderman both said 'worst-case scenario' (i.e., 'wet and busy'), and no one disagreed, so that became the design condition. The flood protection specialist added that they should incorporate flexibility, to which the alderman responded by suggesting that expanding the existing road and adding more flood defense would best meet these criteria. The 'flexibility' of this approach was attractive to most of the group.

Climate change was not the only uncertainty the group grappled with. As discussed previously, the group concluded that they would need more information on various fronts before they could make a decision. These uncertainties were, in part, a product of new options being introduced for which no one had information. They also resulted from a reticence on the senior engineer's part to share information with confidence. While senior engineers in other groups spoke with certainty, the senior engineer here was very careful to caveat most information he shared, even when in his confidential instructions, saying things like "just to be clear, I won't stand behind those figures very much; they are just back of the envelope numbers". He later stated, "as head of the group that was in charge of developing the cost estimates, we should be careful taking that with too much definiteness until we do our engineering designs". This reticence to provide any more certainty was consequential; as the deliberations were drawing to a close, the Port Authority representative was keen to know that they could meet their goals, but the senior engineer was unwilling to confirm. This was a key factor in preventing a definitive final agreement. During the exercise debrief, a participant reflected that they "had a lot of questions, and felt like there wasn't a whole lot of information that was available". The pricing information they wanted was, in fact, in the senior engineer's instructions, but he emphasized the uncertainty around it, downplaying its value.

The senior engineer was also relatively hesitant to explicitly state his preference for one option over the others, presenting himself as a neutral resource person. In contrast, the flood protection specialist was much more confident in the data she presented and willing to express explicit support for an option. In her opening remarks, she stated, "We really don't want to compromise on the climate risks associated with the different types of builds and the different options we have on the table related to the roadway, [so] we do want to put out there that option D would be the most attractive for us". While the senior engineer's cautiousness generated some feeling of uncertainty, the flood protection specialist's strong assertions contributed to the prominence her preferred option received.

Similar to the first scenarios group, this group was very creative in proposing various options not in their instructions. They extensively deliberated on whether it might be wiser to move the port inland along the river due to flooding concerns. While they did not have information on what costs that might entail or how feasible it would be, they earnestly considered different components, like how a land swap might be orchestrated with the state and how a transplanted facility might link more effectively with the north-south-running A1 motorway. The chair introduced the idea of using a different construction technique, like tunneling the road. The idea of charging tolls on the roads was also introduced as a way to pay for a more expensive option.

As in the first scenarios group, there was substantial focus on the impact any highway might have on the community of Bloomland. While the alderman role's confidential instructions state a preference for the below-grade option, in both groups the players went off-script and were reticent to accept any highway without making sure it was not going to destroy the community. In the words of the alderman in this group,

> I understand that this is very important for business and industry throughout the district, but I have to say that [any road] is going to significantly impact the Bloomland neighborhood [because] it will bifurcate the neighborhood – we've done it all throughout the country, all throughout the world, and we know this is going to be an issue, so that's my main concern.

As a participant reflecting on the experience noted, there is a legacy of highway projects destroying neighborhoods under the banner of 'urban renewal' in Boston and other cities starting in the 1940s. The idea of any highway passing through this neighborhood seems unappealing. These concerns were not as prominent in Singapore or Rotterdam.

Another interesting feature is that, similar to the first scenarios group, participants not only accepted the presence of interest group representatives, but also deferred to them for information. For example, when discussing sea level rise forecasts in 10 or 20 years, the senior engineer actually looked to the environmental NGO representative and asked if her organization had done any sort of analysis. This is perhaps unsurprising in Boston, where an NGO – The Boston Harbor Association (now known as Boston Harbor Now) – has been a key facilitator and generated widely cited inundation maps (TBHA 2010). The environmentalist was also quick to mention a potential lawsuit in this group, saying that they were strongly opposed to the wetland route and prepared to go to court. As in the first group, this threat did not offend others, but rather had substantive influence on what seemed palatable or realistic as an option.

Risk assessment group #1

This group recommended expanding the existing highway, with new dedicated truck lanes so that freight can move with less congestion. They also decided to invest in rail, but passenger service first and freight only later if and when deemed appropriate. In contrast, most other groups focused on freight rail. Last, they committed to starting this work on an accelerated schedule and prescribed a phased approach, with the passenger rail coming online as soon as possible to alleviate congestion during road reconstruction. This approach was also presented as a *flexible* way to proceed in the face of *uncertainty*, although the uncertainty was around changing transportation preferences rather than climate change.

This outcome with dedicated truck lanes and passenger rather than freight rail was, in large part, a result of the port representative's intransigence and her ability to leverage that to extract a more favorable outcome. Throughout most of the deliberations, she was unwilling to entertain anything other than a new road, questioning the accuracy of the figures given for the estimated capacity increase that improved freight rail might provide. Even when others were looking for creative ways to accommodate her, she remained unsatisfied. Her inflexibility started to notably irk other participants. A participant from a similar agency to the port authority, but who was playing a different role in this exercise, commented that "The Port Authority certainly has a lot of money . . . so your concern should also be governmental relations and community benefits, and the community absolutely would not support [that] option, [so] I think the Port Authority needs to hear the community's position on this pretty clearly". Nonetheless, her aggressive gambit worked insofar as the outcome was shaped in many ways in response to the attention she demanded. While not her first choice, passenger rail should take cars off the road, and she gained the dedicated lanes for her trucks. Afterwards, the participant from a similar authority reflected,

> Well, working for [an agency like this] myself, I know you would gin up your own money to do your own thing. There would be no discussion – you wouldn't take priority over what the town wants. You'd have to be patient and attentive to what they say.

This suggests that her inflexibility was not altogether realistic, as in reality, economically self-sufficient public authorities like this need to be attentive to community concerns. They also get things done in environments with constrained resources by investing themselves rather than waiting for government agencies. An example of this in Boston would be the Silver Line bus rapid transit running to the airport; Massport bought the buses and is compensating their operations to facilitate free boarding at the airport (Mohl 2013).

Despite her intransigence, the port representative did seem to recognize the need to find allies, saying things like "as long as there is not opposition from the residents, because we need to move forward quickly" when asked if she would support an option. In fact, she drew serious concerns out of the alderwoman, who had been silent on her constituents' strong opposition to the elevated road option. The fact that it took a direct inquiry to invoke feedback on the option from the alderwoman is informative; in the real world, bringing actors to the table is the first step in robust multi-stakeholder deliberative process, but ensuring that they have the capacity and confidence to fully engage is also critical. The woman playing this role came from a neighborhood organization and appeared unsure of when and how she should intercede in a fast-paced discussion that was ostensibly focusing on the 'technical' merits of different proposals. Others, including the port representative, clearly understood the implicit 'rules of the game', whereas she seemed not to. Her muted involvement had other implications on how the 'zone of possible agreement' took shape.

While the port representative and senior engineer largely dominated the deliberations, others did make important contributions. For example, the flood protection specialist's disclosure that renovating the existing road would allow for concurrent dike reconstruction, likely attracting additional government funding, was instrumental in making that option popular. Similarly, strong opposition from the environmentalist and municipal traffic project manager to the alternative route through the wetland quashed it relatively quickly.

The senior engineer assumed a facilitative role, volunteering to map out the options and levels of support on a flipchart, interjecting regularly to confirm the statements of others, and proposing a straw poll. This was not because the deputy director was doing a poor job – she employed effective facilitation techniques and avoided stating her preferences to maintain an air of neutrality. The senior engineer simply pivoted into being a second facilitator and was able to dominate with his data. Others deferred to him for information. His approach represents a stark contrast to the senior engineer in the second scenarios group, who was very careful to highlight the uncertainty in his data. Both were looked to with authority, so the lack of confidence in the numbers of the senior engineer in the other group led participants to believe there was too little clarity to make a decision. In this case, the senior engineer played down any uncertainties, leading the group to feel confident that they could make a decision.

This group was also very creative. The environmentalist recommended a hybrid road-rail option with cargo moving by rail from the port to a transfer hub somewhere to the west of the city, at which it could be transferred to truck. The deputy director proposed a dedicated 'freight haul road' running through the existing rail right-of-way. The port representative objected to the former because of the added logistical issues and cost, but supported the latter. In fact, the latter was gaining substantial traction and looked like it might be the final agreement, until the senior engineer reviewed his notes and found a stipulation that the rail right-of-way is not large enough for a highway and any widening would likely face stiff opposition.

Compared to the scenarios groups, this group acknowledged the climate risks much more explicitly. The port representative downplayed their importance, stating that they need to focus more on the present, but others referred to the risk assessment when deliberating. Funding was less prominent of an issue than in the other three groups, but still talked about. For example, when a stakeholder said 'if only money wasn't an issue', the deputy director responded: "But it is! Money is an issue – always is".

Risk assessment group #2

The second risk assessment group reached consensus on an option that involved fully climate proofing the existing A3 while rebuilding it, enhancing freight rail service (also with climate proofing) and adding a new passenger rail service. This package emerged quite late in the deliberations, but ultimately satisfied everyone, including the port representative. She was hesitant, but took getting more capacity online as quickly as possible as her primary concern and was convinced that this option could be executed rapidly, especially given that all of the parties were enthusiastic about it.

The total budget for this package is $3.25 billion. The National Transportation Agency has a hard budget cap of $2.5 billion, but the alderwoman committed to providing the additional $750 million from the city's budget. As in the other Boston groups, financing was highlighted as a factor, with the deputy executive director emphasizing in his opening remarks that 'money matters'. This was repeated at various points when the group considered more expensive options. For this reason, the ultimately more expensive final agreement only emerged as a viable option very late in the deliberations when, seemingly out of nowhere to the others, the alderwoman said, "Well, my community actually kind of likes this idea, because we have been crossing our fingers and kind of hoping for something to go with the rail and, in fact, we are happy to throw $750 million on the table [for] that plan". She had been holding back on revealing the availability of these extra funds, and this disclosure changed everything, providing for a comprehensive option with substantial transportation capacity improvements that incorporated climate resiliency and satisfied most other interests expressed at the table.

The deputy director played an extremely dominant role in this group. Employing active listening techniques, he would confirm the statements of others and frequently and methodically chart the course to the next step. He engaged participants in the process of evaluating each option against a range of criteria, took numerous straw polls, made sure to call on parties for their opinions and had another participant track key elements on a flipchart. In general, his techniques could be considered quite strong.

> We are not reaching a technical decision; we are trying to reach broad consensus as a group that can be followed up on in greater detail. . . . What we really want to do is engage each other from our own perspectives, understand each other's perspectives, and reach a reasonable type of agreement that we can all live with,

said the deputy director. He was also a consensus builder. For example, recognizing that the port representative was still unhappy as they finalized the package, he asked if the group could "offer something to [the port] that would appease some concerns?" This actually yielded what participants framed in the debrief as "a side negotiation between the community and the port", in which the alderwoman admitted she had some more money beyond the $750 million she had already put on the table and offered a further $250 million to the Port Authority for something like a "big fancy crane".

As in the other exercise runs in Boston, the parties were very explicit in identifying their interests and positions. The port representative focused on a better transportation link north; the alderwoman emphasized quality of life and raised the idea of a community benefits agreement; and the environmentalist and flood protection specialist both spoke of the valuable wetland and goal of reducing pollution, and thus championed public transit. As in the other risk assessment group, the port representative made strong demands; after they were finished deliberating, a participant reflected that "it seems like they would have deeper pockets". As discussed in the previous section, port authorities in the United States would typically contribute to infrastructure projects, not insist that less-well-funded government agencies construct the infrastructure of their choosing for them. Here, too, the alderwoman stated opposition to any road through Bloomland, despite her confidential instructions suggesting that she would prefer one below grade. Again, this reflects negative associations with highway projects.

While explicit in expressing their interests and positions, the participants did employ negotiation techniques and made calculated statements in efforts to sway opinion and form alliances. For example, the environmentalist attempted to kibosh the wetland route not by focusing on the environmental impacts, but rather the high cost. While ultimately unsuccessful, the port representative and alderwoman clearly recognized some shared interests and formed an informal alliance.

A common theme across all four groups in Boston was the readiness of the environmentalists to threaten a lawsuit and the degree to which the others acquiesced to that threat. In this case, as soon as the wetland option was introduced, the representative stated, "While we really appreciate being part of this process, I think if [that] were the path we walk down, we would not have much choice but to challenge that in court". Later on, when assuaging the port representative, the alderwoman said not to worry because they have lots of money for lawyers to beat back 'fringe interests'. Reflecting post-exercise, the participant that filled the environmentalist role reflected, "I do think it's interesting what lawsuits and uncertainty can do to projects; with very little 'real' leverage you can create quite a bit of leverage". In a similar vein, a participant reflected in a follow-up interview that "People brought to the table assumptions around legal protections, the costs of litigation, the fierceness of the [regulatory] protection". This underscores the interdependency that the threat of lawsuits can create, giving ostensibly weak parties leverage in deliberations vis-à-vis more powerful parties and influencing the zone of possible agreement.

As in the other risk assessment group, the chair outlined the climate risks up front. This was the only group in which a player (the alderwoman) explicitly assumed the role of being a climate skeptic. Early on she said, "Well, I would challenge anyone to show me proof . . . I understand that there is always a risk of flooding, but your topnotch engineering has always maintained the best quality of life, and that's what I'm interested in, because that's what my citizenry values the most." However, when it came to the specifics, she said, "If you are generally talking about higher quality construction and flood risk reduction, then I support that. It's just this climate stuff that I don't believe in". This may be reflective of decision-making in the United States, where it can be more effective to frame *resiliency* efforts without mentioning the term *climate change*.

Fragmented governance: Boston's neo-pluralist, neo-liberal model

Decision-making in Boston occurs within a *neo-pluralist* governance paradigm. In this model, various interest groups continuously compete over the evolution of policies within more or less distinct policy domains, ultimately shaping them via the relative influence of their various positions and their differing levels of power (Dahl 1962; Lindblom 1977; McFarland 2007). These interest groups are composed of both governmental and non-governmental actors, with the government holding varying degrees of autonomy and authority in different situations. Furthermore, the state is not a single actor, but manifests as a set of actors with varying interests across different levels of government, and even different agencies and departments within the same administration. Other interest groups include corporate lobby groups and nonprofit advocacy organizations. Groups with shared interests and perspectives cluster in what Sabatier and Jenkins-Smith (1999) call 'advocacy coalitions'. The range and complexity of actors varies, depending on the 'policy niche', with groups often trying to carve specific niches for the purposes of control (Lowery and Gray 2004). While consensus is frequently pursued, and reached, in a neo-pluralist paradigm, the interactions between coalitions are often adversarial in nature.

The paradigm under which governance occurs in Boston may also be characterized as *neo-liberal* insofar as there is comparatively less state intervention in what is an overwhelmingly market-oriented economy, a strong ethos of fiscal austerity in government spending and substantial skepticism of the government's ability to solve problems (Harvey 2007; Jahn 1998). The state plays a major role in the provision and management of infrastructure, but these activities are typically framed in the service of the private economy and private companies under contract do much of the actual work.

Fragmentation

A key characteristic of the neo-pluralist model is the fragmented nature of governance and decision-making. Solof (1998, 5) put it best, stating that "The United States may be one nation under God but, politically, it is fractured into a multitude of jurisdictions – states, counties, municipalities, school districts, election wards and more". There are at least four levels of government in the Boston area – municipal, regional, state (Massachusetts) and federal – with different responsibilities and relationships to one another in different sectors. Compared to other parts of the world, these various actors do not always coordinate effectively. In the context of climate change, an interviewee reflected that it is "ridiculous that everyone is doing their own vulnerability assessments, and everyone is coming up with their own climate predictions. We are all right here together!" That interviewee went on to say that it is 'tricky', because responsibility is often unclear. Another participant with knowledge of decision-making in the Dutch context compared the two in the exercise debrief, saying,

> What I have seen from the Netherlands versus here is that there you have a very good network at the national level, regional level, and here there are a lot of different groups coming up with very good out of the box ideas with more transparency, but you don't catch all of the mistakes that you would with the better network.

The emerging set of key actors around climate change is largely ad hoc and not intentional in design. An issue like adaptation may be more appropriately dealt with at the regional level, given that most of the impacts will be regionally felt, and adaptive options extend across and impact multiple municipalities. However, the regional level is the weakest in Massachusetts. In the words of a participant:

> From an institutional standpoint, many of us have been concerned that in the Boston area compared to Rotterdam and Singapore, there is nothing between the municipality and the state in terms of decision-making. . . . We are lacking on both the transportation and on the climate change side from lacking an effective regional planning network, and it all has to be negotiated between the communities and the state, and that is a pretty big gap to have to deal with.

The region is highly fragmented into over 100 different municipalities, ranging in size and nature from the largely urban city of Boston with over 600,000 people, to low-density 'country suburbs' on the edge of the metropolitan area (MAPC 2017). As a 'home rule' state, municipalities have substantial autonomy in planning and decision-making. They must operate within state and federal laws and go to the Massachusetts Legislature for approval on certain matters, and are enticed to make certain decisions around issues to receive state and federal grants, but otherwise make their own laws and decisions (Department of Revenue 2015). Regional agencies typically have little power. As discussed later in this chapter, the Metropolitan Planning Organization (MPO) exerts influence insofar as transportation projects may only receive federal funding if they are prioritized through its process. The Metropolitan Area Planning Council (MAPC) coordinates planning across the region and is an important source of information and technical support, but does not have any legal authority to compel municipalities to cooperate or to unilaterally implement planning changes (Commonwealth of Massachusetts 2015; MAPC 2017).

Fragmentation in the Boston area is not just a matter of numerous municipalities. There is also fragmentation in service delivery among agencies at the same level of government. There are at least six state and local agencies involved in transportation planning in Boston, plus private contractors, federal agencies and other stakeholders. The City of Boston itself divides responsibility for its road infrastructure between at least two departments – Transportation and Public Works. "There is a constant issue with BTD and DPW kind of overlapping in some areas," reflected an interviewee.

It is notable that having multiple levels of government is not in and of itself unique to the United States. As discussed in the Rotterdam chapter, there are also agencies at four levels – national, provincial, regional and local – in the Netherlands. However, the fragmentation in terms of the number of different jurisdictions and overlapping responsibilities in infrastructure and service provision is unparalleled.

Litigation

Debate over how litigious the United States is, and whether this is a point of pride or scourge, is ongoing. In the context of major infrastructure projects in Boston's recent history, lawsuits have played very important roles. The extensive Boston Harbor cleanup – which took over two decades, cost \$4.5 billion and involved the construction of various infrastructure, including the state-of-the-art Deer Island Sewerage Treatment Plant – was precipitated by a suit filed against the State of Massachusetts and the U.S. Environmental Protection Agency in the 1980s by the Conservation Law Foundation (CLF) (Shelley 2011). A once highly polluted harbor is now swimmable and fishable. The CLF is a prominent environmental non-governmental organization based in Boston. A settlement between the CLF, the Commonwealth (i.e., state), and the City of Somerville was the impetus behind an extension of the Green Line (metro) through Somerville, despite the transit agency's financial woes (Somerville 2015). Interviewees noted the influence that litigation, and the threat thereof, has on planning and decision-making; according to one involved in planning and project development,

> It can change a lot of agreements that happen; if you don't think about what the law department is going to require you to do, you are going to be stuck having what you just spent three years doing sitting on a shelf for a year and a half while they figure out the legalities and insurance around it.

Low trust in government

Whether justified or not, one characteristic of governance in the United States is relatively low trust in government institutions. In 2016, only 39% of U.S. respondents in a global survey by Edelman (2016) indicated that they trust government. In contrast, 49% of Dutch respondents and 74% of Singaporean respondents indicated that they trust their governments (Edelman 2016).[3] The lack of trust has implications on what citizens entrust the government to do and what proportion of their income they are willing to give the government to provide services. The protracted debate over health care and the role of the government in ensuring universal, afford-able access in particular is evidence of this. Reflecting on how people view the role of government in the United States versus the Netherlands, a participant opined,

> In the Netherlands, people buy into taxes and services differently, and they expect the decisions will be made at the top and they accept it, because they believe that [agencies] are making decisions to prepare effectively, while in the U.S. it's more "yes we'll give you some tax money, but we [will hold you] accountable for every cent you spend", and that level of accountability, mixed with our political cycles and how people get elected comes into play.

In contrast to the low degree of trust in government, 57% of U.S. respondents stated that they trust NGOs, and 51% stated that they trust the business com-munity (Edelman 2016).[4] It is impossible to tease out causality, but this contrast in the level of trust in government versus civil society and the private sector is not surprising, given the prominent roles both NGOs and businesses play in plan-ning, decision-making and service provision in the United States. It is noteworthy that trust in the media in the U.S. was only 47%, which is right at the 27-country average, but below Singapore (60%) and the Netherlands (55%) (Edelman 2016).

Government underfunding, poor quality infrastructure

The United States has been highly criticized for the poor quality of its infrastruc-ture (*The Economist* 2011; Markovich 2014; National Economic Council and the President's Council of Economic Advisers 2014). The American Society of Civil Engineers (ASCE) gave the country a D+ grade overall for the 'condition and performance' of its infrastructure in its latest review, with a D- for public transit infrastructure, D for levees, D for dams, D for roads, B for rail, and C+ for bridges (ASCE 2017). The ASCE (2017) also criticizes the state of infrastructure in Mas-sachusetts, noting that 14.4% of bridges are rated structurally deficient; 292 dams are considered to be high-hazard potential; and there is a roughly $1.4 billion capi-tal expenditure gap in the state's schools. The ASCE (2017) calls on all levels of government and the private sector to "close the two trillion dollar 10-year invest-ment gap"; establish a "clear vision for our nation's infrastructure"; and invest in new technologies that will meet the "triple bottom line", providing economic, social and environmental benefits. Current inadequacies have economic and social consequences – Americans spend hours in traffic, businesses incur additional costs and traffic fatalities result, in part, from poor road conditions (National Economic Council and the President's Council of Economic Advisers 2014).

U.S. transportation infrastructure is not only in poor shape in absolute terms, but also relative to other countries. The World Economic Forum's (2014) Global Competitiveness Report 2014–2015 ranked Singapore second, the Netherlands fourth and the United States twelfth overall for their infrastructure systems; and the Netherlands fifth, Singapore sixth and the United States sixteenth for the 'quality of roads' subcomponent. The World Economic Forum report emphasized infrastructure as one of the 12 'pillars' of economic competitiveness, suggesting that the U.S. is losing out because of its poor performance in this area.

The poor state of infrastructure is, in large part, a product of relatively lower expenditures. In 2014, $279 billion was spent on transportation infrastructure in the U.S. (by all levels of government), which represents approximately 1.6% of GDP and $870 per capita (CBO 2015). In contrast, Singapore spent approximately 10.9 billion SGD (8.2 billion USD) on transportation infrastructure in 2015, which represents approximately 2.7% of GDP, and 1,980 SGD (1,490 USD) per capita (MOF 2015). Not only is transportation infrastructure spending lower in the United States relative to elsewhere in the industrialized world, it is also significantly lower, as a share of GDP, than it was during the years of infrastructure expansion in the 1950s through 1970s (Markovich 2014).

Underinvestment in infrastructure is reflective of the smaller role for and proportion of the economy entrusted to government. General government expenditures as a percent of GDP in 2014 were 40.1%, which is relatively low by OECD (i.e., developed world) standards; in contrast, the ratio in the Netherlands is 50.4% (Heritage Foundation 2015). Furthermore, if defense spending is excluded, this is reduced to approximately 31% in the U.S. (Center on Budget and Policy Priorities 2015). It must be acknowledged that this rate is still quite high compared to Singapore at 17%, which is one of the lowest in the world; however, in Singapore expenditures on social security and healthcare, which are typically among the most expensive programs, come in large part from the government-managed but individually funded Central Provident Fund (CPF 2015; MOF 2015).[5]

The role of private contractors

Much of the actual construction and maintenance of the road network in the Boston area – ranging from design and engineering, through paving to snow removal – is conducted by private contractors (Boston Public Works Department 2014; MassDOT 2017a). In the context of climate adaptation, MassDOT's Central Artery Vulnerability Assessment is being conducted by external consultants. An interviewee noted that this is the norm with environmental and other assessments and modeling; agencies have to hire consultants to do most of this work because of the specific expertise and work involved. While not inherently good or bad, there are potential downsides. One is that the underlying models remain the intellectual property of the consultants – every time MassDOT or another agency want to tweak parameters and do another run, they must pay the consultants to do so. Another is that consultants are brought in on a project-by-project basis and typically expected to solve a problem and move on.

> Often there are consultants working on a project, and I think it's often hard for them to admit that they haven't solved the problem, so they are going to act like they solved the problem with whatever they are proposing, and I don't think that they would feel like they should say "it's enough for now",

reflected a participant, noting how it can impede flexibility. While agency staff may be reticent to 'stick their necks out', interviewees asserted that consultants are probably even less likely to.

The Rotterdam chapter introduced various models of public-private partnerships. Privatized infrastructure provision, including both transportation and water infrastructure, is prevalent elsewhere in the United States, but not in the Boston area. While private contractors play a central role in infrastructure construction in the Boston area, they are typically selected through conventional project-by-project bidding processes run by city and state agencies, with the respective agencies maintaining ongoing ownership and management.

Strong role of non-governmental actors

Non-governmental organizations are extremely influential players in the Boston area. Their involvement includes lobbying for their preferred options, providing technical support and providing interfaces to their respective constituencies. Two organizations that have been particularly active in Boston on climate adaptation and transportation infrastructure respectively are Boston Harbor Now and A Better City (ABC). While certainly not the only important organizations in these domains, they are illustrative of the impact non-governmental actors can have.

Neighborhood-level community organizations are important actors, organizing residents, advocating on their behalf and engaging in service delivery. An example is Neighborhood of Affordable Housing (NOAH) in East Boston, which undertakes a wide variety of activities, including affordable real estate development, homeowner and renter counseling and support, youth programs and English classes (2017). In the area of climate adaptation, NOAH has run workshops to raise awareness and facilitate preparedness (Douglas et al. 2012; Lynds 2015). While neighborhood organizations work with and lobby government agencies, it is notable that they do not place all of their faith in them, including on climate adaptation. In the words of an interviewee from a neighborhood organization,

> We do value the relationships we have with officials, but we can't focus too much [on them]; our resources are limited as well as our capacity . . . Sometimes we need them for certain things, but sometimes it's not effective . . . If I have a conversation in front of Dunkin' Doughnuts in [a local] square with a resident who has an issue, his feedback in that 10-minute conversation on the street to me is a lot more valuable than me going to [the local city councilor]. For example, when we are doing climate change adaptation, if I know that resident can't get out of his house in the third-floor apartment and he is in a flood zone, then I know that's what I have to address, as opposed to [the councilor] saying "yeah, this is what the city can do". To me, [the resident's] information is much more important to see how we are going to move forward with a lot of things in the community.

Institutional and business alliances like the Medical Academic and Scientific Community Organization (MASCO 2011) in Boston's hospital and university-rich Longwood area are a very different type of neighborhood organization, but are impactful for many of the same reasons – in particular, their integral service delivery and interface between their members and government. MASCO has its own planning staff that works with government agencies, providing additional capacity and advancing members' interests on transportation, infrastructure, open space, development and construction issues. Vis-à-vis climate risks, MASCO manages a Joint Operations Center to coordinate communications and resources during emergencies, and closely coordinates with the Boston Water and Sewer Commission, the state Department of Conservation and Recreation, and other agencies around flooding and other issues. For example, MASCO has access to stormwater gauge and other information so that they can proactively warn their members of potential flooding conditions. MASCO reciprocates by providing data on what floods in practice to inform infrastructure improvements over time.

What is notable is that these organizations are seen as legitimate actors, engaging in governance either with or in lieu of the state. They gain this legitimacy and access by providing services that the government agencies they work with are unable to; serving as conduits between their constituents and government agencies, and as neutrals among agencies; providing legitimacy in both directions (i.e., of government initiatives to their constituents and of constituent interests to the government); and by allying with agencies with shared interests.

The neo-pluralist model suggests that, these organizations are often initiated and maintained by 'political entrepreneurs' with strong personalities and agendas; nurtured by 'patrons', which include foundations and governments; are products of social movements that evolve to become institutionalized; exist as actors within 'issue networks'; and provide exclusive benefits to their members, encouraging membership (McFarland 2007). These characteristics largely hold true for the advocacy organizations discussed in this chapter. Despite the lack of power Boston Harbor Now (formerly TBHA) ostensibly has, past-president Vivien Li and the organization wield significant influence via their networks and political entrepreneurship. For example, Li had a seat on the influential Boston Conservation Commission, was a co-chair of the City of Boston's 2014 Climate Action Plan Steering Committee and chaired MassDevelopment's Brownfields Advisory Group. She was highly regarded and influential in the development community – sometimes as a friend and sometimes as a foe to developers – and was even named one of the 50 most influential women in Boston commercial real estate in 2014 (Bisnow 2014; Grillo 2012). The organization is dependent on key patrons, including the Barr Foundation; foundations often play a central role in funding the work of nonprofits in the United States. TBHA evolved out of environmental concerns, and in particular the health of the Boston Harbor in the 1970s, representing the institutionalization of a social movement (TBHA 2015). The organization has been successful to some extent because it is part of various 'issue networks' – in the area of climate change adaptation, it found itself in a productive alliance with the City, among other actors. It has marshaled external resources for research and thought leadership and extended the credibility of municipal efforts among those who might be skeptical of the City.

Box 5.1   A Better City: the prominence of non-governmental actors in governance

A Better City (ABC) was formed in 1989 as the Artery Business Council out of fear among the business community that the massive Central Artery/Tunnel project – often referred to as the 'big dig' – would massively disrupt their operations. The group evolved into an innovative partnership with similarities to the Traffic Management Company discussed in the Rotterdam chapter, although, and it is important to note, driven by the private sector rather than public sector. ABC became a critical conduit for information in both directions, a source for creative ideas on how the project could minimize disruptions to commerce and life in Boston and a coordinator between the various business and institutional actors in the city and the project team.

The organization was successful in ensuring that utility services were maintained, traffic was able to flow and so on, thanks in large part to well-placed and technically knowledgeable membership and a strong core staff. Politically, the group used its access and influence to prevent the Artery project from becoming a 'political football', successfully lobbying for various policies, funding and other government decisions that would facilitate smooth implementation. ABC was very successful vis-à-vis the big dig for a few reasons: the large and complex nature of the project; the significant resources the group had, both in terms of staff and members that had the ear of political leaders; the 'responsiveness and staying power' this staff and membership afforded, including strong technical expertise; their broad perspective and ability to tackle issues ranging from project planning to political lobbying; and tactical flexibility in employing different means to achieve their goals, working with various other actors (Luberoff 2004a, 2004b).

Post big dig, the group changed its name and became an organization with a wider mission (ABC 2017): "A Better City is a diverse group of business leaders united around a common goal – to enhance Boston and the region's economic health, competitiveness, vibrancy, sustainability and quality of life." Its 130 members 'across multiple sectors' pay high dues to fund a professional staff and ensure that the organization is well resourced (ABC 2017; Luberoff 2004a). The organization advocates for and provides technical expertise on various issues, including the public transit system. For example, it has long championed the proposed Urban Ring bus rapid transit line, lobbying for it and providing technical reports that support the case. In fact, ABC co-chaired the MBTA's

Urban Ring Working Committee. Politically, the organization played a leadership role in the ultimately unsuccessful effort to defeat a state ballot initiative in the 2014 election that eliminated automatic annual increases in the gas tax. Opposing what is de facto a tax cut may seem counterintuitive for a business organization, but ABC argued that the tax revenue is important for the greatly needed investments in the transportation system.

ABC is so highly regarded that it is asked to facilitate among agencies. The South Boston Waterfront Sustainable Transport Plan is an example of this (ABC 2015). The complex planning process was a partnership among the Massachusetts Convention Center Authority, Massport, the City of Boston and the Massachusetts Department of Transportation and engaged various other stakeholders. According to an interviewee, "The South Boston Waterfront Transportation Planning Process is a great example [of multi-stakeholder collaboration], because it's four agencies working together, with a neutral party [i.e., ABC] kind of managing it". When asked why ABC is coordinating, the interviewee responded: "The fact that they are a non-governmental, [and President and CEO] Rick Dimino is a former Commissioner of the [Boston] Transportation Department, he's been in that advocacy role for 15–20 years though, so he is neutral enough, and he has good relationships with all the key players; it's an advocacy group that advocates for the city, and urban health and projects [that all can support]."

As discussed further later in this chapter, ABC is also engaging in various climate adaptation initiatives; among other activities, Dimino served on the Mayor's Climate Action Leadership Committee. Furthermore, ABC's role in coordinating and representing constituency interests in the face of an unprecedented infrastructure project like the big dig may be illustrative of the roles this kind of organization can play as cities and regions begin to address unprecedented climate risks.

ABC exhibits neo-pluralist characteristics as an advocacy organization. Like Vivien Li and TBHA, ABC it is led by a highly regarded and politically savvy 'political entrepreneur' that came out of public service and remains integrated into various political institutions. Underscoring the importance of networks among advocacy organizations, Dimino was actually vice-chair of the TBHA board. While not a social movement in the strictest sense, ABC's emergence out of concern among the business community that the Central Artery project would be excessively disruptive suggests how organizations like this manifest as the institutionalization of shared concerns among previously unorganized groups. ABC is successful in part because it allies itself with other groups, including key city and state agencies. ABC's membership comes from the corporate and institutional sectors; it is not clear what 'exclusive benefits' they get, except for the opportunity to interact within a network of firms concerned about similar issues.

Stakeholder interactions and decision-making

Given the fragmented nature of governance in the Boston context, it is not surprising that participants opined that engagement with other stakeholders is an important element of decision-making. The average response to the question of 'how important is it that you engage with other decision-makers and stakeholders as you plan and make decisions?' was 6 before and 6.5 after the exercise on a 7-point Likert scale from not at all (1) to very (7). The statistically significant increase from pre- to post-exercise suggests that participation increased the already high value participants place on multi-stakeholder deliberations.[6]

In contrast to Singapore, participants emphasized engagement *both* across agency lines and with external stakeholders. As discussed in the previous section, non-governmental organizations play key roles in governance in the Boston context. In addition to providing resources, external stakeholders can actually bestow legitimacy on processes.

However, many were quick to note that engagement is often imperfect. One participant reflected that even within government,

> as agencies, we all operate in our silos, whether at the same level of government or different; we do our own thing and in order to break out of that and understand and appreciate what the other agencies are doing I think you have to meet somehow, and these working groups are a good forum for that.

Vis-à-vis external stakeholders, participants noted that community forums and other forms of engagement are quite standard, but that they often happen too late to have profound implications on planning and decision-making.

Structured forms of multi-stakeholder decision-making are quite common in Boston; 79% reported prior experience with 'facilitated multi-stakeholder decision-making processes'. In contrast, 57% of participants in Rotterdam and only 41% in Singapore reported they have. Those who have participated in this kind of process in the past rated their experiences very highly, with an average of 5.6 on a 7-point Likert scale. This is a notably higher average than in Singapore (4.7) or Rotterdam (4.6). Some reported that the processes they have participated in were more or less similar to that they experienced in the RPS exercise, while to others, this was something new. A participant with extensive experience in community planning reflected afterwards,

> What you staged for us felt foreign to me in a very pleasant way because we were such a disparate group and the points of view were quite different, and I know that was part of the exercise, but it was refreshing because I haven't had that experience professionally. . . . I've been through many a charrette, tabletop meetings, community presentations, forums for constituents, and it didn't have the feeling you created for us with the various players at the table, so my takeaway personally, I came away thinking wouldn't it be nice if some of our projects really did have this type of [interactions with a mix of different people].

In terms of how frequently they interact with others, participants from inside government reported very regular interactions with counterparts from other agencies – at least daily, on average. They reported less frequent interactions with stakeholders outside government, but still at least monthly, on average. According to respondents, the formality of these interactions is a mix of formal and informal, which is similar to what was reported in Rotterdam and Singapore. Fourteen characterized their interactions as 'mostly formal meetings, but some informal', twelve as 'mostly informal interactions, but some formal' and only one each as 'only formal' and 'only informal'.

Shifting administrations, shifting priorities

Another characteristic of governance in the United States is the instability from administration to administration. Each election offers the opportunity (or threat) to completely change – and sometimes reverse – the priorities of government, and replace not only the political class but also the senior bureaucrats. This may reflect healthy democratic institutions, but it is disruptive to the implementation of long-term policy agendas.

> A lot of [what shapes the currency of issues] is varying shades of politics – whether it is the governor's priority, whether there are concerns with equity with each town or city or region getting their fair share, what 'fair share' is, that sort of thing,

said an interviewee. In contrast, the People's Action Party's more than 55 years of single-party rule in Singapore has provided stability in government policy, making about-faces and major bureaucratic changes rare. Healthy democratic institutions in the Netherlands have witnessed changes in administration, but there is typically more consistency from one to the next in both bureaucratic personnel and policies, especially around issues like infrastructural investments.

At all levels in the United States, administrative changes can precipitate shifts in the degree to which issues like climate change are given attention and how they are approached. In Boston, former Mayor Thomas Menino, who had championed the city's climate efforts, retired in 2013 after 20 years in office. Interviewees noted that his long tenure – and the strong networks and political capital that afforded him – allowed him to champion longer-term issues like climate change. In the words of one,

> If you are not somebody like Mayor Menino, God rest his soul, that was able to establish himself for a long time and have a bit of an iron fist with [longer-term] stuff that he knew needed to get done or wanted to get done, it's really difficult to get it done without paying and he even had to pay many times over the years after making certain decisions.

Menino's successor, Marty Walsh, appears to concur that the issue is important. However, there have been changes, including in senior staffing. Similarly at the state level, a new governor, Charlie Baker, assumed office in January of 2015, shifting the state from a Democratic to a Republican administration. Baker appointed a new cabinet and has different priorities than previous governor, Deval Patrick, emphasizing, among other things, tighter fiscal management. While it is still early in his administration, newly elected President Donald Trump is certainly promising to radically upend the status quo, including reducing regulations and significantly cutting funding to agencies like the Environmental Protection Agency and National Oceanic and Atmospheric Administration, which play key roles on the issue of climate change.

Creativity

The very creative options that emerged from the four groups that participated in the A New Connection in Westerberg exercise in Boston – which included routes, technologies and changes to the port not introduced in the instructions – suggest that participants were thinking 'outside the box'. While the United States certainly does not hold a monopoly on creativity, this pattern is not altogether surprising in a country that prides itself on fostering innovative thinking. While there is no perfect way to measure and compare countries based on their level of creativity, one attempt to do so – based on the dimensions of 'technology, talent, and tolerance' – found that the U.S. ranked second behind only Australia (Florida, Mellander and King 2015).[7]

Climate vulnerabilities

Boston faces substantial flooding risks. It has been ranked the eighth most vulnerable coastal city in the world in terms of potential economic losses due to flooding, with estimated average annual losses of 237 million USD today and over 700 million by 2050, even with some adaptation (Hallegatte, Green, Nicholls and Corfee-Morlot 2013). Climate models suggest that the mean sea level in the Boston area could rise between one and two feet by 2050, and three and six feet by 2100 (Douglas et al. 2013). The region has already experienced a rise in sea level of approximately one foot since 1900, which is about 50% more than the global average; this is largely due to subsidence, but changes in ocean circulation may also be playing a role (Horton et al. 2014). Sea level rise is a relatively slow-moving phenomenon, but becomes a much more immediate problem when compounded with the surge from a tropical cyclone (i.e., hurricane), nor'easter or other storm event. While no single storm event can be linked to climate change, the frequency, intensity and duration of hurricanes in the North Atlantic has been increasing over the past 30 years, and the trend is projected to continue with rising sea surface temperatures and other climatic changes (Walsh et al. 2014). While rarely making landfall, hurricanes seem to be tracking further north and have greater intensity (Northeast Climate Impacts Assessment 2006). Flooding risks are particularly acute when sea level rise, storm surge and very high tides (i.e., 'king tides') culminate. The potential impacts are stark – what is a 100-year event today could become a 5-year storm by 2050 and the high-tide norm around 2100 (Douglas et al. 2013; Kirshen et al. 2008).[8] It is conceivable that within 50 years, a 100-year surge hitting at high tide after 2.5 feet of sea level rise could inundate 30% of the city (Douglas et al. 2013).

The *Climate Ready Boston: Municipal Vulnerability to Climate Change* report found acute flooding vulnerabilities among the city's infrastructure, including most of the schools (many of which are designated emergency shelters); many of the police and fire stations; 1,500 units of public housing, which are on properties deemed to be 'high-priority' vulnerable; and approximately 132 miles of road, which are vulnerable at mean higher high water (MHHW) plus five feet, and an additional 300 miles vulnerable at MHHW plus 7.5 feet (Spector and Bamberger 2013). Some of these assets already experience flooding, with others increasingly at risk as sea levels rise and temperatures increase.

Sea level rise and coastal storms are not the only water-related threat to the Boston area. The Northeast of the United States has seen increases in average annual precipitation in recent decades, and this trend is expected to continue (Northeast Climate Impacts Assessment 2006; Walsh et al. 2014). Furthermore, the region has experienced a disproportionally high increase in extreme precipitation relative to the rest of the United States over the past 50 years – there was a 71% increase in the volume of precipitation during 'very heavy events' from 1958 to 2012 – and this trend is also expected to continue (Walsh et al. 2014). The models suggest that increases in the frequency and intensity of precipitation events will be particularly concentrated in the spring and winter (Horton et al. 2014). With shifting conditions, the winter precipitation may fall as rain or snow; some winters may see little or no snow while others see heavy and prolonged bouts (Walsh et al. 2014). Experience with the record-breaking winter of 2015, in which 110 inches of snow overwhelmed communities, crippling the region's aging transportation infrastructure and costing the state's economy over one billion dollars, suggests that more intense winter precipitation could be highly problematic. Intense precipitation as rainfall in other seasons can overwhelm stormwater infrastructure, causing flooding that damages property and disrupts infrastructure systems (Douglas et al. 2013). Infrastructure in the Boston area was not constructed to handle the type of flashflood event that seems to be increasingly common. More frequent and intense precipitation can also swell rivers, leading to flooding (Walsh et al. 2014).

Average summer temperatures have been record breaking in recent years, and the trend is expected to continue and possibly intensify (Walsh et al. 2014). Heat waves may become an increasingly significant threat with climate change. In fact, the City of Cambridge's (2015) Climate Change Vulnerability Assessment suggests that the risks associated with extreme heat are more acute than those associated with flooding, at least in the short to medium term; the region may, on average, face up to three times as many days above 90°F than it does currently in the 2030 timeframe, and by 2070 it could experience almost three months over 90°F, compared with less than two weeks on average now. Put differently, Massachusetts' heat index could be similar to that of present-day South Carolina in the 2070–2099 timeframe, making a typical summer day feel 12–16°F warmer (Northeast Climate Impacts Assessment 2006). Heat waves threaten both public health and the stability of infrastructure systems. While many places in the United States and around the world experience much hotter temperatures and more intense heat waves than Boston can expect in the medium term, their built environments and cultural norms are tailored to those conditions (Horton et al. 2014). As experiences in recent years in both the U.S. Midwest and Northern Europe have shown, extreme temperatures in regions with typically moderate climates can result in catastrophic loss of life and disruption to society.

Climate change is also shifting the ranges of various species, including disease vectors like mosquitoes and ticks that carry West Nile virus, Eastern equine encephalitis and other public health threats (Douglas et al. 2013).

The impacts of climate change are not felt evenly across the population. While expensive oceanfront property is often vulnerable, so are marginalized populations living in flood-prone areas; poorer-quality housing; situations with greater exposure to ground-level ozone and other pollutants; without air conditioning; and with less access to resources and alternatives (Horton et al. 2014). There are clear relationships between various socioeconomic variables – including race and ethnicity, age, gender, economic status and educational attainment – and vulnerability (Horton et al. 2014). The working class and largely immigrant neighborhood of East Boston is among the most vulnerable in the city (Douglas et al. 2013). Community organizations and academics from local universities are working with marginalized communities, including in East Boston, to increase understanding and enhance their adaptive capacity, but they often have the least access to resources, alternatives and information (Douglas et al. 2012; Lynds 2015).

Infrastructure planning, decision-making, and adaptation to climate change

The Commonwealth of Massachusetts, City of Boston (and other municipalities in the metro region) and other actors are increasingly aware of the threats climate change poses and are examining how they might increase their resilience, but relatively few concrete adaptive measures have been implemented thus far (Horton et al. 2014). While Hurricane Sandy was a wakeup call, bringing substantial attention to the issue, it has not translated, thus far at least, into significant investments or major policy changes in the Boston area. In the words of an interviewee,

> With Hurricane Sandy we were lucky, [having] missed it by five hours. [If it had hit us], we wouldn't be having this conversation, we'd be having another. But, how long has it been since Hurricane Sandy, [and] how much has Boston really prepared?

The risks were well documented before Sandy and yet the storm caught many off-guard, suggesting that the lack of action is not simply the result of insufficient awareness among decision-makers and other stakeholders (Horton et al. 2014). Nonetheless, the high degree of attention being given to examining the risks posed by climate change and nascent groundwork should not be underappreciated. Interviewees were quick to point out that it takes time, but efforts are advancing. All levels of government and many non-governmental actors are involved in various efforts to appraise the region's vulnerabilities and are starting to devise adaptive strategies. In fact, one characteristic of climate preparedness in the Boston area is that there are *so many* efforts underway. Lack of coordination and the incomplete institutionalization of these efforts may be challenges to their ability to affect change, but they represent conscious efforts to prepare for climate change. Another characteristic of the climate adaptation efforts in the greater Boston area is the outsized role played by nonprofit organizations.

This section provides a nonexhaustive overview of various efforts underway at the federal, state and local levels. Given that adaptation will typically need to integrate into wider systems of infrastructure planning and decision-making, it also provides a brief introduction to the institutional arrangements in the Boston area. Insights from the Harboring Uncertainty project are integrated throughout.

Participants were asked a series of questions to better understand their views on climate change vis-à-vis infrastructure planning and decision-making. Interestingly, participants reported the highest level of awareness of 'climate change and the risks it may pose' in Boston, compared to Singapore and Rotterdam. The average response pre-exercise was 6 on a 7-point Likert scale from 'not at all' at 1 to 'very' at 7. In comparison, the average was 5 in Rotterdam and 4.3 in Singapore. Unsurprisingly, the highest rankings (i.e., 7s) were from those directly working on climate and/or sustainability issues. The lowest rankings – two 4s – were from participants that work in transportation agencies (one state, one federal). The higher average responses hold when actors are compared with counterparts in similar positions and organizations in both Singapore and Rotterdam (see Figure 5.1).

In general, participants expect climate change to be a fairly significant factor in their organizations' planning and decision-making over the next 10 years, with an average ranking of 5.7 (pre-exercise) on a 7-point Likert scale. In comparison, the averages in Rotterdam and Singapore were 4.9 and 4 respectively. There was notable variation across participants, with those working on water and/or coastal issues giving the highest responses and those working on land transportation issues lower. The average response was very similar (5.6) to the question of the degree

Position	Rotterdam	Singapore	Boston
Transportation agencies	2, 3, 3, 5, 6, 7 (4.3 avg.)	3, 5, 5, N/A (4.3 avg.)	4, 4, 5, 6, 7, 7, N/A (5.5 avg.)
Engineering consulting	3, 5, 5, 6, 6 (5 avg.)	N/A	5, 5, 5, 6, 6, 6, 7 (5.7 avg.)

Figure 5.1 Comparative awareness of climate risks by position. Self-assessments of participants on a 7-point Likert scale from 'not at all aware' at 1 to 'very aware' at 7

Used with permission of author

to which climate change is already on their organizations' radars. Looking at individual responses, an interesting – albeit not surprising – pattern is that those working directly on climate issues gave much higher answers than did their colleagues in the same organizations that are not. This suggests a discrepancy in how far nascent climate resiliency initiatives are permeating into these organizations. Follow-up interviews largely confirmed this, with participants reflecting that climate resilience and other emergent issues are clearly rising in profile, but not yet fully integrated into planning and decision-making on the ground. "Institutionalizing a different approach is still a challenge", reflected a participant, adding that

> even with MassDOT, as progressive as they are and having all this healthy transportation and climate change goals . . . they are still working on how to change their project prioritization process to acknowledge all that other stuff, because really, they are still looking at capacity, safety, the condition of the pavement and the bridge ratings.

Participants in Boston were asked to assess and rank why climate change is not a higher priority in infrastructure planning and decision-making. As Figure 5.2 illustrates, the top three reasons are resource constraints, competing priorities and undefined responsibility.

Resource constraints were a recurring theme during the workshop and throughout the interviews. It is clear that many see already inadequate funding for infrastructure as a particularly acute problem when resiliency efforts are asking agencies

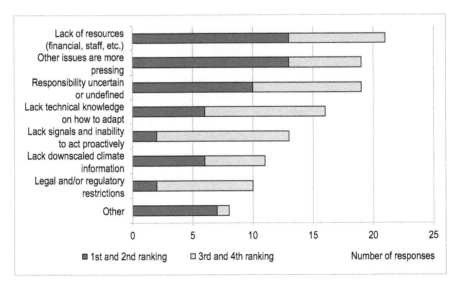

Figure 5.2 Reasons why climate change is not a higher priority
Used with permission of author

to do more. "Resource constraints are a bigger issue than climate change uncertainty", opined a participant, going on to ask, "How do you add all of these elements to a project that you can't afford to begin with?" The same participant added that, unfortunately, enhanced climate resiliency is often deemed 'not worth it' when resources are tight and value engineering begins.

Resource scarcity directly exacerbates competition among priorities. Participants reflected that the competing priority is often getting badly needed infrastructure projects done without further complication and delay. "A lot of bridge projects are accelerated almost to the case of being an emergency, so I don't know that [future climate vulnerability is] ever anybody's first question", said a participant. Resource constrains are, however, not the only factor behind competing priorities. Interviewees discussed the very real tradeoffs that manifest between enhancing climate resilience and community impacts, not dissimilar to the tradeoff between the below-grade and elevated road options in the exercise. Two different interviewees working on road projects in vulnerable coastal environments reflected that perhaps they could do more to elevate or protect infrastructure, but that would change its relationship to the surrounding environment.

Undefined responsibility is all the more problematic in a fragmented institutional environment like that found in the Boston area; there are so many agencies with overlapping jurisdiction that it is often not clear who should take the lead on an emerging issue like climate adaptation. Ultimately, participants reflected that there is not one single barrier, but rather many confounding factors limiting the further integration of climate resiliency into planning and decision-making. Interestingly, lack of downscaled climate information ranked quite low as a barrier. This is notable because insufficient information is often assumed to be a critical barrier. The eight 'other' barriers participants noted were "lack of concern and misinformation"; "cost/benefit issues for clients"; "political priorities"; "not a priority with public or elected government"; "conflicting priorities"; "how to revamp [old infrastructure]"; "denial"; and "standard of care in engineering field creates disincentive to create new technical approaches or document uncertainties – to do so creates professional liability". Many of these underscore resource scarcity, the lack of prioritization and challenges to institutionalization.

In terms of how *confident* participants are that they and their organizations will be able to manage the risks and uncertainties climate change poses, participants entered the workshop with a middling average ranking of 4.4 on a 7-point Likert scale. This is slightly higher than the averages in Singapore (3.8) and Rotterdam (3.7), but still low. It is notable that the average was lower among the six individuals working for transportation agencies that answered this question, at 3.5.[9] In contrast, the average was 5 among those actively working on climate adaptation projects, suggesting that they have confidence in their work to help prepare for a changing climate. The aforementioned barriers to integration explain much of the skepticism. Another reason is widespread belief that extensive climate adaptation activities will only be implemented in response to climate-related events. However, relatively slow progress in integrating adaptation into project-level planning and decision-making after supposed wakeup calls like Hurricanes Katrina and Sandy suggests that even responding reactively can be a challenge.

Participants were generally skeptical of the ability of agencies to conduct the kind of wide, comprehensive and integrated planning that may be necessary to holistically address an issue like climate change. In the words of one,

> Comparing to Singapore or even the Netherlands, [their] ability to have a land-use planning and transportation conversation with the decision-makers, and . . . to actually come up with an action plan is a lot more nimble than it is here with all of the multiple veto points, and the fact that we really don't do much land-use planning to begin with.

This same participant used the failure to implement true high-speed rail in the United States as an example of the relative inability of government to advance complex projects, especially when they involve controversial actions.

In contrast to Singapore and Rotterdam, there was not a statistically significant increase in participants' average confidence from pre- (4.4) to post-exercise (4.5). However, participants were also asked to self-report on whether the exercise changed their level of confidence. Twelve of 29 reported no change, two reported feeling less confident and the remaining fifteen reported increased confidence. This suggests that the exercise experience did make many participants feel more confident.

Participants in Boston were also asked how confident they are that *other* stakeholders will be able to manage the risks and uncertainties climate change poses to our infrastructure systems. Interestingly, the average response here was notably lower than when participants were asked about themselves and their own organizations – 3.6 versus 4.4 on a 7-point Likert scale. This would suggest that participants have more confidence in their own organizations than they have in others.

Adaptation planning

As discussed previously, a major feature of governance in Boston, and the wider United States, is fragmentation across levels of government and various agencies. Given this complexity, a fully comprehensive overview of all the various adaptation activities underway and pieces of the puzzle in how infrastructure is managed is beyond the scope of this chapter. Some elements are highlighted, while others are admittedly disregarded.

Boston was an early mover on the climate change issue. The city joined ICLEI-Local Governments for Sustainability's Cities for Climate Protection Campaign in 2000 and has been a leader in passing energy efficiency and green building ordinances. The earliest efforts focused exclusively on climate mitigation, but by the middle of the last decade it was becoming evident that at least some degree of climate change is inevitable, and substantial change likely, necessitating adaptive measures. In 2007, then Mayor Thomas Menino released an executive order on climate action that directed city departments to integrate climate change into their planning, projects and review processes (Spector and Bamberger 2013). Follow-up activities included departmental reviews of the potential risks to infrastructure and programs, a new climate preparedness questionnaire for all large projects under review by the Redevelopment Authority, the explicit consideration of flooding and heat island impacts in open space and infrastructure planning, and the gradual integration of adaptation into the city's climate action efforts. Hurricane Sandy, which largely spared Boston but wreaked havoc in New York and New Jersey in the fall of 2012, brought much greater attention to the issue. Shortly thereafter, the mayor created a Climate Preparedness Task Force involving the heads of various relevant agencies. The results of this process were released via the 2013 'Climate Ready Boston: Municipal Vulnerability to Climate Change' report, which emphasized integrating climate preparedness with capital planning; updating emergency management plans; coordinating closely with regional, state and national partners; and better engaging and educating communities (Spector and Bamberger 2013). The report mapped the acute vulnerability of much of the city's facilities and infrastructure, including its transportation network and critical emergency services.

The Climate Ready Boston report informed an evolving *Climate Ready Boston* action plan, under the Greenovate banner. The latest (2016) Climate Ready Boston report updates the risk assessment for the city, paying particular attention to eight neighborhoods with pronounced vulnerabilities, and proposes 11 strategies:

1 Maintain up-to-date projections of future climate conditions to inform adaptation.
2 Expand education and engagement of Bostonians on climate hazards and action.
3 Leverage climate adaptation as a tool for economic development.
4 Develop local climate resilience plans to coordinate adaptation efforts.
5 Create a coastal protection system to address flood risk.
6 Coordinate investments to adapt infrastructure to future climate conditions.
7 Develop district-level energy solutions to increase decentralization and redundancy.
8 Expand the use of green infrastructure and other natural systems to manage stormwater, mitigate heat, and provide additional benefits.
9 Update zoning and building regulations to support climate readiness.
10 Retrofit existing buildings against climate hazards.
11 Insure buildings against flood damage.

These strategies fall under four 'layers' – *prepared and connected communities, protected shores, resilient infrastructure* and *adapted buildings* (Greenovate Boston 2016). Some of these strategies resemble those found in Rotterdam's plan, which is not surprising given that they belong to the same networks – including 100 Resilient Cities – and have engaged in extensive knowledge exchange. Others respond to

Boston's specific context; the sixth is particularly important given the complex, fragmented institutional environment. It is noteworthy that, while led by the City of Boston, the Climate Ready initiative involves a range of actors from the public and private sectors; the steering committee includes members from the City, the state Office of Coastal Zone Management, and the Green Ribbon Commission. The latter is an arms-length "group of business, institutional, and civic leaders in Boston working to develop shared strategies for fighting climate change in coordination with the City's Climate Action Plan" (Boston Green Ribbon Commission 2017). Its funding largely comes from foundations and corporate partners. This type of arrangement is relatively unique. According to the *Boston Globe*,

> It's rare to get CEO engagement in this kind of enterprise, which Boston's commission has. Plus, the private sector has more financial resources than the city. Close collaboration between city and commerce has already contributed to slowing emissions and could help Boston take measures to prepare for the impact of climate change.
>
> (Fitzgerald 2014)

While the City of Boston is a key player, it is only one of over 100 municipalities in a metropolitan region with 4.5 million residents (MAPC 2017; U.S. Census Bureau 2014). Many of the communities in the region have minimal or no climate change initiatives. Cambridge is a notable exception, with a series of initiatives, including their own Climate Change Vulnerability Assessments (City of Cambridge 2015, 2017). Cambridge, like Boston, recognizes that the jurisdictionally fragmented planning environment is a substantial challenge. Its most significant sea level rise and storm surge threat is via flanking of the Amelia Earhart dam, which is not even in the city but rather neighboring Somerville and is operated by the Department of Conservation and Recreation (a state agency), with regulatory oversight from the Army Corps of Engineers (a federal agency) and others (City of Cambridge 2017).

The Metropolitan Area Planning Council (MAPC 2017) – which brings together representatives of all municipalities along with state appointees – plays a regional coordination role in various areas, including land-use planning and transportation. The MAPC established a goal for the region of being "prepared for and resilient to natural disasters and climate change" in their MetroFuture Regional Plan (MAPC 2008, 22). In pursuit of this goal, the organization developed a Metro Boston Regional Climate Change Adaptation Strategy Report, which assesses the vulnerabilities and outlines a strategy in various thematic areas, including 'protecting critical infrastructure' and 'protecting the coastal zone' by, among other things, investing in shoreline restoration projects and evaluating coastal retreat and associated land acquisition measures (MAPC 2015). Unsurprisingly for a regional coordinating council, two of the 'guiding principles' for this MAPC effort are facilitating 'effective regional partnerships' between municipalities, state government and the private sector, and 'strengthened communication across institutions and communities'. Interviewees reflected that the MAPC could play an important role in cording across municipal boundaries and enhancing best practices, particularly among smaller member communities, but the organization is very limited in its authority. It does not have the jurisdiction, or the influence, to impose a comprehensive and integrated approach to climate vulnerability on the region.

A significant proportion of the infrastructure in the metro Boston area – including the public transportation system, the arterial road network, much of the coastal defenses and the freshwater and wastewater treatment systems – is managed by state agencies. Agencies are at various stages in their climate adaptation work, although few are making concrete efforts to enhance resiliency thus far. The Global Warming Solutions Act, which was passed by the Massachusetts Legislature and signed by former Governor Deval Patrick in 2008, focused largely on greenhouse gas emissions reductions, but Section 9 is explicitly adaptation focused. It mandated the creation of an adaptation advisory committee, with representation and expertise from transportation, water, energy and other infrastructure systems; manufacturing; low-income communities; land conservation, coastal management and ecosystems; and local government (Commonwealth of Massachusetts 2008).

In response, the Secretary of Energy and Environmental Affairs convened an Advisory Committee. Much of the work was done through thematic subcommittees, including one focused on 'Key Infrastructure', which was co-chaired by representatives of the Departments of Environmental Protection and Transportation and included members from other agencies, academia, NGOs, utilities and engineering consulting (EEA 2011). This process culminated in the release of the Massachusetts Climate Change Adaptation Report in 2011. The report outlines the threats the Commonwealth faces and introduces both cross-sectoral and sector-specific strategies for adapting to them. For Key Infrastructure, the report makes some general recommendations, like "Explore Possible Changes in Land Use, Design, Site Selection, and Building Standards" and "Identify Lead Times for Adaptive Construction" (EEA 2011, 55). In the area of transportation infrastructure, the report enumerates various potential strategies, ranging from 'no regrets strategies', like "maintain existing transportation infrastructure to minimize the chances of flooding or other damage that might occur before final or more permanent adaptation plans can be implemented", to 'long-term strategies', like "enhance water-based transit options in affected coastal and riverine areas as a long-range transport alternative and as an interim back-up to damaged infrastructure" (EEA 2011, 58–59).

The report was intended as an initial step in the Commonwealth's efforts; it guided agencies and other stakeholders as they started to engage in, or enhance existing, vulnerability analysis and planning for short-, medium- and long-term adaptive responses. Agencies have engaged in adaptation efforts to varying degrees, although few have moved beyond examining the risks and some have not even done that yet. According to an interviewee, the ultimate "goal is not to have one person in each organization that is 'the climate person', but rather to have everyone informed and the issue infused throughout organizations". This is an aspiration yet to be realized. It is notable that the Executive Office of Energy and Environmental Affairs, which plays a key coordinating role, had a dedicated Policy Advisor for Climate Change Adaptation, but she moved on after the change in administrations in 2015, and it is not clear how much of a priority adaptation is in the current (Baker) administration.

The federal government in the United States plays important roles in the management of various infrastructure systems. It directly owns and operates very little infrastructure in the Boston area, yet is quite influential through both regulatory and financial channels. It has also supported, at least historically, the development and dissemination of best practices in newly emerging areas like climate resilience. The Obama Administration advanced action on climate change in various respects, including via Executive Order 13653, which mandated: "Modernizing Federal Programs to Support Climate Resilient Investment"; "Managing Lands and Waters for Climate Preparedness and Resilience"; the creation of an interagency Council on Climate Preparedness and Resilience; and the creation of a State, Local, and Tribal Leaders Task Force on Climate Preparedness and Resilience (The White House 2013). This task force provided a set of recommendations to the president in November of 2014, emphasizing the key roles the federal government must play in adapting to climate change, particularly vis-à-vis local, state and tribal agencies. The first recommendation was *Building Resilient Communities* (State, Local, and Tribal Leaders Task Force on Climate Preparedness and Resilience 2014). The president's Climate Action Plan, which was released in 2013, also put adaptation front and center (Executive Office of the President 2013). The administration also established itself as an important clearinghouse for climate data with the http://climate.data.gov and http://toolkit.climate.gov portals, which contain a wealth of data from various agencies. The U.S. Global Change Research Program, which is chartered under the Federal Advisory Committee Act, brings together various key experts from both inside and outside government to generate comprehensive National Climate Assessments. The adaptation chapter of the latest assessment largely focuses on enumerating the risks, but does include a small section on potential 'response strategies', ascribing various tasks to federal agencies, like "ensuring the establishment of federal policies that allow for 'flexible' adaptation efforts and take steps to avoid unintended consequences" (Bierbaum et al. 2014, 675). However, all of these initiatives are now vulnerable to elimination with the Republican Party controlling the White House (executive branch) and both houses of Congress; many Republicans are skeptical of climate change and concerned about 'overregulation', and President Donald Trump has vowed to significantly cut the budgets of most agencies working on climate issues.

Land transportation infrastructure

At least nine different agencies and other stakeholder groups are directly involved in land transportation infrastructure planning, decision-making, operation and maintenance in Boston. Table 5.1 enumerates these actors and the key roles they play; it reflects the main players, but is not fully comprehensive or reflective of

Table 5.1 Key actors involved in land transportation in Boston

Agency/stakeholder group	Roles
U.S. Department of Transportation; especially the Federal Highway Administration (FHWA) and Federal Transit Administration (FTA)	• Finance infrastructure projects • Technical support (including through research centers like the Volpe Center) • Statutory oversight
Massachusetts Department of Transportation (MassDOT); especially the Highway and Mass Transit Divisions	• State-level road infrastructure, including all interstate highways • Regulatory oversight of other transportation infrastructure
Massachusetts Bay Transportation Authority (MBTA)	• Public transportation system operator in the greater Boston area. Operates most services directly, but some privately contracted (including commuter rail) • Under but operated at arms-length to MassDOT
Massachusetts Department of Conservation and Recreation (DCR)	• Operate and maintain various parkways (e.g., Storrow Drive)
Boston Region Metropolitan Planning Organization (MPO)	• Regional transportation planning and coordination (see below) • Establish priorities for state and federal transportation funds
Boston Transportation Department (City of Boston)	• Planning and oversight of non-state-controlled road infrastructure in Boston • Emphasis on 'complete streets' (i.e., pedestrian and cyclist amenities)
Public Works Department (City of Boston)	• Responsible for construction and maintenance of city roads • Oversight of private contractors
Private construction, maintenance and/or operating contractors	Various contractors in different sectors, including: • Over 100 different private contractors do construction, repaving and other road-related work for the city • Numerous construction and maintenance contracts awarded by state agencies (roads and transit) • Contracted system operators like Keolis (MBTA commuter rail lines)
Private transportation operators (e.g., MASCO, Bridj, taxi fleets)	• Institutional/business alliances like the Medical Academic and Scientific Community Organization in Longwood run private shuttle networks, as do large institutions like MIT and Harvard • Private, for-profit shuttle taxi and shuttle services
Stakeholder interest groups (e.g., A Better City; Livable Streets Alliance)	• Lobby government agencies for transportation investments and preferred design options • Provide supporting research and thought leadership • Coordinate constituencies
Neighboring municipalities (e.g., Brookline, Revere)	• Neighboring municipalities run interconnected urban road networks

Used with permission of author

the complexities involved. Planning and decision-making inherently involves various other agencies and stakeholder groups. For example, the City's Complete Streets initiative involves coordination between the Transportation Department, the Public Works Department (which owns and maintains the infrastructure), the Boston Water and Sewer Commission (which is responsible for the drainage infrastructure), the Planning & Development Agency, and other actors (Boston Transportation Department 2014). Table 5.1 also excludes the political actors involved in the decision-making process. Political leaders at the local, state and federal levels play important roles both directly, by approving projects, allocating funds for them and so on, and indirectly, based on the leadership and broad directives they give the bureaucracy. Table 5.1 does not reflect the full breadth of regulatory oversight either. For example, many projects will be subject to the Massachusetts Environmental Protection Act and/or National Environmental Policy Act, meaning they must go through environmental impact assessment processes under the purview of other agencies.

Funding comes through various mechanisms. Unlike in Singapore, transportation-related fees and taxes do not cover expenditures, with substantial proportions made up from general government revenues. For example, while Singapore's public transportation system is self-supporting from an operations perspective, fares constitute only 31% of the MBTA's revenue, with the largest proportion coming from state sales taxes (42%) (Garvin, Cloutier and Butler 2015). On the road side, tolls are collected on some state highways, but they contribute only $357 million in revenues, which would cover only 23% of the highway proportion of the MassDOT budget (MassDOT 2014). In total, tolls, gas taxes and other user fees cover approximately 59% of state and local road spending (Henchman 2014). In contrast, revenues from tolls, registration fees and other direct user fees exceed road infrastructure expenditures in Singapore (May 2004). The federal government provides approximately 32% of funds for capital outlays in Massachusetts, with the remainder coming from state and local revenues (National Economic Council and the President's Council of Economic Advisers 2014). The federal government also lends money at very low interest through programs like the Transportation Infrastructure Finance and Innovation Act.

State and local governments are dependent on federal transportation dollars, leaving them vulnerable to politically charged congressional approval. Instability also exists at the state and local levels, as new administrations often establish different priorities than their predecessors and change their priorities over time. In the words of an interviewee,

> We can't even function sustainably! We are year to year to year. You program for so much each year, and that's all you get, and then your governor or your leader changes and you reset, so there is no long term thought about sustainability.

Given the plethora of actors involved, some level of coordination around transportation infrastructure planning and decision-making is essential. The Boston Region Metropolitan Planning Organization (MPO) plays an important role here. MPOs are federally mandated organizations that bring together key stake-holders to make coordinated transportation planning decisions to allocate scarce federal and state funds – it is typified as 'continuing, comprehensive and coordinated' (3-C) transportation planning (Solof 1998). Parties from different levels of government and other stakeholder groups are expected to develop shared visions for their regions and reach consensus around which investments will best advance their shared goals. The Boston MPO's region encompasses 101 cities and towns in eastern Massachusetts, with a population of approximately three million people (MPO 2015a). Federal Highway Administration and Federal Transit Administration representatives sit as nonvoting members. The MPO's primary responsibility is three separate but related planning processes: A 'Long-Range Transportation Plan', which sets the broad vision for the region for at least 20 years; the 'Transportation Improvement Program', which is the list of prioritized projects for the next four years; and the 'Unified Planning Work Program', which is a database of transportation infrastructure projects underway in a given year.

The MPO attempts to be holistic in its analysis, considering regional trends, and plans for land-use planning, development and employment. In many ways, it is a logical channel through which climate adaptation may be integrated into transportation infrastructure planning and decision-making. Interviewees reflected that MPOs could play important leadership roles on issues like this.

> Some MPOs really want to be regional planners and regional leaders, and when they see a topic that they can make a contribution on and be supported politically and publicly, that's all good stuff as long as it doesn't put a major strain on them; and if there is a really important new public need that has come along, like climate resilience wasn't something they would have thought of 5–10 years ago and now they are, it allows them to play a more significant role,

reflected one interviewee. Another asserted that MPOs can be more flexible than most government agencies, allowing them to agilely respond to emerging threats. The first interviewee noted that MPOs across the country vary widely in capacity, support and goals, and urged caution in 'overloading' these organizations with additional goals. MPO staff spoken with through this research emphasized both the relevancy and their nascent interest in considering climate resilience factors. However, they are not yet included in their evaluations. It is notable that mitigation and other environmental concerns are well accounted for in the 35 criteria applied to projects proposed for inclusion in the TIP (MPO 2015b). According to a staff person,

> we transportation planners for decades have been concerned with what comes out of tailpipes; mitigation is considered more naturally, it's about getting people out of their cars and so on, [whereas] this is relatively newer and different.

Another MPO staffer suggested that it might be a matter of it taking time to permeate through the institutional environment. Of course, there are barriers. "You need to recognize that this is a *very* financially constrained environment", reflected an interviewee.

The Massachusetts Department of Transportation (MassDOT) directly or indirectly oversees much of the transportation infrastructure in the state, including roads and public transit. The impacts of climate change are on the agency's radar, although activity so far has largely been investigatory in nature. A Federal Highway Administration-funded pilot project titled 'Climate Change and Extreme Weather Vulnerability Assessments and Adaptation Options of the Central Artery' is particularly notable (Bosma et al. 2015). Billions were spent on this critical web of infrastructure relatively recently – the project was completed in 2007 – yet it appears to be vulnerable to flooding from coastal storm surge. The vulnerability assessment, which was conducted in partnership with experts from academia and a private consulting firm, involved the development of very sophisticated flooding models constructed using a range of scenarios and Monte Carlo methods to get probabilistic analyses of the risks in 2030, 2070 and 2100. It also generated a set of adaptation options. The key conclusions were (Bosma et al. 2015, viii):

- The interconnected and complex nature of urban environments requires interaction with multiple stakeholders at various steps in the assessment.
- The lack of redundancy and the critical nature of each structure make the CA/T system potentially extremely vulnerable.
- Results of the modeling and vulnerability assessment yielded almost immediate project and engineering design implications that may not have been realized without the high-resolution modeling and analysis.
- In complex systems like the CA/T, the number and spatial extent of vulnerable Structures increase over time as SLR rises and the intensity of some storms increase, suggesting that local adaptation options may be most applicable in the near-term and regionally based adaptations (safeguarding multiple Structures for multiple stakeholders) will become more cost-effective and necessary solutions in the long-term.

With the assessment done, the project team is now working with their counterparts in operations to discuss how they can move forward. According to an interviewee directly involved, it has become a discussion around risk tolerance, confounded by limited resources and competing priorities. MassDOT is also conducting wider vulnerability assessments, looking at other factors across the wider Commonwealth. Again, however, this is slow to translate into concrete action. In the words of an interviewee:

> I don't see anything happening yet, besides the vulnerability assessment. I think it's a struggle, because we are being asked by districts that are building projects along the water, "how are we supposed to build for resiliency?" [But]

as we heard in the [Harboring Uncertainty] workshop, there are no standards, and consultants say we are not putting our necks out to say what the standards are . . . [So the question is], is it MassDOT guidance? Are we going to update our design manuals, and when does that warrant the investment?

It is noteworthy that MassDOT is substantially further along on its climate *mitigation* work (i.e., reducing greenhouse gas initiatives). Efforts are championed and supported by an internal initiative called GreenDOT, that advances sustainability throughout the organization, supporting lobbying for and supporting integration into planning, design, construction and operations (MassDOT 2017b).

According to an interviewee, the team acts as a 'bridge' between internal units of MassDOT and external stakeholders, including environmental nonprofits and regulatory agencies. It is unclear what role GreenDOT will play in integrating climate resilience into the agency, but it is both an option moving forward and a model of how internal champions can facilitate the integration of new issues – like responding to climate change – into large government agencies that can be slow to change.

It is also notable that the complex modeling conducted for the Central Artery Assessment drew the interest of other key stakeholders, including the Cities of Boston and Cambridge and other state agencies. In fact, these municipalities and some other state and federal agencies officially joined the project, expanding the scope so that they could benefit from the results for their own analysis and planning. This reflects a desire both for information and for some degree of coordination. "The public can't be told the Charles will rise 2 feet if you live in Boston, and 3 feet if you live in Cambridge because both have ranges but decide to use different numbers", reflected an interviewee from a different agency, adding, "We don't want to look like bozos! We need a consensus range [so that] consultants and agencies are all playing with the same deck of cards". MassDOT is not the logical coordinator or clearinghouse for information on the impacts of SLR and storm surge, but de facto became so because they initiated this project that has wider implications than the highway assets they originally set out to examine.

In this complex environment, there are many other important actors. The Massachusetts Bay Transportation Authority (MBTA) is the subsidiary of MassDOT responsible for the public transit system in the greater Boston area; it is the fifth-largest mass transit system in the United States. The MBTA recognizes its acute vulnerabilities to climate change, is in the process of assessing the threats posed to its assets and is making climate change adaptation a criteria in capital investment planning. Unfortunately, the MBTA is an old system with almost $9 billion in debt and $7 billion in deferred maintenance (Gurley 2015). Outdated equipment and poor maintenance greatly exacerbated the challenges the MBTA faced during record snowfall in the winter of 2015; substantial portions of the system were crippled for days, riders were stranded during regular breakdowns and the CEO ultimately resigned amidst the uproar (Dungca 2015). As discussed earlier in this chapter, this kind of disruptive weather may become increasingly common with climate change. The Massachusetts Port Authority (Massport) is the separate agency responsible for operating Boston's main international airport, two smaller airports in the area and commercial port facilities throughout Boston Harbor. It is a public authority with a board appointed by the governor of Massachusetts, but is completely self-financing. Many of its facilities, including the airport, which is built on fill in the harbor, are vulnerable to climate risks. Massport has committed to an ambitious multi-million-dollar program to both mitigate greenhouse gas emissions and address the risks posed by climate change (Abel 2015). It has a Resiliency Program with a dedicated program manager and working group comprised of key individuals from across the organization (Massport 2015b). It is notable that Massport can operate much more nimbly, with relative autonomy and an independent and healthy budget. According to more than one interviewee, a challenge for Massport is the vulnerabilities in the systems they depend on, but that are beyond their control, including key highway and public transportation links.

The U.S. Department of Transportation directly manages virtually no infrastructure in the Boston area. However, it can be very influential in disseminating best practices; in supporting those best practices with grants, including both thematic grants, like those for adaptation pilot projects, and stipulations included in federal block grants; and via its regulatory oversight.

> The DOT can take the 'bully pulpit' when it gets behind an issue; for example, former Secretary LaHood focused on the distracted driving issue, which led to political pressure to take it seriously. . . . Leadership is really important to promoting the prominence of an issue, and thus the amount of attention given to it,

reflected an interviewee. The vulnerability assessment above is an example of the support the USDOT has been providing. Various reports and guidance documents have also been generated, many of which are available via their Transportation and Climate Change Clearinghouse (http://climate.dot.gov). The agency also released a Climate Adaptation Plan, which enumerates the threats climate change poses to the nation's transportation infrastructure, and introduces programs, policies and plans the agency is putting in place to address them (USDOT 2014). With a recent change in administration in Washington, however, priorities are unclear going forward; on the one hand, President Trump has called for substantial investments in infrastructure, while on the other he and other Republicans have downplayed climate change as an issue. Resiliency and climate adaptation are unlikely to be priorities.

Flood protection infrastructure

While somewhat less fragmented than the transportation sector, flood protection and coastal zone management responsibilities are also divided among various agencies at different levels of government. This section introduces some of these agencies and the challenges they face, paying particular attention to how they are integrating climate adaptation.

At the federal level, there are three key agencies engaged in flood protection: the U.S. Army Corps of Engineers (USACE), the Federal Emergency Management Agency (FEMA) and the National Oceanic and Atmospheric Administration (NOAA). The USACE is the branch of the Department of Defense responsible for many large public works projects, including substantial flood control and coastal defense infrastructure (USACE 2015a). USACE coastal defense infrastructure includes levees, dams, seawalls and beach nourishment. The USACE is engaged in various efforts to understand the potential impacts of climate change on coastal environments, including infrastructures, and how they might respond from engineering and planning perspectives (USACE 2015b). In general, the Corps is trained on reducing coastal flood risks by providing engineered solutions, or assisting others in doing so with their extensive expertise. The USACE has faced challenges and controversies, including the failure of their levees to protect the city of New Orleans during Hurricane Katrina in 2005, causing catastrophic damage and loss of life, which was attributed in large part to shortcomings in their planning, design, construction and management (Andresen et al. 2007). Partly in response to those infrastructure failures, the USACE has made 'building climate resilience' a priority (USACE 2015a). In response to Hurricane Sandy, the Corps released the 'North Atlantic Coast Comprehensive Study: Resilient Adaptation to Increasing Risk' (NACCS), which introduces a 'risk management framework' and directly accounts for climate change scenarios (USACE 2015b).

NOAA's Office for Coastal Management is focused on 'making communities more resilient', which involves providing explicit support as they adapt to climate change (OCM 2015). The Office is largely focused on providing data and other resources to state and local decision-makers, rather than direct coastal management. Programs like Digital Coast provide more detailed analysis so that stakeholders may make more informed decisions. In accordance with the Coastal Zone Management Act of 1972 and other regulations introduced since, the Coastal Zone Management Program works with state agencies in various areas, including coastal conservation, pollution control and marine spatial planning. One channel through which the OCM influences state and local agencies and other actors is grants, which typically match state or local funding.

FEMA is often associated with disaster response, both immediately following catastrophic events and with the recovery in the months and years following. For example, the Agency facilitated the distribution of over $10 billion for Hurricane Sandy recovery (FEMA 2015a). FEMA also plays important roles before disasters via its preparedness activities, which include mapping vulnerabilities and providing grants and technical assistance to help communities reduce them. FEMA's 'National Flood Insurance Program: Flood Hazard Mapping' is very influential, as it establishes flood insurance rates and requirements in coastal areas (FEMA 2015b). Changes to the maps, which may become more common and important with climate change, typically invoke substantial pushback due to the implications for property owners and municipalities. The Flood Insurance Program plays important roles in providing insurance to potentially vulnerable property owners, and sets standards around how communities must enhance their resilience in order for property owners to qualify, and for other forms of assistance.

At the state level in Massachusetts, three agencies have primary responsibility for flood protection: the Office of Coastal Zone Management (CZM), The Department of Environmental Protection (DEP), and the Department of Conservation and Recreation (DCR), which are all branches of the Executive Office of Energy and Environmental Affairs. The state exercises control over activities in coastal zones through Chapter 91, The Massachusetts Public Waterfront Act, which "seeks to preserve and protect the rights of the public, and to guarantee that private uses of tidelands and waterways serve a proper public purpose" (DEP 2015). Most activities that impact coastal zones require authorization under Chapter 91.

The CZM is responsible for supporting adherence to federal and state guidelines on coastal zone management, providing both technical support and assistance to help municipalities and other stakeholders meet those standards. The CZM receives substantial financial support from the federal government to carry out its mission. Climate change is a significant issue for the CZM Office; the extensive 'StormSmart Coasts' program is providing technical assistance and grants to municipalities and coastal landowners to help them enhance resilience in the face of climate change. The CZM also maintains a 'barrier beach inventory', along with guidelines for their management; and inventories of both public and private seawalls and other coastal structures (CZM 2015). The latter is informative in understanding Boston's coastal conditions, documenting that (DCR 2009; Fontenault, Vinhateiro and Knee 2013):

- 58% of the Boston Harbor coastline is protected, mostly by seawalls and revetments;
- approximately a third of this infrastructure is privately owned and two-thirds public, with municipalities owning 40% and the state 60%;
- the structural condition of over one third of this infrastructure has been graded 'C' or lower; and
- it would cost approximately $47 million to bring just the publicly owned infrastructure up to an 'A' grade, not including additional protection to address increasing climate risks.

One thing the CZM lacks is regulatory authority; there is little the agency can do to require municipalities and private landowners to make more resilient decisions. "We can't require anything that is stricter than the building code, so the building code says what level you have to be at with your first floor, and you can't require anything higher than that", noted an interviewee, adding that "you can [only] use incentives, and I think that's something that [is] a limitation". The interviewee noted that even with municipal harbor planning, the city does the plan, and CZM and EEA approve those plans for development along the water with requirements that they consider climate risks, but no concrete standards on what that means:

> It's a performance standard – it's not "you have to build at this level", it's "how is this public amenity, this public realm going to perform in the

future?" and nobody knows what the level is going to be exactly, so it's sort of using best guesses and what the proponent sees as how risk averse they want to be.

The DCR is responsible for the actual management and operations of much of the state-owned infrastructure, including many of the seawalls along the coast; approximately 1,500 dams directly, plus oversight of hundreds more; parks and public lands (DCR is the largest landowner in Massachusetts); approximately 500 lane miles of parkways and other roads; and water resource protection (DCR 2017). This includes the Charles River and Amelia Earhart dams, which are vital for flood control in the Boston area (Bourne Consulting Engineering 2009). According to DCR interviewees, the organization is starting to look at climate data in their projections and consider how climate change vulnerabilities might influence the ways in which they evaluate projects, prioritize and invest. A substantial hurdle is that the agency already faces $1 billion in deferred maintenance, so is challenged with making difficult choices. Another issue they grapple with is the question of which assets to armor and which to, in the words of an interviewee, "abandon to climate change" over time, especially given that this is not simply a technical question, but also a political one. DCR interviewees also noted that adaptation could compete with other priorities. For example, the DCR has been reconstructing the Nahant Causeway just north of Boston because of flooding problems and might have elevated it further, but came up against permitting limitations; in particular, environmental regulations limited the degree to which they could enlarge the causeway. "These tensions cannot be resolved using the traditional permitting guidelines because they are not complex, not comprehensive", reflected an interviewee.

As noted above, the City of Boston is a major owner of coastal infrastructure. Most of this is under the purview of the Boston Planning & Development Agency (formerly known as the Boston Redevelopment Authority). The agency is responsible for directing and regulating planning in and around the coastal zone and is directly involved in various waterfront projects. Climate risks are being considered in some instances, but whether the responses are satisfactory is debatable. One interviewee noted the South Station expansion and associated air rights project as an example in which the risks could be substantial, as the site is right on the water, and it is not clear that they were truly considered.

Non-governmental organizations play various roles in coastal planning. Boston Harbor Now (formerly TBHA) continues to play a major role in highlighting coastal vulnerabilities and facilitating conversations on how to increase resilience. The organization remains an important clearinghouse for information and has been a key partner in various initiatives, including the 2016 Climate Ready Boston report (Boston Harbor Now 2017).

In contrast to the Netherlands, in which most stakeholders have faith in the robust coastal flood defense network, American coastal defenses have been called into question, including by government agencies directly (see Andresen et al. 2007; USACE 2015b). Widespread distrust in their efficacy is, at least in part, a product of relatively recent failures, including with Hurricanes Katrina and Sandy. There is some debate around whether the solutions should be 'harder', like sea-walls with massive gates closing off Boston Harbor, similar to those in the Netherlands, or 'softer', like restoring wetlands and coastal retreat (Bennett 2010). Decision-making is complicated by budgetary, institutional and political constraints and competing interests, including concerns over the environmental consequences of certain options. Despite, or perhaps because of, the fragmented nature of decision-making, agencies emphasize coordination and are tied together through funding and overlapping responsibilities.

Like Singapore, Boston also faces significant inland flooding threats. The Boston Water and Sewer Commission (BWSC) is perhaps the furthest along among agencies in terms of concrete actions to enhance climate resilience. The BWSC's three-year Capital Improvement Program released in 2014 notes that they "reviewed all aspects of the Commission Sewer System, including the Commission's design standards, assets, mapping, maintenance and operational practices and future impacts of climate change on the Commission's facilities" (Boston Water and Sewer Commission 2014, 9). According to interviewees and presentations made by staff, the BWSC has already implemented some measures to both understand and respond to climate risks, including the installation of gauges throughout their stormwater network to track patterns and identify problems in real time. They share this data with key stakeholders via an intranet to warn them when flooding may be imminent.[10] Acknowledging that complete protection is impossible and may not be most effective in all cases, the BWSC is emphasizing rapid recovery. For example, a pumping station may flood, but the key systems should be protected and spare parts on hand so that it may be brought back online quickly. The BWSC is also building some flexibility into the system; for example, they are building redundant pipes into a new pumping station so that they may increase capacity quickly and cheaply in the future as necessary. Possible reasons why the BWSC and its state counterpart, the Massachusetts Water Resource Authority, are further along than other agencies in preparing for the risks posed by climate change seem to include the direct relevance of climate change, and particularly water-related threats; the proactive steps of strong internal champions that are senior enough to access resources; the relative autonomy these agencies have, particularly when it comes to funding (both are funded primarily through user fees); and the relatively closed nature of their systems.

Uncertainty: challenges and solutions in Boston

Harboring Uncertainty participants were asked 'how significant of a problem is uncertainty (not just from climate change) to you as you plan and make decisions (1 being not at all and 7 being very)?' The average response was 5.3 pre-exercise, which is very similar to the averages in Rotterdam (5) and Singapore (5.1). As in Rotterdam and Singapore, participants reported that uncertainty is a pervasive feature of decision-making.

The uncertainty I am dealing with so often is around things like "will we get this type of developer or that one", "this land use or that"; it's that kind of uncertainty, not [climate change] uncertainty, environmental uncertainty,

said one participant. In the context of the exercise, another reflected that it was frustrating to have 'linear projections' on various fronts, including growing traffic, that do not account for uncertainties, like the potential for a significant mode shift from private to public transportation. Participants generally understood uncertainty in broad terms in the exercise runs. One framed it in terms of 'risk': "We focused on risk quite a bit, without necessarily always calling it risk; we were thinking of climate risk as well as economic risk, other environmental risk, community risk". The risks associated with different options are multifaceted and uncertain.

Participants were also asked to identify the degree to which uncertainty is a factor in how their organizations view and plan for climate change adaptation. At 5, the average response was very similar to that for uncertainty in general in the pre-exercise survey; participants did not see uncertainty in the context of climate adaptation as any more or less significant of a factor than uncertainty is in general in decision-making. However, it is notable that there was a statistically significant increase in the average ranking of how much of a factor uncertainty is in climate adaptation from pre- to post-exercise.[11] This would suggest that the exercise enhanced participants' perceptions of how much of a factor uncertainty may be as they start to tackle adaptation challenges.

As in Singapore and Rotterdam, participants' reflections overwhelmingly focused on governance challenges rather than scientific uncertainty. In the words of one, contrasting the high degree of uncertainty around if and how resilience will be institutionalized to the decreasingly important uncertainty around the impacts of climate change,

I think we have to distinguish between uncertainty in terms of what the actual degree of climate change is, and uncertainty with respect to what our responses are. We are uncertain overall to what our responses are; in terms of regional responses, we have a lot of uncertainty in terms of what approaches we will take. . . . I think there is much more of a consensus on the likelihood of flooding and so forth, but in terms of what to do about it, that's another piece of the uncertainty question.

To some, uncertainty is merely an excuse for inaction. A participant that is actively involved in advancing the integration of climate change into planning and decision-making asserted that climatic uncertainty is actually relatively small, given all of the other imperfect models and variables that inform decision-making. He also suggested that differences in the professional norms of those generating climate models, versus other models, is consequential; climatologists are scientists trained to acknowledge the uncertainties upfront, while traffic and economic forecasters are trained to generate models for policymaking that typically do not emphasize their uncertainties. Another challenge is that – whether real or perceived – the uncertainties around climate change are inhibiting the establishment of standards, which is problematic for engineers. In the words of one,

> [We] engineers are great at "here is a set of standards, now design to those standards". . . . [An official] said "well there is so much uncertainty, there can't really be standards, so give it your best shot", [but] I think that problem is really significant; there is so much uncertainty associated with sea level rise and climate change that I think it's really hard to understand what is going to work best.

It is difficult for consultants, and in particular civil engineers accustomed to working within concrete parameters, to work with climate models that are seen to be uncertain and dynamic. In addition to professional standards and norms, uncertainty is interwoven with many of the other barriers to action, including resource constraints. Reflecting on the exercise, a participant said,

> So this is all just a reality of resources. Even in [this exercise], we talked about the budget first and really nothing was allowed to go above the budget. If you took climate change out of the picture, we still really can't afford the infrastructure we need. So, when you talk about uncertainty it's really difficult when there are so many needs, even absent climate change issues, how do we even begin. We are talking about allocating very, very scarce resources, and I don't know if there is a 1% chance or a 10% chance, but . . . we are fighting over a very small pie, so these uncertainty issues become much harder to deal with, because it's hard to allocate resources to things that frankly that very well could happen.

Managing uncertainty in Boston

Asked how they and their agencies typically deal with uncertainties, participants responded as follows:[12]

- seven participants said 'follow official policies or guidelines' (19%);
- sixteen 'consult experts for their best projections' (43%);
- four 'plan for worst-case scenario' (11%);
- ten 'maintain flexibility' (27%); and
- two listed 'other' approaches (5%), which were:

  - "follow existing FEMA maps and precipitation data, and attempt to get clients to think about planning and designing for future changes in climate, flooding and rainfall"; and
  - "prioritize resilient approaches".

This range of responses is relatively similar to those in Rotterdam. Singapore was notably different, with a higher proportion reporting that they 'plan for

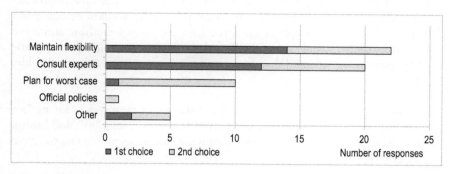

Figure 5.3 Preference ranking of how agencies should deal with uncertainties
Used with permission of author

worst-case scenario'. Post-exercise, participants were asked to rank how they think uncertainty *should* be dealt with. As illustrated in Figure 5.3, 'maintain flexibility' was the most popular option. As in Rotterdam and Singapore, this preference was largely echoed throughout the exercise debrief and follow-up interviews. Flexibility is seen as a way to advance despite resource constraints and in light of the fact that building to the expected worst-case scenario may never be enough. "Flexibility is crucial, because building it to the worst-case scenario, I think we still won't always be prepared, and B, we don't have the resources for it", reflected a participant.

Some did note that flexibility has a downside, particularly when it involves taking a 'wait-and-see' approach. The pros include an ability to be responsive to dynamic conditions and ongoing learning; the cons include potentially being underprepared when extreme events occur. In general, participants saw the popularity of flexible options in the exercise as reflective of the real world, in which some iterative steps are being taken but little or no grand adaptive responses, and characteristic of decision-making in Boston.

> It's really interesting, and maybe some of it is the bias of people who operate within the Boston and Massachusetts environment that the preference was more for the conservative, closer to status quo, but making improvements to existing infrastructure, and hardening and improving the capacity of that,

reflected a participant. "We are very used to working under confinement", added another. Participants also noted that there are substantial barriers to institutionalizing flexibility in practice. One is the more or less linear and phased process of infrastructure planning, construction and maintenance, which involves different actors at different times. "In transportation planning, the demands for funding drive a level of predictability in terms of time frames, which [are] completely oblivious to [the benefits of] flexibility and changes in terms of actual demand", reflected a participant. Another barrier is the previously discussed constraints placed by professional norms and standards; in the words of a participant, "Flexibility isn't really an option when you have to stamp something and leave your liability on it". Regulatory and political constraints were also cited as barriers. One participant reflected that we are perhaps just not good at being flexible, saying,

> Most people want there to be a clear-cut answer, or clear way of saying "we are finished, we are done, we have arrived at a certain solution", and I think you have to be comfortable saying that we're not necessarily going to arrive at a particular solution.

'Consult experts' was a close second in Boston, while it was the third most popular option in Singapore and second but far behind 'maintain flexibility' in popularity in Rotterdam. This may reflect a preference for getting 'an answer' to the question of which risks should be accounted for to avoid blowback – legal and otherwise – later. In making a case for the need for experts who can provide concrete scientific data to base decisions on, a participant reflected,

> You need to make a compelling case for new funds, or different sources of funds . . . and that is where the risk and the engineering and the management comes in, once you are able to establish that as a point of reference, then you can get into the debate. . . . We don't have this benign dictatorship where the engineer arrives at the king and the king makes the decision on the best interest of the populace, there is no king. There is a planning process, but it is going to have to factor in the technical data before it gets into the consensus building.

Decision support: multiple scenarios

Eighty-six percent of Harboring Uncertainty project participants reported prior experience using multiple scenarios as a way to manage uncertainty. As in both Singapore and Rotterdam, this suggests widespread use of scenarios as a decision-support tool. Participants were also asked how useful the consideration of multiple scenarios is (or might be) in their work; they were very positive, with an average response of 6 pre-exercise on a 7-point Likert scale. The workshop debrief and follow-up interviews provided greater clarity on the value of, and challenges in using, scenarios in practice. One theme that emerged is the value of scenarios in making salient that there are multiple possible futures. "It was new for me, but new in a good way; good that we could see a world in which very different things could happen", reflected a participant. Scenarios invite participants to think about different things that could happen, rather than asking them to accept or reject a single forecast of the future. Contrasting the scenarios version of the exercise to the risk assessment version during the debrief, a participant reflected that scenario planning inevitably engages people in the discussion, and gives [them] a concrete understanding, whereas the risk assessment is kind of abstract numbers that you have to take at face value, or you dispute, but the scenarios really change how people think and get them talking to each other about it.

He went on to add, "it's more time consuming, but there is a lot more benefit that comes out of it". As discussed earlier in this chapter, the scenarios groups in the RPS exercise had a harder time reaching agreement than those given a unitary risk assessment. Reflecting on why that might have been, a participant asserted that the scenarios provide 'more choice'. He went on to suggest that the risk assessment groups were dealing with "the cold hard facts that [they] were given, and [thus] were less able to think outside the box". Others noted that scenarios might be more or less appropriate in different circumstances. Said one,

> It is easier to do for a long-range vision document, long-range future plan, but on a project or even corridor level it's harder to change. . . . If you want to look at different infrastructure solutions, you don't want to be changing the environmental assumptions.

Learning from the RPS exercise

As discussed in more detail in Chapter 6, participants were asked a series of questions post-exercise to gather feedback on how much the RPS mirrored their realities and was valuable in their opinion as a learning tool. In terms of how similar the 'situation or problem presented' is to their own worlds, the average ranking was 5 on a 7-point Likert scale from 'very different' (1) to 'very similar' (7). This is similar to Rotterdam (5.2) and higher than Singapore (4.4). The 'characters' involved were also seen to be similar, with an average ranking of 5.4. In comparison, the average was 4.6 in Singapore and 5 in Rotterdam. As discussed above, non-governmental actors play major roles in planning processes in the United States – particularly in emerging domains like climate adaptation – so the prominent roles taken on by these actors in the exercise were not as foreign as in Singapore. Participants also found the divided interests among actors ostensibly representing the same organization – namely the alderman and municipal Department of Traffic project manager – to be an accurate reflection of reality:

> One of the things I thought was interesting [was that] there were a couple of different people from the city, and they had different viewpoints, which I thought was entirely appropriate because it's so realistic! I think that's part of our challenge, is that even within one organization you can have two different people at the table with third parties and they disagree with each other.

The 'interaction between the characters' was seen as relatively similar to participants' realities at 4.8. As discussed earlier in this chapter, agencies are increasingly engaging with one another and other stakeholders in collaborative processes, but their deliberations are not exactly like those facilitated in the exercise. In fact, participants found the collaborative 'method of decision-making' less realistic, with an average ranking of only 3.9.

Participants in both risk assessment and scenarios groups reported that these respective 'tools introduced' were somewhat although not entirely similar to those they employ in the real world, with an average of 4.4 for the former and 4.6 for the latter. The 'options or solutions' presented in the game were also somewhat realistic to participants, with an average of 4.6. Participants reflected that the idea of building a new highway was not realistic in Boston, making it less realistic, but that elements reminded them of the previously discussed Central Artery (i.e., 'big dig') project.

Participants almost universally reported that they learned something from participating in the exercise, with only one of 26 answering 'no' when asked in the follow-up survey. What they learned varied, but the vast majority reported more process- and negotiation-related findings than any substantive observations around climate change. 'Perspective taking' was a common theme, and in particular the value of playing a role other than your own. As one participant put it:

> It gives [you] an appreciation, a respect for other people's roles. It's going to take a lot of different perspectives to figure out solutions for different aspects of climate change and adapting, and having an engineer by training play a political figure in an exercise, they have to be that person that they get annoyed with, and they have to take it on to some degree, so a forced way of getting people to look beyond themselves and get a wider perspective, and that has to be helpful.

An engineer from a public agency that participated similarly noted the value for technical actors in understanding that issues are not as simple as they might seem, and involve more than scientific facts and rigid standards:

> Unless you sit with various stakeholders at the table, you will not know what their sensitivities are. . . . As an engineer you know [what] the legislation says . . . but unless you sit down with them you would never know their concerns so you need a mixture of political actors, engineers, public relations, and those are the kinds of things you are not taught in [engineering] school!

Participants also reflected that the exercise exposed them to an alternative process for deliberating among stakeholders. "I wish that the approach to decision-making were more like that in the real world; ultimately, decisions are made somewhat mysteriously, and I don't think that they are made so openly as part of [this type of] consensus building group", reflected a participant. Another participant noted that this kind of exercise could be particularly germane when initially bringing together multiple stakeholders, saying,

> It seems like it would be particularly useful when someone is setting up a new working group or something, giving them an opportunity to open up and

understand each other; it's kind of a non-threatening environment . . . so it is useful as a way to open mindsets.

Conclusion

Climate risks are increasingly on the radars of agencies and other stakeholders in Boston and the wider Massachusetts and U.S. context, but few concrete adaptive measures have been taken thus far. Various agencies have produced guidance documents and require project proponents to consider the risks associated with climate change. However, these are typically not strict standards and the degree to which they are taken seriously varies.

One challenge is that governance is fragmented across multiple agencies at four different levels of government, and coordination is relatively weak. Planning and infrastructure management are piecemeal in nature, with various pieces of the puzzle under different agencies. In general, there is insufficient coordination among the different actors, especially at the regional scale.

Another challenge is that climate change is politicized; changes in administration can have significant impacts on how much attention the issue gets. 'Leadership' is a theme across all three cities, but means different things in each case. In Singapore, it is the top-down definition of priorities. In Boston, it is bold political action to take a long-range perspective, despite the fact that it may not be easy. Participants opined that this is unfortunately uncommon. However, inter- and intra-agency leadership does not always manifest by force; it can also result from having strong networks, being persuasive and exuding political clout. While leadership matters, as in Singapore, interviewees also emphasized the importance of background work done by mid- and lower-level staff to prepare for the emergence of issues like climate resilience before they arrive on the policy agenda, so that the scaffolding is in place when issues emerge.

Adding to the institutional complexity is the prominence of external stakeholders, including both advocacy and business organizations. These organizations play substantial roles, particularly around nascent issues like climate adaptation. They can be complementary to government, even leading what in other places might be agency-led efforts. An example is the central role that Boston Harbor Now has played in documenting the city's climate risks and advancing conversations on possible solutions. Civil society organizations can also play antagonistic roles, including through litigation when their interests are threatened. In general, lawsuits feature prominently as an instrument for resolving disputes around what should be done, when, and by whom. In the context of climate adaptation, lawsuits have not been a factor thus far in Boston, but they may very well emerge as parties feel that their interests are being unfairly impacted or ignored. The threat of lawsuits certainly played prominently in the role-play simulation exercise conducted with stakeholders.

Underinvestment in infrastructure is an unfortunate reality in the United States, reflecting unwillingness to put resources into maintaining high standards. This has implications on how projects are prioritized and what is deemed possible.

A common theme among the interviews conducted for this research is that it is really hard to integrate climate resiliency at the project level when proponents are already extremely stretched for resources and are often doing the work to address acute deficiencies as quickly as possible. Funding was a prominent issue in all four groups that played the role-play simulation exercise, while it was much less so in Singapore and Rotterdam. Participants reflected afterwards that this is unsurprising, given that it is such a prominent issue in their real-world planning and decision-making. One reason for the scarcity of resources for public sector projects is the relative lack of faith in the state. In both the Netherlands and Singapore, citizens trust the government to provide high-quality infrastructure and accept the commensurate taxes and fees to pay for it. In the U.S., average trust in government is lower, as are government revenues and expenditures on infrastructure. It seems probable that this will have significant implications on the ability of agencies to adequately prepare for the impacts of climate change.

As in Singapore and Rotterdam, participants see uncertainty as a pervasive factor in their governance and decision-making. To some, climate uncertainty is nothing more than an excuse for inaction. For others, it is a factor insofar as agencies are providing ranges of possible futures when engineers and decision-makers are used to working with unitary, if still imperfect, forecasts and design standards. They are unsure of how to proceed and feel bounded by professional norms, client expectations, and the fear of lawsuits or other blowback. In general, participants reflected that uncertainty is a product of many factors, including resource constraints, and competing interests and priorities. They widely favor 'flexibility' as the best way to proceed in the face of uncertainty. However, some cautioned that flexibility can end up devolving into a reactive, wait-and-see approach that leaves the region unprepared. Furthermore, there are substantial barriers to institutionalizing flexibility, including the aforementioned piecemeal nature of planning and decision-making. Project design and funding processes are typically linear in nature, leaving little room for ongoing learning and adaptation. Here too, professional norms typically dictate that engineers and other technical experts 'get it right' the first time; according to interviewees, they are reticent to put their stamp on something that is 'good enough' for the time being and expected to change in an iterative fashion.

A common theme across the three cities is that the multiple scenarios groups largely ignored them, implicitly or explicitly defaulting to the 'worst-case scenario'. The one exception was the group in Boston that methodically considered each infrastructure option against each scenario. However, when it came time to make a decision, the chair suggested that they should decide which scenario they should be designing for, which led them to plan for the worst-case scenario and put the other possible futures aside. Despite the marginalization of the scenarios, there were notable differences when compared to the groups that did not have them. Most clearly, both scenarios groups failed to reach agreement within the time allotted, whereas both risk assessment groups did. During the debrief conversation, participants reflected that, even when not explicitly acknowledged, the scenarios provided license to accept the notion that the future is very uncertain.

In contrast, the risk assessment version forced participants to either accept or reject a forecast of future conditions. Risk assessment forecasts simplify decision-making insofar as they provide a unitary set of parameters to which infrastructure planning and design can respond. On the other hand, such assessments make assumptions that may be grossly incorrect. Multiple scenarios acknowledge these uncertainties, but in turn do not provide users concrete, fixed design parameters to work with as they execute. This can be disconcerting.

Finally, participants overwhelmingly reported that they learned from the experience. The lessons learned were largely process related. Participants learned the value of perspective taking and exploring the interests and priorities of others. More technically oriented participants reported that it was valuable to see why the politics matters too. The workshop modeled a multi-stakeholder, collaborative approach to decision-making. Many participants reflected that this was interesting and appealing to them, and that this kind of effort may be valuable in their own contexts as they grapple with emerging issues, like how to adapt to climate change. More specifically, they learned how these processes could be more or less effective, including the value of getting interests on the table and of good facilitation.

As in Singapore and Rotterdam, these findings suggest that the wider governance regime significantly influences how climate change is being integrated into planning and decision-making in Boston, and may evolve further moving forward. Many reflect what one might expect in a neo-pluralist and neo-liberal planning environment. Decision-making in Singapore is heavily influenced by the pursuit of 'national interests'. Stakeholders – particularly those inside government – are expected to coalesce around these interests and make policy choices that align with them. In the Netherlands, there is a tradition of seeking consensus, often referred to as the 'polder mentality' and relatively strong levels of trust in government. In contrast, decision-making in the United States may be characterized as the pursuit of solutions that satisfy or arbitrate between multiple interests that persist in tension. Both in the exercise conducted under this research and in the real world, stakeholders are forthright in expressing and pursuing their interests. Consultative processes are designed into infrastructure projects to provide forums for interest-driven feedback. Even relations among government agencies and levels of government can be interest-driven and at times adversarial. Whether adversarial or collaborative, adaptation efforts will need to explicitly account for different interests if they are to minimize opposition and ultimately be successful.

Notes

1 An additional 36 individuals were interviewed either before or after the workshop but did not participate. Interviews served to shed light on how infrastructure planning and decision-making happens in practice in the Boston region; what is being done to adapt to climate change; who the key players are; and, after the workshop, to ground truth the themes that emerged.

2 The Boston Harbor Association (TBHA) merged with the Boston Harbor Island Alliance in 2016 and took Boston Harbor Now as a new name.

3 Respondents were asked to indicate how much they trust government on a 9-point Likert scale, on which 1 means "do not trust them at all" and 9 means "trust them a great deal"; a top four ranking is counted as 'trust' (Edelman 2016).

4 This compares to 62% in Singapore and 49% in the Netherlands for NGOs, and 60% and 56% respectively for the business community (Edelman 2016).

5 While direct expenditures may be less, the Singaporean model actually gives the government *greater* control over the economy, as the Central Provident Fund is a major economic actor.

6 Hypothesis: Exercise participation will increase participants' opinions on the importance of engagement. Question asked: 'How important is it that you engage with other decision-makers and stakeholders as you plan and make decisions?' The results were significant at the $p = 0.025$ level, using a Wilcoxon matched pairs signed ranks test ($N = 16$, $T = 25$; two-tailed hypothesis). Therefore, the null hypothesis can be rejected.

7 It is noteworthy that both Singapore (ninth) and the Netherlands (tenth) ranked very highly in this index.

8 In other words, the chance of the given level of flooding occurring in any particular year could increase from ~1% to 20% by 2050, and then become the twice-daily norm by 2100.

9 The phrase "that answered this question" is used intermittently, because two participants, including a transportation planner actively working on adaptation projects, were late so did not complete pre-exercise surveys. In some other cases, participants chose not to answer certain questions.

10 According to interviewees on both the BWSC and institutional side, this communication is not simply one way. The users of this data provide feedback on if, when and how flooding actually occurs so that they can hone in on problem spots.

11 Hypothesis: Exercise participation will shift respondents' opinions on how much of a factor uncertainty is in climate change adaptation. Question asked: 'To what degree is uncertainty a factor in how your organization views and plans for climate change adaptation?' The results were significant at the $p = 0.05$ level, using a Wilcoxon matched pairs signed ranks test ($N = 22$, $T = 58.5$; two-tailed hypothesis). Therefore, the null hypothesis can be rejected.

12 Note that the number of responses (39) is greater than the number of respondents ($N = 30$) because some chose more than one option, although asked to 'choose only the most common or important'.

Works cited

AAPA [American Association of Port Authorities] (2013). *U.S. Port Ranking by Cargo Tonnage 2013.* Port Industry Statistics. www.aapa-ports.org/Industry/content.cfm?ItemNumber=900&navItemNumber=551

ABC [A Better City] (2015). *South Boston Waterfront Sustainable Transportation Plan.* www.abettercity.org/docs/2015.01.15%20SBoston%20Waterfront_ExecSumm_ONLY_PB.pdf

ABC (2017). *About Us – Our Mission.* www.abettercity.org/about-us/mission

Abel, D. (2015, May 4). Logan airport drafts climate change plan: Targets energy use, emissions; Aims to protect against sea rise. *The Boston Globe.* www.bostonglobe.com/metro/2015/05/03/logan-plans-major-changes-address-climate-change/KXnlO6Q0DwqlqessUZd12H/story.html?s_campaign=8315.

Andresen, C.F., J.A. Battjes, D.E. Daniel, B. Edge, W. Espey, Jr., R.B. Gilbert, T.L. Jackson, D. Kennedy, D.S. Mileti, J.K. Mitchell, P. Nicholson, C.A. Pugh, G. Tamaro, Jr. and

R. Traver (2007). *The New Orleans Hurricane Protection System: What Went Wrong and Why.* A Report by the American Society of Civil Engineers Hurricane Katrina External Review Panel. Alexandria, VA: American Society of Civil Engineers.

ASCE [American Society of Civil Engineers] (2017). *2017 Infrastructure Report Card.* www.infrastructurereportcard.org

Bennett, D. (2010, June 6). Defending Boston from the sea: A massive ocean barrier. Hidden holding tanks. With sea levels rising, urban planners start envisioning a more waterproof city. *The Boston Globe.*

Bierbaum, R., A. Lee, J. Smith, M. Blair, L.M. Carter, F.S. Chapin, III, P. Fleming, S. Ruffo, S. McNeeley, M. Stults, L. Verduzco and E. Seyller (2014). Ch. 28: Adaptation. *Climate Change Impacts in the United States: The Third National Climate Assessment.* J.M. Melillo, T.C. Richmond and G.W. Yohe, Eds. U.S. Global Change Research Program. pp. 670–706. doi:10.7930/J07H1GGT

Bisnow (2014, November 7). *Boston Power Women 2014: Part 2.* www.bisnow.com/archives/newsletter/boston/3321-boston-power-women-2014-part-2

Bosma, K., E. Douglas, P. Kirshen, K. McArthur, S. Miller and C. Watson (2015). *MassDOT-FHWA Pilot Project Report: Climate Change and Extreme Weather Vulnerability Assessments and Adaptation Options for the Central Artery.*

Boston Green Ribbon Commission (2017). www.greenribboncommission.org

Boston Harbor Now (2017). www.bostonharbornow.org

Boston Public Works Department (2014). *About.* www.cityofboston.gov/publicworks/about.asp

Boston Transportation Department (2014). *Boston Complete Streets.* www.bostoncompletestreets.org

Boston Water and Sewer Commission (2014). *Boston Water and Sewer Commission Capital Improvement Program 2015–2017.* www.bwsc.org/ABOUT_BWSC/reports/PDFs/CIP%202015-2017.PDF

Bourne Consulting Engineering (2009). *Massachusetts Coastal Infrastructure Inventory and Assessment Project – Boston Harbor.* Prepared for the MA DCR. www.mass.gov/eea/docs/czm/stormsmart/seawalls/boston-harbor/boston.pdf

CBO [Congressional Budget Office] (2015, March). *Public Spending on Transportation and Water Infrastructure, 1956 to 2014.* www.cbo.gov/sites/default/files/cbofiles/attachments/49910-Infrastructure.pdf

Center on Budget and Policy Priorities (2015). *Policy Basics: Where Do Our Federal Tax Dollars Go?* www.cbpp.org/research/policy-basics-where-do-our-federal-tax-dollars-go

City of Cambridge (2015). *Climate Change Vulnerability Assessment – Part 1.* www.cambridgema.gov/CDD/Projects/Climate/climatechangeresilienceandadaptation.aspx

City of Cambridge (2017). *Climate Change Vulnerability Assessment – Part 2.* www.cambridgema.gov/CDD/Projects/Climate/climatechangeresilienceandadaptation.aspx

Commonwealth of Massachusetts (2008). *An Act Establishing the Global Warming Solutions Act.* Acts of 2008, Chapter 298. https://malegislature.gov/Laws/SessionLaws/Acts/2008/Chapter298

Commonwealth of Massachusetts (2015). *Chapter 40B – Regional Planning.* General Laws, Part I – Administration of the Government, Title VII – Cities, Towns and Districts. https://malegislature.gov/Laws/GeneralLaws/PartI/TitleVII/Chapter40B

CPF [Central Provident Fund Board] (2015). *CPF Overview.* http://mycpf.cpf.gov.sg/CPF/About-Us/Intro/Intro.htm

CZM [Office of Coastal Zone Management] (2015). *StormSmart Coasts – Helping Communities and Homeowners With Coastal Erosion, Flooding, and Storm Damage.* www.mass. gov/eea/agencies/czm/program-areas/stormsmart-coasts/

Dahl, R.A. (1962). *Who Governs? Democracy and Power in an American City.* New Haven, CT: Yale University Press.

DCR [Department of Conservation and Recreation] (2009). *Massachusetts Coastal Infrastructure Inventory and Assessment Project Coastal Hazards Commission Infrastructure Plan Working Group Summary Report.* Boston, MA: DCR Office of Waterways. www.mass.gov/ eea/docs/czm/stormsmart/seawalls/public-inventory-report-2009.pdf

DCR [Department of Conservation and Recreation] (2017). www.mass.gov/eea/agencies/ dcr/

DEP [Department of Environmental Protection] (2015). *Chapter 91, The Massachusetts Public Waterfront Act.* www.mass.gov/eea/agencies/massdep/water/watersheds/chapter-91-the-massachusetts-public-waterfront-act.html

Department of Revenue (2015). *What Is Home Rule?* Division of Local Services, Technical Assistance Section. www.mass.gov/dor/docs/dls/mdmstuf/technical-assistance/best-practices/homerule.pdf

Douglas, E.M., P.H. Kirshen, V. Li, C. Watson and J. Wormser (2013). *Preparing for the Rising Tide.* Boston, MA: The Boston Harbor Association.

Douglas, E.M., P.H. Kirshen, M. Paolisso, C. Watson, J. Wiggin, A. Enrici and M. Ruth (2012). Coastal flooding, climate change and environmental justice: Identifying obstacles and incentives for adaptation in two metropolitan Boston Massachusetts communities. *Mitigation and Adaptation Strategies for Global Change*, 17: 537–562.

Dungca, N. (2015, February 25). MBTA, Keolis shake up leadership: Struggling commuter rail operator names veteran to oversee operations; T taps interim successor for general manager. *The Boston Globe.*

Economist (2011, May 12). Banyan: Low expectations. *The Economist.* www.economist. com/node/18681827.

Edelman (2016). *2016 Edelman Trust Barometer: Global Results.* www.edelman.com/ insights/intellectual-property/2016-edelman-trust-barometer/global-results

EEA [Executive Office of Energy and Environmental Affairs and the Adaptation Advisory Committee] (2011). *Massachusetts Climate Change Adaptation Report.* Boston, MA: The Commonwealth of Massachusetts. www.mass.gov/eea/waste-mgnt-recycling/air-quality/ green-house-gas-and-climate-change/climate-change-adaptation/climate-change-adaptation-report.html

Executive Office of the President (2013, June). *The President's Climate Action Plan.* Washington, DC: The White House. www.whitehouse.gov/sites/default/files/image/ president27sclimateactionplan.pdf.

FEMA [Federal Emergency Management Agency] (2015a). *Sandy Recovery Office.* www. fema.gov/sandy-recovery-office

FEMA (2015b). *FEMA Flood Map Service Center.* https://msc.fema.gov

Fitzgerald, M. (2014, April 6). How Boston is – and should be – preparing for rising seas; Five things the city is doing now, and five more things it ought to be doing. *The Boston Globe.*

Florida, R., C. Mellander and K. King (2015). *The Global Creativity Index 2015.* Toronto: The Martin Prosperity Institute.

Fontenault, J., N. Vinhateiro and K. Knee (2013). *Mapping and Analysis of Privately-Owned Coastal Structures Along the Massachusetts Shoreline.* South Kingstown, RI: RPS asa (for the Massachusetts Office of Coastal Zone Management). www.mass.gov/eea/docs/czm/stormsmart/seawalls/private-coastal-structures-2013.pdf

Garvin, P., C. Cloutier and D. Butler (2015, March 2). How the MBTA makes and spends its money: A breakdown of the 2015 fiscal year budget. *The Boston Globe.*

Greenovate Boston (2016). *Climate Ready Boston – Final Report.* City of Boston.

Grillo, T. (2012, May 11). Vivien Li: Waterfront champion. *Boston Business Journal.* www.bizjournals.com/boston/real_estate/2012/05/vivien-li-waterfront-champion.html.

Gurley, G. (2015, March 11). Tackling MBTA's debt problem: Earlier decisions made bad situation worse. *CommonWealth Magazine.* http://commonwealthmagazine.org/transportation/tackling-mbtas-debt-problem.

Hallegatte, S., C. Green, R.J. Nicholls and J. Corfee-Morlot (2013). Future flood losses in major coastal cities. *Nature Climate Change,* 3: 802–806.

Harvey, D. (2007). *A Brief History of Neoliberalism.* Oxford, UK: Oxford University Press.

Henchman, J. (2014, January 3). *Gasoline Taxes and User Fees Pay for Only Half of State & Local Road Spending.* Washington, DC: Tax Foundation. http://taxfoundation.org/article/gasoline-taxes-and-user-fees-pay-only-half-state-local-road-spending.

Heritage Foundation (2015). *2015 Index of Economic Freedom.* www.heritage.org/index/explore?view=by-variables

Horton, R., G. Yohe, W. Easterling, R. Kates, M. Ruth, E. Sussman, A. Whelchel, D. Wolfe and F. Lipschultz (2014). Ch. 16: Northeast. *Climate Change Impacts in the United States: The Third National Climate Assessment.* J.M. Melillo, T.C. Richmond, and G.W. Yohe, Eds. Washington, DC: U.S. Global Change Research Program. pp. 16–1–nn.

Jahn, D. (1998). Environmental performance and policy regimes: Explaining variations in 18 OECD-Countries. *Policy Sciences,* 31: 107–131.

Kirshen, P., C. Watson, E. Douglas, A. Gontz, J. Lee and Y. Tian (2008). Coastal flooding in the Northeastern United States due to climate change. *Mitigation and Adaptation Strategies for Global Change,* 13: 437–451.

Lindblom, C.E. (1977). *Politics and Markets: The World's Political Economic Systems.* New York, NY: Basic Books.

Lowery, D. and V. Gray (2004). A neopluralist perspective on research on organized interests. *Political Research Quarterly,* 57(1): 163–175.

Luberoff, D. (2004a, August 1). The Big Dig gave birth to a business association that redefined civic leadership. *CommonWealth Magazine.*

Luberoff, D. (2004b, May 3). *Civic Leadership and the Big Dig.* Rappaport Institute for Greater Boston, Working Paper 11. Cambridge, MA: John F. Kennedy School of Government, Harvard University.

Lynds, J. (2015, March 11). Many homeowners unaware of living in flood zones. *East Boston Times-Free Press.* www.eastietimes.com/2015/03/11/many-homeowners-unaware-of-living-in-flood-zones.

MAPC [Metropolitan Area Planning Council] (2008). *MetroFuture Regional Plan.* www.mapc.org/sites/default/files/MetroFuture_Goals_and_Objectives_1_Dec_2008.pdf

MAPC (2015). *Metro Boston Regional Climate Change Adaptation Strategy Report.* www.mapc.org/sites/default/files/RCCAS_full_report_rev_030515_clean.pdf

MAPC (2017). www.mapc.org

Markovich, S.J. (2014, October 14). *Transportation Infrastructure: Moving America.* CFR Backgrounders. Council on Foreign Relations.

MASCO [Medical Academic and Scientific Community Organization] (2011). *Programs and Partnerships.* www.masco.org/programs/programs-and-partnerships

MassDOT [Massachusetts Department of Transportation] (2014, June 30). *Basic Financial Statements, Required Supplementary Information and Supplementary Schedules*. www.massdot. state.ma.us/portals/0/docs/InfoCenter/financials/financial_060314.pdf

MassDOT (2017a). *Doing Business With Us*. www.massdot.state.ma.us/highway/ DoingBusinessWithUs.aspx

MassDOT (2017b). *Environmental Stewardship*. www.massdot.state.ma.us/planning/Main/ SustainableTransportation/EnvironmentalStewardship.aspx

Massport [Massachusetts Port Authority] (2015a). *About the Port of Boston*. www.massport. com/port-of-boston/about-port-of-boston

Massport (2015b). *Resiliency*. www.massport.com/business-with-massport/resiliency/

May, A.D. (2004). Singapore: The development of a world class transport system. *Transport Reviews: A Transnational Transdisciplinary Journal*, 24(1): 79–101.

McFarland, A.S. (2007). Neopluralism. *Annual Review of Political Science*, 10: 45–66.

MOF [Ministry of Finance, Government of Singapore] (2015). *Analysis of Revenue and Expenditure: Financial Year 2015*. www.singaporebudget.gov.sg/data/budget_2015/ download/FY2015_Analysis_of_Revenue_and_Expenditure.pdf

Mohl, B. (2013, February 14). A silver lining. *CommonWealth Magazine*. http://common wealthmagazine.org/transportation/005-a-silver-lining/.

MPO (2015a). www.ctps.org

MPO (2015b). *TIP Evaluation Scoring*. www.ctps.org/drupal/data/html/plans/TIP/TIP_ Evaluation_Scoring.html

National Economic Council and the President's Council of Economic Advisers (2014). *An Economic Analysis of Transportation Infrastructure Investment*. Washington, DC: The White House. www.whitehouse.gov/sites/default/files/docs/economic_analysis_of_ transportation_investments.pdf

NOAH [Neighborhood of Affordable Housing] (2017). *About*. http://noahcdc. org/?q=about

Northeast Climate Impacts Assessment (2006). *Climate Change in the U.S. Northeast*. Cambridge, MA: Union of Concerned Scientists.

OCM [Office for Coastal Management] (2015). *National Oceanic and Atmospheric Administration*. http://coast.noaa.gov

The President's State, Local, and Tribal Leaders Task Force on Climate Preparedness and Resilience (2014, November). *Recommendations to the President*. Washington: The White House. www.whitehouse.gov/sites/default/files/docs/task_force_report_0.pdf

Sabatier, P.A. and H.C. Jenkins-Smith (1999). The advocacy coalition framework: An assessment. *Theories of the Policy Process*. P.A. Sabatier, Ed. Boulder, CO: Westview. pp. 117–166.

Shelley, P. (2011, July 1). A Long Journey to a Cleaner Boston Harbor. *CLF Scoop*. Boston, MA: Conservation Law Foundation. www.clf.org/blog/massachusetts/ clf's-peter-shelley-reflects-on-his-long-journey-to-a-cleaner-boston-harbor

Solof, M. (1998). *History of Metropolitan Planning Organizations*. Newark, NJ: North Jersey Transportation Planning Authority. www.njtpa.org/getmedia/b95661af-dfd4-4e3d- bb87-39e617619c7b/MPOhistory1998.pdf.aspx

Somerville (2015). *OSPCD – Green Line Extension*. www.somervillema.gov/departments/ ospcd/green-line-extension

Spector, C. and L. Bamberger (2013). *Climate Ready Boston*. Boston, MA: Climate Preparedness Task Force, City of Boston.

TBHA [The Boston Harbor Association] (2010). *Boston Harbor Sea Level Rise Maps*. http://tbha.org/boston-harbor-sea-level-rise-maps

TBHA (2015). *About Us.* http://tbha.org/about-us

USACE (2015b, January). *North Atlantic Coast Comprehensive Study: Resilient Adaptation to Increasing Risk – Main Report.* www.nad.usace.army.mil/Portals/40/docs/NACCS/NACCS_main_report.pdf

USACE [United States Army Corps of Engineers] (2015a). *Headquarters.* www.usace.army.mil

U.S. Census Bureau, Population Division (2014). *Annual Estimates of the Resident Population: April 1, 2010 to July 1, 2014.* http://factfinder.census.gov/faces/tableservices/jsf/pages/productview.xhtml

USDOT [United States Department of Transportation] (2014). *U.S. Department of Transportation Climate Adaptation Plan 2014: Ensuring Transportation Infrastructure and System Resilience.* www.dot.gov/sites/dot.gov/files/docs/2014-%20DOT-Climate-Adaptation-Plan.pdf

Walsh, J., D. Wuebbles, K. Hayhoe, J. Kossin, K. Kunkel, G. Stephens, P. Thorne, R. Vose, M. Wehner, J. Willis, D. Anderson, S. Doney, R. Feely, P. Hennon, V. Kharin, T. Knutson, F. Landerer, T. Lenton, J. Kennedy and R. Somerville (2014). Ch. 2: Our changing climate. *Climate Change Impacts in the United States: The Third National Climate Assessment.* J.M. Melillo, T.C. Richmond, and G.W. Yohe, Eds. Washington, DC: U.S. Global Change Research Program. 19–67. doi:10.7930/J0KW5CXT

The White House (2013, November 1). *Executive Order – Preparing the United States for the Impacts of Climate Change.* www.whitehouse.gov/the-press-office/2013/11/01/executive-order-preparing-united-states-impacts-climate-change

World Economic Forum (2014). *Global Competitiveness Report 2014–2015.* www.weforum.org/gcr

6   Role-play simulation exercises for social learning and collaborative problem solving

Introduction

Role-play simulation exercises and other varieties of serious games have been promoted as means to engage multi-stakeholder groups and help them work through complex issues, like how they might integrate climate adaptation into their infrastructure planning and decision-making (Rumore, Schenk and Susskind 2016). The Harboring Uncertainty project, which undergirds the findings in this book, used an exercise to rapidly yet vividly introduce new issues, bring stakeholders together and provide a space for experimentation and dialogue. A corollary goal was to assess this relatively novel approach to action research. That is, to examine whether exercises live up to the claims made that they bring benefits to both communities engaged and researchers developing and deploying them, and why or why not.

As this chapter explains, Harboring Uncertainty participants were given a shared hypothetical challenge to address, assigned roles other than those they fill in the real world to facilitate perspective taking, and provided both shared general and role-specific confidential instructions to frame the issues and their interests and perspectives. The challenge presented is a transportation infrastructure decision complicated by the release of new information on the potential impacts of climate change. Rather than ignoring these new threats because of their uncertainty and absence from the regulations and norms traditionally followed, the transportation agency in the fictitious case has decided to assemble various stakeholders to collaboratively consider how they might respond. Parties are challenged to consider potential climate threats and possible responses, including issues of uncertainty and responsibility, while protecting their various interests.

The outcomes of the Harboring Uncertainty project suggest that RPS exercises can provide valuable insights and learning opportunities. As discussed in this chapter, participation led to statistically significant increases in participants' recognition of climate risks, recognition of uncertainty as a factor and confidence in their ability to manage risks and uncertainties. Participation also increased the importance participants place on engaging with others, heightened awareness of their interdependencies and enhanced recognition of the need to account for various interests and priorities in decision-making. Participants also reported enhanced appreciation for the importance of good process design and effective engagement in deliberations. From a research perspective, the paths the various groups who played the exercise followed, which were video recorded and coded for analysis, and the outcomes they reached yielded various insights. Furthermore, the exercise served as a valuable inflection point that informed the debrief conversations and individual interviews that followed.

This chapter examines these findings and provides guidance on how researchers, consultants, community officials and others might employ RPS exercises and other types of serious games, in their planning processes and research. It is also honest about some of the shortcomings and challenges that require attention when exercises are being used.

Why use serious games?

Planning and decision-making increasingly involves addressing complex challenges in ambiguous institutional environments in which responsibility is unallocated, scattered or unclear; the rules and norms of decision-making are weak; and science and technical information is contested (Hajer 2003). The solutions often require 'collaborative boundary work', which involves stakeholders constructing arrangements that promote collective and coordinated individual actions across traditional domains of planning and policymaking (Quick and Feldman 2014). Collaborative techniques that can advance this work are, as discussed in Chapter 8, well established. They typically place emphasis on stakeholder group representation and the application of good process to help groups generate outcomes that are seen as 'fair, efficient, stable and wise' (Susskind and Cruikshank 1987; Innes and Booher 2010).

A frequent challenge is how to instigate these collaborative efforts. That is, how to bring the necessary stakeholders together, particularly when they do not feel invested and the connections to their traditional areas of responsibility are unclear. This is particularly acute when the challenges being addressed are not yet strongly felt, as is often the case when attempting to proactively advance climate change adaptation planning. Actors both inside and outside of government are often stretched for time and other resources, reducing their proclivity to engage in processes that they do not see as immediately relevant to their work and interests.

This chapter makes the case for using RPS exercises, and serious games in general, to overcome this challenge and instigate productive boundary work, building bridges and establishing new foundations for groups to collaborate in ambiguous institutional environments. Exercises can offer low-cost, low-risk opportunities to engage stakeholders and introduce them to emerging challenges and opportunities in sandbox-like simulated environments (Schenk 2014; Schenk and Susskind 2014). Serious games can effectively put participants into situations that they may face in the future; expose them to tools, approaches and potential solutions that they might consider adopting; and help them to appreciate the interests and perspectives of others (Rumore, Schenk and Susskind 2016). RPS exercises are being used in various contexts to help groups advance climate adaptation planning by facilitating both individual and social learning, catalyzing collective action, providing venues for the brainstorming of new ideas and exploring how stakeholders might react in various hypothetical yet entirely plausible circumstances (Mendler de Suarez et al. 2012; Schenk 2014; Susskind et al. 2015).

Serious games for action research

In the context of the Harboring Uncertainty project, an RPS exercise was employed to serve dual purposes as an instrument for *action research* (Schenk and Susskind 2014). The insights gleaned from the exercises were intended to be informative to both those who participated, as they start to grapple with climate adaptation in their real-world planning and decision-making, and to this research, as we look to build theory and enhance our understanding in this complex and evolving policy arena.

The findings discussed in this chapter suggest that exercise participation was an impactful experience for those who participated. The findings discussed throughout the rest of this book suggest that exercises, complemented by various other research tools, can be insightful from a research perspective. In addition to learning directly from participants' interactions within the exercise runs, the exercise experience served as a valuable inflection point, initiating informative reflection and conversation.

This experience using RPS exercises to induce reflection among participants suggests that this might be a viable approach to action research in various contexts, because it can provide a valuable short circuit in the action-reflection cycle (see Figure 6.1). Participants can simulate an 'action' step, experimenting at low

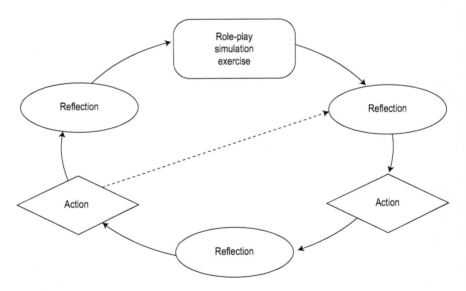

Figure 6.1 Role-play simulation exercises in the action-reflection cycle
Source: Schenk and Susskind 2014 (with permission)

cost and when real action is not yet feasible. In this context, participants considered how they might respond to uncertain climate risks in project-level decision-making before most of them have been asked to do so in reality. This challenged them to collaboratively reflect on how they could manage uncertainty, highlighted some of the factors that they would need to take into account and introduced alternative approaches to both decision-making and the framing of uncertainty, including the use of multiple scenarios.

Role-play simulation exercises and other serious games

Evidence from Turkey and the Fertile Crescent suggests that games may be as old as human civilization. While they have served as entertainment throughout history, honing our skills and wits and proving our mettle to our peers, they have often also provided important side benefits. Games typically reflect the societies that created them while concurrently providing opportunities to examine values and norms. *Serious games*, with the explicit purpose of engaging players to vividly convey lessons, foster meaningful reflection and/or develop skills may also be ancient, but their modern incarnation is rooted in 20th-century military 'war gaming' and the education arena of the 1960s (Abt 2002; Mayer 2009). Serious games engage participants to tackle fictional yet realistic challenges that generate insights with real-world implications. They are used in a wide range of contexts; in the public policy and planning arenas, serious games are being used to help groups make better urban planning decisions, explore budgeting options, experiment with different approaches to energy policy and examine the healthcare system (Dolin and Susskind 1992; Mayer 2009; Tucker 2012). They are now being used to engage decision-makers and other stakeholders around climate change issues, including how they might advance adaptation and enhance resilience (Mendler de Suarez et al. 2012; Rumore, Schenk and Susskind 2016; Susskind et al. 2015).

Serious games vary widely in style, complexity and audience. Some are intended to quickly yet vividly convey relatively simple but highly important messages to participants. An example of this is the 'Humans vs. Mosquitoes' game, which only requires a few tokens and can be played in minutes, yet can deliver important lessons around climate change, disease transmission and the assessment of risks (Humans vs. Mosquitoes 2014). Its simplicity means it can be used virtually anywhere and with any audience – from schools in Vietnam to senior officials at global climate negotiations. Other serious games involve sophisticated computer-based decision-support systems, require significant background understanding or preparation, and can take hours or days to play. For example, decision-makers from multiple agencies and other relevant organizations were brought together in 2013 to participate in a sophisticated exercise that examines how to protect lower Manhattan from sea level rise and storm surges; while physically together and able to speak directly to each other, participants deliberated within a graphics-rich computer environment that can simulate the potential consequences of different decisions (Tygron 2015). The role-play simulation exercises developed for and used with residents and public officials in four communities as part of the New

England Climate Adaptation Project fall somewhere in between – participants must read approximately10 pages to prepare and the exercises are designed to take about two hours to play and debrief, but they are intentionally accessible to most people and require no additional equipment or expertise (Susskind et al. 2015).

Role-play simulation (RPS) exercises are a variety of serious game that put participants not only into a simulated situation, but also into a role other than that they hold in the real world. They take on and are expected to represent the interests of a different party in order to facilitate perspective taking. Participants are provided with shared general instructions that establish the context, and role-specific confidential instructions that further introduce their respective character's interests and priorities and provide information that the player may or may not want to share as the deliberations unfold. RPS exercises are much like traditional games in that they have fixed rules that establish the bounds of what is possible, while resembling role plays in that participants are assigned to fill specific roles that allow for some flexibility but ultimately define who they are, including their interests and general outlook on the situation (Susskind and Corburn 1999). Exercises are typically facilitated by a trainer or professional neutral that refrains from guiding the deliberations but helps participants reflect on their experiences and what they suggest about their own situations, including potential alternatives that may not have been on their radars previously. In this sense, exercise debriefings are typically an integral part of the RPS experience, as that is when participants can collectively reflect on what they learned.

Research suggests that RPS exercises can be profoundly impactful for educational and community engagement purposes, including in the context of climate adaptation. Exercises can enhance understanding among participants of the challenges they face, increase their *collaborative capacity* and help them to engage in *social learning* (Rumore, Schenk and Susskind 2016). More specifically, exercises can vividly illustrate challenges to increase awareness and foster appreciation for the need for action and help parties to appreciate the nature of the risks they face. Exercises can also increase confidence among participants that they can do something. Increasing 'collaborative capacity' involves highlighting the interdependences that exist among different stakeholders – and thus the need to engage with others – and identifying opportunities for collective action rooted in collaborative decision-making (Rumore, Schenk and Susskind 2016). This can reflect increased empathy or simply the utilitarian realization that parties cannot succeed alone. It can also involve learning about ways in which parties can more effectively deliberate, including developing mastery of new decision-support tools. 'Social learning' involves the provision of 'safe spaces' for parties to meet, come to appreciate their respective interests and priorities, and initiate important discussions. Only time can tell if this social learning translates into concrete action, but case evidence suggests that it can (Rumore, Schenk and Susskind 2016).

Despite the successes using RPS exercises to facilitate social learning, increase collaborative capacity and initiate action, we need to be honest about the limits of RPS exercises. While they can influence the ways in which parties view a situation and help them to better understand the range of possibilities, they are ultimately presenting very simplified simulations of reality and thus rarely lead to *the answer*. Insights learned, tools and approaches introduced and new options identified must subsequently go through the complex gamut of real-world policy-making – with all of the politics and other constraints involved – if they are to gain traction. Exercises can provide valuable points of departure, but rarely escort participants to the ultimate conclusion. Furthermore, previous work suggests that in order for exercises to be impactful, they need to be realistic and relevant to those playing; be facilitated by a third party that can help participants reflect and make sense of the outcomes; provide clear instructions, including the role-specific confidential instructions introduced earlier in this chapter; and be played by the actual stakeholders that are facing, or may face, a situation like that simulated (Susskind and Schenk 2014).

The Harboring Uncertainty project

This chapter illustrates the value of serious games by drawing from the Harboring Uncertainty project. The project engaged infrastructure managers and other stakeholders in three coastal cities – Singapore, Rotterdam and Boston – to explore how they might more effectively integrate climate change into their planning and decision-making. The primary research questions were: As infrastructure managers and other stakeholders grapple with complex and uncertain risks, like those posed by climate change, how are they likely to make decisions in practice? Furthermore, how can we support more effective decision-making? In the spirit of action research, an RPS exercise was used to engage stakeholders. The exercise provided a window of opportunity for the participants to examine various issues, instigating reflection and discussion. It helped the groups to collectively consider climate risks and how they might adapt to them, and it fostered reflection around their current and potential future decision-making processes and support tools.

While using the RPS exercise as a research instrument, the Harboring Uncertainty project also sought to examine the efficacy of this approach. That is, to test the assertion that exercises that bring stakeholders together to wrestle with simulated challenges can enhance their awareness of the issues being examined and how they might be resolved both technically and in terms of governance. More specifically, the project examined the following hypotheses related to the use of RPS exercises:

- *Increased recognition of climate risks* – On average, participants' levels of understanding of how significant of a threat climate change poses to their infrastructure will increase.
- *Increased recognition of uncertainty* – In addition to increased recognition of the need to consider climate change adaptation, participants' recognition of the importance of uncertainty as a factor will also increase.
- *Increased confidence* – In general, participants will leave feeling more confident that they, and other stakeholders, can and will find ways to address the risks posed by climate change.

- *Increased understanding of interdependence* – Participants will gain new appreciation for their interdependence with other stakeholders and of the role of interests in deliberations. They will subsequently conclude that multi-stakeholder processes, like those simulated in the exercise, can effectively bring them together to address shared challenges.
- *Increased appreciation for good process* – Participants will gain appreciation for the importance of good process design in effective deliberation. They will also gain enhanced understanding of how both process features and the tactics of participants can shape the outcomes.

The exercise developed for the Harboring Uncertainty project, which is introduced in the next section, was run with 76 participants across the three cities. The outcomes for each of the 10 groups that completed the exercise are summarized in Table 2.2 in Chapter 2. The exercise put participants into a simulated environment to quickly expose them to an emerging issue (climate risks in this case); possible responses; potential decision-support tools and alternative methods of decision-making (the use of scenarios in particular in this case); and the various interests and perspectives of different stakeholders. They could learn and experiment in a low-cost, simulated environment. As discussed in Chapter 1, the exercise runs were video recorded, transcribed and coded for analysis. From a research perspective, both how each group concluded and the paths that brought them there were informative. Using a mixed-methods research approach, the runs were complemented by preliminary and follow-up interviews, pre- and post-exercise surveys, debrief conversations and extensive background research. The debrief conversations, follow-up interviews and post-exercise surveys captured the broader reflections that the exercise invoked.

The exercise: A New Connection in Westerberg

Numerous RPS exercises have been developed for use in a wide variety of contexts when multi-stakeholder groups are facing shared challenges. The exercise specifically designed for the Harboring Uncertainty project is called A New Connection in Westerberg. It is a relatively simple exercise that takes approximately 90 minutes to run, excluding the time required for preparation and debriefing, but that highlights many of the challenges around integrating climate risks into infrastructure planning and decision-making, particularly at the project level. The same exercise was run in all three cities to allow for direct comparison of the processes and outcomes among the different groups.

A New Connection in Westerberg was developed based on best practices in RPS design, building on the extensive experience of affiliates of the MIT Science Impact Collaborative, the Program on Negotiation at Harvard Law School and associated organizations. An early version was piloted with student volunteers to test the mechanics. More polished versions were then piloted with participants in Boston and Rotterdam similar to those who would later participate in the project, to test its resonance and viability with those in the case cities.

A New Connection in Westerberg places participants in a fictitious yet realistic situation in which a group of stakeholders from various government agencies and key external constituencies have been brought together by the National Transportation Agency as a special 'A39 Climate Change Evaluation Group'. Their task is to consider if and how they can reconcile the still-uncertain climate risks recently detailed in a report called the *Westerberg Climate Impacts Assessment* with plans to construct a new highway (the A39), which may be vulnerable if certain design options are chosen. The primary choices before them are if, how and where the road should be constructed. The initial options presented are to build the road below grade (which is the status quo approach), elevate the road, reroute the road through a wetland, or cancel the project and invest in rebuilding an existing road. The above- and below-grade options are illustrated in Figure 6.2. Other options, like enhancing freight and/or passenger rail service and investing in remedial measures to lower the risks and/or negative impacts associated with the various options, emerge during deliberations.

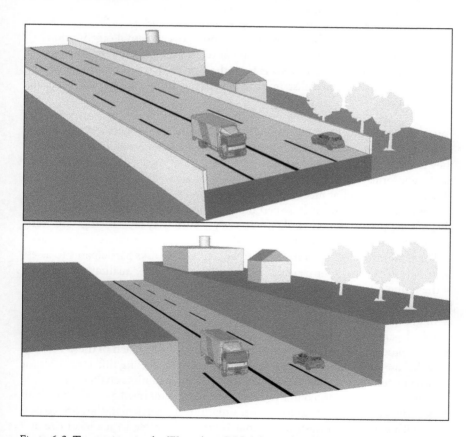

Figure 6.2 Two options in the Westerberg RPS (elevated and below-grade road)
Used with permission of author

There are tradeoffs among the options given to the exercise participants, with differentiated costs and benefits associated with each for the various stakeholders. Divergent interests, costs and benefits, and perceptions of uncertain risks all must be addressed. The exercise is not simply about better understanding the threats posed by climate change and identifying the optimal response against some externally imposed criteria, but rather about vetting options against uncertain scientific information *and* the very real concerns and interests of the various stakeholders. The option that seems best to one group may be untenable to others, necessitating broad deliberation as decisions are made. For this reason, the exercise mimics a multi-stakeholder collaborative effort, in which the various parties are explicitly instructed to seek consensus around how to move forward while protecting the interests of their respective constituencies. To this end, each participant in the Westerberg exercise fills one of seven roles:

- regional deputy director from the National Transportation Agency
- Westerberg District alderman (i.e., city councilor)
- project manager from the city's Department of Traffic
- executive director of an environmental non-governmental organization
- director of community and government relations from the Port Authority
- senior engineer for new projects from the National Transportation Agency
- flood protection specialist from the National Infrastructure and Planning Agency

Participants are given shared general and individual role-specific 'confidential instructions' that outline their interests and provide additional information that they may or may not want to share with the rest of their groups, as they wish. Sharing information may help to clarify matters and facilitate the identification of creative options that meet various interests and priorities. On the other hand, parties may be reluctant to share certain information – like funds they have available but are prepared to use only if necessary – until they are sure they are going to get what they need in return.

There are two versions of the Westerberg RPS – one asks participants to assess their options against four plausible but mutually exclusive, qualitative scenarios of the future, while the other provides a more conventional single risk assessment forecast of future climate conditions. These versions were run with roughly equivalent groups of participants in each of the case cities, with allocation done on a matched-pair basis to the degree possible. As discussed in Chapter 7, the differences in process and outcomes between the groups playing each of these versions provided an opportunity to explore the implications of using different tools for framing uncertainty as stakeholders consider their adaptation challenges.

While the case presented in the exercise is highly simplified, participants in all three cities could relate it to their own situations. In particular, they are coastal cities with extensive infrastructure that is very vulnerable to sea level rise and storm surge inundation. While they are at different stages in the process of planning and integrating adaptive measures into their infrastructure systems, all three are grappling with how to respond. While the agencies and levels of government are different across the three cities (most notably, Singapore has a single level of government), the roles in the exercise are somewhat similar to those that might be involved in similar real-world situations in the three countries. Similarities and differences in the institutional arrangements and modes of decision-making across the three cities are discussed in Chapter 2.

Learning from Westerberg: the value of exercises

As discussed previously, the A New Connection in Westerberg exercise was employed, along with a suite of complementary research methods, to examine climate adaptation-related issues in the context of infrastructure planning. Among the goals of the wider Harboring Uncertainty project was to test the efficacy of exercises for this kind of action research. It explored their potential benefits both for those who are engaged as participants and as a way to glean insights for research purposes. The findings presented in the next five sections suggest that RPS exercises can provide both rich insights and a valuable learning experience for multi-stakeholder groups convened to collectively examine emerging challenges like adapting infrastructure to climate change. All five RPS-related hypotheses introduced earlier in this chapter were affirmed. There were statistically significant increases from pre- to post-exercise in participants' recognition of climate risks, recognition of uncertainty as a factor and confidence in their ability to manage the risks and uncertainties. There was also a statistically significant increase in the importance participants place on engaging with others, heightened awareness of their interdependencies and enhanced recognition of the need to account for various interests and priorities. Participants also reported enhanced appreciation for the importance of good process design and effective engagement in deliberations.

Increased recognition of climate risks

As discussed throughout this book, awareness of the risks that climate change poses to our infrastructure systems is increasing. Nonetheless, it is not yet widespread throughout the various agencies and other stakeholder groups that are necessary if sufficient adjustments are to be made to the ways in which planning and decision-making takes place. This may be particularly true at the local level in many regions around the world and among those engaged in project-level decision-making rather than higher-level strategic planning.

One of the most prominent claims made of RPS exercises, and serious games in general, is that they can provide forums for the rapid, yet vivid, introduction of emerging issues, like the risks posed by climate change. The argument is that by immersing participants in realistic simulated environments, RPS exercises can make the risks more tangible and salient, putting those risks into perspective (Rumore, Schenk and Susskind 2016). Embedding simple information, like risk projections and the cost estimates associated with different adaptive responses, can help participants to understand and more effectively engage with the choices to be made.

The Harboring Uncertainty project's results support this assertion. Participants were asked to self-report their level of awareness of 'climate change and the risks it may pose' on a 7-point Likert scale both before and after the exercise. In aggregate across the three cities, there was a statistically significant increase, suggesting that participation increased recognition of the risks posed by climate change.[1] Looking at each case city separately, the shift was statistically significant in Singapore, while the less pronounced increases were not statistically significant in Boston or Rotterdam. This may be explained in large part by the already high levels of recognition among participants in Boston and Rotterdam before the exercise; there was less opportunity for significant increases in recognition. Looking across the individuals who participated, the most significant increases in all three cities were typically among those who started with the lowest levels of awareness. This suggests that the greatest value RPS exercises have as tools for increasing recognition is among those with relatively little prior exposure. Given that we are at an important juncture when climate risks – whether explicitly labeled as such or not – need to be 'mainstreamed' broadly into infrastructure planning and decision-making, RPS exercises may prove invaluable for spreading the word (Haywood et al. 2014; Romsdahl 2011). A Harboring Uncertainty participant underscored this by emphasizing that it

> makes a difference for stakeholders, whether they are working [on climate issues], or not, interested in it, or not, [and] the most important [factor] is that it's easy, understandable, [information is] easily available [allowing for] the mainstreaming, to take [climate risks] into consideration with some other developments, but not as the main issue itself.

Increased recognition of uncertainties

Uncertainty is a pervasive factor in decision-making, especially in the context of climate adaptation. While it is necessary for decision-makers and other stakeholders to find ways to work through uncertainty, it is important that they first acknowledge its presence and nature. Harboring Uncertainty participants were asked both before and after the exercise two questions around uncertainty as a factor in their planning and decision-making: how much of a factor it is in general, and how much of a factor it is in their organizations' climate adaptation efforts. The average responses were high to both questions: 5.2 pre- and 5.3 post-exercise for the question of uncertainty in general, and 4.6 pre- and 5.6 post-exercise for the question of uncertainty as a factor in adaptation. These are on a 7-point Likert scale from 'not at all' at 1 to 'very' at 7.

Participants reflected that uncertainty is a factor throughout planning and decision-making, and not simply when it comes to climate adaptation. Said one participant in the Netherlands,

> [There] are so many things, like how much is the population going to grow, how much is car use going to develop, what is the economic development

going to be – there are so many interests that you have to deal with . . . so this climate change is just one aspect of a very, very wide range of aspects that you have to value, that you have to judge as a politician.

Nonetheless, as illustrated in Figure 6.3, there was a statistically significant increase in how much of a factor participants felt uncertainty is in the context of climate adaptation from before to after the exercise.[2] There were statistically significant increases in all three cities, not just in aggregate. This suggests that participating in the RPS exercise, on average, increased perceptions of how much of a factor uncertainty is in adaptation planning. This finding may have implications as stakeholders increasingly engage in adaptation planning efforts; matters may not be as straightforward as they perceive them to be a priori.

Uncertainty – both technically and as a governance challenge – manifested as a factor in the A New Connection in Westerberg RPS exercise runs in all three cities. The implications uncertainty had included downplaying the risks the fictitious community of Westerberg might face, fostering paralysis and allowing parties to shape the uncertain future to best meet their own interests and priorities.

Uncertainty was used by some as an excuse to discount the risks associated with climate change. For example, when arguing for the below-grade road option, which may be considered the most vulnerable to climate change, one participant said, "the downside is the risk of flooding due to climate change in the next 20 years, but uncertainty about this is big". The assertion was that uncertain climate risks should not stand in the way of what is otherwise the best option for their

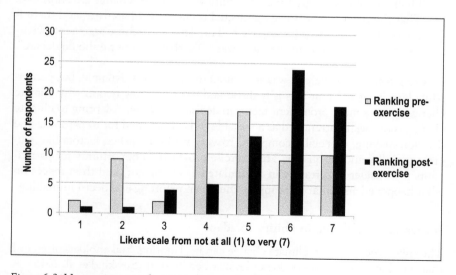

Figure 6.3 Uncertainty as a factor in climate adaptation
Used with permission of author

constituency. Similarly, in opposition to an option that might be deemed more climate proof but have greater impacts on the adjacent neighborhood, the alderman in one group said that the elevated road is "unacceptable for the municipality . . . For years we have tried to minimize the effects of roads on local citizens, and now we would change that completely for one uncertainty?!" These comments underscore the notion that uncertainty is a problem not only in a technical sense, but also insofar as it can be used as an excuse to discount risks. Uncertainty around climate change was a factor because it provided a convenient argument; decisions need to be made between competing priorities, and parties see certain activities proposed to address climate change as counter to their interests, so discount their necessity by invoking uncertainty.

Uncertainty was also a reason for delaying action, as parties asserted that they needed better information before they could make decisions. In the case of a group in Rotterdam, the flood protection specialist expressed her unwillingness to accept any option without "a very clear risk analysis of the pros and cons" of the different choices, including an assessment of the uncertainties around both climate and traffic projections. She ultimately called for more research. It is not clear if parties were genuinely arguing for a delay in decision-making because of uncertainty, or simply using uncertainty as an excuse because a delay was in their interest; their comments would suggest a little of both. "It was too attractive for some people to say 'let's do more research' instead of making a decision right now", said a participant during an exercise debriefing.

Reflecting on why other interests won out in the end from her perspective, one participant said,

> I had the impression that the uncertainties in climate change are enormous. That the old arguments [e.g., projected traffic growth] are true, and there is no room for discussing [them], we had no debates on those arguments whatsoever, while on climate change it was "OK, that's where we should debate".

To some degree, the exercise was structured to invoke this dynamic, but participants largely agreed that this is realistic and perhaps a key reason why climate change is not a more prominent factor in decision-making. Adapting to climate change is not well entrenched as a variable to be accounted for in planning and decision-making, especially compared to very well-established factors like efficient mobility and air quality. The exercise provided an opportunity for participants to consider uncertainty in a simulated environment, and then reflect on what happened and what it means for their own planning and decision-making.

Increased confidence in ability to adapt

The risks associated with climate change can be daunting. Stakeholders often feel that they have few options or do not know where to start (Susskind et al. 2015). A problem that is often framed as global in nature can seem unsurmountable at the local level. Yet, climate adaptation is largely a local or regional challenge, requiring locally appropriate responses. RPS exercises may provide invaluable confidence-building experiences, increasing participants' sense that they, and their counterparts in other organizations, can successfully adapt to the threats posed by climate change.

Participants in the Harboring Uncertainty project were asked both before and after the exercise how confident they are that they and other stakeholders will be able to manage the risks and uncertainties climate change poses. There was a statistically significant increase from pre to post, suggesting that, on average, participation boosted participants' confidence.[3] Exercise participation provided them with an opportunity to see that realistic solutions to tackle climate risks are possible, that we can make sense of the risks, including by deploying useful decision-support tools and planning ahead for potential future actions, and that their colleagues and counterparts in other agencies and organizations are also starting to think about what should be done and how. A participant in the Netherlands who has done work on transportation infrastructure and climate change was pleasantly surprised by how quickly and easily other participants with less experience in this area grasped the issues and started deliberating on responses, stating that her increased confidence "was based on [our] discussions that people were aware that it might happen, that we don't know for sure how much, and when, but let's, well, save some money already so that when it happens we can interfere". Another Dutch participant reflected that "people [were] very constructive in looking for solutions; some of the stakeholders were not supposed to believe in climate change, but the others were very positive, at least in their roles".

While the exercise did increase the confidence of many participants, the average response across the three cities was middling even post-exercise at 4.4 on a 7-point Likert scale. This reflects persistent concern among participants that they and their fellow agencies and other stakeholders may not be up to the task.

> People don't decide until a disaster happens; you can see that in New York – we already predicted years ago which areas would be flooded with [Hurricane Sandy] and we knew exactly which subways were going to be flooded, but nobody did anything! So, that's why I think you can tell them, but they want to see it with their own eyes – they will wait until a disaster happens, and then they will react,

said a participant expressing a widely held sentiment.

> The real issue is that we don't really exactly know how much things will change, whether or not Singapore will be drowned, or [when] part of Singapore will be under water, so, in terms of that . . . climate could change faster than we think,

said another participant, expressing concern that we may not be able to prepare quickly enough.

In addition to comparing pre- and post-exercise surveys, participants were asked on the post-exercise survey to reflect and explicitly self-report on whether the exercise changed their level of confidence.[4] Across the three cities, 32 reported increased confidence, 6 reported feeling less confident, and the remaining 33 reported no change. These responses reinforce the conclusion that the exercise increased confidence for many more people than it decreased, but a substantial proportion saw no change. It is noteworthy that this exercise was not explicitly designed to increase confidence among participants, but rather to foster reflection on whether or not they should feel confident. An exercise with that goal may very well generate much more substantial increases.

The exercise experience did instigate valuable reflection among participants around *why* they are not more confident. When queried during the debrief sessions and follow-up interviews, deficient professional capacity was regularly cited. One dimension of this is lack of proficiency in adaptive or flexible design and planning. Participants characterized the traditional approach that most engineers are trained to take as 'deterministic' in nature; they see the systems they work within as more or less predictable, and predetermined based on a relatively understandable set of variables. As discussed further in Chapter 8, flexibility requires a substantially different perspective on how systems work and how decision-making should be approached.

Participants' reflections suggest that mechanisms of what DiMaggio and Powell (1983) call 'institutional isomorphism and collective rationality' may also be driving adherence to common norms and dissuading creativity; agencies are pressured to provide consistent and dependable service with no surprises, so mimic others to avoid risks. External standards also drive conformity. As discussed futher in chapter 8, another major factor is the limited time and resources agencies have to consider new variables like 'deep uncertainty', and possible new solutions, like integrating flexibility.

Another factor is persistent discussion around whether climate change is even worthy of attention. "The [persistence of] different opinions, and [the fact that] not everybody has the same level of knowledge about climate change", in the words of a participant who went on to say,

> it's partially different levels of knowledge, and also different levels of involvement with the issue . . . like with everything, you have people on the front and people in the middle, and people at the back, and I think it's mainly to do with that – not everybody is on the same level of knowledge, and not everybody has [the necessary] institutions.

The same participant went on to argue that it is also about prioritization:

> I think every organization has its own aims, and what I notice in the past years is that climate has not been an issue, or less of an issue because of political reasons mainly, and the economic crisis – less money available, and climate is one of the first things to be dropped off.

Increased understanding of interdependence and interests

Adapting to climate change is typically a collective risk management task that requires the integration of science and policy and the reconciliation of different interests, priorities and perspectives (Moser and Ekstrom 2010; Susskind 2010). Decision-makers and other stakeholders typically need to appreciate and understand the interdependent nature of their respective pieces of the planning and policymaking puzzle, including around interconnected infrastructure systems (Bollinger et al. 2014). Multi-stakeholder deliberations can provide opportunities for parties to collectively examine the risks and possible solutions and identify ways forward despite significant and persistent uncertainties.

Harboring Uncertainty project participants were asked both before and after the exercise how important is it that they engage with other decision-makers and stakeholders as they plan and make decisions. The average response across the three cities was 5.8 pre- and 6.3 post-exercise on a 7-point Likert scale. This is a statistically significant increase, suggesting that participation increased the already high value they place on multi-stakeholder deliberation.[5] The importance of broad engagement was universal across the three cities, with average responses (post-exercise) of 6.4 in Rotterdam, 6 in Singapore and 6.5 in Boston. However, opinions on *who* should be engaged varied across cities. In Boston, actors from outside government are extensively involved in adaptation planning efforts. In contrast, participants in Singapore agreed that better cooperation among government agencies is important, but are wary of involving external stakeholders.

One reason why participants deemed multi-stakeholder engagement to be important is because it facilitates the incorporation of various factors into planning and decision-making that might otherwise be disregarded or downplayed. This includes strongly held sentiments that, if ignored, could lead to strong opposition and thus implementation challenges later. For example, in the A New Connection in Westerberg exercise runs, the option of routing the highway through a wetland was discounted early in most cases because of strongly expressed environmental concerns. In Boston, the mere threat of a lawsuit from the environmental non-governmental organization representative was sufficient to make this option less attractive to others; agencies did not want to ignore these concerns and potentially face substantial delays and legal costs defending their choice in court. The exercise underscored how important it is to understand the various interests and interdependencies, and how they shape what is possible. Even in Singapore, where individual interests were typically downplayed, participants reflected on the value of understanding the different factors at play as they attempt to deduce what is in the 'national interest'. All four groups implicitly or explicitly identified nurturing the economy as a key national priority, and subsequently spent substantial time looking for creative ways to address the concerns expressed by the port representative.

Participants also learned via the exercise that getting the various parties together and factors on the table could allow for greater creativity. For example, the flood protection specialists in most groups introduced the possibility of accessing additional funds if the reconstruction of a dike on which part of the existing motorway runs is done concurrently as a joint project. This had tremendous sway in deliberations, but would not have come up if the Transportation Agency had just tackled this problem unilaterally. In Boston, one of the participants that filled the Transportation Agency regional deputy director role reflected afterwards that this was key to her becoming a proponent of the highway rebuilding option, as she saw this as an opportunity to save her agency some money while achieving their transportation goals. Others affirmed that this is realistic in resource-constrained environments in which funding is often the issue. In Rotterdam, this combined dike and road project was framed as 'work with work', which is a concept being promoted by agencies as they institutionalize adaptation. In all cases across the three cities in which agreement was reached, or almost reached, the outcomes were framed as 'compromises' or 'creative solutions' that reconciled different interests and integrated different factors.

The exercise also underscored how beneficial it is for participants from different sectors and backgrounds to appreciate each other's epistemologies. In particular, participants reflected that there is value in bringing technicians, policy makers and other stakeholders together to enhance their mutual understanding of how and why each reaches certain conclusions and makes the decisions they do. Participants in both the Netherlands and Singapore reflected that it is uncommon for technical experts to be at the table in multi-stakeholder forums, but that there is benefit to be had in including them so that they can be more responsive to the needs of decision-makers, and vice versa. "The experts are generally very good in their respective areas, so what they need is someone to come in and challenge their assumptions", said a participant in Singapore. This is a call for enhanced and appropriate science-policy interactions, which RPS exercises can play a role in initiating and facilitating.

Increased appreciation for good process

Bringing multiple stakeholders together may be an important precursor to effective decision-making in complex and ambiguous institutional environments, including those involving infrastructure planning and climate change-related risks. However, simply convening officials from various agencies and levels of government and other non-governmental actors is no guarantee of success. Given their very different interests, priorities and deeper epistemologies, the various actors may very well flounder and fail to engage in productive work, if good process is not provided.

The Harboring Uncertainty exercise runs drove home how important good process design and management is, and the implications that different process choices and participant behaviors can have on the trajectory and outcomes. Ninety-seven percent of workshop participants reported that they learned something from the RPS exercise.[6] When asked what they learned, participants' responses were overwhelmingly process related. This was universal across the three case cities and across the groups, including both more technically oriented and more policy-oriented participants coming both from within and outside government. The exercise invoked significant reflection around what good process might look like and its importance as groups grapple with emerging challenges like adapting to climate change. While many of the differences in process and outcomes may be attributed to differences across the three case cities and risk assessment versus scenarios versions of the exercise, there were also features that can best be attributed to the choices different meeting chairs (i.e., those filling the regional deputy director of the Transportation Agency role) and other actors made.

How deliberations are structured – including the agenda followed – can have significant implications. For example, despite the fact that scenarios were explicitly included in the instructions for participants who played that version of the exercise, they were largely ignored by all but one of those five groups. This was, at least in part, because they were not explicitly integrated into the agenda; most chairs did not create the space for their use. A second example of the impacts the structure of deliberations can have is a group that played the risk assessment version of the exercise in Rotterdam. It was the only group that leaned towards a below-grade road option, which can be explained by the fact that it was presented as the default and focused on inordinately. The same group ultimately failed to reach agreement because the chair stipulated that unanimous consent was required, even though this was not stated in his instructions. One party, the flood protection specialist, was able to hold out and block an agreement that everyone else was ready to accept. These examples underscore the degree to which the agenda and process decisions made can influence the outcomes, highlighting the value of good process design.

The performance of chairs varied widely, with implications on the trajectory and outcomes. While efforts were made to put participants with some experience running meetings into that role, a couple of chairs were not very confident. In one instance, the chair essentially stepped back from the process, allowing the group to proceed more or less organically without her involvement. This allowed another player (the environmentalist) to step in and dominate. In contrast, the chair of a different group employed strong facilitation techniques – he proposed an agenda and helped the group stick to it, systematically called upon parties to make sure that all voices were heard, employed active listening techniques to confirm what parties were saying, had another participant track key variables on a flipchart, and held straw polls at various junctures to get a sense of where the group was. Participants reflected afterwards that astute facilitation helped make the process smooth and ultimately successful in reaching agreement. Some facilitators showed more bias than others did. A couple explicitly declined to express their preferences in order to remain, in their words, neutral. In contrast, some clearly attempted to steer their groups in certain directions. An example is the aforementioned chair that informed the group that she wanted an option involving renovating the existing road because it would save her agency money. She was quick to discount other options based on her perspective.

The performance of other parties also had implications. Despite the fact that non-governmental actors would rarely even be at the table in this type of deliberation in Singapore, the environmental NGO representative in one of the scenarios groups dominated both qualitatively, by driving the discussion, and quantitatively, with the highest frequency of interventions. She championed an option that involved renovating the existing road and enhancing rail, and she was able to convince other participants by making fact-based arguments that supported her cause and discredited some of the assertions of the port representative. For example, she convinced them that new technologies, like advanced traffic management systems, were rapidly evolving and could address congestion much more efficiently and effectively than could building new roads. When asked during the debrief how she was able to leverage so much influence, other participants said that she was making sound, rational arguments. "Our NGO talks like a professor", said one. This underscored for participants the degree to which the performance of actors can influence the outcomes.

Whether parties representing stakeholder interest groups get their issues on the agenda and effectively fight for them can have major implications. The aldermen and -women (i.e., city councilors) were generally influential in Boston, but one seemed unsure of when and how she should intercede in the fast-paced deliberations to express her concerns around the elevated road – which is the most important issue to that role – and almost neglected to voice them. In fact, her opinion only came out when the Port Authority representative directly asked her about this issue. An alderwoman in Singapore expressed her concerns, but ultimately accepted an elevated road because she was convinced that it was for the greater good of the wider populace. She reflected afterwards on what this experience taught her about the impact an individual can have on deliberations:

> I thought the character of the individual also impacts the decision at the end, because I sort of conceded defeat, [saying] "Okay, yeah, I agree with you, so okay". I know that I'm not supposed to go towards that direction, but I sort of agreed because I feel that we should think holistically. So, I thought the character of that particular individual, apart from their role, also influences how things go.

In contrast, a port representative in Boston was so obstinate with her demands that she started to irritate other parties at the table, yet ultimately gained more for her constituency than did her counterparts in other groups in Boston, including dedicated trucking lanes on the highway and a promise of funding from the city for 'a fancy crane or something'. Experiences like this suggest that persistence can indeed pay.

The Port Authority representative's querying of the more withdrawn alderwoman in the Boston case discussed above is an example of wider attempts at coalition building. This was a common strategy among those who played the Port Authority role, particularly among the Boston groups. Port representatives realized that they needed to get other parties on board if they were to see an acceptable agreement reached and implemented quickly, which was a priority for them. In another Boston group, the port representative worked to build a relationship with the alderman, explicitly stating at one point that from my perspective, I'm really going to have to agree with the alderman, because when this goes out for public meetings, we want the community to be happy and to not hold this up due to their issues with this going through the community.

In general, after the exercise participants reflected that the exercise taught – or reminded – them how much value there is in working to understand and account for the interests of others. "We should have asked more questions to come to a better decision", said a participant in Rotterdam. Another reflected that this dynamic is realistic, stating that: "I also experienced this as a real-life experience, because that's the way we do discussions – everyone starts talking, giving up solutions [instead of listening]".

Considerations in the use of serious games

The findings from the Harboring Uncertainty project suggest that RPS exercises, and perhaps serious games writ large, can be a powerful addition to the toolkits of those seeking to advance action on complex and uncertain issues like adapting to climate change. However, there are caveats to be drawn both from this and other experiences using exercises to facilitate learning and dialogue and engage in action research. It is also important to note that much more work is necessary to test the efficacy of RPS exercises – and serious games in general – in different situations and with different approaches. The Harboring Uncertainty project took a particular approach; future research might experiment with others, including the use of more sophisticated game engines to provide feedback and help participants visualize the threats they face and implications of different possible decisions. There may also be variability in the efficacy of serious games – or different types of serious games – across different cultures and contexts. The Harboring Uncertainty project engaged stakeholders in three different cities around the world, but for all the differences, there are actually important similarities, not least in terms of their professional cultures. While work remains, the following challenges and considerations deserve attention as serious games are adopted and further tested.

Recruitment challenges

Potential exercise participants need to believe that the experience will provide value if they are going to be convinced to participate. As discussed earlier in this chapter, participants in this Harboring Uncertainty project overwhelmingly reflected afterwards that they found it to be a useful experience. However, some actual and potential participants were skeptical ahead of time. Parties do not necessarily believe 'a game' can be useful. One way to both provide value and entice participants is by promoting workshops featuring exercises as opportunities for parties with a shared emerging challenge, like adapting to climate change, to meet and get a better understanding of the opportunities and barriers they face and a sense of each other's perspectives and interests. The Harboring Uncertainty workshops achieved this to some degree, although some participants reflected that they could have been better targeted towards groups of relevant stakeholders. For example, the workshop in Boston could have been run with parties involved in the Metropolitan Planning Organization's transportation planning processes, plus some additional stakeholders with relevance to the issue, perhaps even under the auspices of the MPO. That would have provided more focus and value to participants facing a shared, real-world challenge. RPS exercises should focus on a particular challenge or issue and serve as opportunities for parties to meet and advance their thinking, which they can subsequently translate to their shared real-world situation. In general, exercise conveners are more likely to be successful if they can make the case that the experience will be relevant and credible to participants.

Relevance and credibility

RPS exercises are most effective when they get at the actual issues and dynamics that participants are or will be wrestling with in the real world. They must be credible to participants such that they are relatable while introducing them to something novel so as to invoke fresh reflection. Participants in this Harboring Uncertainty project were asked in the post-exercise survey to assess the accuracy of the A New Connection in Westerberg RPS in various respects, including who was at the table, the options available and the method of decision-making. The results varied from city to city and question to question, but largely validated that the exercise approximated their realities and/or presented a plausible future. The credibility of the exercise was a product of extensive background research and testing, which took substantial time. It also required the application of best practices in exercise design. The importance of credibility and resonance with participants suggests that there is significant value in creating or tailoring exercises for each context, rather than simply using preexisting exercises off the shelf. This does, however, require substantial resources. While valuable for comparative research purposes, a downside in the Harboring Uncertainty project was that the same exercise was used across all three cities, inherently compromising its fidelity to each individual case. The design process attempted to compensate by drawing elements from across the three and including commonalities to the degree possible, but some things were foreign to participants. The clearest example of this is that the exercise includes roles from two levels of government, while there is only one level in the city-state of Singapore. The efficacy of RPS exercises for action research is at least somewhat contingent on good design that resonates with participants while presenting something new to invoke reflection.

On the other hand, discrepancies between present and plausible future realities in each case city and the situation presented in the exercise were not fatal. Value was extracted by reflecting on what was unrealistic in the exercise runs and why. As discussed further below, this required thorough debriefing with participants. In general, no matter how good the design, exercises are imperfect and simplified reflections of reality. Interpretation and translation are absolutely required if they are to be valuable to both participants and researchers.

First step, not the final decision

As discussed earlier in this chapter, RPS exercises are most suitable as groups start to explore new challenges, engage stakeholders that do not have extensive histories of working together, and experiment with new tools and approaches to assessing risks and making decisions. They are good conversation starters. Exercises can also be very effective for groups to practice their skills and test preparedness for rare but highly impactful events – hence the popularity of military drills (i.e., 'war games') and mock catastrophe exercises for first responders. Exercises are typically less appropriate for arriving at a final decision around how to proceed with policymaking, planning or infrastructure investment decisions. They are, by necessity, typically gross simplifications of reality, and thus must be understood within the wider context of decision-making, which, for better or worse, involves a variety of considerations that may not be accurately reflected in an exercise. This includes the political dimension of decision-making, in which elected officials need to balance different interests and consider what is politically feasible. It also includes the legal dimension; exercises usually contain some constraints, but it is virtually impossible for them to reflect all of the legislative and regulatory constraints on real-world decision-making, not to mention the additional burdens associated with defending decisions through court challenges. In addition to political and legal complexities, exercises usually cannot convey or contain all of the technical considerations that will ultimately factor into real-world decision-making. Ideally, they reflect the most salient scientific and technical information and can equip participants to engage in conversations around *the facts*, but they are not comprehensive. Exercises are typically best understood as valuable pieces of wider strategies of social learning and collaborative problem solving, and not as solutions in their own right as groups grapple with how to proceed in the face of complex issues. Debriefing and fostering wider reflection on the lessons learned through exercises can be a critical piece of making exercises useful for participants.

Importance of debriefing

Experiences in the Harboring Uncertainty project suggest that many of the lessons learned by participants do not come directly from the exercise, but rather from *reflecting* on what happened during the debriefings. It is during the debriefings that participants can collectively process and make sense of what happened and draw useful conclusions to inform their own practices. This suggests that RPS exercises can indeed offer a valuable inflection point, introducing various issues and concepts, but that much of the learning comes from drawing insights from the experience that can inform decision-making back in the real world. Researchers and facilitators employing exercises need to both leave ample time for debriefing and provide a framework that will invoke reflection on the relevant themes. From a research perspective, supplementary research tools – which included pre- and post-exercise surveys, interviews and background research in the case of the Harboring Uncertainty project – are also very important for triangulating findings.

Debriefing requires thoughtful facilitation, which typically involves walking a fine line between letting participants independently work through what they learned, often yielding insights not previously known to the facilitator, and helping them organize their thoughts and keeping them trained on the core issues (Dennehy et al. 1998). When using games for research purposes, working through validity and reliability issues with participants might follow a phased framework that involves questions to help participants 'cool down'; working through the chain of events with them; looking for counterfactuals and their importance; determining the internal validity of the key variables in the exercise and confounding variables that shaped the outcomes; assessing the generalizability of the findings; discussing how realistic the exercise was; assessing the robustness of what happened against what might have happened under different conditions; and determining if, how and why lessons learned might be applied in the real world (van den Hoogen et al. 2016). Harboring Uncertainty exercise debriefings loosely followed some guiding questions to get at these dynamics. For example, the questions, 'How substantial of a challenge was uncertainty in the exercise? How did you manage it?' were asked to foster discussion around whether uncertainty was a barrier to action, and why, which was one of the key research objectives.

Effective debriefing often also requires a certain degree of interrogation. Some of the turns and outcomes in the A New Connection in Westerberg exercise runs were likely unrealistic, compared to the real-world situations the participants were coming from. An example is the influence the environmental NGO representative had in one of the Singapore runs. Nonetheless, discussion around why the environmentalist was influential when similar actors would not be at the table in a parallel real-world situation was informative. In that case, the particular player's ability to make what others perceived to be strong, factual arguments won them over. Participants reflected that they did not think 'greenies' would engage in the same way in the real world. However, they felt that the power of the 'logical' argument to win the day in their rationalist paradigm was realistic and, this experience provided food for thought as adaptation evolves and arguments are made around how it should be integrated into planning and decision-making and who should be at the table.

Extracting wider lessons for policymaking and planning

As discussed earlier in this chapter, the Harboring Uncertainty project explicitly focused on action research. That is, on meeting the dual objectives of providing a valuable experience for participants while concurrently drawing wider lessons to inform our growing understanding of how to effectively advance climate adaptation, and planning and policymaking in other situations rife with complexity, uncertainty and institutional ambiguity (Schenk and Susskind 2014). The lessons drawn from the project, which underscore this book, suggest that serious games can play a significant role in the research process. However, as discussed in the previous section, most of the learning comes not from what happens within the exercise, but from how participants reflect afterwards. This highlights the importance of other, complementary, research tools, including pre- and post-exercise surveys, debriefings and follow-up interviews.

Steps can also be taken to enhance the efficacy of exercises from a research perspective. Chief among them is designing exercises to intentionally invoke deliberation – and later reflection – around key variables. For example, multiple scenarios were introduced in one version of the A New Connection in Westerberg exercise to experiment with if and how participants would use them, compared to groups that were given a single risk assessment forecast. This approach – designing two different versions of the exercise, assigning participants to the respective versions with an eye towards keeping the groups as similar as possible (to minimize the confounding variables), and including questions in the surveys, debriefings and follow-up interviews – was taken to explicitly generate research insights. In the context of action research, it is important to be deliberate when integrating various elements into the exercise; some should be designed to generate research insights, others to convey lessons to participants, and still others to accomplish both.

Conclusion

In the spirit of action research, the Harboring Uncertainty project employed an RPS exercise in an effort to provide value to those who participated, while generating research insights (Schenk and Susskind 2014). This chapter has examined whether exercises can be impactful for those engaged, and in what ways. The answer to the first question seems to be a resounding 'yes' – RPS exercises can be a valuable tool for researchers that aim to directly engage in reflection and problem solving with stakeholders. In terms of the *ways* in which they are impactful, the evidence collected from pre- and post-exercise surveys, debriefing conversations and follow-up interviews suggests that participants learned a great deal from participating. There were statistically significant increases from pre- to post-exercise in key areas, including participants' perceptions of how significant of a factor uncertainty is in climate adaptation, how important they feel it is to engage with other decision-makers and stakeholders, and their self-reported awareness of climate change and the risks it may pose. Participants were nearly unanimous in reporting that they learned from the experience. Key themes that emerged when asked what they learned include the importance of good process and how different process design and actions on the part of participants can shape the outcomes; the importance of bringing parties together and getting information on the table to generate wise and broadly supported solutions; and the nature of uncertainty in decision-making and how it might challenge them to reconsider the ways in which they make decisions.

Notes

1 Hypothesis: Exercise participation will increase participants' awareness of climate risks. Question asked: 'How aware would you say you are of climate change and the risks it may pose?' The results were significant at the $p = 0.001$ level, using a Wilcoxon matched pairs signed ranks ($N = 26$, $T = 61$; one-tailed hypothesis). Therefore, the null hypothesis can be rejected.

2   Hypothesis: Exercise participation will shift respondents' opinions on how much of a factor uncertainty is in climate change adaptation. Question asked: 'To what degree is uncertainty a factor in how your organization views and plans for climate change adaptation?' The results were significant at the $p = 0.01$ level, using a Wilcoxon matched pairs signed ranks ($N = 47$, $T = 193$; two-tailed hypothesis). Therefore, the null hypothesis can be rejected. There was not a statistically significant shift in participants' perceptions of 'uncertainty in general' as a factor in decision-making. However, as noted, the average response was high both before and after.

3   Hypothesis: Exercise participation will increase participants' confidence in their ability to manage the risks and uncertainty posed by climate change. Question asked: 'How confident are you that you and other stakeholders will be able to manage the risks and uncertainties climate change poses?' The results were significant at the $p = 0.05$ level, using a Wilcoxon matched pairs signed ranks ($N = 41$, $T = 300$; one-tailed hypothesis). Therefore, the null hypothesis can be rejected.

4   The Likert scale question asked was: 'How has your confidence in the ability of your organization and other stakeholders to adapt to the risks climate change poses changed as a result of your participation in this exercise (1 being less confident, 7 being more confident and 4 being neutral)?'

5   Hypothesis: Exercise participation will increase participants' opinions on the importance of engagement. Question asked: 'How important is it that you engage with other decision-makers and stakeholders as you plan and make decisions?' The results were significant at the $p = 0.005$ level, using a Wilcoxon matched pairs signed ranks ($N = 43$, $T = 253.5$; one-tailed hypothesis). Therefore, the null hypothesis can be rejected.

6   Of the 68 participants who answered the question, 'Did you learn anything from the exercise that you might be able to apply to your own planning and decision-making?' 66 answered positively.

Works cited

Abt, C.C. (2002) *Serious Games*. Lanham, MD: University Press of America.

Bollinger, L.A., C.W.J. Bogmans, E.J.L. Chappin, G.P.J. Dijkema, J.N. Huibregtse, N. Maas, T. Schenk, M. Snelder, P. van Thienen, S. de Wit, B. Wols and L.A. Tavasszy (2014). Climate adaptation of interconnected infrastructures: A framework for supporting governance. *Regional Environmental Change*, 14: 919–931.

Dennehy, R.F., R.R. Sims and H.E. Colins (1998). Debriefing experiential learning exercises: A theoretical and practical guide for success. *Journal of Management Education*, 22(1): 9–25.

DiMaggio, P.J. and W.W. Powell (1983). The iron cage revisited: Institutional isomorphism and collective rationality in organizational fields. *American Sociological Review*, 48(2): 147–160.

Dolin, E.J. and L.E. Susskind (1992). A role for simulations in public policy disputes: The case of national energy policy. *Simulation & Gaming*, 23(1): 20–44.

Hajer, M. (2003). Policy without polity? Policy analysis in the institutional void. *Policy Sciences*, 36: 175–195.

Haywood, B.K., A. Brennan, K. Dow, N.P. Kettle and K. Lackstrom (2014). Negotiating a mainstreaming spectrum: Climate change response and communication in the Carolinas. *Journal of Environmental Policy & Planning*, 16(1): 75–94.

Humans vs. Mosquitoes (2014). http://humansvsmosquitoes.com/

Innes, J.E. and D.E. Booher (2010). *Planning With Complexity: An Introduction to Collaborative Rationality for Public Policy*. New York, NY: Routledge.

Mayer, I.S. (2009). The gaming of policy and the politics of gaming: A review. *Simulation & Gaming*, 40(6): 825–862.

Mendler de Suarez, J., P. Suarez, C. Bachofen, N. Fortugno, J. Goentzel, P. Gonçalves, N. Grist, C. Macklin, K. Pfeifer, S. Schweizer, M. van Aalst and H. Virji (2012). *Games for a New Climate: Experiencing the Complexity of Future Risks*. Pardee Center Task Force Report. Boston, MA: The Frederick S. Pardee Center for the Study of the Longer-Range Future.

Moser, S.C. and J.A. Ekstrom (2010). A Framework to Diagnose Barriers to Climate Change Adaptation. *PNAS*, 107(51): 22026–22031.

Quick, K.S. and M.S. Feldman (2014). Boundaries as junctures: Collaborative boundary work for building efficient resilience. *Journal of Public Administration Research and Theory*, doi:10.1093/jopart/mut085

Romsdahl, R.J. (2011). Decision support for climate change adaptation planning in the US: Why it needs a coordinated internet-based practitioners' network. *Climatic Change*, 106: 507–536.

Rumore, D., T. Schenk and L. Susskind (2016). Role-play simulations for climate change adaptation education and engagement. *Nature Climate Change*, 6: 745–750.

Schenk, T. (2014). Boats and bridges in the sandbox: Using role play simulation exercises to help infrastructure planners prepare for the risks and uncertainties associated with climate change. *Infranomics: Sustainability, Engineering Design and Governance*. A.V. Gheorghe, M. Masera and P.F. Katina, Eds. Berlin, Germany: Springer.

Schenk, T. and L. Susskind (2014). Gaming for action: Role-play simulation exercises for participatory action research on climate change adaptation. *Action Research for Adaptation Practices: Developing and Applying Knowledge for Governance*. A. van Buuren, J Eshuis and M. van Vliet, Eds. London, UK: Routledge.

Susskind, L. (2010). Responding to the risks posed by climate change: Cities have no choice but to adapt. *The Town Planning Review*, 81(3): 217–235.

Susskind, L. and J. Corburn (1999). Using simulations to teach negotiation: Pedagogical theory and practice. *PON Working Paper*, 99-3. Cambridge, MA: Program on Negotiation at Harvard Law School.

Susskind, L. and J. Cruikshank (1987). *Breaking the Impasse: Consensual Approaches to Resolving Public Disputes*. New York, NY: Basic Books.

Susskind, L., D. Rumore, C. Hulet and P. Field (2015). *Better Safe Than Sorry: Helping Costal Communities Anticipate and Manage Climate Change Risks*. London, UK: Anthem Press.

Susskind, L. and T. Schenk (2014). Can games really change the course of history? *Négociations*, 2(22): 29–39.

Tucker, D. (2012). Gaming Our Way to a Better Future. *Wilson Center Policy Brief*. Washington, DC: The Wilson Center.

Tygron (2015). *Showcase Lower Manhattan*. www.tygron.com/showcases/showcase-lower-manhattan

van den Hoogen, J., J. Lo and S. Meijer (2016). Debriefing research games: Context, substance and method. *Simulation & Gaming*, 47(3): 368–388.

7 Uncertain decision-making
The use of multiple scenarios

Introduction

Uncertainty is a very real factor in much of our planning and decision-making. This is particularly true when advancing climate adaptation, as there is typically substantial uncertainty within the scientific and technical information available, conditions are stochastic and dynamic in nature, and systems models point towards a wide range of possible futures. Furthermore, as discussed throughout this book, much of the uncertainty is not even scientific in nature; the complex institutional environments that policymaking and planning take place in, particularly around nascent issues like climate adaptation that have not yet been institutionalized, can be a significant source of uncertainty.

Despite persistent uncertainty, policy makers, planners and other stakeholders need to find ways to make recommendations and decisions at various stages throughout the infrastructure design and implementation process. We cannot simply throw our hands in the air and stop developing and managing our infrastructure systems because we lack complete information. This chapter illustrates the daunting challenge of working through uncertainty in project-level decision-making. In particular, it examines the use of multiple scenarios as products to inform decision-making.

Scenario planning has been advanced as a powerful way to both highlight and bracket uncertainties; users devise multiple possible futures (i.e., scenarios) and seek solutions that are robust against the range of them. Most of the existing literature focuses on the *scenario planning process*. This chapter takes a different point of view, exploring how the scenarios that come out of planning processes might inform decisions being made down the line. That is, it considers how groups might actually use the resulting scenarios in practice when they must make project-level decisions and were not part of the initial scenario-building process. It enhances our understanding of the value and possible limitations of scenarios as *products*.

The Harboring Uncertainty project introduced in the first chapter of this book is the primary source of data for this chapter. Seventy-six stakeholders in three coastal cities – Singapore, Rotterdam and Boston – were engaged to explore how they make decisions in the face of significant and persistent uncertainties, in particular those emanating from climate change, and how they might improve their decision-making in practice. Half of the exercise groups were given multiple plausible scenarios of the future, and the other half a single probabilistic forecast of the risks posed by climate change. Lessons are drawn from their comparative experiences.

The findings suggest that the value of multiple scenarios, particularly as inputs for project-level decision-making, is mixed in practice. Virtually all stakeholders engaged liked the idea of considering multiple possible futures in their planning and decision-making. However, insights drawn from the role-play simulation exercise runs and debriefing conversations suggest that it can be challenging to figure out how best to use them in practice, particularly when it comes time to make decisions at the project level. The use of multiple scenarios seems to accentuate uncertainties and make them more explicit, for better *and* worse. They encourage users to consider the implications of an uncertain future but do not inherently provide the tools they need to make sense of those implications and move forward. One substantial challenge is that stakeholders at all levels are typically used to working with single design standards or conditions, and the scenarios call them into question. Even if the traditional standards should be questioned, it can be uncomfortable to confront uncertainty. Discomfort does not always breed constructive responses. In the exercise runs conducted with Harboring Uncertainty participants, some responded by quickly defaulting to a single scenario, often the worst case, while others were paralyzed. Neither of those options entails the productive consideration of their implications. This does not in any way obviate the value of scenario planning as a process, but it does suggest that we need to be realistic about the limitations of the products (i.e., scenarios).

Background: scenarios and scenario planning

In the context of strategic planning, scenarios are future worlds that are entirely plausible. They represent potential trajectories that could come to pass if key conditions (i.e., 'drivers of change') evolve in one way rather than another. While individually unlikely, a range of scenarios is supposed to illustrate the breadth of possible futures vis-à-vis the important factors in any given situation. The consideration of multiple scenarios is promoted as a way to better understand and bracket unresolvable uncertainties. As illustrated in Figure 7.1, scenario planning, which is the process of constructing and evaluating scenarios, involves identifying bounding conditions, drivers of change and key uncertainties, and using them to develop a range of possible futures (i.e., scenarios) that the robustness of options can be evaluated against (Schoemaker 2004). This is often, although certainly not always, a multi-stakeholder effort, rather than done by a single or small team of experts. Scenario planning processes generate multiple internally consistent possible futures against which decisions can be evaluated (Chermack, Lynham and Ruona 2001; Cornelius, Van de Putte and Romani 2005). Rather than predicting the future, users recognize that there are various possible futures and consider the robustness of their options against each of them

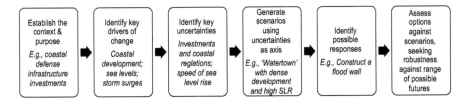

Figure 7.1 The scenario planning process
Source: Adapted from Aldrich 2011; Schoemaker 1995

(Schoemaker 2004). Scenarios can help decision-makers overcome 'overconfidence' and 'tunnel vision' (Schoemaker 1995).

Scenario planning was first prominent in the private sector, with Royal Dutch Shell being an early adopter. It is, however, gaining traction among government agencies in various sectors and at all levels around the world as a way to make sense of, and proceed despite, uncertainty around the future. Looking across a wide range of cases, Chakraborty and McMillan (2015) have devised a 'scenario typology for planning practitioners' with the following major components:

- Organizational structure – unitary, strong leader or loose coalition
- Scope – single issue, comprehensive or problem-oriented
- Scenario type – normative, predictive or explorative
- Outcome – awareness, vision or policy recommendation
- Stakeholder engagement – general public, government agencies or interest groups
- Participation extent – inform only, seeking feedback or joint fact-finding
- Engagement medium – web-based, face-to-face or hybrid
- Scenario construction and analysis tools – qualitative, planning support systems or computer modeling
- Resources – statutory or recurring, opportunity-based or fundraised

This typology provides a useful way to systematically design and examine scenario planning efforts. Based on their coding of 68 projects using this typology, Chakraborty and McMillan (2015) consider when and by whom various process design choices might be made and explore the tradeoffs between different options. They also identify common relationships across the categories, provide examples of processes that fall into the various categories and note that some may fall into more than one basket for each component. While they are careful to avoid definitive judgements on which design choices might be more or less appropriate, noting that each case will demand a different process, future empirical analysis might shed further light on which approaches are more or less successful in different contexts.

While increasingly popular in various planning contexts, scenario planning has gained particular attention in the context of climate change adaptation as a way for groups to systematically consider multiple vulnerabilities, structure decisions and encourage robust responses (Lempert 2012; Moore, Seavy and Gerhart 2013). Adaptation often does not require absolute certainty, but benefits from an understanding of the range of what is possible. Applications of scenario planning abound, including in the Netherlands, Singapore and the United States. Scenarios are even being devised at the global level as a way to assess climate impacts (IPCC 2012).

Regions like the Snohomish Basin in Washington State (USA) are using climate change as one 'driver of uncertainty', coupled with another – the "relationship between society and nature" in that case – to construct 'stories' about what the future might look like (Alberti, Russo and Tenneson 2013). Participants in the Snohomish process used the scenarios to explore potential future challenges to and opportunities with the provision of ecosystem services. Municipal agencies like Denver Water are using scenarios to make sure they are considering multiple plausible futures as part of their 'integrated resource planning' efforts (Quay 2010). This led them to adopt a series of 'flexible adaptation strategies'. Some efforts, like the Las Cienegas National Conservation Area process initiated by the U.S. Bureau of Land Management, are integrating scenario planning into larger ongoing efforts that feature other approaches, such as collaborative adaptive management (Caves, Bodner, Simms, Fisher and Robertson 2013).

In the Netherlands, the Rotterdam Climate Change Adaptation Strategy features four 'delta scenarios': *full*, with moderate climate change and high growth; *steam*, with high growth and rapid climate change; *calm*, with low growth and socioeconomic decline; and *hot*, with rapid climate change and socioeconomic decline (Rotterdam Climate Initiative 2013). These scenarios are derived, in part, from the Royal Netherlands Meteorological Institute's Climate Scenarios (KNMI 2014). The city's more recent 'Resilience Strategy' discusses multiple scenarios, but gives particular prominence to an aspirational 'Rotterdam tomorrow: A resilient future scenario' (Rotterdam Climate Initiative 2016). The vision presented is one in which the city is the undisputed 'water capital of the world', having capitalized on climate change as an 'opportunity' to reinvent itself and export its know-how as "Europe's most innovative learning city". In general, scenario planning is widely employed in Rotterdam and throughout the Netherlands to frame discussions around a variety of topics, ranging from security policy to the opportunities for a 'data-driven smart city' (Nenciu, van der Duin, Janssen, Snijders and Hulstijn 2016).

Boston's current climate change adaptation efforts are considering multiple emissions scenarios; they do translate them into SLR projections but do not involve multi-factor scenarios based on two or more axes of uncertainty (Douglas et al. 2016; Greenovate Boston 2016). The different emissions scenarios are primarily used to describe when there is more or less uncertainty, and how that uncertainty increases the further we look into the future (Douglas et al. 2016).

In Singapore, scenarios are widely used by the strategic planning and 'foresight' units within various agencies. The Centre for Strategic Futures in the Prime

Minister's Office prepares high-profile national scenarios using a foresight process they call 'scenario planning plus' (Centre for Strategic Futures 2016a). One of the Centre's more recent projects generated 18 'Driving Forces Cards', which illustrate some of the key trends that are likely to shape Singapore, and in particular its public administration, over the next 20 years. They fall into different thematic categories, including the 'Future of Technology' and the 'Future of Singaporean Society', and are designed to be conversation starters as agencies engage in thinking about multiple possible futures. One of the cards focuses on 'Climate Change and the Global Carbon Regime'; it very briefly summarizes the risks climate change may pose and Singapore's commitments (Centre for Strategic Futures 2016b).

In the context of transportation infrastructure, the Federal Highway Administration in the United States is encouraging and supporting the uptake of scenario planning among agencies based on the premise that by using "the scenario planning technique, transportation agencies can make better decisions about how to develop a transportation system that responds to a wide range of factors and trends" (Volpe Center 2011a, i). Federal Highway Administration–funded pilot projects have experimented with the use of scenario planning, including a multistakeholder effort to advance integrated land-use and transportation planning while considering the impacts of climate change on Cape Cod in Massachusetts (Volpe Center 2011b). The U.S. Department of Housing and Urban Development (HUD) has also encouraged the adoption of scenario planning techniques to advance integrated land-use and transportation planning through their Sustainable Communities Regional Planning Grants program (Chakraborty and McMillan 2015). Boston's Metropolitan Planning Organization is using four scenarios based on different potential investment approaches in their long-range transportation planning process (MPO 2015).

Critiques of scenarios and scenario planning

Various critiques have been leveled at the use of scenarios, including that (Chakraborty and McMillan 2015; Chermack et al. 2001; Schoemaker 1998, 2004):

- processes and scenarios can be subjective in nature;
- they can inadequately consider uncertainties;
- the limited number of scenarios can be problematic;
- conversely, too many scenarios can overwhelm;
- they often default to a single preferred or seemingly likely future;
- they do not always adequately involve various stakeholders, including the public, and gather an adequate range of perspectives;
- processes are prone to political interference and constraints;
- a lack of political and/or agency leadership support can render useless; and
- it is often unclear how the scenarios connect and will translate into better decisions in practice.

Bartholomew (2007) analyzed 80 different integrated transportation and land-use scenario planning efforts in the United States and found that they frequently fell short, with the outcomes already predetermined, only cursory stakeholder involvement, substandard assessment methods and unclear outcomes. Zegras and Rayle (2012) examined the use of scenario planning in transportation and urban planning in Portugal and found that it has only modest impacts on participants' propensity to collaborate in the future, in part because of challenges like 'vague problem definition'.

Even proponents acknowledge the challenges and limitations. Chakraborty, Kaza, Knaap and Deal (2011) are bullish on their use in regional planning, but find that groups often fail to adequately consider uncertainty and end up default-ing to a single scenario. Quay (2010) asserts that scenario planning is a powerful tool, but notes that it requires an ongoing commitment to monitoring and incre-mental decision-making, multi-agency and stakeholder engagement, and real changes in governance frameworks. As discussed elsewhere in this book, these conditions are often particularly weak in the context of climate change adaptation of interconnected infrastructures that involves weak institutions and significant uncertainty.

Hypotheses: the advantages and disadvantages of using scenarios

The benefits and challenges associated with scenario planning are relatively well understood, but a recurring theme is the dearth of research on – and thus evidence for if and how – the scenarios generated influence actual planning, policy formu-lation and project-level decision-making at later stages. Those involved in sce-nario planning processes are not always the same as those making decisions down the line, so the question is what value the scenarios have when the scenario plan-ning effort is over and decisions are being made. This chapter explores whether the provision of multiple possible futures (i.e., scenarios) makes a difference in how decision-makers and other stakeholders evaluate project-level choices. The Harboring Uncertainty research project it draws from did not examine scenario planning as a process, but rather the value of the scenarios as products.

The initial hypothesis was that using multiple scenarios as a tool for framing uncertainty and making decisions can enhance climate change adaptation plan-ning efforts. The findings discussed in this chapter suggest that the benefits are not so straightforward, as groups may find it challenging to inject multiple sce-narios into project-level decision-making. Six sub-hypotheses were examined; in some cases, the findings seem to affirm the central hypothesis while in others they illustrate the complications associated with considering multiple possible futures when making infrastructure decisions.

One sub-hypothesis was that scenarios would draw greater attention to the process design (i.e., the institutional arrangements for decision-making). The premise was that the introduction of scenarios as a new component would open up the entire process to greater critique. That is, when groups were challenged to consider options against multiple scenarios to assess robustness, this would invoke some participants to challenge the entire decision-making process and how the group operates. The supposition was that a Pandora's Box of attention to process design would be opened, resulting in delays, frustration and/or more pressure on the facilitators. As discussed below, elements of this did emerge in this project. To the degree that they were considered at all, the scenarios complicated decision-making.

A second, very much related sub-hypothesis was that new forms of discourse would emerge because of the emphasis placed on uncertainty. The supposition was that the explicit attention paid to uncertainty when using scenarios would focus the discourse on making the best choice in the face of multiple possible futures, rather than on parties justifying their respective positions on the basis of, or focusing on discrediting, a single forecast. This did *not* emerge in the research; as discussed below, the parties did not deeply consider the scenarios and thus avoided any substantial shifts in discourse and the framing of uncertainty.

A somewhat contradictory sub-hypothesis to the previous was that parties might use scenarios as ammunition. That is, parties will use the scenarios that best justify their respective positions to further make their cases, discounting the scenarios that contradict their positions or better advance others'. As a result, rather than diminishing disagreements and facilitating consensus around the best path forward, scenarios might contribute to more persistent disagreement, especially insofar as they embrace rather than reduce uncertainty. The findings suggest that this is a concern; parties did, in fact, default to the scenario that affirmed their respective worldviews, rather than genuinely considering multiple possible futures.

A fourth sub-hypothesis was that different coalitions among different stakeholders might emerge when the scenarios are introduced. The suspicion was that the scenarios could lead to different alliances than would otherwise emerge, as parties that would otherwise be compelled to plan for the (single) forecast provided are given more license to consider alternative options. This may lead to parties taking different positions and thus forming different relationships with others. Here, too, the findings suggest that this may be a factor – to some degree, participants did indeed ally with others with shared visions of the most likely future.

The introduction of multiple scenarios may take many participants, and especially those trained as engineers, outside of their comfort zones because of the lack of a single variable forecast of future conditions on which decisions can be based. A sub-hypothesis was thus that engineers are trained to work with estimates and associated probability distributions, adding additional factors of safety as prescribed, and thus would be uncomfortable with multiple possible futures. This may be particularly true when the scenarios are qualitative in nature, with no probabilities attached, and thus cannot easily be translated into engineering parameters. A corollary expectation was that participants would ultimately default to the single scenario they deem most appropriate or disregard the others altogether. As noted above and discussed more extensively later in this chapter, participants did, for the most part, default to a single scenario. However, it is not clear that this phenomenon was any more or less prevalent among engineers versus policy experts and other stakeholders.

A final sub-hypothesis was that the explicit recognition of multiple possible futures would lead to the favoring of flexibility. Because multiple scenarios accentuate uncertainty, the suspicion was that flexibility would emerge as a way to remain agile, rather than adopting other responses to uncertainty, like using a single worst-case scenario or deferring to experts. As discussed below, the findings strongly suggest that the presentation of multiple scenarios can, in fact, encourage stakeholders to seek flexible pathways forward.

Methods: examining the value of scenarios

As discussed more extensively in the first chapter of this book, the research undergirding the findings in this chapter employed an experimental design. Seventy-six infrastructure planners, decision-makers and other stakeholders in Singapore, Rotterdam and Boston were involved in a role-play simulation exercise to examine, among other things, how they would handle the introduction of multiple scenarios into a simulated decision-making process. The exercise is discussed in greater detail in chapter 6. These cities were chosen for various reasons, including their significant coastal vulnerabilities under climate change, highly developed infrastructure networks and very different public administration and policy arrangements. The RPS exercise placed participants in a simulated environment not radically different from their own situations, yet abstracted for the purposes of both simplification and freer experimentation. As discussed below, half of the groups in each city were given exercise instructions that included multiple scenarios, while the other half were given a single risk assessment forecast. This allowed for the comparison of process and outcomes, as the exercises and groups were otherwise largely the same.

From a research perspective, participants completed pre-exercise surveys when they first arrived for the half-day workshops in each city. They were then provided instructions for the RPS exercise, which is called A New Connection in Westerberg. General instructions set the scene: participants became members of a taskforce grappling with how they might revise transportation infrastructure plans – and in particular plans to build a new road into and out of a congested port area – in light of new information on the potential impacts of climate change. Each participant was also assigned a role, of which there were seven, ranging from a senior engineer from the National Transportation Agency to the director of community and government relations from the Port Authority. The participants were given the hypothetical situation, assigned their roles and asked to deliberate.

As noted previously, there are two versions of the exercise, which were played by different but similarly constituted groups of participants in each city. One version includes the multiple qualitative scenarios presented in Figure 7.2. The other includes a risk assessment forecast that introduces the various climatic variables and their potential impacts, providing some probabilities around how they might affect infrastructure, but does not include scenarios. Running

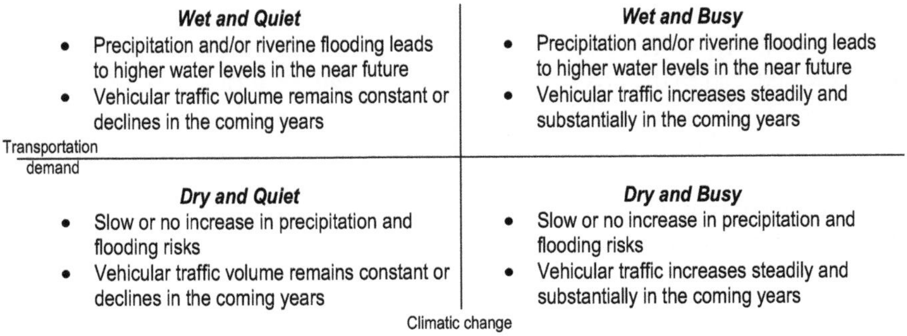

Wet and Quiet	**Wet and Busy**
• Precipitation and/or riverine flooding leads to higher water levels in the near future • Vehicular traffic volume remains constant or declines in the coming years	• Precipitation and/or riverine flooding leads to higher water levels in the near future • Vehicular traffic increases steadily and substantially in the coming years

Transportation
demand

Dry and Quiet	**Dry and Busy**
• Slow or no increase in precipitation and flooding risks • Vehicular traffic volume remains constant or declines in the coming years	• Slow or no increase in precipitation and flooding risks • Vehicular traffic increases steadily and substantially in the coming years

Climatic change

Figure 7.2 Scenarios presented in the scenarios version of the Westerberg exercise
Used with permission of author

otherwise identical versions of the exercise with groups comprised of participants assigned to be relatively similar in composition allowed for examination of the differences in process and outcomes when multiple scenarios are introduced. That is, it allowed for significant control of confounding variables so that the effects of the independent variable (i.e., the presence or absence of scenarios) could be better understood.

The exercise runs took approximately 90 minutes and were video recorded, transcribed and coded for analysis. As discussed in Chapter 6, the RPS provided a low-cost way to foster reflection and facilitate experimentation, including with the use of scenarios, around a planning challenge that was relatively new for most people involved. Debrief discussions – which were also recorded and coded – immediately followed the exercise runs in each city. These discussions were informal in nature, loosely following a set of guiding questions. This phase was critical from both an educational perspective for the participants and a research perspective, as much was learned from reflecting on participants' experiences, what they suggest about how agencies and other stakeholders might advance climate adaptation, and what might be more or less realistic and appropriate in their respective real-world institutional environments. Participants were invited to further reflect during one-on-one interviews in the days following each workshop. These interviews dug further into their experiences in the exercise and how they relate to participants' own organizations and their roles vis-à-vis climate change adaptation.

Last but not least, from a research perspective, participants completed surveys at the end of each workshop. The pre- and post-exercise surveys provided descriptive statistics, including demographic information (pre-exercise survey) and feedback on the RPS experience (post-exercise survey). Wilcoxon matched pairs signed-rank tests were used to test the significance of participants' shifts from before to after the exercise on a range of questions.

Findings: using multiple scenarios in decision-making

The findings from the Harboring Uncertainty project suggest that those engaged in decision-making around infrastructure investments can find the injection of multiple scenarios disquieting. They underscore the uncertainties, clouding users' perceptions of the future. This can be a good thing, insofar as the uncertainties are real and deserve attention. However, individual and collective responses are not always productive. The findings suggest that the added complication can paralyze decision-making, as users become frozen rather than finding ways to make decisions despite persistent uncertainties. Conversely, others simply ignore the multiple scenarios and default to planning for a single scenario (i.e., possible future). While this provides a pathway forward, it can obviate the benefits of generating scenarios in the first place. It can also precipitate arguments around *which* future is most likely or concerning, and thus should be planned for, which is not the intention of scenario planning processes.

Scenario planning is touted as a way for agencies to assess the robustness of their proposals when confronted with uncertainties, including those associated with climate change. The assertion is that projects and policies vetted against a range of possible futures will be more robust. This research suggests that there are advantages, disadvantages and significant challenges to using scenarios in practice. They can make uncertainties more explicit, providing a vivid and accurate sense of the range of possible futures. However, the consideration of multiple futures does not always fit well with planning and decision-making processes accustomed to using single forecasts for their design conditions. The use of scenarios, particularly in project-level decision-making, is not yet well-understood. Despite the increasing use of scenario planning, it is virtually always conducted within broader, more strategic-level processes and not at the project level.

While not a normal part of planning and decision-making, especially at the project level, scenario planning processes have been conducted in all three countries in which the Harboring Uncertainty project was conducted. In fact, most participants reported previous experience using multiple scenarios – 86% of participants in Boston, 82% in Singapore and 93% in Rotterdam. However, these experiences were all at a more strategic level rather than project level. Reflecting on their previous experiences with scenarios, participants were positive. Asked how 'useful' the consideration of multiple scenarios is in their work, the average responses among those who reported prior experience using them were 6.2 in Boston, 5.6 in Singapore and 5.8 in Rotterdam (on a 7-point Likert scale). Participants also reflected positively on the value of scenarios when asked. "[It was] good that we could see a world in which very different things could happen", reflected a participant in Boston. Scenarios are valuable because "it's not wise to have all your eggs in one basket, [and they allow you to] pursue multiple alternatives simultaneously, and give you a framework for decision-making going forward because there are so many unknown variables", reflected another participant, adding that they facilitate the creation of "if–then statements to prepare for multiple possible futures".

Table 7.1 Comparison of the scenarios versus risk assessment versions of the exercise

	Scenarios	Risk assessment
Process	Largely *ignored scenarios*. Most groups implicitly or explicitly defaulted to the worst-case scenario (i.e., 'wet and busy')	Parties either *accepted or rejected* forecast, based on their interests
	However, *accentuated uncertainty* (for example, the scenarios groups took longer on average)	Some debate around why these forecasts should be questioned as more tenuous than others used in decision-making
Outcomes	Greater *difficulty reaching agreement*. Three of five groups concluded with *calls for more research*	Mix of outcomes: B+, two D+s, and two no agreements (one almost an A+)
	Favored D+ option (chosen in two groups, two others leaning towards and still on table for fifth), which may be seen as the *most flexible*	No agreements were *impasses in negotiations*, rather than calls for more research

Despite the positive opinions of participants, the experiences they had during the RPS exercise runs suggest that the benefits are far from decisive. The key outcomes of the10 groups across the three cities are summarized in Table 2.2 in the second chapter and discussed in greater detail within the case (i.e., city) chapters. The differences across the10 exercise runs may be attributed to various factors. Nonetheless, comparing and contrasting the five groups that used the version with multiple scenarios against the five groups that used the version with a single risk assessment reveals some patterns in terms of both the processes they followed and the outcomes they reached; these differences are summarized in Table 7.1.

Multiple scenarios ignored

The instructions provided to those who participated in the scenarios version of the exercise clearly instructed them to go through a process that involved comparing their options against each of the scenarios to assess their robustness. Despite this, only one of the five groups that played that version explicitly used the scenarios, methodically evaluating the various infrastructure options against each of them as part of their decision-making process. Furthermore, even in that case (in Boston), the chair concluded the exploratory phase of their deliberations by suggesting that they focus in on one scenario as they shift to decision-making, stating:

> So now is when we craft a recommendation . . . We talked about a lot of things, but if we had to come up with a recommendation, what do you think it should be? A, B, C or D? [And] what are we planning for? What type of scenario are we planning for?

All of the other groups largely disregarded the scenarios, typically implicitly or explicitly defaulting to the worst-case scenario (i.e., 'wet and busy'). This observation controverts the hypothesis that the scenarios would draw greater attention to the process design, upending it. Instead, participants, at most, considered the various scenarios but then defaulted to the procedural tasks of assessing their options and making decisions using what they saw as the single most likely or appropriate scenario to plan for. Participants later reflected that they did not use the scenarios when it came time to make decisions, because they felt that they needed to base their decision-making on something concrete; the worst-case scenario was believable to them and encouraged them to make 'robust' decisions. Participants noted that planning for the worst-case scenario is typically not the standard practice in the real world, given limited resources and the subsequent need to satisfice, but nor is the use of scenarios when making concrete decisions. Agencies often find ways to get by, try to remain flexible and balance the costs and benefits, but they do not explicitly consider multiple possible futures.

Uncertainty accentuated

While the scenarios did not precipitate fundamental changes to the decision-making processes followed in most cases – and even the one group that did explicitly consider their options against the scenarios defaulted to a single standard when it came time to make decisions – their presence did seem to have an impact on the discourse. The scenarios implicitly, if not always explicitly, emphasized the presence of uncertainty. On average, the scenarios groups had a harder time reaching agreement and concluded with more calls for research. The debriefings and follow-up interviews suggested that this reflected the challenges associated with embracing uncertainty and finding ways to make decisions in spite of it. Participants reflected that there are advantages and disadvantages to introducing multiple scenarios. They can draw warranted attention to uncertainties, but this can make the process of arriving at a decision more difficult. A participant in Boston reflected in the debriefing that the scenarios groups took longer because they had 'more choice'. Another added that:

> I think scenario planning inevitably engages people in the discussion, and gives people a concrete understanding, whereas the [single] risk assessment is kind of abstract numbers that you have to take at face value, or you dispute, but the scenarios really change how people think and get them talking to each other about it. So, it's more time consuming, but there is a lot more benefit that comes out of it.

A different participant reflected that the risk assessment group that he was a part of was tasked with dealing with the 'cold hard facts' they were given, and were 'less able to think outside the box'. Participants could either accept or challenge the veracity of the forecasts, but the emphasis was not on arriving at a shared sense of uncertainty and how to work through it.

The influence of scenarios on deliberations

Interestingly, the injection of scenarios did not seem to change the coalitional dynamics among participants, compared to those seen in the groups that played the risk assessment version of the exercise, refuting that hypothesis. Nor did the scenarios serve as particularly potent ammunition. In fact, interests-driven contention over the forecasts was clearer in the risk assessment runs, with parties more strongly accepting or rejecting the information given based on their interests and priorities. This might have been because it was easier to decipher their interests vis-à-vis the concrete numbers given, and because the single forecast posed a clearer threat to some than more abstract scenarios and notions of uncertainty.

Some participants did emphasize the uncertainties and risks more than others did, both in the real world and in the exercise. A participant involved in infrastructure planning in the Netherlands reflected that they "take into account that there are different scenarios, but [conclude that] it's good to take into account the worst-case scenario, because the cost may be slightly more, [but] if we don't do it, there [can be] a lot more damage". This reflects a general predilection to robustness and risk aversion. In contrast, a port representative in an exercise run in Boston stated, in character, "I don't care about the future. I have the [transportation] problem now!" During the debriefing, participants reflected that this is a realistic sentiment, given limited resources and acute problems already confronting decision-makers and other stakeholders. Ultimately, the positional and coalitional dynamics varied across the groups, but these differences were attributable to other factors and not to whether the groups played the scenarios vs. non-scenarios version of the exercise. In many cases, they suggest differences across the three cities.

Difficult decisions

Participants reflected that it is difficult to make decisions using multiple scenarios. The outcomes summarized in Table 7.1 would seem to affirm this; three of five scenarios groups concluded with no agreement but rather calls for 'more research'. In contrast, only one of the non-scenarios groups completely failed to reach agreement; this is attributable to the chair's requirement that the group reach complete unanimity. In general, the scenarios groups had a harder time reaching agreement and tended to be deliberating right down to the wire, while the non-scenarios groups typically reached agreement much more easily.

Decision-makers, planners, engineers and other stakeholders are used to working with and designing towards fixed standards, not ranges or multiple possible conditions. "If you want to look at different infrastructure solutions, you don't want to be changing the environmental assumptions", said a participant in Boston. The findings support the hypothesis that engineers and technicians are uncomfortable with multiple scenarios rather than fixed standards. The deeply engrained practice of working with fixed design standards and hard criteria is a substantial barrier to the consideration of multiple scenarios and integration of flexible approaches.

The qualitative and basic nature of the scenarios presented in the exercise may also have reduced their value. A participant in the Netherlands reflected that the scenarios were very 'abstract', requiring users to be 'very visionary' to understand what the implications might be. It is notable, however, that many of the scenarios being developed for climate adaptation planning – including those developed within Rotterdam's adaptation effort – are similar in style.

Flexible solutions recommended

The agreements that scenarios groups *did* reach, or were gravitating towards when the exercise concluded, were all variations of an option that involved expanding the existing roadway, rather than constructing a new one; climate proofing the existing infrastructure; and enhancing freight and/or passenger rail. They prescribed taking these steps in phases as conditions evolve and new information emerges. These recommendations are very flexible in nature, emphasizing adaptive planning as a way to proceed despite persistent uncertainties. This supports the hypothesis that, by fostering greater appreciation for the presence of multiple possible futures, scenarios guide groups towards more flexible approaches. Unfortunately, as discussed further in Chapter 8, institutionalizing flexible approaches is unlikely to be easy in practice.

Scenario planning as a process

While difficult to use in project-level decision-making, many participants reflected that the value of scenarios is in the *process* of scenario planning, which encourages them to think methodically and consider various potential future conditions. Their value is not in arriving at concrete decisions, but rather as an important step in the process of understanding the planning environment before decisions are made. Interviewees emphasized that you still have to make decisions based on concrete numbers, but that scenarios can help you identify which numbers are most appropriate and prepare for both changing conditions and deviations from those numbers as you move forward. In the words of a participant in Singapore:

> So, for example, in the exercise, yes, we come up with the four scenarios, but then after that we ran those four scenarios into yet another set of considerations, which is "okay, are there any down sides?" "No, so, what we can we do?" We selected the worst-case scenario, and then we based our decision on that. So, in a way, it's sort of also part of that analytical process.

The research findings from this project suggest that scenarios may be invaluable, insofar as uncertainty is a real and increasing challenge that decision-makers and other stakeholders must acknowledge and work with. However, the findings also underscore the real challenges to the use of scenarios in practice. It may be necessary to accept that there are multiple possible futures, but this represents a significant departure from the status quo of designing infrastructures to fixed, unitary design conditions.

Conclusion: the scenarios paradox

Experiences with participants in the Harboring Uncertainty project revealed a paradox – they almost universally expressed support for and interest in using scenarios to frame uncertainty, yet largely ignored them in the RPS exercise runs. To the degree that they did seem to influence the deliberations, it was by accentuating the presence of uncertainty, complicating matters and making reaching agreement harder. The debriefings and interviews provided some insights into this contradiction, resulting in some recommendations around the opportunities and limitations for the use of scenarios in practice.

Participants with prior experience using scenarios reflected that it is really the *process of scenario planning* that they find useful. Scenario planning can provide decision-makers and other stakeholders with a better understanding of the nature and breadth of the uncertainties they face, but the richness comes from engaging in the interactive process of identifying the key drivers, sources of uncertainty and other factors, and then collectively devising the scenarios (Chakraborty and McMillan 2015). The exercise simply presented four already devised scenarios, making them less vivid for the participants.

Many participants stated that they ultimately need a single design condition or standard to plan and design towards when it comes to making concrete investment decisions. For certain variables like future sea level and precipitation patterns, they said that we should 'pick a number'. The scenarios version of the RPS exercise did not provide a single design standard that they could work with, causing participants to either default to the worst-case scenario (i.e., 'wet and busy') or conclude that there was too much uncertainty to make a decision. Participants identified various reasons why they feel that they need unitary standards, including professional and organizational standards and norms, and questions of liability and responsibility. These findings underscore the substantial challenges associated with using scenarios but do not mitigate the importance of acknowledging uncertainty in planning and decision-making, and the value multiple scenarios can provide in illustrating these uncertainties.

A recommendation in response to these findings is that proponents of scenario planning should be realistic about the benefits of both their processes and the products they generate. Scenario planning can provide tremendous value as groups grapple with developing a shared understanding of the uncertainties they face. However, the resulting scenarios may have limited currency in separate decision-making processes, particularly in the public sector and when it comes to project-level decision-making. Scenarios may be informative, but they are not directly transferrable. The fact that the greater value is in the process underscores the importance of engaging decision-makers and other key stakeholders directly in scenario planning efforts if they are to be influential.

Another recommendation is that processes grappling with significant uncertainties establish provisional standards for decision-making, while explicitly recognizing that they are contingent. This necessitates flexibility and adaptive management as conditions change and new information emerges. The debate between 'picking a number' because it is necessary for making project-level decisions and rejecting standards because of persistent uncertainties may be a false dichotomy. Participants in this research stated that they need parameters like design storms when making decisions, while acknowledging that these standards do not need to be fixed. In fact, it is accepted that they change over time as conditions change, new knowledge is accrued and risk tolerances shift. Scenario planning can help planners, decision-makers and other stakeholders to appreciate the range of possible futures and map potential pathways forward, while accepting that decisions will continue to be made based on the standards of the day. This can encourage greater attention to the maintenance of flexible pathways and the provision of ongoing monitoring. As discussed in the next chapter, decision-making will require other, complementary approaches, like adaptive management to enact flexibility in decision-making.

Works cited

Alberti, M., M. Russo and K. Tenneson (2013). *Snohomish Basin 2060 Scenarios. Adapting to an Uncertain Future. Decision Support for Long Term Provision of Ecosystem Services in the Snohomish Basin, WA*. Seattle, WA: Urban Ecology Research Laboratory, University of Washington.

Aldrich, S. (2011). An introduction to scenario planning. *Local Communities Adapting to Climate Change: Managing Risk in Decision Making, June 20th, 2011*. Cambridge, MA: Lincoln Institute of Land Policy and the Consensus Building Institute (course).

Bartholomew, K. (2007). Land use-transportation scenario planning: Promise and reality. *Transportation*, 34(4): 397–412.

Caves, J.K., G.S. Bodner, K. Simms, L.A. Fisher and T. Robertson (2013). Integrating collaboration, adaptive management, and scenario-planning: Experiences at Las Cienegas national conservation area. *Ecology and Society*, 18(3): 43.

Centre for Strategic Futures (2016a). www.csf.gov.sg

Centre for Strategic Futures (2016b). *Driving Forces Cards 2035*. www.csf.gov.sg/docs/ default-source/default-document-library/csf-df-cards.pdf

Chakraborty, A., N. Kaza, G.-J. Knaap and B. Deal (2011). Robust plans and contingent plans. *Journal of The American Planning Association*, 77(3): 251–266.

Chakraborty, A. and A. McMillan (2015). Scenario planning for urban planners: Toward a practitioner's guide. *Journal of the American Planning Association*, 81(1): 18–29. doi:10 .1080/01944363.2015.1038576

Chermack, T.J., S.A. Lynham and W.E.A. Ruona (2001). A review of scenario planning literature. *Future Research Quarterly*, Summer 2001: 7–31.

Cornelius, P., A. Van de Putte and M. Romani (2005). Three decades of scenario planning in shell. *California Management Review*, 48(1): 92–109.

Douglas, E. et al. (2016). *Climate Change and Sea Level Rise Projections for Boston*. The Boston Research Advisory Group Report prepared for Climate Ready Boston.

Greenovate Boston (2016). *Climate Ready Boston – Final Report*. Boston, MA: City of Boston.

IPCC [Intergovernmental Panel on Climate Change] (2012). *Workshop Report of the Intergovernmental Panel on Climate Change Workshop on Socio-Economic Scenarios*. O. Edenhofer, R. Pichs-Madruga, Y. Sokona, V. Barros, C.B. Field, T. Zwickel, S. Schloemer, K. Ebi, M. Mastrandrea, K. Mach, C. von Stechow, Eds. Potsdam, Germany: IPCC Working Group III Technical Support Unit, Potsdam Institute for Climate Impact Research. pp. 51.

KNMI [Royal Netherlands Meteorological Institute] (2014). *KNMI '14 Climate Scenarios for the Netherlands*. De Bilt, NL: KNMI, Ministry of Infrastructure and the Environment.

Lempert, R.J. (2012). *Climate Scenarios that Illuminate Vulnerabilities and Robust Responses*. RAND Infrastructure, Safety, and Environment Working Paper, WR-919-NSF.

Moore, S.S., N.E. Seavy and M. Gerhart (2013). *Scenario Planning for Climate Change Adaptation: A Guidance for Resource Managers*. Point Blue Conservation Science and California Coastal Conservancy.

MPO [Boston Region Metropolitan Planning Organization] (2015). Scenario Planning Results. *Charting Progress to 2040: The Boston Region's Next Long-Range Transportation Plan*. www.ctps.org/Drupal/data/html/plans/lrtp/charting/Charting_Progress_Scenario_Planning/index.html

Nenciu, G., P. van der Duin, M. Janssen, D. Snijders and J. Hulstijn (2016). *Future Scenarios of Data-Driven Smart Cities*. https://stt.nl/stt/wp-content/uploads/2016/08/Future-Scenarios-of-Data-Driven-Smart-Cities.pdf

Quay, R. (2010). Anticipatory governance. *Journal of the American Planning Association*, 76(4): 496–511.

Rotterdam Climate Initiative (2013). *Rotterdam Climate Change Adaptation Strategy*. www.rotterdamclimateinitiative.nl/documents/Documenten/20121210_RAS_EN_lr_versie_4.pdf

Rotterdam Climate Initiative (2016). *Rotterdam Resilience Strategy: Ready for the 21st Century*. Rotterdam: City of Rotterdam.

Schoemaker, P.J.H. (1995). Scenario planning: A tool for strategic thinking. *Sloan Management Review*, 36(2): 25–40.

Schoemaker, P.J.H. (1998). Twenty common pitfalls in scenario planning. *Learning From the Future*. L. Fahey and R.M. Randall, Eds. New York: Wiley & Sons. pp. 422–431.

Schoemaker, P.J.H. (2004). Forecasting and scenario planning: The challenges of uncertainty and complexity. *Blackwell Handbook of Judgment and Decision Making*. D.J. Koehler and N. Harvey, Eds. Malden, MA: Blackwell Publishing. pp. 274–296.

[John A.] Volpe [National Transportation Systems] Center (2011a). *FHWA Scenario Planning Guidebook*. FHWA-HEP-11-004. U.S. Department of Transportation, Federal Highways Administration.

Volpe Center (2011b). *Interagency Transportation, Land Use, and Climate Change Cape Cod Pilot Project – Cape Cod Commission Action Plan*. U.S. Department of Transportation, Federal Highway Administration.

Zegras, C. and L. Rayle (2012). Testing the rhetoric: An approach to assess scenario planning's role as a catalyst for urban policy integration. *Futures*, 44: 303–318.

8 Moving forward
Flexible and collaborative governance

Introduction

Two recurring themes throughout this book are (1) the favoring of *flexibility* as a response to uncertain and dynamic conditions and (2) the importance of good *process* in robust, multi-stakeholder deliberative efforts initiated to tackle emerging challenges, such as adapting to climate change. This concluding chapter introduces models and approaches that might help groups advancing climate adaptation to integrate both flexibility and strong deliberation into their efforts, while not shying away from discussing the substantial challenges they face.

In the end, each case will call for its own unique approach to the integration of climate adaptation into infrastructure planning, decision-making and ongoing management. However, elements of flexibility, broad stakeholder engagement and facilitated deliberation may be helpful in a wide variety of situations. More flexible and collaborative approaches to governance can help agencies and other stakeholders to move forward one step at a time in the face of persistent uncertainties, dynamic conditions and unclear institutional arrangements. They can help groups reach consensus on the broad goals and devise mechanisms for ongoing monitoring, evaluation and identification of widely supported options.

The nature of governance

Planning and decision-making involves both formal and informal interactions among stakeholders. Processes are typically bounded by various rules and regulations. However, a great deal of the groundwork happens more informally among actors across different agencies and other stakeholder groups, but within shared and well-established institutional environments. These are characteristic of what Sabatier and Jenkins-Smith (1999) call *policy subsystems*. An example would be the network of actors involved with and revolving around the Boston Region Metropolitan Planning Organization, which coordinates transportation infrastructure decision-making. Contesting *advocacy coalitions* operate as factions within these subsystems – for example, public transit advocates versus those who favor investments in roads. Actors are familiar with each other and regularly interact to discuss issues and advocate for certain options as planning and decision-making evolve. These processes are punctuated by formal decision-making moments and mandated steps like public meetings, but feature substantial informal elements. Interactions across policy subsystems are often sporadic, but important. Decisions made in parallel or succession have implications on each other, even if they are not well coordinated.

The nature of deliberations within policy subsystems varies across the three cities examined through the Harboring Uncertainty project. In Singapore, there is coordination across agencies, but non-governmental actors are largely absent. While informal deliberations take place behind closed doors at the staff level, there is general deference to hierarchies when decisions are to be made. Decision-making in Boston is typified by significant fragmentation across various agencies and levels of government. Non-governmental actors play significant roles as both partners with and adversaries to government agencies. In general, deliberations involve more interests-based bargaining, rather than the deference to 'national priorities' seen in Singapore. The situation in Rotterdam is somewhat more collaborative and consensus seeking rather than adversarial – reflecting the 'polder model' discussed in Chapter 3 – but still involves the expression of different interests and priorities. While there are multiple agencies, levels of government and non-governmental stakeholders involved in infrastructure management, their interactions are seemingly more coordinated than in Boston and non-governmental actors are typically relatively less involved. Despite these differences, the importance of strong policy subsystems to craft options and negotiate tradeoffs is constant across the three cities.

Lack of coordination can be problematic when issues span subsystems or fall between the cracks. Institutionalizing climate change adaptation into planning and decision-making in a tangible way is often emblematic of this. Stakeholders find themselves in what Hajer (2003) calls an *institutional void*. That is, they are in territory that is not wholly governed by the rules and norms of any existing institutional arrangement (i.e., policy subsystem). Standards and regulations around how future climate risks should be integrated into planning and decision-making are starting to emerge, but significant work remains in translating them into practice, particularly at the project level. The institutional void is also characterized by ambiguity around responsibility. It is unclear how to effectively and efficiently amend existing institutions – or facilitate the creation of either permanent or temporary new ones – when new issues like climate change emerge. It is often unclear to whom the various actors within an institution that has evolved to manage a particular type of infrastructure within a certain jurisdiction should look when grappling with how to adapt. Collaborative planning processes aim to make these interactions more explicit by bringing stakeholders together. The argument is that resolving complex problems that cross traditional institutional lines demands a concerted and collective focus on new ways of thinking, sources of information and flexibility over time.

Good process: collaborative governance

Emerging or evolving policy subsystems can benefit from strong process support. This often involves what Quick and Feldman (2014) call *collaborative boundary work* to bridge across existing institutional arrangements. Multi-stakeholder collaborative processes are normatively advanced as a powerful way to engage the range of decision-makers and other stakeholders associated with a particular problem or management challenge, bringing them together to collectively analyze the situation, solicit and evaluate information, and seek out solutions that are both robust and widely supported (Ansell and Gash 2008; Innes and Booher 2010; Margerum 2011; Susskind and Cruikshank 1987).

While far from the norm, collaborative practices are being implemented in various places and under a variety of conditions. Research suggests that deliberative processes can foster new discourses to advance adaptive action (Hobson and Niemeyer 2011). The ways in which these processes are structured – and how actors engage – can have significant implications. In the context of the role-play simulation exercise run with Harboring Uncertainty project participants, the ways in which the various chairs structured their meetings and the approaches each individual adopted had significant implications on the outcomes. Participants reflected that it was eye opening for them to see how influential group dynamics, the decisions the chairs made, the coalitions that formed and other negotiation strategies were on the outcomes. This underscores the importance of good process design and facilitation, if adaptation planning efforts are to be successful and widely supported.

Prior collaborative multi-stakeholder efforts – including both the Maasvlakte 2 Port of Rotterdam expansion and Traffic Management Company processes discussed in Chapter 3 – provide models of what might work as actors assemble to advance climate change adaptation. These processes, along with others, seem to suggest that the following factors are important for success:

- getting the right people to the table;
- scoping processes widely enough to capture systemic complexity, but narrowly enough that they remain relevant to and able to handle specific decisions that need to be made;
- general buy-in from participants and organizational support (including provision of the necessary resources);
- appropriate process design and facilitation; and
- ensuring that processes have the support of the ultimate decision-makers, and that there are direct avenues from any outcomes back into decision-making.

Getting the right people to the table can be a challenge. Outside government, stakeholder groups are often large and diffuse. Intermediary stakeholder organizations can thus play critical roles representing constituencies. They can also translate and legitimize emerging ideas and activities among their constituents – as these organizations are often ahead of the curve – and serve as clearinghouses for information and other resources in both directions. Deltalinqs (the port businesses' association) in Rotterdam and A Better City in Boston are examples of such organizations. They concurrently serve as both advocates for the business community and leaders and strong partners to government on various initiatives, including around infrastructure and climate change. An important caveat is that not all stakeholder groups necessarily have robust representation. Certain groups, like business and environmental interests, are often better represented than others are, including heterogeneous and hard-to-represent groups like 'neighborhoods'. Furthermore, the capacity of organizations varies from place to place; the weakness of civil society organizations is cited as one reason why government agencies do not engage them more in Singapore. However, this is a self-fulfilling prophecy – organizations need to be nourished and granted legitimacy if they are going to engage as partners in deliberative efforts.

Consensus building approach

Collaborative planning takes a variety of forms in practice. The consensus building approach (CBA) emphasizes convening representatives from the various stakeholder groups in face-to-face meetings to identify creative solutions that substantially meet everyone's interests and concerns (Susskind, McKearnan and Thomas-Learner 1999). Common characteristics of the CBA include the involvement of neutral third-party facilitators; the preparation of situation or conflict assessments, based on interviews, prior to convening; an emphasis on the various underlying and priority-ranked interests of each party and how they might be traded across for mutual gains; and the creation of single-text documents by the group to ensure that actionable and genuinely supported plans are developed. While each situation will demand a slightly different approach, general steps in the CBA are outlined in Figure 8.1. Other schools of collaborative planning typically employ similar techniques, emphasizing the effective engagement of multiple stakeholders to facilitate widely supported pathways forward. The aforementioned Maasvlakte 2 consultative process around expanding the Port of Rotterdam more or less followed this process, arriving at an outcome that the various constituencies involved – the port and associated businesses, environmentalists, recreational interests, and others – could live with (WesselinkVanZijst 2015).

While notable criticisms of collaborative planning exist (Few, Brown and Tompkins 2007; Foster 2002; Layzer 2008), there is substantial evidence that it can lead to better outcomes when the conditions are right (Ansell and Gash 2008; Innes and Booher 2010; Margerum 2011). An important question is if, and how,

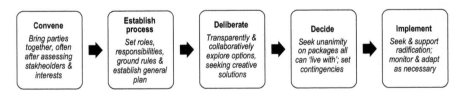

Figure 8.1 The consensus building approach

Source: Adapted from Susskind et al. (1999), Consensus Building Institute (2008)

collaborative planning can make a difference in situations rife with complexity and uncertainty, such as those present under climate change. The CBA has been framed as a way of engaging with and more successfully managing complex systems, yet more work is necessary to fully appreciate the benefits, limitations and barriers of collaborative governance in such situations (Innes and Booher 1999). Few et al. (2007) suggest that the uncertainty and long-term nature of climate change exacerbates the problems associated with the power imbalances present in all participatory processes. Whether it is true that asymmetric power ultimately dooms the efficacy of collaboration in the adaptation arena remains an open question worthy of more attention. Margerum (2011) suggests that collaborative processes are more successful when embedded within the institutional fabric of management and decision-making processes and across networks of processes. An important corollary question is how to better embed multi-stakeholder collaboration into existing institutional regimes. The relative lack of uptake thus far suggests that this is not easy. On the other hand, more explicitly engaging the full range of stakeholders may become all the more necessary as climate adaptation moves from general assessment and planning to project-level decision-making; the stakes become higher and the impacts on winners and losers more pronounced when concrete infrastructure and land-use decisions are in play.

As discussed in Chapter 6, participants in the Harboring Uncertainty project almost universally reported that they learned from the role-play simulation exercise that they participated in. Most of the lessons learned were process-oriented and underscored the value of facilitated consensus-building efforts. In fact, there was a statistically significant increase in the importance participants place on engaging with other stakeholders as they plan and make decisions, from an average of 5.8 pre-exercise to 6.3 post on a 7-point Likert scale.[1] Broad support for stakeholder engagement was universal across the three cities, although there were differences in opinion around who should be involved. In particular, participants in Singapore were much more reticent to accept non-governmental actors at the table. The exercise presented a somewhat familiar environment for some but was foreign to others; the idea of directly involving non-governmental actors was new to participants in Singapore, which is one factor behind their reticence to accept their presence. In contrast, processes in Boston typically involve non-governmental actors. There, the refreshing difference for many was the structured nature of the process, with explicit facilitation and an emphasis on seeking consensus.

One key lesson for exercise participants was the importance of having all parties and decision-makers in the room. One benefit of this identified by participants is that it can facilitate greater creativity and allow for new options to emerge. "In [our] case, resources committed by the community helped to arrive at a consensus", reflected one. Another is to clarify interests; "If we do bring all the stakeholders into the conversation, decision-making and planning is more thorough and not as much 'assumption' is made about varied interests." Multi-stakeholder processes can support perspective taking, allowing participants to "see the world as others see it, [and] take a more mediated approach to conflict resolution and consensus building". "I learned how to look beyond the best options identified for the role I played and find mutual gains among members of the group", reflected another participant, while caveating that this process can take time and resources. To some, the exercise underscored the value of "getting all the cards on the table" in a negotiation. Many emphasized that they appreciated the facilitated and structured nature of the deliberations in the exercise. The "importance of process and ability of the facilitator" really matters. It is "important to bring together stakeholders early to evaluate options and risk systematically; preparing for flexibility and many possible futures is an important lens through which decisions can be made", reflected a participant.

Bridging the science-policy interface: joint fact-finding

This research also shed light on the divide between the technical and political branches within government agencies. Interests dominate the political, whereas data dominates the technical. This divide can be inconsequential when each 'side' feels like it has legitimacy in the eyes of the other, and is getting what it needs from them. Technicians are asked for models (e.g., traffic models and economic growth forecasts). When the system is functioning smoothly and the level of contention is low, these models are accepted by the political side and inform their decision-making, which is also necessarily informed by other considerations, including competing interests and priorities. Decision-makers do not want to know about the minutia of the models, they just want a best guess of the future. Participants reflected that the exercise helped them to gain new appreciation across this divide; this is just one of the benefits of bringing technical and political actors together within multi-stakeholder processes.

The relationship between technical experts and decision-makers can become strained when the *facts* become contested and/or the uncertainty becomes pronounced. It is in these situations that scientific and technical information becomes a part of deliberations, rather than merely an objective set of facts informing them. Harboring Uncertainty participants expressed varying opinions on the place and legitimacy of scientific and technical information in the decision-making process. Some feel that models should be deferred to as neutral sources of information. Participants in Singapore were particularly bullish on the value of data to inform 'objective' decision-making. In contrast, many others – especially in Rotterdam and Boston – emphasized the political nature of models and other forecasts, asserting that they are often manipulated or interpreted to support particular outcomes. Participants asserted that decision-makers are typically not given the full suite of information, nor do they treat models as neutral information. A participant in the Netherlands reflected, "With alternative forecasts and alternative scenarios, the unfavorable ones are discarded very early in the process; the further down in the decision-making process you go, the less objective the information is, the less well-balanced". Many participants concurred that the use of models and forecasts can quickly become political. "[Models are] a way of calculation, and you can calculate anything you want, and if there is a little bit too much, you change the rules!" Addressing the abusing and misusing of technical information may require different relationships between scientific and technical experts and the decision-makers and other stakeholders that use their products. Persistent uncertainty and unclear standards only accentuate this need.

Joint fact-finding (JFF) can be an effective way to mediate between science and policy in a wide range of situations, including in the context of adaptation. Scientific and technical information must be *salient*, *legitimate* and *credible* to stakeholders if it is to be usable (Cash et al. 2002). Corburn (2009) argues that we need processes of co-production, in which climate science is not treated as separate from, but rather integrated into, collaborative processes aimed at crafting solutions. JFF is a way to operationalize co-production and enhance saliency, credibility and legitimacy in practice. JFF is appropriate when there are factual gaps and it is not immediately clear, or parties do not agree on, how those gaps should be filled. It can help when scientific and technical information is a necessary ingredient in a decision-making process, but there are questions around how that data should be framed, collected and interpreted. As outlined in Figure 8.2, the process typically involves (Karl, Susskind and Wallace 2007; Matsuura and

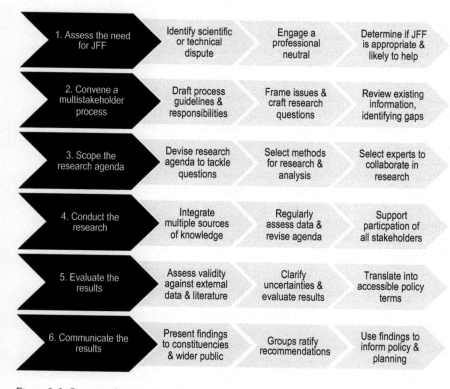

Figure 8.2 Steps in the joint fact-finding process

Source: Matsuura and Schenk 2017, 5 (used with permission of authors). Adapted from Consensus Building Institute 2011

Schenk 2017): convening multiple stakeholders and establishing the research questions; devising a research agenda appropriate to the questions, including identifying the right methods and experts; conducting the research, integrating multiple sources of knowledge; assessing the results vis-à-vis the germane policy and planning questions; and disseminating the results. Stakeholders are directly involved in framing research questions; working with technical experts to design, and often implement, their research programs; and receive the outcomes within wider collaborative forums (Adler, Bryan, Mulica and Shapiro 2011; Karl et al. 2007; McCreary, Gamman and Brooks 2001). Stakeholders will not always agree on what is important and are likely to interpret the data differently, but can explicitly focus on these differing values and interpretations and on uncertainties remaining in the data. JFF has been employed to collectively identify disagreements or gaps in the data and devise broadly supported ways of answering questions in a wide variety of contexts, ranging from desalinization in California to nuclear safety in post-Fukushima Japan (see cases in Matsuura and Schenk 2017).

Climate adaptation may complicate the traditional JFF model, as persistent uncertainty and dynamic conditions make the arrival at a set of stable 'facts' impossible. Nonetheless, this research suggests that decision-makers need technical information on which they can base their decisions at various points. Rather than one-off efforts, iterative JFF processes may continue indefinitely, facilitating ongoing learning. Instead of *the facts*, stakeholders may need to find ways to arrive at *facts for now* – acknowledging their contingent and imperfect nature – and *facts for use* – emphasizing their salience, credibility and legitimacy for decision-making (Schenk 2017). This is a strategy of *satisficing* rather than waiting for perfect information before moving forward (Simon 1956). Iterative JFF involves ongoing monitoring and evaluation so that stakeholders are kept abreast as conditions change and/or new information emerges. Of course, iterative JFF is only effective insofar as the wider decision-making forums it is supposed to feed information into are also ongoing and structured to be flexible and responsive to changing facts. The next section discusses how flexibility can be institutionalized into governance arrangements, including how approaches like *collaborative adaptive management* can marry ongoing fact-finding to ongoing, multi-stakeholder deliberative forums.

Flexibility and other approaches to managing uncertainty

As discussed throughout this book, uncertainty is a pervasive factor in planning and decision-making, including around our infrastructure systems. In the context of adapting to climate change, uncertainty does not emanate solely from scientific and technical uncertainties like our emissions trajectory or the interactions between various emissions scenarios and sea level rise, although those uncertainties certainly have implications. Uncertainty is also a consequence of institutional ambiguities; how agencies and other actors will respond to climate risks remains largely unclear and influenced by a myriad of interconnected forces.

Decisions made (or not) in one arena have implications in others. Uncertainty is in large part a governance challenge. There are various possible ways to respond to uncertainties about the future: decision-makers may focus on robustness, building to the worst-case scenario; take a more passive reactive wait-and-see approach; or incorporate flexibility into their plans and decisions, intentionally leaving windows for adaptation as events unfold and learning occurs. Each of these approaches offers advantages and disadvantages and may be more or less appropriate in different circumstances.

The reactive approach involves responding to events or changing conditions as they unfold (Berrang-Ford, Ford and Paterson 2011). It can be appropriate when the risks of waiting are deemed tolerable, the costs of being proactive would be high and uncertainties obscure the assessment of options. Regardless of whether it is optimal, the reactive approach is often the default; actors are motivated when they experience events firsthand (Measham et al. 2011).

Robust infrastructure is able to handle the anticipated range of possible futures without requiring significant modification – it is designed to be strong, rather than nimble (Birkmann et al. 2010). This approach is appropriate when the consequences of not taking precautionary action could be severe, the costs associated with taking action now are low (or provide important co-benefits) and/or there is relatively little uncertainty. In the Dutch context, the Delta Works, which protect most of Holland with dikes and other flood control infrastructure from up to 1-in-10,000-year flood events, is an example of robustness (Ministerie van Verkeer en Waterstaat 2007). This extremely robust level of protection is deemed necessary because the consequences of flooding could be catastrophic in an extremely densely populated region below sea level. In Singapore, the government has invested aggressively in increasing water independence via extensive rainwater catchment and storage, desalinization, and the NEWater wastewater recycling system (PUB 2015). Singapore has a bilateral agreement to purchase water from Malaysia and thus these efforts may not be necessary, but the country identified water security as a national priority and thus chose to invest in an extremely robust approach. This approach can also yield co-benefits, as they have greater leverage when negotiating water prices with Malaysia.

A flexible or adaptive approach involves taking action today but explicitly keeping as many options open as possible for adjustments in the future as conditions change and new information emerges (National Academies 2014). It is most appropriate when doing nothing is risky, but uncertainty about the future makes taking decisive action now difficult. In the context of climate adaptation measures, it represents a middle way between the 'anticipatory' and 'proactive' versus the 'responsive' and 'reactive' dichotomy (Smit et al. 1999).

As illustrated in Figure 8.3, participants in the Harboring Uncertainty project widely favored flexible approaches as a means to deal with uncertainties. They cited various reasons for this, including the ability to move forward, yet remain adaptive, and to avoid expensive investments immediately in resource-constrained environments. They saw flexibility not merely as a response to climate-related uncertainties, but to the whole gamut of uncertainties present in most

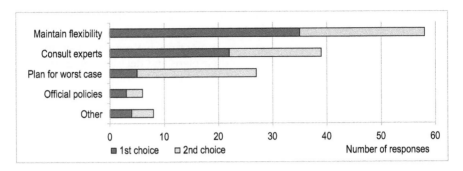

Figure 8.3 Preference ranking of how agencies should deal with uncertainties
Used with permission of author

infrastructure systems. Yet, as discussed further below, flexibility does not always fit well within our governance arrangements.

Infrastructure involves the articulation of built systems, and thus is in large part a matter of engineering and design. If infrastructures are to be flexible and adaptive, they typically need to be designed accordingly. Rather than reducing uncertainties as much as possible and building to the best estimates of future conditions with the standard risk factors – based on the assumptions that the future can be well enough understood and will be relatively stable – infrastructure is built such that it can respond to changing conditions and increasing understanding over time (de Neufville and Scholtes 2011; Taneja 2013). Taneja defines the concept as follows (2013, 73–74):

> A flexible or adaptable [infrastructure] can be altered or employed differently, with relative ease, so as to be functional under new, different, or changing requirements, in a cost-effective manner (which essentially means, to maintain, or even improve service levels, with little or no extra investment).

Rather than building infrastructure that is insufficient and difficult to enhance to meet actual needs, or 'white elephants' that are overbuilt and waste resources, infrastructures are adapted to efficiently and effectively meet the requirements placed upon them in as close to real time as possible. Empirical analysis suggests that, while flexibility has a cost, adaptive approaches can provide significant value (Cardin and de Neufville 2008; de Neufville and Scholtes 2011).

While flexibility in design and engineering may be wise and empirically defensible in the face of significant uncertainties, it does represent a change from the status quo, and thus hurdles must often be overcome. In general, embracing flexibility may be as much a governance challenge as it is a design challenge. Infrastructure systems can only be flexible and dynamic if couched within wider institutions that are structured to monitor and adapt them over time.

Adaptive policymaking – also known as dynamic adaptive policymaking – is a flexible approach to planning and decision-making that allows for decisions to be made today while creating the structures for ongoing monitoring and evaluation and subsequent adjustments over time (Marchau, Walker and van Wee 2010; Rahman, Walker and Marchau 2008). It represents a departure from the design-build-forget model that, unfortunately, seems to dominate much of our infrastructure management. Rahman et al. define this approach as follows (2008, 44):

> This approach allows implementation to begin prior to the resolution of all major uncertainties, with the policy being adapted over time based on new knowledge. It is an innovative way to proceed with implementation of long-term policies despite the uncertainties. The approach makes adaptation explicit at the outset of policy formulation. Thus, the inevitable policy changes become part of a larger, recognized process and are not forced to be made repeatedly on an ad-hoc basis. Adaptive policies combine actions that are time urgent with those that make important commitments to shape the future, preserve needed flexibility for the future, and protect the policy from failure.

They liken the approach to a ship travelling a long distance between two ports. The destination port (i.e., the goal) remains constant, but the exact route is sure to change during the journey in response to weather conditions, vessel traffic and other factors. The steps in the adaptive policymaking approach include (Rahman et al. 2008): establishing the objectives, constraints and policy options; devising a 'basic policy', including what is necessary for it to succeed; adding an adaptive layer to the basic policy by identifying the ways in which it may be vulnerable, what actions may be taken in response to threats and other changes, and the 'signposts' that will be monitored to track performance and facilitate rapid response; and implementing the policy, which includes maintaining monitoring systems so that the policymaking process may be reinitiated if and when certain triggers are reached. Various tools, including the use of scenarios, can support this adaptive approach. Marchau et al. (2010) illustrate how a dynamic adaptive approach may be applied in transportation policymaking, outlining potential applications in road pricing, high-speed rail, and airport planning in the Netherlands. Unfortunately, these examples are largely aspirational, reflecting the challenges associated with implementing adaptive approaches in practice.

Adaptive policymaking is just one model in a suite of tools proposed for integrating flexibility into planning and policymaking. The dynamic adaptive policy pathways approach builds on adaptive policymaking, factoring in adaptation tipping point and adaptation pathways techniques which, among other things, add explicit consideration of the timing of actions and additional feedback mechanisms and emphasize the proactive mapping of various pathways that may be followed, depending on conditions at predetermined tipping points (Walker,

Haasnoot and Kwakkel 2013). Haasnoot et al. (2013, 485) illustrate how the dynamic adaptive policy pathways approach could be applied in the Rhine Delta in the Netherlands to take "into account the deep uncertainties about the future arising from social, political, technological, economic, and climate changes". Once again, however, the example illustrates how such an adaptive approach could enhance management, but it is not being applied in practice. This underscores the dearth of examples from practice and suggests that there are substantial barriers to implementation.

Collaborative adaptive management (CAM), which is typically promoted as an approach to natural resource management, is similar in many ways to the aforementioned processes; agencies are expected to remain responsive to changing conditions (e.g., ecosystem or species health) and newly emerging information over time (Doremus et al. 2011; Holling 1978; Lee 1993; Williams and Brown 2012). CAM emphasizes ongoing research and knowledge creation – rather than simply monitoring – as an important element of enhancing understanding. At its best, it also emphasizes the need for collaboration among decision-makers, scientists and other stakeholders. The steps in the CAM process are outlined in Figure 8.4. CAM has been applied to the management of infrastructure and natural resources around the world – including the Glen Canyon Dam in the United States – with admittedly mixed success; a major shortcoming is that processes often fail to translate new information into concrete management changes (Camacho 2009; Susskind, Camacho and Schenk 2011).

There are a myriad of other tools and approaches intended to support more flexible and adaptive planning, decision-making and infrastructure management. Anticipatory governance emphasizes systemic efforts to analyze possible futures with tools like scenario planning so that a range of 'flexible adaptation strategies' may be proactively developed (Fuerth 2009; Quay 2010). Fuerth (2009, 29) defines anticipatory governance as "a system of institutions, rules and norms that provide a way to use foresight for the purpose of reducing risk, and to increase capacity to respond to events at early rather than later stages of their development". He goes on to suggest that the basic elements are "a system for generating foresight in the form of alternative constructs about the future; a system for incorporating foresight into policy-making and policy-execution; and a system to provide feedback connections between results and estimates". Anticipatory governance has been institutionalized into the way some infrastructure is managed, including by municipal agencies in the United States (Quay 2010). Other tools such as mediated modeling may also be employed to support groups as they work through complex and dynamic situations (van den Belt 2004).

In general, these adaptive approaches are designed to move planning and decision-making from the 'predict and act' paradigm to one of 'monitor and adapt' when conditions are highly uncertain and dynamic in nature. Walker et al. (2013) identify the following 'key principles' for success: a wide range of uncertainties should be explored in a dynamic way; short-term targets and long-term goals must be linked; and short-term actions should be taken, while a range of possible

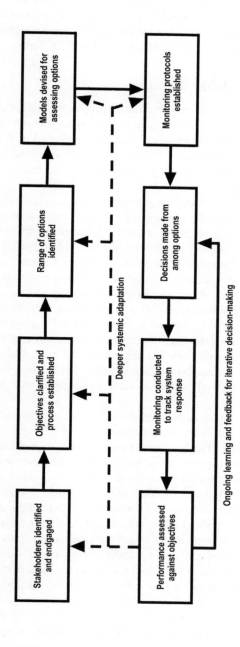

Figure 8.4 The collaborative adaptive management process

Source: Schenk (2017, p. 88). Used with permission. Adapted from Williams and Brown (2012, p. 13).

options are left open for the future. Quay (2010) adds that decision-support tools like scenarios can help to anticipate the range of possible futures; issues like capital planning and financing must be considered; cooperation is required to create the necessary monitoring regimes; and flexible decision-making systems need to be properly institutionalized if they are to be sustained into the future.

Barriers to flexible and adaptive approaches

The limited uptake and success in institutionalizing more flexible and adaptive approaches into our planning, policymaking and infrastructure management suggests that there are substantial barriers. Participants engaged in the Harboring Uncertainty project identified various barriers to taking more flexible approaches in practice, emphasizing that the paradigm shift from 'predict and act' to 'monitor and adapt' is no simple task.

It is difficult for officials to shift from a mentality of focusing on the product to one in which, in the words of a participant, "systems are not designed with a deterministic future in mind, but with a completely uncertain future in mind and the control room capabilities . . . to monitor where things are going and be able to adapt". Officials and other stakeholders may need to be ready accept less robust infrastructure today with the understanding that adaptive measures will take place as necessary down the road. Actors are often risk adverse and enjoy a sense of satisfaction when an infrastructure project is 'done'. If adaptive approaches are to succeed, agility may need to be framed as more 'resilient', as opposed to risky; actors sold on the benefits of viewing infrastructure projects as ongoing and iterative, rather than emphasizing their completion as the goal; and institutional arrangements shifted to accommodate these changes. Participants recognized the monumentality of this – "[Is it] realistic to expect a paradigm shift like this; how do you do it?" asked one.

Adaptive approaches must be squared with the web of laws and regulations that bound planning and decision-making processes, which typically reflect the 'predict and act' paradigm. The hurdles are many: decision-making and regulatory control is fragmented across agencies and levels of government; at each step, agencies rely upon internal methods of analysis and data collection and are reticent to involve other stakeholders until late in the process; the incentives discourage the monitoring and evaluation of decisions previously made; and adaptive capacity is minimal (Camacho 2009). Unfortunately, these barriers to flexibility are often encouraged by regulations, rather than occurring in spite of them. Regulations are also typically difficult and slow to change. "Detailed [standards] are fixed in law, [and] it takes a long time to change them", said a participant. From air quality to design standards, regulations typically stipulate explicit minimum requirements or thresholds because they provide concrete benchmarks against which activities can be measured. Adaptive approaches may call for flexibility in these standards to allow for more contextually efficient and effective responses, rather than the application of 'one size fits all' solutions.

Another hurdle is fragmentation among agencies and other actors. This is particularly problematic in pluralist institutional environments, like in the United States. Flexible approaches will often involve actions that straddle boundaries of responsibility, requiring substantial coordination. By their nature, they also involve ongoing engagement. Traditionally, different actors are responsible for different parts of the system and for initial construction versus maintenance. These divisions delimit areas of competence and responsibility and are not always easily worked across. Projects go through more or less linear steps from initial planning through project proposal and budgeting, design, permitting and negotiation to construction, involving various actors. For example, a new highway in the United States may be proposed by a state department of transportation, based on internal demand models and/or external political pressures; go through a metropolitan planning organization process for coordinated regional planning and approval; involve private engineering firms for evaluation and design work; receive funding from the Federal Highway Administration; require permitting from both federal and state environment agencies and other authorities; and ultimately be constructed by private contractors chosen through a competitive bidding process. Later, maintenance will typically involve a variety of actors, some of whom are the same as those involved in capital planning and construction and some that are completely different. A flexible approach requires tighter integration among those responsible for the various steps of design, funding, project review, construction and maintenance. On a related note, actors must take responsibility for ongoing monitoring. The 'control room' monitoring functions must be strong, if adaptations are going to be timely and effective. "At any given time, situational awareness is a precondition – [you must] know where you are, and what your circumstances are", reflected an interviewee. This requires resources and staff competencies.

Complicating matters further, the different pathways that adaptive systems may follow as conditions evolve can involve the introduction of new actors and regulations. For example, a potentially vulnerable coastal road might initially be constructed with flood-resistant materials; be adapted with enhanced drainage capacity when flooding intensifies and a tipping point is reached; and then require the construction of protective berms when flooding becomes even more pronounced. The initial material requirements are relatively easily stipulated in the 'request for proposals' for construction. Enhancing the drainage capacity is likely to invoke additional permitting under regulations and is probably more easily done if the potential need was considered during the initial design and construction. Nonetheless, it is still within the domain of a transportation agency. New protective berms will likely require further environmental and water management permitting and invoke questions of responsibility – is a berm the responsibility of the transportation agency, or the agency (or agencies) with responsibility for flood control and/or coastal zone management? Different pathways will require that different actors be at the table and on board. Truly flexible approaches may require coordination with actors who have no role with the initial project, but who may be called upon if certain adaptive measures are initiated down the road. It raises new questions around who is responsible and thus must be engaged.

Flexible approaches may be more economically efficient over time, but decision-makers need to be convinced of the value. According to participants, the approach a decision-maker takes will depend on the (real or perceived) relative costs and benefits.

> If we can work in climate change when we make a project, and it is cheaper, we will do it then; when it is cheaper to be flexible, then we will be flexible; and when it is cheaper to see what happens and react in the future, then we will do that – money is the basic parameter for making these kinds of choices,

said a participant. Comparing the costs and benefits of different approaches is difficult, however, when potential future adaptive measures are typically less elaborated and costs will change over time. In general, estimating potential future costs in an adaptive system may be challenging, but nonetheless expected by decision-makers. "The decision-maker needs to know, wants to know, what is the cost of the extras if we are going to [implement them] in five or ten years", said one participant. Financing adaptive approaches also involves challenges related to the questions of responsibility outlined in the last section: will the funding be available if and when tipping points are reached, and who should be funding adaptive measures when the agency with primary responsibility may change, depending on the pathways followed?

Infrastructure projects are typically financed through capital planning processes that involve the one-time allocation of funds. In the United States, these funds often come, at least in part, from a different level of government – federal funding is integral to most infrastructure projects implemented by state and local agencies. For highways, for example, the Federal Highway Administration is a major source of money. These funds typically need to be spent within a certain window of time and come with explicit conditions that need to be met. Adaptive approaches may require less initial capital outlay, but require funding if and when tipping points are reached and adaptive measures required. The question is, can managers count on the support being there when needed? Should funders like the Highway Administration allocate more than is needed for initial construction and allow recipients to bank some for later adaptive measures? Or, develop funding mechanisms explicitly for adaptive measures? How much should be allocated, given the uncertainties around what will be necessary and how much it will cost? Interviewees reflected unequivocally that current funding mechanisms are not designed to accommodate ongoing, adaptive approaches. Furthermore, the availability of funds and relative priority of different infrastructures fluctuates over time based on the economy, political dynamics and other factors, making delaying investments risky when the money is on the table.

It is notable that it may be easier to inject flexibility into some infrastructure systems than others. Agencies in systems with less fragmented responsibilities, dependence on external financing and/or regulatory oversight can make decisions with greater independence, and thus they can act more nimbly. Participants reflected that this might explain why flexible approaches have gained traction in some sectors and not others. The Boston Water and Sewer Commission and Massachusetts Water Resources Authority are two agencies in the Boston area at the forefront of taking concrete adaptive measures; while both depend on external actors, they have relatively stable funding streams (water and sewer charges) and relatively autonomous infrastructure networks. The Port of Rotterdam has been a leader in experimenting with more flexible approaches; it is a state-owned but independently operated corporation with a strong funding stream and relative autonomy over its planning and decision-making. None of these organizations operates in a vacuum, but they are less dependent on others compared to many other infrastructure managers.

Adaptive approaches to making decisions are no more value free and immune from the interests of different stakeholders than are conventional approaches. Assessments of the adaptive management of natural resources suggest that processes can flounder when the interests of the various stakeholders are not accounted for in process design and there are subsequently poor incentives for actors to engage (Camacho 2009; Susskind, Camacho and Schenk 2011). There is no reason to believe that matters would be any different in the context of infrastructure systems or when climate change is the driving force of uncertainty. Measham et al. (2011) identify the heterogeneity of interests among stakeholders, the fact that adaptation is only one objective among many, even for proponents, and the fact that interests manifest via politics as key barriers to effective climate change adaptation. Planners and decision-makers cannot merely view uncertainty and dynamic conditions as technical problems (Birkmann et al. 2010). Flexibility can be a viable strategy, but must account for the interests and perspectives of the various stakeholders.

Engineers, technicians and other professionals engaged in infrastructure planning have largely been trained, and are most experienced, within the 'predict and plan' paradigm. As discussed earlier in this book, participants were somewhat skeptical when asked how confident they are that they and other stakeholders will be able to manage the risks and uncertainties associated with climate change. Many cited deficient professional capacity – and lack of proficiency with planning and designing flexibility in particular – as the reason for their lack of confidence. An engineer from Rijkswaterstaat, the Dutch agency responsible for both transportation and water infrastructure, opined,

> We have to reeducate our engineers, because our engineers are educated in a linear world – things are true or not true. They learn to discuss risks, but they didn't learn to discuss uncertainty. So, that's a way of thinking that they didn't learn.

Training is only one factor in the perpetuation of deterministic norms within professions and the organizations they populate. As discussed in Chapter 6, 'institutional isomorphism and collective rationality' may also be driving adherence to common standards and practices (DiMaggio and Powell 1983). 'Coercive isomorphism' may be a product of the pressures put on infrastructure agencies by their political masters to provide consistent and dependable levels of service with no surprises; standards imposed by other organizations, like the conditions the Federal Highway Administration imposes when funding state and local projects; and the pressures agencies put on the consultants that often do the design and assessment, especially in the United States. "Flexibility isn't really an option when you have to stamp something and leave your liability on it", opined an engineering consultant in Boston. DiMaggio and Powell (1983, 151) explicitly identify "uncertainty [as] a powerful force that encourages imitation". Flexibility typically involves moving beyond mimicry, which is both professionally risky and not necessarily incentivized.

In addition to the ways in which professionals are trained and the institutional, organizational and professional norms they adhere to, another factor is the limited time and resources they have to consider new variables like 'uncertainty' and possible solutions like flexibility. Even if engineers appreciate the stochastic nature of systems and would like to act more flexibly, they do not necessarily have the time and resources to do so and subsequently default to deterministic approaches as a way to 'satisfice'. As a participant in the Netherlands said, "[We] just have the manuals, and the standards, and follow them blindly, you don't think, you don't have time to think!" While it may be more efficient in the long run, the tighter the resource constraints, the harder it is to step back and think about how to act more flexibly.

These substantial challenges will need to be overcome if more flexible and adaptive approaches are to take hold. This is a tall order, but they may be necessary as agencies struggle to make wise choices despite limited resources, dynamic conditions and imperfect knowledge. As a first step, actors engaged in infrastructure planning and decision-making need to appreciate the dynamic nature of their systems. Institutional norms then need to be disrupted, creating opportunities to modify the status quo. Actors also need to see the value in and incentives to making this paradigmatic shift. That is, they need to be convinced of the 'value of flexibility' and feel reassured that they will not be punished for taking a new approach (de Neufville and Scholtes 2011; Taneja 2013).

Conclusion

Unfortunately, there are no easy answers to the question of how actors engaged in infrastructure planning, decision-making and ongoing maintenance can disrupt existing norms and inject more flexibility into their institutional arrangements. The integration of more deliberative processes that engage all of the relevant actors in a coordinated fashion may help. Many, though certainly not all, of the barriers identified above are ultimately coordination challenges. Even those that are not would benefit from broadly inclusive processes that can foster consensus around goals and facilitate ongoing deliberation around how decisions made reconcile with different interests and priorities.

As is emphasized throughout this book, the challenges of implementing more flexible, adaptive and broadly inclusive approaches will be different in each place. In Singapore, strong hierarchies, relatively straightforward and clearly delineated institutional arrangements, high government capacity, and the dearth of strong interest-group opposition may make the integration of more flexible approaches easier. However, non-governmental actors are unlikely to be at the table, which can have implications on which ideas are heard and whose interests are served. In contrast, the complex web of actors and acute resource scarcities are likely to make the injection of flexibility challenging in Boston. Decisions are often contested, so a stream of ongoing decision-making could precipitate grid-lock. On the other hand, the complex web of actors can be valuable insofar as there is a predilection towards broad involvement in planning and decision-making. That is not to say that deliberative processes could not be much better organized in practice. Rotterdam falls somewhere in between in many ways. A historical predilection towards robustness may make a turn towards flexibility difficult to institutionalize, but some projects, like the 'Room for the River' initiative, suggest that it is possible. The Dutch 'polder mentality' may predispose institutions to strong deliberation, but it is not clear that they are always broadly inclusive or well organized.

Each region and associated set of institutions will face its own challenges as it attempts to institutionalize flexibility, engage in multi-stakeholder deliberation and generally advance the adaptation of its infrastructure systems. This book has given a flavor of how adaptation is happening and might continue to evolve in three cities with different governance regimes; the barriers they face to greater action in practice; and some of the tools and approaches they might employ as they advance their agendas. It is hoped that others can learn from their experiences, while tailoring to their own needs and conditions.

Note

1 Hypothesis: Exercise participation will increase participants' opinions on the importance of engagement. Question asked: 'How important is it that you engage with other decision-makers and stakeholders as you plan and make decisions?' The results were significant at the $p = 0.005$ level, using a Wilcoxon matched pairs signed ranks ($N = 43$, $T = 253.5$; one-tailed hypothesis). Therefore, the null hypothesis can be rejected.

Works cited

Adler, P.S., T. Bryan, M. Mulica and J. Shapiro (2011). *Joint Fact Finding: A Strategy for Bringing Science, Policy and the Public Together When Matters Get Contentious*. Joint Fact Finding Conference Proceedings. Tokyo: Department of Public Policy, University of Tokyo. www.mediate.com/articles/AdlerJoint.cfm

Ansell, C. and A. Gash (2008). Collaborative governance in theory and practice. *Journal of Public Administration Research and Theory*, 18(4): 543–571.

Berrang-Ford, L., J.D. Ford and J. Paterson (2011). Are we adapting to climate change? *Global Environmental Change*, 21: 25–33.

Birkmann, J., M. Garschagen, F. Kraas and N. Quang (2010). Adaptive urban governance: New challenges for the second generation of urban adaptation strategies to climate change. *Sustainability Science*, 5: 185–206.

Camacho, A.E. (2009). Adapting governance to climate change: Managing uncertainty through a learning infrastructure. *Emory Law Journal*, 59(1): 1–78.

Cardin, M.-A. and R. de Neufville (2008). *A Survey of State-of-the-Art Methodologies and a Framework for Identifying and Valuing Flexible Design Opportunities in Engineering Systems*. Working Paper. Cambridge, MA: Massachusetts Institute of Technology.

Cash, D., W. Clark, F. Alcock, N. Dickson, N. Eckley and J. Jäger (2002). *Salience, Credibility, Legitimacy and Boundaries: Linking Research, Assessment and Decision Making*. John F. Kennedy School of Government, Harvard University Faculty Research Working Papers Series, RWP02–046.

Consensus Building Institute (2008). *Consensus Building Essential Steps*.

Consensus Building Institute (2011). *Key Steps in the Joint Fact-Finding Process*. www.cbuilding.org/sites/cbi.drupalconnect.com/files/JFF_2011.pdf

Corburn, J. (2009). Cities, climate change and urban heat island mitigation: Localizing global environmental science. *Urban Studies*, 46(2): 413–427.

de Neufville, R. and S. Scholtes (2011). *Flexibility in Engineering Design*. Cambridge, MA: MIT Press.

DiMaggio, P.J. and W.W. Powell (1983). The iron cage revisited: Institutional isomorphism and collective rationality in organizational fields. *American Sociological Review*, 48(2): 147–160.

Doremus, H., W.L. Andreen, A. Camacho, D.A. Farber, R.L. Glicksman, D. Goble, B.C. Karkkainen, D. Rohlf, A.D. Tarlock, S.B. Zellmer, S. Jones and Y. Huang (2011). *Making Good Use of Adaptive Management*. Center for Progressive Reform. White Paper #1104.

Few, R., K. Brown and E.L. Tompkins (2007). Public participation and climate change adaptation: Avoiding the illusion of inclusion. *Climate Policy*, 7(1): 46–59.

Foster, S. (2002). *Environmental Justice in an Era of Devolved Collaboration*. Harvard Environmental Law Review, 26; Fordham Law Legal Studies Research Paper, No. 17. http://ssrn.com/abstract=291510

Fuerth, L.S. (2009). Foresight and anticipatory governance. *Foresight*, 11(4): 14–32.

Haasnoot, M., J.H. Kwakkel, W.E. Walker and J. ter Maat (2013). Dynamic adaptive policy pathways: A method for crafting robust decisions for a deeply uncertain world. *Global Environmental Change*, 23: 485–498.

Hajer, M. (2003). Policy without polity? Policy analysis and the institutional void. *Policy Sciences*, 36: 175–195.

Hobson, K. and S. Niemeyer (2011). Public responses to climate change: The role of deliberation in building capacity for adaptive action. *Global Environmental Change*, 21: 957–971.

Holling, C.S. (1978). *Adaptive Environmental Assessment and Management*. Laxenburg, Austria: International Institute for Applied Systems Analysis.

Innes, J.E. and D.E. Booher (1999). Consensus building and complex adaptive systems. *Journal of the American Planning Association*, 65(4): 412–423.

Innes, J.E. and D.E. Booher (2010). *Planning With Complexity: An Introduction to Collaborative Rationality for Public Policy*. Milton Park, UK: Routledge.

Karl, H.A., L.E. Susskind and K.H. Wallace (2007). A dialogue, not a diatribe: Effective integration of science and policy through joint fact finding. *Environment: Science and Policy for Sustainable Development*, 49: 20–34.

Layzer, J.A. (2008). *Natural Experiments: Ecosystem-Based Management and the Environment*. Cambridge, MA: MIT Press.

Lee, K.N. (1993). *Compass and Gyroscope: Integrating Science and Politics for the Environment*. Washington, DC: Island Press.

Marchau, V.A.W.J., W.E. Walker and G.P. van Wee (2010). Dynamic adaptive transport policies for handling deep uncertainty. *Technological Forecasting & Social Change*, 77: 940–950.

Margerum, R.D. (2011). *Beyond Consensus: Improving Collaborative Planning and Management*. Cambridge, MA: MIT Press.

Matsuura, M. and T. Schenk (2017). *Joint Fact-Finding in Urban Planning and Environmental Disputes*. London and New York: Routledge.

McCreary, S.T., J.K. Gamman and B. Brooks (2001). Refining and testing joint fact-finding for environmental dispute resolution: Ten years of success. *Mediation Quarterly*, 18: 329–348.

Measham, T.G., B.L. Preston, T.F. Smith, C. Brooke, R. Gorddard, G. Withycombe and C. Morrison (2011). Adapting to climate change through local municipal planning: Barriers and challenges. *Mitigation and Adaptation Strategies for Global Change*, 16: 889–909.

Ministerie van Verkeer en Waterstaat (2007). *Water veiligheid, Begrippen begrijpen*. Den Haag, NL: Ministerie van Verkeer en Waterstaat, Directoraat-Generaal Water.

National Academies [Committee on U.S. Army Corps of Engineers Water Resources Science, Engineering, and Planning: Coastal Risk Reduction; Water Science and Technology Board; Ocean Studies Board; Division on Earth and Life Studies; National Research Council] (2014). *Reducing Coastal Risk on the East and Gulf Coasts*. Washington, DC: The National Academies Press.

PUB [Singapore Public Utilities Board] (2015). *Our Water, Our Future*. www.pub.gov.sg/Documents/PUBOurWaterOurFuture.pdf

Quay, R. (2010). Anticipatory governance. *Journal of the American Planning Association*, 76(4): 496–511.

Quick, K.S. and M.S. Feldman (2014). Boundaries as junctures: Collaborative boundary work for building efficient resilience. *Journal of Public Administration Research and Theory*, doi:10.1093/jopart/mut085

Rahman, S.A., W.E. Walker and V. Marchau (2008). *Coping With Uncertainties About Climate Change in Infrastructure Planning – An Adaptive Policymaking Approach*. Final Report. Rotterdam, NL: Ecorys Research and Consulting.

Sabatier, P.A. and H.C. Jenkins-Smith (1999). The advocacy coalition framework: An assessment. *Theories of the Policy Process*. P.A. Sabatier, Ed. Boulder, CO: Westview. pp. 117–166.

Schenk, T. (2017). Facts for now, facts for use: Satisficing and adapting in joint fact-finding. *Joint Fact-Finding in Urban Planning and Environmental Disputes*. M. Matsuura and T. Schenk, Eds. London and New York: Routledge.

Simon, H.A. (1956). Rational choice and the structure of the environment. *Psychological Review*, 63(2): 129–138.

Smit, B., I. Burton, R.J.T. Klein and R. Street (1999). The science of adaptation: A framework for assessment. *Mitigation and Adaptation Strategies for Global Change*, 4: 199–213.

Susskind, L., A. Camacho and T. Schenk (2011). A critical assessment of collaborative adaptive management in practice. *Journal of Applied Ecology*, doi:10.1111/j.1365-2664.2011.02070.x

Susskind, L. and J. Cruikshank (1987). *Breaking the Impasse: Consensual Approaches to Resolve Public Disputes*. New York, NY: Basic Books Inc.

Susskind, L., S. McKearnan and J. Thomas-Learner, Eds. (1999). *The Consensus Building Handbook*. Thousand Oaks, CA: Sage.

Taneja, P. (2013). *The Flexible Port*. Delft, NL: Next Generation Infrastructure Foundation.

van den Belt, M. (2004). *Mediated Modeling: A System Dynamics Approach to Environmental Consensus Building*. Washington, DC: Island Press.

Walker, W.E., M. Haasnoot and J.H. Kwakkel (2013). Adapt or perish: A review of planning approaches for adaptation under deep uncertainty. *Sustainability*, 5: 955–979.

WesselinkVanZijst (2015). *Maasvlakte 2*. www.wesselinkvanzijst.nl/cases/maasvlakte-2

Williams, B.K. and E.D. Brown (2012). *Adaptive Management: The U.S. Department of the Interior Applications Guide*. Washington: Adaptive Management Working Group, U.S. Department of the Interior.

Index

For Product Safety Concerns and Information please contact our EU
representative GPSR@taylorandfrancis.com
Taylor & Francis Verlag GmbH, Kaufingerstraße 24, 80331 München, Germany

www.ingramcontent.com/pod-product-compliance
Ingram Content Group UK Ltd.
Pitfield, Milton Keynes, MK11 3LW, UK
UKHW021616240425
457818UK00018B/596